Puritan Profiles

54 Influential Puritans at the time when
the Westminster Confession of Faith was written

William S. Barker

Mentor

William S. Barker is Vice-President for Academic Affairs and Professor of Church History at Westminster Theological Seminary in Philadelphia, Pennsylvania. An ordained minister of the Presbyterian Church in America, he served as Moderator of the General Assembly in 1994. He holds the A.B. from Princeton University, M.A. from Cornell University, B.D. from Covenant Theological Seminary, and Ph. D. from Vanderbilt University. He has previously served on the faculty and administration of Covenant College and of Covenant Theological Seminary, and as a pastor of a suburban and of an urban church. He and his wife, Gail, have two children and four grandchildren.

© William S. Barker
ISBN 1-85792-154-2
Published in 1996, reprinted 1999

Mentor
is an imprint of
Christian Focus Publications,
Geanies House, Fearn, Ross-shire,
Scotland, IV20 1TW, Great Britain.
Cover design by Owen Daily

'But grow in the grace and knowledge of
our Lord and Savior Jesus Christ. To him be glory
both now and forever! Amen.' (2 Peter 3:18)

To
Gail Kern Barker
Christiana mea carissima

Contents

TIME-LINE

1603   Death of Elizabeth; accession of James I
1604   Hampton Court Conference

1611   Authorized Version of the Bible

1620   Pilgrims to Plymouth Colony, Massachusetts on the 'Mayflower'

1625   Death of James I; accession of Charles I

1628   May--Petition of Right
       Founding of Massachusetts Bay Colony at Salem
1629   March--Dissolution of Parliament by Charles I

1633   William Laud made Archbishop of Canterbury

1637   Imposition of Prayer Book on Church of Scotland

1638   February 28--Signing of the National Covenant
       November-December--General Assembly of Glasgow

1639   First Bishops War

1640   April--Short Parliament
       Second Bishops War; Scottish Army marches into England
       September--*Et Cetera* oath
       November 3--Long Parliament opens

1641   October--'Irish Massacres'
       November 27--Parliament passes Grand Remonstrance

1642   August 22--Charles I raises standard at Nottingham
       October 23--Battle of Edgehill

1643   **June 12--Ordinance passed by Parliament for calling Assembly of Divines**
       July 1--Assembly convenes
       August 17--Solemn League and Covenant approved by Scottish Parliament
       September 25--Solemn League and Covenant subscribed by members of Assembly and Parliament and Scottish Commissioners

1643	October 12--End of revision of Thirty-Nine Articles
	October 17--'Church Government' under discussion

1644   **May 24--Report and debate on 'Directory for Public Worship'**
July 2--Battle of Marston Moor
August 20--Committee appointed on 'Confession of Faith'
November 8--'Form of Church Government' sent to Parliament
December 9--Self-Denying Ordinance proposed

1645   **January 3--'Directory for Public Worship' passes House of Commons**
January 23--Resolutions passed by House of Commons containing substance of Presbyterianism
June 14--Battle of Naseby
July 7--Assembly sends up 'Directory for Church Government'

1646   April 27--Charles I escapes to Scots at Newark
April 30--Committee from House of Commons with Jus Divinum Queries
December 4--'Confession of Faith' presented to Parliament

1647   **April 26--Scripture proofs for 'Confession' given to Parliament**
August 6--Army marches into London
August 27--'Confession' approved by Church of Scotland
October 15--'Larger Catechism' completed
November 11--Charles I flees, ending up at Carisbrooke Castle, Isle of Wight
November 25--'Shorter Catechism' presented to House of Commons

1648   **April 14--Catechisms presented in final form**
April 30--Outbreak of Second Civil War
August 17--Battle of Preston
December 6--Pride's Purge of Parliament

1649   January 20--Trial of Charles I opens
January 30--Execution of Charles I
February 22--Last numbered Plenary Session of Assembly
September 11--Battle of Drogheda

1650   September 3--Battle of Dunbar

1651   September 3--Battle of Worcester

1652   **March 25--End of Assembly's work of sitting as a committee to examine candidates for the ministry**

1653   April 20--Dissolution of 'Rump' of Long Parliament
July--Inception of 'Barebones' (or Nominated) Parliament
December 16--Oliver Cromwell becomes Protector

1657   May 8--Cromwell rejects kingship
June 26--Cromwell installed as Lord Protector

1658   September 3--Death of Oliver Cromwell

1660   Restoration of Charles II

1662   August 24--Act of Uniformity excludes Nonconformists from Church of England

1669   First Indulgence of Charles II

1672   Second Indulgence of Charles II

1685   Charles II becomes Roman Catholic on deathbed; accession of his Roman Catholic brother, James II

1688   James II flees from 'Glorious Revolution'; accession of William III and Mary

1689   Act of Toleration

Chapter 1

Introduction

Question: What is the chief end of man?
Answer: Man's chief end is to glorify God, and to enjoy him for ever.

Question: What rule hath God given to direct us how we may glorify and enjoy him?
Answer: The word of God, which is contained in the scriptures of the Old and New Testaments, is the only rule to direct us how we may glorify and enjoy him.

Question: What do the scriptures principally teach?
Answer: The scriptures principally teach what man is to believe concerning God, and what duty God requires of man.

Question: What is God?
Answer: God is a Spirit, infinite, eternal, and unchangeable, in his being, wisdom, power, holiness, justice, goodness and truth.

So begins the Westminster Shorter Catechism. For those of us who memorized it in childhood, along with scores of Bible verses, it proved to be a precious introduction to Christian theology. In more mature years we typically moved to the Westminster Confession of Faith, some devouring its systematic setting forth of Christian teaching in a single sitting upon their first enthusiastic encounter with its thirty-three concise chapters. Usually only later in our development did we come to appreciate the Larger Catechism, some four or five times as long as the Shorter Catechism, and with its detailed expositions of the Ten Commandments and of the Lord's Prayer, valuable helps to one's devotional meditation and Bible study. For those who became involved in the ministry and government of the church, lay as well as clergy, the Westminster Assembly's Directory for the Publick Worship of God and Form of Presbyterial Church-Government still possess helpful insights and advice, even though most modern denominations have modified them over the years.

Where did these documents come from, and how were they produced? The Westminster Assembly of Divines (or clergymen) was a group of one hundred and twenty-one English Puritan ministers, assisted by six Scottish commissioners and thirty laymen, ten from the House of Lords and twenty from the House of Commons. They met from July 1, 1643 to February 22, 1649, with an average of sixty to eighty in attendance, as an advisory body to Parliament for the further reformation of religion and the church in England, Ireland, and Scotland.

The political context was one of Civil War, as the Parliamentary forces, eventually led by Oliver Cromwell, were already engaged militarily with the Cavalier army of King Charles I by October 23, 1642. The immediate roots of this conflict lay in the uprising of the Scots, rallying behind their National Covenant of 1638, against the imposition by Charles and Archbishop of Canterbury William Laud of Episcopacy, Anglican liturgy, and Arminian doctrine. But the more remote roots go back to tensions between the Stuart monarchy – beginning with James I in 1603 – and the English Puritans, leading up to the Short Parliament of the spring of 1640 and the Long Parliament starting in November 1640, and even to the back-and-forth development of the English Reformation under the Tudor monarchs Henry VIII, Edward VI, Mary and Elizabeth I in the sixteenth century. The Westminster Assembly comes at the culmination of the era of the Protestant Reformation and represents a consummation of that movement's effort to understand and apply the Bible's teaching.

Philip Schaff says of the Westminster Assembly: 'It forms the most important chapter in the ecclesiastical history of England during the seventeenth century. Whether we look at the extent or ability of its labors, or its influence upon future generations, it stands first among Protestant Councils.' [1]

Almost a century later, John Leith claims even more:

> The place of the Confession in the history of Christian doctrine is such that a grasp of its significance is crucial for an understanding of the contemporary theological situation. The Confession was not only the conclusion of one hundred and twenty-five years of Protestant theology; it was also in a real sense, along with other seventeenth-century statements of the faith, the conclusion of sixteen centuries of theological work.[2]

The results of the Westminster Assembly, ironically, were only of a limited nature in England itself. The subsequent political circumstances of Cromwell's Commonwealth and Protectorate in the 1650s favoring Independency or Congregationalism, and of the Restoration of the Stuart monarchy in the person of Charles II in 1660 restoring Episcopacy, prevented the establishment of Presbyterianism for more than a very brief time, or in any complete fashion. All of the Assembly's major documents, however, were adopted readily by the General Assembly of the Church of Scotland and also eventually by the Scottish Parliament. As Presbyterianism was conveyed to other parts of the world, including America, the Westminster Standards were adopted in those various places.

But the work of the Westminster Assembly was influential not only among Presbyterians. Again, John Leith comments:

> The Westminster Confession was adopted with a few modifications as the Savoy Declaration of the English Congregational churches. It was adopted by the Congregational Synod of Cambridge, Massachusetts in 1648, and with the Savoy modification, by the Synod of Boston in 1680, and by the Congregational churches of Connecticut at the Synod of Saybrook in 1708. It was adopted with modification by the London Baptists in 1677 and in America as the Baptist Confession of 1742 (Philadelphia).

He goes on to add: 'Certainly the number of children who received their religious instruction from the Shorter Catechism must be estimated in the millions.' [3] Philip Schaff says further:

> The Westminster Confession together with the Catechisms, is the fullest and ripest symbolical statement of the Calvinistic system of doctrine. In theological ability and merit it is equal to the best works of the kind, and is not surpassed by the Lutheran Formula of Concord or the Roman Decrees of the Councils of Trent and the Vatican [I]. Its intrinsic worth alone can explain the fact that it has supplanted the older Scottish standards of John Knox and John Craig in the land of their birth, and that it was adopted by three distinct denominations: by the Presbyterians in full, and by the Congregationalists and the Regular Baptists with some slight modifications .... Altogether it represents the most vigorous and yet moderate form of Calvinism.[4]

If all of this is even nearly the case, then we naturally want to know how this Assembly did its work and what sort of people were involved. The latter subject is the main focus of this book, but, before considering the people, it is necessary to give a brief sketch of the general course of the Assembly's work with the main turning-points over its five-and-a-half years.

The members of the Assembly, all being Calvinists, were essentially agreed in doctrine. They were also all agreed in wanting to change the prelacy of the existing Episcopal system of church government, although some held out hope for a modified form of Episcopacy. It was also apparent before the beginning of the Assembly that some of the Puritan brotherhood, particularly those who had experienced Congregationalism while in exile in the Netherlands, were in favor of Independency within a national church. The Scottish delegation, naturally, favored the Presbyterian system of church government as it had been established in their homeland in the days of John Knox and of Andrew Melville. One of the first major turning-points came as a result of a deteriorating military situation in 1643 that led to the Solemn League and Covenant. This was a political and ecclesiastical agreement between Parliament and Scotland, adopted on September 25, 1643, to bring the Scottish armies into alliance with the Parliamentary forces and to commit the English Puritans to reform the church in accord with the Scriptures and the best Reformed churches (such as the Presbyterian Church of Scotland). The Scottish commissioners entered the Assembly just as it was giving up its effort to revise the Thirty-Nine Articles of the Church of England, its major task of the summer of 1643, and was turning to the pressing matters of worship, ordination, and church government. Through much of 1644 and 1645 the focus was upon church government, with the Independent minority raising many arguments in the 'Grand Debate' but finally yielding to the Presbyterian majority, who were aided by the arguments of the Scots who, though not voting members, were free to enter into all the debates of the Assembly and its committees.

A second major issue for the Assembly had to do with Church discipline and the Erastianism of some of its members, but especially of Parliament. Erastianism takes it name from Thomas Erastus, a sixteenth-century physician-theologian influential in Zurich and Heidelberg. He taught that the civil government has the responsibility to exercise jurisdiction over all matters, whether civil or ecclesiastical, and to punish all offences, even the church's excommunication being subject to civil approval. Although all the Westminster divines were still committed to the concept of an established national church, the majority of them, like John Calvin, maintained the prerogative of the church, in administering the keys bestowed by Christ, to determine who could come to the Lord's Supper and enjoy the fellowship of the church and who could be excluded for reasons of scandal or heresy. The 'crisis of the Assembly' occurred in March and April 1646, when the Assembly protested against the system of commissioners for dealing with appeals from church discipline that Parliament was preparing to institute, and Parliament charged the Assembly with 'breach of privilege'. Parliament issued 'Nine Queries' concerning the *jus divinum*, or divine right, of church government, which were ultimately answered outside the Assembly by the London Presbyterian ministers' *Divinum Regiminis Ecclesiastici* of December 2, 1646. The crisis passed as the political-military situation shifted, but Parliament never did approve parts of the Confession of Faith relating to the civil magistrate.

Military victories by the Parliamentary forces at Marston Moor on July 2, 1644, increasing the influence of Cromwell and hence of the Independents, and at Naseby on June 14, 1645, destroying the King's military hopes, affected the balance of power within Parliament and between Parliament and the Army. The Army took power in London in the summer of 1647, and the Scots invaded on behalf of the Stuart King in the spring of 1648, producing the Second Civil War. Cromwell defeated the Scottish armies, and on December 6 'Pride's Purge' removed Presbyterians from Parliament, leaving the 'Rump Parliament'. In January 1649 Charles I was tried, and he was executed on the 30th.

In the midst of these complex events the Assembly was meanwhile pursuing its work on the Confession of Faith and the Catechisms, first in committees and then in the full Assembly. The Confession was completed on November 26, 1646, with the Scripture proofs added and sent to Parliament on April 26, 1647. The Larger Catechism was completed on October 15, 1647, the Shorter Catechism on November 25, 1647, and both presented in final form on April 14, 1648. The Scots had returned home before the end of 1647, and the Assembly continued to function mainly for the examination of candidates for the ministry.

The dramatic and exciting twists and turns of the history surrounding the Assembly contribute a context that makes the doctrinal standards less abstract, but the people who produced them add an even more personal dimension. Acquaintance with the remarkable persons who

generated these documents, although they are little known even to
church historians, adds a human element to what can otherwise seem
like mere propositions of theology. It is hoped that the biographical
sketches contained in this book will first of all prove edifying, both by
providing exemplary models of Christian commitment and also by
stimulating greater interest in, and study of, the Westminster Confession and Catechisms themselves.

My first challenge was to determine which of the members of the
Assembly were most involved and most influential. Out of the one
hundred and twenty-one originally nominated by Parliament (two for
each English county, one for each Welsh county, two each for the
Universities of Oxford and Cambridge, four for London, and one for
each of the Channel Islands), plus almost twenty more who replaced
those who died or did not participate, and also the thirty members of
Parliament and the six Scottish commissioners, I have selected forty-
six (including the non-voting assistant John Wallis) plus three New
Englanders as well as the Irish Anglican Archbishop James Ussher who
were invited but did not come. Also included are four famous contemporary Puritans who were not members of the Assembly but had
significant connections with it. I have been guided in my selection by
the amount of participation in debates, the preaching activities before
Parliament, the theological influence through writing or teaching at the
Universities, the particular role played in producing the Confession or
Catechisms, and the unique role of the clergy in the city of London. An
argument certainly could be made for including some that I have left
out, but I believe that it is not difficult to justify the inclusion of each
one that does appear here.

A second task was to determine the distinctive contribution of each
figure. The more I studied each one, the better I came to know his
emphases and style as well as his particular gifts. As a result I have
grouped them in the categories shown in the Table of Contents. These
divisions are certainly not to be viewed as hard-and-fast or necessarily
definitive. John Arrowsmith, for example, could just as fairly be put in
the category of notable theologians and Edmund Staunton among the
noted preachers. In the introductions to each chapter I seek to mention
others who deserve to be included in that category.

It should also be acknowledged that I have not had the opportunity
to read many of the primary sources, but my work is largely derivative
from many excellent secondary sources. At the same time, where

possible, I have quoted from the Westminster divines themselves so that one may hear the voice of the Assembly. The copious end-notes are intended to guide those who are interested to test my conclusions or to pursue further research. Certainly such figures as Stephen Marshall, Cornelius Burgess, Edmund Calamy, William Gouge, Thomas Gataker, Herbert Palmer, Thomas Goodwin and Alexander Henderson deserve modern full-length studies. As will be apparent to anyone who peruses the end-notes, I am especially indebted to the works on the Assembly by Robert S. Paul, John Richard de Witt, S.W. Carruthers and Alexander F. Mitchell. For biographical information I owe much to the standard reference works, such as A.G. Matthews' *Calamy Revised* and the *Dictionary of National Biography*, in which the entries on Assembly members that I have used are almost half by Alexander Gordon, no other contributor doing more than two. The 1979 Yale Ph.D. dissertation by Larry Jackson Holley contains much helpful biographical information for the period up to 1643, but also several errors. James Reid's *Memoirs of the Westminster Divines* (1811, 1815) is an invaluable source of information not to be found elsewhere, but it also tends to be fulsome and excessively devotional. I have relied on him to be the channel, nevertheless, for accounts from earlier biographers such as Samuel Clarke, Thomas Fuller, Daniel Neal and Benjamin Brook. A more concise source for much of the same information is the anonymous *History of the Westminster Assembly ... and Biographical Sketches of Its Most Conspicuous Members* published in 1841, which the minutes of the Presbyterian Board of Publication at the Presbyterian Historical Society in Philadelphia show most likely to be by Archibald Alexander of Princeton Theological Seminary.

Every reader will probably find one of these Puritan figures with whom to identify. Some were laymen: in this collection John Selden, Archibald Johnston of Warriston, John, Lord Maitland, and Sir Henry Vane, Jr. Of the divines, some were military chaplains, some were teachers, some were pastors; some were imprisoned, exiled, or plundered by soldiers; some were unmarried, some had numerous children; some were aged, some were still youthful; some were from humble and poor backgrounds, some were from the upper classes; all of the divines were both preachers and theologians. In the providence of God an amazing and fascinating group of men, supported no doubt by some amazing and fascinating women of whom we get only glimpses, were brought together to produce materials that have been of great usefulness to the church of Jesus Christ, documents that are far better known than the individuals who produced them. It is my hope that an acquaintance with the individuals will stimulate an even greater knowledge of the documents they produced and of the Scriptures and the great Author to which they point. In giving thanks for them, may we glorify and enjoy their God and ours.

Notes

1. Philip Schaff, *The Creeds of Christendom,* 3 vols., 6th ed. (New York and London: Harper & Brothers, 1877, 1931) I, 728.
2. John H. Leith, *Assembly at Westminster: Reformed Theology in the Making* (Richmond, Va.: John Knox Press, 1973), 12.
3. *Ibid.,* 11-12
4. Schaff, *Creeds of Christendom,* I, 788.

Chapter 2

The Officers of the Assembly

Those chosen to be officers of the Westminster Assembly clearly were recognized as leaders among the Puritan clergy. The Prolocutor, or presiding officer, was appointed by Parliament. The Assessors, or assistants to the Prolocutor, were chosen by the Assembly itself. In addition to the six that served in these two positions who are described in this chapter, Parliament also appointed two Scribes who were divines but not voting members of the Assembly, Henry Roborough and Adoniram Byfield, both members of the London clergy. In December of 1643 the young John Wallis was appointed by Parliament as Amanuensis or assistant to the Scribes, and he is described in Chapter 8 on the notable scholars.

William Twisse (c.1578 -July 19, 1646)

Parliament appointed the Prolocutor, or presiding officer, of the Westminster Assembly. The choice of Dr. William Twisse was unanimous in both the House of Lords and the House of Commons. This no doubt reflected two things: his international reputation as an orthodox Reformed scholar and his moderate spirit. The Scottish delegate Robert Baillie suspected that the latter was the main motivation of the political powers:

> The man, as the world knows, is very learned in the questions he has studied, and very good, beloved of all, and highlie esteemed; but merely bookish, and not much, as it seems, acquaint with conceived prayer, [and] among the unfittest of all the company for any action; so after the prayer he sitts mute. It was the canny convoyance of these who guide most matters for their own interest to plant such a man of purpose in the chaire.[1]

Twisse was known to be one who favored a reformed episcopacy and who had managed to avoid repression by the monarchy. On the other hand, his Calvinistic credentials were clear from his published opposition to Arminianism, and his strong sabbatarian views marked him as a Puritan. As one of the oldest members of the Assembly, he was widely respected, but his waning energies, and finally failing health, kept him from playing a very active role in the debates.

Born at Speanhamland near Newbury, in Berkshire, about 1578 (according to some, perhaps as early as 1576), Twisse was the son of a well-to-do clothier. His grandfather was German, and Twisse may have been fluent in that language, as shown by his later travels. Admitted to Winchester School in 1590, his religious convictions developed there. He entered New College, Oxford as probationer fellow in 1596 and continued there for the next sixteen years, receiving his B.A. on October 14, 1600, his M.A. on June 12, 1604 (after which he was ordained), and his B.D. on July 9, 1612.

Twisse had gained some attention through his Thursday catechetical lectures in the college chapel and his Sunday sermons at St. Olave's, attracting both town and gown in Oxford. He gained the appreciation of the University, however, through an unusual incident. A Jew who taught Hebrew to Oxford students, Joseph Barnatus, had persuaded several University doctors, including the Warden of New College, that he had converted to Christianity, and Twisse was to preach at his baptism. On the day before, however, having filled his purse, he ran away. Dragged back to Oxford, he declined baptism, and Twisse put aside his prepared sermon and preached instead on God's judgment on rebellious backsliding. 'He acquitted himself on this remarkable occasion in such a learned and masterly manner, that he was applauded and admired by the whole University.'[2]

Shortly thereafter King James I chose him to be chaplain to his daughter Elizabeth, Queen of Bohemia, to accompany her with her husband to Heidelberg from April to June 1613. Upon his return he became rector of Newtown Longville, Buckinghamshire. While there he continued with his studies, receiving his D.D. on July 5, 1614. It was also while there that he refused in 1618 to read the King's 'Book of Sports' because of his sabbath convictions. However, James ordered the bishops not to disturb him, perhaps because of the service he had rendered to the Princess Elizabeth or possibly because the King knew that Twisse's reputation was such both at home and among the Reformed churches abroad that to treat him harshly 'would redound greatly to their own disgrace'.[3]

Twisse's reputation had indeed grown through his publications. In 1618 he aided Sir Henry Savile in the publication of the fourteenth-century Augustinian Archbishop of Canterbury Thomas Bradwardine's *De Causa Dei contra Pelagium*. In 1632 he published *Vindiciae Gratiae, Potestatis ac Providentiae Dei*, written against the Arminians and Jesuits. In 1641 appeared *Of the Morality of the Fourth Commandment*, which would be re-issued posthumously in 1652 as *The Christian Sabbath Defended*. In 1646 he published *An Examination of Mr. Cotton's Treatise concerning Predestination*, a response to the views of John Cotton, a close friend. But his main work was *Animadversiones de Predestinatione*, published by Andrew Rivet in 1649, in which he answered all of the arguments of Arminius, Corvinus, and others against the Elizabethan Calvinist William Perkins. Also appearing posthumously were his *The Riches of God's Love* in 1653 and 'Fifteen Letters to Joseph Mede', originally written between November 1629 and July 1638 to the Cambridge chiliast expressing his own premillennial views and other matters.[4]

On October 4, 1620 Twisse was installed as rector of Newbury, his home town, and he remained in that post until appointed to the Westminster Assembly. He steadfastly declined numerous other invitations that stemmed from his international reputation. These included

one to a chair of divinity at the University of Franeker in the Nether-
lands, where William Ames taught. He once explored a change in order
to reduce his duties as age took its toll and conferred about it with
Archbishop William Laud, with whom he had been acquainted at
Oxford. When Laud offered to help, saying he would assure King
Charles I that Twisse was no Puritan, he decided to stay where he was.

Twisse's moderation was apparent even though he was recognized
abroad as the most scholarly opponent of Arminian theology. When the
Westminster Assembly opened on July 1, 1643, Twisse preached a
sermon before both Houses of Parliament, the members of the Assembly, and a large congregation in Westminster Abbey on John 14:18, 'I
will not leave you comfortless: I will come to you.' Thomas Fuller
reports of this sermon, which is not extant:

> In his sermon he exhorted them faithfully to discharge their high
> calling to the glory of God and the honour of his church. He much
> bemoaned that one thing was wanting, namely, the royal assent to
> give comfort and encouragement to them. Yet he hoped that by the
> efficacy of their fervent prayers it might in due time be obtained,
> and that a happy union might be procured betwixt him and the
> parliament.[5]

Twisse was regarded as the most able disputant in England, his strength
coming from his courtesy and thorough understanding of his opponent's position. As a controversialist, however, he preferred to carry on
disputations in writing:

> And, for this, he gives the following reasons: - Because, these
> things may be done more quietly by writing; the managers of the
> controversy will then be kept free from foreign discourse; the
> arguments on each side may be more properly and deliberately
> weighed; answers returned with due consideration; and the holy
> things of God may be more decently handled.[6]

It is no wonder that Robert Baillie, though finding much in the way
the Assembly did its business to admire, could groan that 'their
longsomeness is wofull at this time', and William Haller could later
comment that the 'prolocutor, for one thing, ... was not a man to shut
off discussion and force decisions'.[7]

But Twisse's intellectual reputation, his even-handed style, and his good humor helped the Assembly to start aright. Reid comments concerning his writings:

> He often affords considerable entertainment to his reader, by the vivacity of his genius, and the sharpness and elegance of his wit. He sometimes uses jocose or historical diversions, to animate the spirits of his readers, and to preserve them from weariness.[8]

John Owen, even while opposing his view that God could have forgiven sin without satisfaction, referred to Twisse with great respect: 'This great man; our learned antagonist; the learned Twisse; our justly celebrated antagonist; this renowned man; the very illustrious, and the accurate Twisse.'[9]

This trusted leader showed failing health from near the beginning of the Assembly. Members were assigned to visit him in February of 1644 and again in October. On March 30, 1645 he fainted in the pulpit of St. Andrews, Holborn, where he was one of the three lecturers. It was reported on April 1 that he was 'very sick and in great straits'. The Royalist army had deprived him of his living from Newbury, and therefore Parliament had to make a special provision for him. The Assembly assigned members to visit him twice again during 1645 and seven times in 1646 before his death on July 19.[10]

He was buried in Westminster Abbey, and his funeral was attended by the whole Assembly. The funeral sermon was preached by Robert Harris on Joshua 1:2, 'Moses, my servant, is dead.'[11] He had been married twice: first, before 1615, to a daughter of Barnabas Colnett of Combley, Isle of Wight. When he died he was a widower with four sons and three daughters.[12] In his family he had conducted a monthly fast, and regularly 'before dinner and supper, he read a portion of the holy scriptures, expounding the more obscure and difficult passages for the edification of his family'.[13]

Following the Restoration, on September 9, 1661 his remains, along with others, were dug up and thrown into a common pit in St. Margaret's churchyard. Having never sought preferment, Twisse would not have minded. Shortly before his death he had uttered these words as nearly his last: 'Now, at length, I shall have leisure to follow my studies to all eternity.'[14]

John White (Late December, 1574-July 21, 1648)

On Saturday, July 8, 1643, after a day of fasting and prayer, the members of the Westminster Assembly took an oath not to 'maintain any thing in matters of doctrine, but what I think in my conscience to be truth; or in point of discipline, but what I shall conceive to conduce most to the glory of God, and the good and peace of his church', and then they proceeded, according to Parliament's instructions, to select two Assessors, to take the place of the Prolocutor in case of absence or infirmity. The two chosen for this task were John White and Cornelius Burgess.[15]

John White was commonly called 'Patriarch White' or 'the Patriarch of Dorchester', where he had been rector for thirty-seven years. He was among the oldest members of the Assembly, being sixty-eight at its beginning. Like Dr. Twisse the Prolocutor, he too was in declining health, which would leave much of the burden of leadership with the younger Cornelius Burgess. White, however, was able to play a significant role in the Assembly's activities, and the assignments he was given reflect the respect he commanded among the Puritans. At the time of the subscribing of the Solemn League and Covenant in St. Margaret's Church, on September 25, 1643, White led in prayer, 'near upon an hour' according to John Lightfoot's vivid account.[16] Earlier, toward the beginning of the Long Parliament in 1640, White was among only fourteen divines chosen by the House of Lords to serve with a committee of bishops and peers to consider matters relating to innovations in religion.[17]

DEATHS DURING THE ASSEMBLY

Some of the significant members of the Westminster Assembly died during the course of its meetings. The dates of the deaths among the leading figures of the Assembly were as follows:

April 17, 1645	Daniel Featley, age 63
c. March 23, 1646	Thomas Coleman, age c.48
July 19, 1646	William Twisse, age c.68
August 19, 1646	Alexander Henderson, age c.63
November 13, 1646	Jeremiah Burroughes, age c.47
August or September, 1647	Herbert Palmer, age 46
July 21, 1648	John White, age 73
December 16, 1648	George Gillespie, age 35

White had gained this respect through a significant pastoral ministry in Dorsetshire. Born in late December, 1574 in Stanton Saint John in Oxfordshire, he entered Winchester School in 1587 and, like the slightly younger Twisse, went from there to New College, Oxford. He was elected a fellow in 1595, graduated B.A. on April 12, 1597 and M.A. on January 16, 1601.

In 1606 he was appointed rector of Holy Trinity Church in Dorchester, with which he would be associated until his death in 1648. Thomas Fuller comments on his ministry there that 'he absolutely commanded his own passions, and the purses of his parishioners, whom he could wind up to whatever height he pleased on important occasions. He was free from covetousness, if not trespassing on the contrary.'[18] His concern for the poor had a beneficial effect upon the community. Fuller calls him a

> good governor, by whose wisdom the town of Dorchester was much enriched, knowledge causing piety, piety breeding industry, and industry procuring plenty unto it. A beggar was not to be seen in the town, all able poor being set on work, and the impotent maintained by the profit of a public brew-house, and other collections.[19]

Another enterprise engaged White's interest. About 1624 he sought to organize a colony of Dorset Nonconformists in Massachusetts for the sake of religious liberty. He took a lead in seeking a charter and raising funds for the Massachusetts Company, holding a service on the *Arbella* for John Winthrop before he set sail for America in 1629. White is regarded as the author of the *Planters' Plea*, published in London in 1630, one of the earliest accounts of the planting of the colony. A nephew, James White, became a wealthy merchant in Boston, Massachusetts, and Governor Winthrop corresponded with White in 1632 and 1636, urging him to visit the colony.[20]

At the Westminster Assembly, White was one of those who was gradually persuaded of the Presbyterian position.[21] In the early debates on church office he spoke in favor of public reading of the Scripture as a distinct ecclesiastical function.[22] He was one of those originally appointed to the 'Grand Committee', including members of both Houses of Parliament, for the sake of carrying out provisions of the treaty with the Scots.[23] It was White who was designated to present the sensitive petition of the Assembly to Parliament concerning the autonomy of the church in guarding the sacrament of the Lord's Supper from scandalous offenders. In presenting it to the House of Commons on August 8, 1645, White said, 'That there is not a Matter of higher Concernment for the Glory of God, and Peace of this Church, than the Matter of this Petition; nor was anything ever presented to the House with more Zeal, and Tenderness of Conscience.' [24]

White sometimes filled the chair in Twisse's absence in the early months of the Assembly, but he too was subject to illness. Robert Baillie reported on December 7, 1643: 'The one assessour, our good friend Mr. Whyte, hes keeped in of the gout since our coming; the other, Dr. Burgess, a very active and sharpe man, supplies, so farr as is decent, the proloqutor's place.' [25] White was absent again on account of illness in February 1644 and March 1645. [26] In July of 1644 he received leave from the Assembly to 'go down to the country to settle his affairs there', probably as a result of the Cavalier army's having plundered his rectory in Dorchester. [27] Prince Rupert's cavalry had burst into White's house and carried off his library. He had taken refuge in the Savoy Palace until being appointed in place of Daniel Featley as rector of Lambeth on September 30, 1643 and was also given the use of Featley's library until his own books might be recovered. [28]

The burdens of leadership eventually became too great for White in his 70s. On September 23, 1646 Herbert Palmer was appointed Assessor in his place. [29] In November of 1647 he was designated Warden of New College, Oxford, but he declined, being 'sick and infirm, a dying man'. His death occurred on July 21, 1648, and he was buried in the porch of St. Peter's Chapel of his church in Dorchester. [30]

White was married to Ann, sister of Cornelius Burgess. They had four sons, the eldest of whom, John, became rector of Pimperne, Dorset. [31] Among White's published works were *A Way to the Tree of Life: Sundry Directions for the Profitable Reading of the Scriptures* (1647), *David's Psalms in Metre, agreeable to the Hebrew. To be sung in usuall Tunes To the benefit of the Churches of Christ* (1655), and *A Commentary upon the Three First Chapters of the First Book of Moses called Genesis* (1656). This final work was entrusted to Stephen Marshall for publication, but after his death in 1655 Thomas Manton introduced it to the public.

In his four decades as rector of Trinity Church in Dorchester White preached through the whole Bible once and then half of it over again. [32] Pre-eminently a pastor and minister of the Word, he was indeed a Puritan patriarch.

Cornelius Burgess (c. 1589 - early June, 1665)

'A very active and sharpe man' was Robert Baillie's estimate of Cornelius Burgess,[33] one of the two chosen by the Assembly (along with his older brother-in-law, John White) to serve as Assessors, or vice-presidents, to assist the Prolocutor, William Twisse, or serve in the chair in his absence. Twisse and White both being afflicted with illness, Burgess appears to have occupied the chair frequently prior to the death of Twisse in July of 1646 and his replacement by Charles Herle as Prolocutor. Burgess was indeed a leader and a catalyst for much Puritan activity leading up to the Westminster Assembly and following it.

The strength of his convictions and his ability to irritate not only his enemies, but even his allies who opposed him on a particular issue, are shown in his objection to parts of the Solemn League and Covenant that led to his being temporarily suspended from the Assembly. It was August of 1643 and the military situation required an alliance with the Scots, which the Solemn League and Covenant provided. For Burgess, however, some of the provisions for uniformity with the Scottish church raised problems of conscience. What specifically was meant by 'extirpation of popery'? Did opposition to 'prelacy' mean the renouncing of all forms of Episcopacy? Some modifications in the Covenant were made, but Burgess still presented his dissent. When the Assembly would not await his reasons before sending its agreement to Parliament, Burgess added his petition as an individual. The House of Commons required the Assembly to give its answer to the petition, and this caused further debate and frustrating delay. John Lightfoot terms Burgess 'the turbulent doctor' and claims that his petition was 'exceedingly derogatory to the Assembly'.[34] Not only that, but it suggested some sort of partisan motivations: Lightfoot refers to Burgess 'as a wretch to be branded to all posterity, seeking for some devilish ends, either of his own or others, or both, to hinder so great a good of the two nations'.[35] Lightfoot also observed concerning Burgess' dissent: 'This was judged, and that justly, to be intolerable impudency, that the great affairs of two dying kingdoms, should be thought fit by him to stay and wait upon his captiousness.'[36]

But this episode had a happy ending. The Assembly gave its answer on September 2 to the House of Commons, which was satisfied. Burgess said his reasons still expressed his conscientious objections, but he did not want to retard business and offered to withdraw his

petition. This was not acceptable to the Assembly, and the House of
Commons suspended him from his membership 'until he has given
satisfaction to this House and to the Assembly'. By September 8 the
Assembly was satisfied when Burgess apologized for his having
'aspersed' the Assembly, 'but without intention by me, and I am sorry
for it'. After it was pointed out that 'his crime is not his dissenting; in
that every man is free; but his petitioning', the House of Commons was
satisfied and on September 15 restored his membership. It had been a
violation of the rules for an individual, rather than the Assembly as a
body, to petition Parliament. But now, with the modifications, Burgess
was able heartily to subscribe the Solemn League and Covenant, and
he was welcomed back not only to membership, but to a leadership role
in the Assembly.[37]

Burgess had been a leader of the moderate Puritan cause since the
early years of Charles I's reign. Born about 1589 in Batcombe,
Somerset, he entered Oxford in 1611, but his College is unknown.
Transferring to Wadham College, he received the B.A. on July 5, 1615,
and then moved to Lincoln College, receiving the M.A. on April 20,
1618. He became vicar of Watford, Hertfordshire on December 21,
1613, and on January 16, 1626 he was allowed to hold also the rectory
of St. Magnus, London Bridge. He was made one of King Charles's
chaplains, and on June 16, 1627 he was made B.D. and D.D. by Oxford.

To this point his career was marked by success in seeking preferment, but it was soon to be marked by controversy. In 1635 he preached
a Latin sermon to the London clergy at St. Alphage's Church, London
Wall, near to Sion College (with which he had been associated as one
of the original Assistants since 1631 and of which he would be the
President in 1647).[38] In this sermon he stressed the need for bishops to
preach and criticized them for the growth of Arminianism and popery.[39]
He was haled before the Court of High Commission for the 'divers
insolent passages' in his sermon, but this proceeding simply increased
his hostility to the party of Archbishop Laud.[40]

When the Long Parliament opened in November of 1640, Burgess
and Stephen Marshall were chosen to preach to the House of Commons
on the day of fasting, November 17. Together they preached for seven
hours in what would prove to be the first of a significant series of 'Fast
Day Sermons' to the Long Parliament.[41] Burgess preached from Jeremiah 50:5 and emphasized, 'When God vouchsafes any deliverance
to his church, ... then it is most seasonable and most necessary to close

with God by a more solemn, strict, and inviolable, covenant, to be his, and only his for ever.'[42]

Appointed to the House of Lords' committee to consider innovations in religion, Burgess was described by Robert Baillie as the 'mouth' of the eight or ten remonstrants appearing before the committee regarding petitions concerning Episcopacy.[43] Some royalist clergy accused Burgess of instigating the mobs that cried 'No Bishops!' before the walls of Westminster Hall in the winter of 1640-1641:

> Cornelius Burgess, the parson and lecturer of St. Magnus and erstwhile chaplain-in-ordinary to King Charles, is reported to have boasted when he led the 'City rabble' to the very doors of Parliament: 'These are my Band-Dogs; I can set them on, and I can take them off again.'[44]

While that report may be apocryphal, his biographer's judgment is no doubt true: 'There was a spice of the demagogue in his temper; he had the popular ear, and liked leadership.'[45] Edward Hyde, Earl of Clarendon, the Restoration persecutor of Puritans, would later say, 'Without doubt the archbishop of Canterbury [Laud] had never so great an influence upon the counsels at court as Dr. Burgess and Mr. Marshall had then upon the Houses.'[46]

Burgess certainly was influential. The Earl of Essex, a general of Parliament's army, selected him to be chaplain to his regiment of horsemen:

> Such chaplains were highly beneficial to the parliamentary army, to direct their views aright, to afford them aid in their devotion, and to excite them in the performance of their duty, in defence of their liberty and religion, when the situation of public affairs was truly alarming.[47]

As has been mentioned, he was one of the leaders of Sion College, 'and this college would become the focal point of London Presbyterianism during the course of the Assembly, and eventually the home of the Provincial Synod of London'.[48] In the Assembly itself not only was he one of the two Assessors, but he was also convener of the first of the three Committees into which the entire Assembly was subdivided for the sake of bringing considered proposals to the floor for debate and final decisions. As one reviews the records of the Assembly, Burgess appears to be involved in almost every significant activity. He was often assigned the task of putting the official documents of the Assembly into their final form, and he accomplished a 'remarkable feat in reading over the whole of the Larger Catechism at the session of 20 October, 1647'.[49]

He may have had a strong and pleasant voice. On one of the three occasions when the City of London provided a feast for the Assembly, on January 18, 1644, the Divines decided to conclude the banquet with a Psalm: 'The Divines went down [from an upper room to the Hall where the Lord Mayor and other dignitaries were feasting], and the Psalm was sung, Burges "reading the line" in the absence of books, probably because his voice was stronger than the aged prolocutor's.'[50] He had a good knowledge of liturgy, and he may have been responsible for the preservation of some of the finest of English forms, blended with the Scottish, in the Assembly's Directory for Worship.[51]

Burgess had resigned his rectory of St. Magnus in 1641, probably to avoid the charge of pluralism. On March 12, 1644 he was appointed lecturer at the re-opened St. Paul's, with the Dean's house as residence and an income of £400 a year, 'the largest salary paid for a lecturer in this period'.[52] It is no wonder that, when distribution of money was made to the Assembly on April 7, 1645, Burgess joined Edmund Calamy, Stephen Marshall and William Spurstowe in saying they did not need to share in the distribution.[53] His finances did not fare so well, however, after the Assembly. During the trial of the King in January of 1649 he had drafted *A Vindication of the Ministers of the Gospel in and about London from the unjust aspersions cast upon their former actings for the Parliament, as if they promoted the bringing of the King to capital punishment*, which was subscribed by fifty-six other ministers who opposed the King's execution – an action that scarcely gained him favor with Oliver Cromwell.

Although he obtained an appointment as preacher in the cathedral at Wells around 1650, there was a dispute in July of 1656 about his exclusive right to officiate there. With a wife and ten children, he had invested his funds in the purchase of alienated church lands, including the manor of Wells and the deanery which he rebuilt. 'At the Restoration his investment (for which he had been offered over £12,000 in the previous year) was taken from him without recompense.'[54] Afflicted with cancer of the neck and cheek, he retired to his house at Watford, where he attended the church which he had formerly pastored. He was forced to sell most of his library, but his will left his collection of prayer-books, the only treasure left, to his 'dear and much-honoured mother, the renowned university of Oxford'. He was buried on June 9, 1665.[55]

James Reid summarized Burgess's life rightly: 'He possessed ... spirited and manly character .... His active zeal in the service of the church was eminently conspicuous .... Undaunted courage seems to have been the distinguishing characteristic of Dr. Burgess.'[56]

Charles Herle (1598 - September 1659)

When Parliament was informed on Wednesday, July 22, 1646 of Dr. William Twisse's death on the previous Sunday, both Houses immediately agreed on the appointment of Charles Herle as the new Prolocutor of the Assembly.[57] Herle had been one of the most active participants in debate in the Assembly,[58] and, although clearly Presbyterian in his convictions, he showed much sympathy with some of the biblical arguments of the Independents. Thomas Fuller said 'that he was a good scholar, and esteemed by his party a deep divine; and that he was so much the Christian, the scholar, and the gentleman, that he could agree in affection with those who differed from him in judgment'.[59]

Since the Independents were a minority in the Assembly but were favored by many in Parliament, Herle was a natural choice. Many times he defended the rights of the Independents to make their arguments, and he even sided with them on some issues.[60] He apparently maintained close personal relations with some of the Independent leaders. Robert Baillie wrote with some annoyance: '... Mr. Nye, and his good friend, Mr. Herle, hes keept us these three weeks on one point of our Directorie alone ... .'[61] In 1643 he had published *The Independency on Scriptures of the Independency of Churches* in the preface of which he had written:

> ...for the difference betweene us and our brethren that are for Independency, 'tis nothing so great as you seemed to conceive it ...; our difference 'tis such as doth at most but ruffle a little the fringe, not any way rend the Garment of Christ, 'tis so farre from being a fundamentall ....[62]

Herle was one of twelve clergy appointed by Parliament in June 1643 for licensing books on divinity, and it was he who in January 1644 licensed the publication of the Independents' *Apologeticall Narration*, in which they made public their appeal to Parliament concerning congregational church government. William Haller reports:

> Even in giving them leave to print, he declared himself inclined to 'the Presbyteriall way of Church Government.' Nevertheless, he gave them

leave and commended what they wrote as 'seasonably needfull' for the vindication of the Protestant party in general from 'the aspersions of Incommunicablenesse within itselfe' and of the writers 'both against misreportings from without, & some possible mistakings from within.' Their words, he said, were 'full of peaceablenesse, modesty, and candour.'

Haller comments: 'No wonder, in the face of such scrupulous care lest any opposition offered in the spirit of godliness should fail to get a hearing, that the Scots despaired of ever getting the church reformed.'[63]

Not only was Herle fair, but he was a man of real ability. Born in Luxulyan, Cornwall in 1598, of a well-to-do family, he entered Exeter College, Oxford on October 23, 1612 and received the B.A. on July 7, 1615 and the M.A. in June 1618. He apparently served for some years as tutor of James Stanley, Lord Strange, later to be the Earl of Derby. After serving as rector of Creed, Cornwall in 1625, he was presented through the Stanleys with the rectory of Winwick, Lancashire, one of the richest livings in England, on June 26, 1626. The rest of his life was associated with this church, and he was one of the two divines for Lancashire appointed to the Assembly.

In the Assembly he was appointed to the Grand Committee of Parliament for dealing officially with the Scots and also to the committee for composing differences with the Independents, as well as to various other committees. In the Assembly's debate on Erastianism it was Herle, rather than George Gillespie, who gave the immediate response to John Selden's learned speech claiming that Matthew 18 was referring to Jewish civil courts and not to ecclesiastical courts. The more studied responses from Gillespie and Thomas Young came the next day. Alexander Mitchell comments concerning Herle's spur-of-the-moment response that 'judging even from the fragmentary jottings preserved by Byfield, one cannot doubt that it was a very able reply'.[64]

Herle was distinguished most, however, as a preacher. He was called upon to preach four times before the House of Commons and three times before the House of Lords during the 1640s, and at least five of his sermons were published.[65]

John F. Wilson comments that Herle's sermon on the Fast Day of November 30, 1642 'breathed a different spirit' from the militantly political themes up to that time: 'In a sober and reflective manner Herle proposed that "truth" and "peace" were a "Payre of Compasses" to guide church and state.'[66]

He had a high sense of the minister's calling. In the Assembly's discussions of how much education should be required for the ministry, and specifically whether knowledge of Greek and Latin was necessary, Herle said, 'I am of opinion that the pastor's office is to convince; he must be able not only to feed the flock, but to keep off the wolf.'[67] He had pastoral sensitivity to his people's concerns. In the debates on the Preface to the Directory of Worship he warned against an outright condemnation of the Anglican Prayer Book, for 'all the west are exceedingly devoted to this booke'.[68]

He was opposed to the execution of Charles I and therefore retired to Winwick in 1649. In 1651, when the Earl of Derby raised a regiment of soldiers for Charles II, Herle and his household were startled when Lieutenant Arundal arrived with forty horsemen. Expecting to be plundered, Herle discovered that the Earl simply wanted to confer with him. After defeat at the Battle of Warrington Bridge the wounded Arundal was treated at Herle's home. This led to Herle's being investigated in London and being put under temporary restraint.[69]

Mrs. Margaret Herle, buried in the cloisters of Westminster Abbey in January 1647, is thought to have been his first wife. He married as his second wife Dorothy, daughter of John Marshall. He had a large family. After retirement for several years, he died at Winwick and was buried in the chancel of his church on September 29, 1659.

One of his final ministerial acts was to participate, about July 1652, in the ordination of the twenty-two year old John Howe in the parish church of Winwick. The later famous Howe, who also tried and failed to unite Presbyterians and Congregationalists, would sometimes say 'That he thought few in modern times had so truly primitive an ordination; for he considered Mr. Herle as a primitive bishop'.[70]

Herbert Palmer (March 1601 - August or September 1647)

The declining health of John White caused the Assembly to appoint Herbert Palmer as Assessor in his place on September 23, 1646.[71] Palmer had been one of the most active participants in the debates on church government and worship,[72] gradually espousing a Presbyterian position. He had a reputation as 'the best catechist in England'.[73] He was different from most of the members of the Assembly in that he came from an upper-class background and that he remained unmarried.

He was born at Wingham, Kent in March of 1601, younger son of

Sir Thomas Palmer, Knight, or Baronet who had been High Sheriff of Kent and had published a book on foreign travel. Another son of Sir Thomas Palmer by a different wife (and hence a half-brother of Herbert) was Sir James Palmer, who obtained a place in the household of James I and was a personal friend of Charles I when he was Prince of Wales.[74] Herbert Palmer learned French almost as soon as he learned to talk, a knowledge that he would later put to effective use in his ministry. At four or five years of age he began to ask his mother (the eldest daughter of Herbert Pelham of Cawdrey, Sussex) about God. As his gifts developed in youth and he was asked whether he desired to become a lawyer, a courtier, a country gentleman or the like, he replied that he would be a minister of Jesus Christ.[75]

Admitted to St. John's College, Cambridge on March 23, 1616, he received his B.A. in 1619 and his M.A. in 1622 and was chosen as a Fellow of Queen's College on July 17, 1623. He was ordained in 1624 and called to pastoral duties at St. Alphage's Church, Canterbury in 1626. It was in Canterbury that his knowledge of French proved useful, for the minister of the French church there, Philip Delme (who would also serve later in the Westminster Assembly), appreciated his gifts and had him to preach on several occasions. Short of stature and of youthful appearance, Palmer startled an elderly French lady upon his first visit to the church, who said in a loud voice, 'Alas! what shall this child say to us?' But after hearing him pray and preach with fervency and vigor, she lifted up her hands to heaven, praising God for what she had heard.[76]

There were those in the Cathedral of Canterbury who opposed Palmer because of his zeal and piety, claiming that he had gone beyond his office of Lecturer by catechizing and that his Sunday afternoon lecture was drawing 'factious persons' out of other parishes.[77] His high birth and powerful friends, however, tended to protect him. His friends at court almost got him appointed as a prebendary of Canterbury, but he later was thankful that he was removed from the scene of High Church innovations. In February of 1632, with the assistance of William Laud, then Bishop of London, he became vicar of Ashwell, Hertfordshire. In 1632 he was also made a university preacher of Cambridge, having obtained his Bachelor of Divinity in the previous year.

His preaching was characterized by plainness and simplicity, designed to reach the ordinary people. He also encouraged private conference with his parishioners and was known as an excellent casuist, helpful to those who came to him with distressed consciences. He catechized his people publicly and privately, composing and publishing a catechism entitled *An Endeavour of making the Principles of Christian Religion plain and easie* (1640; 6th impression, 1645).

Having a sizeable estate and never marrying, he was charitable in giving Bibles to the poor who could read and for giving money for instruction in reading to those who could not. He welcomed into his home several sons of the nobility and gentry and maintained a tutor to instruct them in the faith. After meals one of the young gentlemen would read a chapter of Scripture and then would be required to repeat from memory the substance of what he had read. He also maintained several poor scholars at Queen's College, Cambridge, of which he was appointed Master on April 11, 1644, and at his death he left a considerable sum of money for that purpose.

In the Assembly Palmer was known for prudence in matters that required deliberation. Not readily persuaded of the office of ruling elder as a matter of divine right, he listened carefully to the Scriptural debate. The Scottish commissioner Robert Baillie tells us:

> When all were tired, it came to the question. There was no doubt but we would have carried it by far most voices; yet because the opposites were men verie considerable, above all gracious and learned little Palmer, we agreed upon a committee to satisfie, if it were possible, the dissenters.[78]

Eventually Palmer was won over to this Presbyterian position.

Thoroughly involved in the work of the Assembly, he left his residence and ministry at Ashwell, but he preached at various churches in London, becoming lecturer at St. James's, Duke Place and then the first pastor of New Church in the parish of St. Margaret's, Westminster (since 1843 represented by Christ Church, Westminster). By appointment of Parliament he was also one of seven who gave the regular morning lecture at the Abbey church of Westminster. He was called upon several times to preach before Parliament, where he did not hesitate to speak candidly to his hearers' spiritual needs. This sometimes incurred their displeasure, but he said:

> ... how much soever they might be superior to him in other respects, yet he was in that place superior to them, as acting in God's name; and therefore would not be afraid to speak, whatever was the will of God

that he should tell them, notwithstanding any displeasure or danger
which might by this means befal him for so doing.[79]

He and his colleague Thomas Hill won the plaudits of Robert Baillie
for their preaching on the Day of Humiliation for both Houses, August
13, 1644: '... two of the most Scottish and free sermons that ever I heard
any where.' Baillie said that 'these two good men laid well about them,
and charged publicke and parlimentarie sins strictly on the backs of the
guilty ....'[80] Among the guilty whom Palmer charged on that occasion
was John Milton for the publication of his treatises on divorce. Arguing
against a policy of toleration, Palmer had asked:

> If any plead Conscience for lawfulness of Polygamy; or for Divorce for
> other causes than Christ and His Apostles mention (of which a wicked
> book is abroad and uncensured, though deserving to be burnt, whose
> Author hath been so impudent as to set his name to it and dedicate it to
> yourselves); or for liberty to marry incestuously – will you grant a
> toleration for all this?[81]

Milton was incensed and responded with his *Tetrachordon* in such a
way that, at least among scholars of English literature, it is Palmer's
reputation that has suffered the greater damage.[82]

But Palmer made a major contribution to a piece of literature that
may have influenced more people than have even Milton's writings –
namely, the Westminster Catechisms. The Scots were not altogether
pleased with Palmer's first effort in the production of the Assembly's
directory of catechizing: 'Mr. Marshall's part anent preaching, and Mr.
Palmer's about catechizing, though the one be the best preacher, and
the other the best catechist in England, yet we now ways like it; so their
papers are passed in our hands to frame them according to our mind.'[83]
Palmer continued to influence the committee work, however, and
although he died before the Catechisms were completed, his method of
catechizing was perpetuated in his younger protegé John Wallis' later
explanation of the Shorter Catechism.[84]

Exhausted from his labors, in his last illness Palmer prayed

> ... for himself, that God would heal the sinfulness of his nature, pardon
> all his transgressions, deliver him from an evil heart of unbelief, and
> from temptation; – teach him to improve all providences, and to live
> upon Christ and the promises. He also prayed much for the nation, for

the church of God, and for all with whom he stood connected. He prayed particularly for Scotland, the churches in France, New England, and foreign plantations.[85]

He died in 1647, at the age of only 46.[86]

His portrait, on page 183 of Samuel Clarke's, *A General Martyrologie*, (London, 1677) 'shows an emaciated visage, sunk between his shoulders; he wears moustache and thin beard, skull-cap and ruff, with academic gown, and leans on a cushion'.[87] He may have been frail and small in physical stature, but he was esteemed by his colleagues and contemporaries as a man of the highest spiritual qualities and of gigantic influence. In summarizing his account of the Assembly, Robert S. Paul says: 'Very early in their London enterprise the Scots had realized that their best hope of success would be to gain the support of men like Herbert Palmer and Cornelius Burgess.'[88]

William Gouge (December 25, 1578 - December 12, 1653)

After the death of Herbert Palmer in August or September of 1647 the Assembly proceeded on November 25 to elect as Assessor in his place Dr. William Gouge, esteemed by that time as 'the father of the London ministers'.[89] Gouge had been one of the most active participants in the work of the Assembly, and he was widely respected both for his affable temperament and for his longevity as a Puritan pastor in the City of London. According to William Haller, he ranked with Richard Sibbes and John Preston among the influential London Puritan ministers of the previous generation.[90]

He was preacher at the large St. Anne's or Blackfriars Church in London, first as lecturer and associate to the rector, Stephen Egerton, (upon the recommendation of Arthur Hildersham) from June of 1608, and then as rector from 1621 until his death at the end of 1653.[91] Called an 'Arch Puritan' by some of his detractors, he was offered more eminent church positions, but he often said that the height of his ambition was to go from Blackfriars to heaven. As a pastor he was recognized as an excellent casuist, ministering effectively to dejected souls and distressed consciences. Among the London ministers he was known for his ability to reconcile differences and also for his charity to the needy.

At the Assembly he was instrumental in resolving the tension with

Cornelius Burgess when that fiery Puritan was suspended by Parliament from the Assembly for his unwillingness to subscribe the Solemn League and Covenant. S.W. Carruthers says that Gouge, 'always a kindly and peaceable soul', reported Burgess' apology to the Assembly.[92] His own attendance was quite regular, and he always carried his Bible or some other book in his pocket so that he might not lose any time during intermissions in the Assembly's business.

This diligence with regard to time was a habit from his youth. Born on December 25, 1578[93] to a family of high estate in Stratford-le-Bow, Middlesex, he went from Eton School to King's College, Cambridge in 1595. There he went through the entire first three years without spending a night outside the walls of the College. During his nine years at King's (receiving the B.A. in 1598, admitted as Fellow on August 25, receiving the M.A. in 1602, and continuing to lecture in logic and philosophy until withdrawing to marry in 1604), he never missed morning prayers in the chapel, which were held at 5:30 a.m. He resolved to read daily fifteen chapters of the Bible, five at each of three

WILLIAM GOUGE

different times of the day. He emphasized the setting apart of the Lord's Day and so regulated his family and household that servants would not have to prepare a meal on Saturday evening or on Sunday.

He usually preached twice on Sunday, and for thirty-five years he also gave a weekly Wednesday forenoon lecture which was well attended by several of the London ministers, leading citizens of London, and even those visiting the city on secular business: 'When the godly Christians of those times came out of the Country into London, they thought not their business done unlesse they had been at Blackfriars lecture.' Gouge had successfully purchased and expanded the church's property to accommodate the crowds: 'So great was the confluence of his hearers that "he was wont (before he began his Sermons) to observe what Pues were empty and to command his Clark to open them for the ease of those who thronged in the Isles".'[94]

As a scholar, not only had he lectured in logic and philosophy at King's College, but he also gave instruction in Hebrew, having been the only steadfast pupil of a Rabbi who had come to Cambridge to teach that language.[95] Gouge had received the Bachelor of Divinity in 1611 and the Doctor of Divinity in 1628. He was appointed by Parliament to be one of those to prepare Annotations on the Bible (sometimes known as the 'English Annotations' or the 'Westminster Annotations' since prepared mostly by Westminster divines, by order of Parliament, at the time of the Assembly); his own part was from 1 Kings to Esther. At the end of his life, in 1653, he was completing a massive commentary on Hebrews, having finished all but the last half-chapter (representing nearly a thousand sermons preached at his church), when he passed cheerfully and quietly to his Lord, thus fulfilling his ambition to go from Blackfriars to heaven. In his last years he suffered from asthma and kidney stones so much that he abandoned preaching, finding it 'a greater difficulty for him to go up into the pulpit, than either to make or preach a sermon'.[96]

Through his long life Gouge was a leader of the Puritan clergy in London. Along with Richard Sibbes in 1626 he had led in raising funds and buying up impropriations in order to support Puritan lectureships.[97] Toward the conclusion of the Westminster Assembly, he was a leader in establishing a Presbytery in London. On May 3, 1647 he was chosen Prolocutor at the first meeting of the Presbyterian provincial assembly of London. In 1649 he served as President of Sion College.

His family represented a Puritan legacy unto the third and fourth

generation. His mother having been sister to two preachers, Samuel and
Ezekiel Culverwell, and having also two sisters married to Puritan
theologians, Dr. Lawrence Chaderton, Master of Emmanuel College,
Cambridge, and Dr. William Whitaker, Master of St. John's, Cambridge, Gouge thus had four notable uncles from the earlier Elizabethan
period. In 1607 he married the orphan daughter of Henry Caulton, a
London merchant, and they had seven sons and six daughters, eight of
whom reached maturity. His eldest son, Thomas (1609-1681), became
a minister in London, was ejected in 1662, and eventually established
Nonconformist schools in Wales. His eldest daughter, Elizabeth,
married a minister, Richard Roberts, who also was ejected in 1662.
Thus Gouge represented a link to the Puritanism of the Restoration era.

Among his several publications were *On Domesticall Duties Eight
Treatises* (1622; 2nd ed., 1626; 3rd ed., 1634) and *A Guide to go to God
... Explanation of the Lord's Prayer* (2nd ed., 1626). His commentary
on Hebrews (1655) has been reprinted as recently as 1980. Three
engravings of his portrait, by John Dunstall, by William Faithorne the
elder and by Stent,[98] have come down to us and show the impressive,
high-browed, white-haired and bearded visage of a Puritan leader.

Notes

1. Robert S. Paul, *The Assembly of the Lord: Politics and Religion in the Westminster Assembly and the 'Grand Debate'* (Edinburgh: T. & T. Clark, 1985) 70 n.57,
quoting from Baillie's *Letters and Journals*, II, 108.
2. James Reid, *Memoirs of the Westminster Divines*, 2 vols. in 1 (Edinburgh and
Carlisle, Pa.: Banner of Truth, 1981; reprint of edition of 1811 and 1815), I, 38; cf.
Dictionary of National Biography, eds. Leslie Stephen and Sidney Lee, 22 vols.
(London: Oxford U. Press 1921-22,) under 'Twisse, William, D.D.', XIX, 1324-
1326.
3. Reid, *Memoirs*, I, 43; Larry Jackson Holley, 'The Divines of the Westminster
Assembly,' (Yale U. Ph.D. diss., 1979), 350.
4. Cf. Paul, *Assembly of the Lord*, 394 n.24.
5. John Richard de Witt, *Jus Divinum: The Westminster Assembly and The Divine
Right of Church Government* (Kampen: J.H. Kok, 1969), 31, quoting Fuller, *The
Church History of Britain*, VI, 250.
6. Reid, *Memoirs*, I, 46, citing Twisse's *The Riches of God's Love*.
7. William Haller, *Liberty and Reformation in the Puritan Revolution* (New York
and London: Columbia U. Press, 1955), 111.
8. Reid, *Memoirs*, I, 50-51. Edmund Calamy also said that 'he was very famous
on account of his wit, learning, and writings' (Reid, I, 49).
9. *Ibid.*, I, 55. Twisse was also a supralapsarian with regard to the order of God's

decrees, but regarded that controversy merely 'a logical nicety' (Reid, I, 54).

10. S.W. Carruthers, *The Everyday Work of the Westminster Assembly* (Philadelphia: Presbyterian Historical Societies of America and of England, 1943), 180; cf. *D.N.B.* XIX, 1326. His signature on a petition to Parliament shows him to have still been active in the Assembly in August of 1645. (Alexander Mitchell, *The Westminster Assembly: Its History and Standards*, 2nd ed. [Philadelphia: Presbyterian Board of Publication, 1897], 306).

11. [Archibald Alexander], *A History of the Westminster Assembly of Divines* (Philadelphia: Presbyterian Board of Publication, 1841), 389.

12. *D.N.B.*, XIX, 1326.

13. Reid, *Memoirs*, I, 52.

14. *Ibid.*, I, 57.

15. Paul, *Assembly of the Lord*, 78.

16. de Witt, *Jus Divinum*, 54, quoting from Lightfoot's *Whole Works*, XIII, 19.

17. Mitchell, *Westminster Assembly*, 101; Paul, *Assembly of the Lord*, 64 and n.37.

18. Reid, *Memoirs*, I, 102, quoting Fuller, *Worthies of England*, II, 340; cf. *D.N.B.*, under 'White, John,' XXI, 59-61. David Underdown, *Fire From Heaven: Life in an English Town in the Seventeenth Century* (New Haven and London; Yale University Press, 1992) says: 'Fanned by the elegant preaching of John White, the new civic spirit was to turn Dorchester, ... into the most 'puritan' town in England ... (5) and comments on the influence of his ministry (92-93, 108, 128).

19. Reid, *Memoirs*, I, 100-101.

20. *D.N.B.*, XXI, 59-60.

21. Paul, *Assembly of the Lord*, 119, 149, 157.

22. *Ibid.*, 141.

23. *Ibid.*, 243 n. 87. The role of the Grand Committee is described in Wayne R. Spear, 'Covenanted Uniformity in Religion: The Influence of the Scottish Commissioners upon the Ecclesiology of the Westminster Assembly' (U. of Pittsburgh Ph.D. diss., 1976), 73-82.

24. de Witt, *Jus Divinum*, 184.

25. Quoted from Baillie's *Letters and Journals*, II, 107-109 in Paul, *Assembly of the Lord*, 558, and also in de Witt, *Jus Divinum*, 35.

26. Carruthers, *Everyday Work,* 180-181.

27. *Ibid.*, 182. Underdown, *Fire From Heaven*, 203-205 describes the Cavalier Army's attack on Dorchester.

28. *D.N.B.*, XXI, 60.

29. de Witt, *Jus Divinum*, 33 n.87.

30. *D.N.B.*, XXI, 60.

31. *Ibid.*, 61. Philip Schaff, *Creeds of Christendom*, I, 741, incorrectly claims that White was 'the great-grandfather of the Wesleys on the maternal side,' but Susannah Wesley was granddaughter of John White 'the Centurator' (1590-1645) who, according to *D.N.B.*, XXI, 59, is frequently confused with John White 'the Patriarch of Dorchester'.

32. Reid, *Memoirs*, I, 100.

33. Quoted in Paul, *Assembly of the Lord*, 558, and de Witt, *Jus Divinum*, 35.

34. Carruthers, *Everyday Work*, 173, 174.

35. de Witt, *Jus Divinum*, 51, quoting from Lightfoot, *Whole Works*, XIII, 11-13.

36. Paul, *Assembly of the Lord*, 93 n.75.

37. This whole incident is described rather fully in Carruthers, *Everyday Work*, 173-175, and in de Witt, *Jus Divinum*, 50-52.

38. Paul, *Assembly of the Lord*, 63 n.32, 78 n.18, 118.

39. Reid, *Memoirs*, I, 69-70; *D.N.B.* under 'Burges or Burgess, Cornelius, D.D.,' III, 301-304.

40. Holley, 'Divines,' 286.

41. Cf. H.R. Trevor-Roper, *The Crisis of the Seventeenth Century: Religion, the Reformation and Social Change* (New York & Evanston: Harper & Row, 1968), Chapter 6 'The Fast Sermons of the Long Parliament,' 294-344, and John F. Wilson, *Pulpit in Parliament: Puritanism During the English Civil Wars, 1640-1648* (Princeton, N.J.: Princeton U. Press, 1969).

42. Reid, *Memoirs*, I. 72.

43. Holley, 'Divines,' 287.

44. Paul S. Seaver, *The Puritan Lectureships: The Politics of Religious Dissent, 1560-1662* (Stanford, Cal.: Stanford U. Press, 1970), 68.

45. *D.N.B.*, III, 303.

46. Trevor-Roper, *Crisis*, 298. William M. Lamont, *Godly Rule: Politics and Religion, 1603-60* (London: Macmillan and New York: St Martin's Press, 1969), 79, comments: 'We still lack good individual studies of ministers who were as important as Burges, Marshall, Calamy, Case, Newcomen and Palmer undoubtedly were.'

47. Reid, *Memoirs*, I, 76-77.

48. Paul, *Assembly of the Lord*, 118.

49. Carruthers, *Everyday Work*, 184.

50. *Ibid.*, 194.

51. Mitchell, *Westminster Assembly*, 242 and n.

52. Seaver, *Puritan Lectureships*, 271; cf. Tai Liu, *Puritan London: A Study of Religion and Society in the City Parishes* (Newark, Del.: U of Delaware Press, 1986), 151-152. He gave up Watford on February 6, 1645 (*D.N.B.*).

53. Carruthers, *Everyday Work*, 62.

54. *D.N.B.*, III, 303.

55. *Ibid.*

56. Reid, *Memoirs*, I, 70, 77.

57. Alexander F. Mitchell and John Struthers, eds., *Minutes of the Sessions of the Westminster Assembly of Divines* (Edmonton, Alberta: Still Waters Revival Books 1991, reprint of 1874 ed.), 258 and n.1.

58. Spear, 'Covenanted Uniformity,' 362, shows him exceeded in number of speeches in the debates on church government through November 15, 1644 by only Thomas Goodwin, Lazarus Seaman, Stephen Marshall, and Herbert Palmer.

59. Reid, *Memoirs*, II, 28.

60. Paul, *Assembly of the Lord*, 146, 151-152 and n.74, 228-229, 235, 352, 363; cf. de Witt, *Jus Divinum*, 30 n.72.

61. Quoted in Paul, *Assembly of the Lord*, 371, from Baillie's *Letters and Journals*, II, 201.

62. Quoted in Paul, *Assembly of the Lord*, 152 n.74.

63. Haller, *Liberty and Reformation*, 140.

64. Mitchell, *Westminster Assembly*, 297 n.1.

65. Wilson, *Pulpit in Parliament*, 113, places him in the second rank of preachers to Parliament, behind only Stephen Marshall, Joseph Caryl, Obadiah Sedgwick, and Richard Vines in frequency.

66. *Ibid.*, 67.

67. Carruthers, *Everyday Work* 151.

68. Paul, *Assembly of the Lord*, 392.

69. Reid, *Memoirs*, II, 26-27; *D.N.B.*, IX, 698.

70. Reid, *Memoirs*, II, 28; *D.N.B.*, IX, 698.

71. de Witt, *Jus Divinum*, 33 n.87.

72. Spear, 'Covenanted Uniformity,' 362, shows him exceeded in number of speeches only by Thomas Goodwin, Lazarus Seaman, and Stephen Marshall.

73. Paul, *Assembly of the Lord*, 363, n.26, quoting Baillie's *Letters and Journals*, II, 148.

74. Holley, 'Divines,' 331, 333; *D.N.B.*, under 'Palmer, Herbert,' XV, 130-132, and 'Palmer, Sir James,' XV, 132.

75. Reid, *Memoirs*, II, 95-97.

76. *Ibid.*, II, 102.

77. *D.N.B.*, XV, 130.

78. Paul, *Assembly of the Lord*, 164, quoting Baillie, *Letters and Journals*, II, 110.

79. Reid, *Memoirs*, II, 114.

80. Paul, *Assembly of the Lord*, 395, quoting Baillie, *Letters and Journals*, II, 220-221.

81. David Masson, *The Life of John Milton*, 6 vols. (Gloucester, Mass.: Peter Smith, 1965, reprint of 1859-80 ed.), III, 263.

82. Masson, *Life of Milton*, II, 163-165, 262-265, 298, and 309-311 provides the details of this exchange. Haller, *Liberty and Reformation*, 127, says that Palmer's was the first public reference to Milton's divorce tracts that is known to us.

83. Mitchell, *Westminster Assembly*, 420-421, quoting Baillie, *Letters and Journals*, II, 148.

84. Cf. Mitchell, *Westminster Assembly*, 420-427, 439 and n.1.

85. Reid, *Memoirs*, II, 114-115.

86. Mitchell, *Westminster Assembly*, 438, says, 'The exact date of his death has not been ascertained even by Dr. Grosart, who has so carefully investigated his history; but by 28th September a successor had been presented to one of the charges held by him.' The last date that the Minutes of the Assembly show him in attendance is August 9. Alexander B. Grosart demonstrated in 1864 that Palmer was the actual author of *The Character of a Christian in Paradoxes and seeming Contradictions*, often attributed to Francis Bacon as 'The Christian Paradoxes' (Masson, *Life of Milton*, II, 520-521 and III, 311 and n.1).

87. *D.N.B.*, XV, 131.

88. Paul, *Assembly of the Lord*, 536.

89. *D.N.B.* under 'Gouge, William, D.D.', VIII, 271-273.

90. William Haller, *The Rise of Puritanism* (New York, Evanston, and London: Harper & Row, 1938), 67.

91. Halley, 'Divines,' 308.
92. Carruthers, *Everyday Work*, 174. Cf. Paul, *Assembly of the Lord*, 94.
93. His son, Thomas Gouge, gives the date of his birth as November 1, 1575 in his life of his father with his father's commentary on Hebrews, but the King's College records give the 1578 date (*D.N.B.*, VIII, 271).
94. Haller, *Rise of Puritanism*, 68, quoting from the funeral sermon by William Jenkyn, his associate for twelve years at St. Anne's. According to Liu, *Puritan London*: 'Sociologically speaking, the parish ... was a rapidly declining parochial community in seventeenth-century London, with an increasingly larger and larger number of the poor and fewer and fewer substantial householders' (59; cf. 41).
95. *D.N.B.*, VIII, 272.
96. Seaver, *The Puritan Lectureships*, 198, quoting Thomas Fuller, *Worthies*, 394.
97. Haller, *Rise of Puritanism*, 80.
98. *D.N.B.*, VIII, 272.

Chapter 3

The Episcopalians

Of the one hundred and twenty-one divines originally appointed to the Westminster Assembly, twenty-eight did not attend, most of them because they were Episcopalians loyal to the King. The one Episcopalian who did attend for any length of time was Daniel Featley. The influence of James Ussher upon the Assembly was great even though he did not attend.

Besides these two who are described in this chapter, other Episcopalians who were invited to the Assembly include: Ralph Brownrigg, Bishop of Exeter; Thomas Westfield, Bishop of Bristol; Henry Hammond; Richard Holdsworth; Robert Sanderson, later Bishop of Lincoln; George Morley, later Bishop of Winchester; John Erle, later Bishop of Lichfield; Henry Hatton; William Nicholson; and Samuel Ward.

Members of the Assembly who later conformed to the Anglican Prayer Book and polity after the Restoration in 1660 include Edward Reynolds, who became Bishop of Norwich; Richard Herrick, or Heyrick; and John Lightfoot. The Amanuensis, John Wallis, also conformed.

James Ussher (January 4, 1581 - March 21, 1656)

Early in 1647 the House of Commons resolved, 'That Dr. James Usher shall have leave to preach at Lincoln's Inn, according to the desire of his petition,' and also, 'That Dr. James Usher shall have leave to go to sit with the Assembly of Divines as one of the said Assembly.'[1] This was a remarkable action since Ussher, Archbishop of Armagh and Primate of the Anglican Church of Ireland, had not only declined his original appointment to the Assembly in June of 1643, but he had boldly preached against the legality of the Assembly because it lacked the King's approval. There is no indication that Ussher ever attended the Assembly, but the fact that such favor could be granted to a committed royalist shows the respect in which he was held by Puritans.

The reasons were at least threefold: his Calvinistic theology, his godliness and his pre-eminent scholarship. He had for a long time associated with a network of Puritan clergymen[2], and his defence of the Anglican Church against the historical claims of the Church of Rome were greatly appreciated. His Irish Articles, adopted by the first convocation of the Irish Protestant clergy in 1615, served as a model for much of the Westminster Confession of Faith, not only in their anti-Roman Catholic sentiment (denouncing the Pope as 'the man of sinne' and rejecting 'the sacrifice of the Masse' as 'most ungodly'), but also in their inculcating of the Puritan view of the Sabbath and in their teaching of absolute predestination and perseverance. At the same time they make no mention of three orders in the ministry or of the necessity of episcopal ordination.[3] Alexander F. Mitchell comments:

> In these articles we have certainly the main source of the Westminster Confession, and almost its exact prototype in the enunciation of all the more important doctrines of the Christian system. In the order and titles of most of the articles or chapters, as well as in the language of many sections or subdivisions of chapters, and in a large number of separate phrases or *voces signatae*, occurring throughout their Confession, the Westminster divines appear to me to have followed very closely in the footsteps of Ussher and the Irish Convocation.[4]

Mitchell also claims an influence of Archbishop Ussher's theology on the Westminster Catechisms.[5] Even though not present at the Assembly, clearly Ussher was an influence upon it.

Ussher was born in Dublin on January 4, 1581. A precocious scholar, he was among the first students to enter the new Trinity

College, Dublin in 1594. Before receiving his B.A. in 1597, he had begun to draw up a Biblical chronology, in Latin, through the Hebrew monarchy, which would become the basis of his famous chronology included in many later editions of the English Bible. In April 1599, when he was still only eighteen years old, he effectively engaged in a disputation at Trinity College with Henry Fitzsimon, a Roman Catholic prisoner in Dublin Castle. This led to a systematic reading of the church fathers which took eighteen years to accomplish.[6]

Ussher was made a fellow in 1599, received his M.A. on February 24, 1601, and was assigned to give the catechetical lecture on the Romish controversy on Sunday afternoons at Christ Church, Dublin. He was ordained deacon and priest on December 20, 1601. In 1602 and again in 1606, and thereafter every three years – staying one month each in Oxford, Cambridge and London, he went to England to purchase books for the Trinity College library. He received the B.D. in 1607 and was appointed the first professor of divinity at Trinity College. In 1609 he made the acquaintance of the scholar and later

From an Original Picture in the British Museum

JAMES USSHER

Parliamentary member of the Westminster Assembly, John Selden.

His first publication was *De ... Ecclesiarum ... Successione* (*The succession and standing of the Christian Churches in the West*), published in 1613, in which he sought to carry on the argument of John Jewel's *Apology for the Church of England* by showing the continuity of doctrine in England over against Roman deviations down to 1270.[7] In 1614 Ussher married Phoebe Challoner, and on March 2, 1615 he was chosen Vice-Chancellor of Trinity College.

It was at this time, when he was thirty-four, that Ussher was assigned the task of drafting the Irish Articles for the Anglican Church in Ireland. Having served at the rectories of Fingles, Assey, and Trim, he was consecrated Bishop of Meath and Clonmacnoise in June of 1621. Granted leave by James I to pursue his studies of British ecclesiastical antiquities, Ussher stayed in England for more than two years, from December 1623 until early 1626. During this time he was appointed Archbishop of Armagh on March 22, 1625.

Between 1628 and 1640 he engaged in correspondence with William Laud, with whom he had cordial agreement in 'love of learning, in reverence for antiquity, and in opposition to Rome' even though he differed with his Arminian theology: 'and though Ussher had none of Laud's passion for uniformity, he fully recognised the duty of allegiance to constituted authority.'[8] He later would attend Archbishop Laud before Laud's execution on January 10, 1645.

In March 1640 Ussher preached before the Irish Parliament and then left Ireland, as it turned out, for the last time. Staying first at Oxford, he was called to London to assist in the ecclesiastical settlement connected with the opening of the Long Parliament in November of 1640. He prepared a draft of a modified scheme of Episcopacy, which gained the favor of some moderate Puritans, eventually of Charles I, and then of Charles II. It was published in 1656, after Ussher's death, as *The Reduction of Episcopacie unto the form of Synodical Government received in the Ancient Church.* On December 22, 1641 he preached before the House of Lords. The rebellion in Ireland having destroyed his property there, except for his library, Ussher was given the Bishopric of Carlisle, the revenue from which he received until the autumn of 1643. He preached in London at St. Paul's, Covent Garden and then moved in 1642 to Oxford, where he preached frequently at St. Aldate's or at All Saints' Church.

When his response to the summons to participate in the Westminster Assembly was to preach against its legality, the House of Commons confiscated his library, but Daniel Featley with John Selden's assistance rescued the books, though many papers and all his correspondence were lost. He left Oxford on March 5, 1645 and took refuge in Wales for a year before returning to London, where he was guest of Elizabeth Mordant, now Dowager Countess of Peterborough, whose husband, John Mordant, first Earl of Peterborough, he had won back from Roman Catholicism more than twenty years earlier.[9]

As mentioned earlier, Parliament approved his appointment at the beginning of 1647 as preacher at Lincoln's Inn, 'one of the most lucrative preaching positions in London'.[10] In November of 1648 he there denounced Parliament's treatment of the King. In January 1649, from Lady Peterborough's house in St. Martin's Lane, 'just over against Charing Cross,' he saw the beginnings of Charles's execution, but fainted when 'the villains in vizards began to put up his hair'.[11]

Oliver Cromwell sought Ussher's advice in the 1650s. Ussher attended Selden's deathbed in November 1654. He gave up preaching after September 1655, due to failing sight and difficulty in speaking from loss of teeth. He died on March 21, 1656. Cromwell ordered a public funeral at Westminster Abbey, the Anglican service being used at the grave.

His several portraits show him in skull-cap and large ruff. 'He was of middle height, erect and well made, of fresh complexion, and wore moustache and short beard.'[12] Gilbert Burnet said of him: 'No man had a better soul.' 'Love of the world seemed not ... in his nature.' 'He had a way of gaining people's hearts and of touching their consciences that look'd like somewhat of the apostolical age reviv'd.'[13] He proved attractive to kings, Cromwell and everyone in between. His biographer concludes:

> His Augustinian theology commended him to the puritans, his veneration for antiquity to the high churchmen; no royalist surpassed him in his deference to the divine right of kings. All parties had confidence in his character, and marvelled at his learning.[14]

Daniel Featley, or Fairclough (March 15, 1582 - April 17, 1645)
Of the dozen-to-twenty Episcopalians invited to the Westminster Assembly, including three Bishops and four later to be Bishops, only

Dr. Daniel Featley participated actively in the Assembly's debates. Although his participation was confined to the summer months of 1643, his role was nevertheless a colorful one, and he continued to play a significant part even after being expelled from the Assembly as a spy for the King.

The charge of being 'a spy and intelligencer to Oxford' was based on correspondence that was intercepted from Featley to Archbishop James Ussher, who was with King Charles's camp in Oxford. The sharing of internal workings of the Assembly was a violation of the pledge that all members had taken at the beginning. Lord Clarendon later said that the King had commanded Featley to leave the Assembly,[15] and it has been suggested that his letter sought preferment from the King.[16] In any case, he had spoken in the Assembly against the Solemn League and Covenant, which was about to be subscribed. Featley was still active in the debates of the Assembly on September 20, 1643,[17] the Solemn League and Covenant was subscribed on September 25, and he was imprisoned on September 30.[18] His church livings were sequestered on October 23, and his incriminating letter was read to the House of Commons on October 30.[19] He would remain imprisoned, in Lord Petre's house in Aldersgate Street, for eighteen months; but even there, as we shall see, Featley would remain active.

Featley had a reputation both as a disputant and as a preacher and writer of devotional material. Born on March 15, 1582 at Charlton-upon-Otmoor, Oxfordshire, son of John Fairclough, cook to Puritan Laurence Humphrey, President of Magdalen College, Oxford, Featley (the first of his family to adopt the vulgarized spelling of his surname) entered Corpus Christi College, Oxford on December 13, 1594 and received his B.A. on February 13, 1601 and his M.A. on April 17, 1605, having become a Fellow September 20, 1602. From 1610 to 1613 he served as chaplain to Sir Thomas Edmondes, the English ambassador at Paris, where he engaged in disputations with French Jesuits. Twenty-one of his sermons preached in France were later published among seventy sermons in a book entitled *Clavis Mystica: A Key opening divers difficult and mysterious Texts of Holy Scripture* (1636).

He was awarded the B.D. on July 8, 1613 and the D.D. in 1617, by which time he had become a domestic chaplain of George Abbot, Archbishop of Canterbury. Featley seems to have been so feisty in debate that in the exercise for his D.D., the regius professor, John Prideaux, 'was so pressed as to lose his temper, and Abbot had some difficulty in effecting a reconciliation'.[20] On February 6, 1619 he took the rectory of Lambeth on his institution by Abbot. In 1622 he married Mrs. Joyce Halloway or Holloway, 'an ancient, grave gentlewoman', already twice widowed and considerably older than he.[21] He ceased to be Abbot's chaplain in 1625, by which time he was rector of Allhallows, Bread Street. He was allowed to exchange that for the rectory of Acton, Middlesex on January 30, 1627. In 1630 he was Provost of Chelsea College.

During the plague of 1625-1626 Featley turned from controversial work to devotional writing, producing *Ancilla Pietatis; or the handmaid to private devotion.*

> Of this, the most popular manual of private devotion in its day, a sixth edition appeared in 1639, besides translations into French and other continental languages. It was a special favourite with Charles I in his troubles.[22]

He was also a contributor, along with such Puritan preachers as Richard Sibbes and John Preston, to a popular anthology of funeral sermons published in 1640 under the title *The House of Mourning.*[23]

It is not surprising, then, that Featley should have been chosen for the Westminster Assembly. Not everyone in the Parliamentary army, however, perceived of him as an ally. On November 12, 1642 some of Essex's troops quartered at Acton 'heard that he was a papist, or that way inclined' and burned down his barns and stables and also did much damage to his church. On February 19, 1643 five soldiers broke into his service at Lambeth intent on killing him. However, Featley had been warned and managed to escape, although two parishioners were slain.[24]

The early work of the Assembly, in July, August and September of 1643, focused on revision of the Thirty-Nine Articles. Featley played an active part in these debates – 'debates probably as important in a doctrinal point of view as any that occurred at a later stage.'[25] His five published speeches in the Assembly are also a main source of information for these early sessions, since neither the Minutes nor John Lightfoot's notes are very extensive for this early period. Of special interest is Featley's contention, over against William Twisse, Thomas Gataker and Richard Vines, that the active, as well as the passive, obedience of Christ is imputed to the believer in his justification.[26]

Even after imprisonment Featley continued to serve the Puritan cause. At Parliament's request he wrote a learned treatise against Roman Catholicism, for which he was allowed three books at a time from his library. He also contributed to the Annotations on the Bible, published in 1645, in which he partially covered the Pauline Epistles. Having held a vigorous disputation with William Kiffin and three other Baptists on October 17, 1642, Featley encountered another Baptist minister, Henry Denne, in prison and published in 1645 what became his best-known work, *The Dippers dipt: or, the Anabaptists duck'd and plung'd over head and ears at a Disputation in Southwark*,[27] describing in lively terms his earlier argument with the Baptists.

By April 1, 1645, when Denne responded with *Antichrist Unmasked*, Featley was already a dying man. He was allowed on bail 'to remove to Chelsea College for change of air. There he died of asthma and dropsy on 17 April 1645, and on the 21st was buried by his own desire in the chancel of Lambeth Church,' honored by a large attendance.[28]

According to Anthony à Wood:

> He was esteemed, by the generality, to be one of the most resolute and victorious champions of the reformed Protestant religion of any of his time; a most smart scourge of the church of Rome; a compendium of the learned tongues, and of all the liberal arts and sciences; and though of small stature, yet he had a great soul, and learning of all kinds compacted in him.[29]

Notes

1. Alexander F. Mitchell, 'Introduction' to *Minutes of the Sessions of the Westminster Assembly of Divines*, eds. Mitchell and John Struthers (Edmonton, Alberta: Still Waters Revival Books, 1991, reprint of 1874 edition), xxxii, n.1, quoting from *Journals of House of Commons*, V, 423.
2. Paul S. Seaver, *The Puritan Lectureships: The Politics of Religious Dissent, 1560-1662* (Stanford, Cal.: Stanford U. Press, 1970), 235.
3. Larry Jackson Holley, 'The Divines of the Westminster Assembly: A Study of Puritanism and Parliament' (New Haven: Yale U. Ph.D. diss., 1979), 352; Philip Schaff, *The Creeds of Christendom*, 3 vols., 6th ed. (New York and London: Harper & Brothers, 1877, 1919), I, 664-665.
4. Alexander F. Mitchell, *The Westminster Assembly: Its History and Standards* (Philadelphia: Presbyterian Board of Publication, 1897), 383 n.1; cf. 121, 382-384. On pages xlvi-xlix of his 'Introduction' to the Minutes of the Assembly Mitchell presents a careful comparison of the nineteen heads of the 104 Irish Articles with the corresponding chapter titles of the Westminster Confession.

5. Mitchell, *Westminster Assembly*, 430.

6. *Dictionary of National Biography*, eds. Leslie Stephen and Sidney Lee, 22 vols. (London: Oxford U. Press, 1921-22), under 'Ussher, James,' XX, 65. Walter Travers, an eminent Puritan of the Elizabethan era, was provost of Trinity College until 1598.

7. *D.N.B.*, XX, 65-66; cf. R. Buick Knox, *James Ussher, Archbishop of Armagh* (Cardiff: U. of Wales Press, 1967), 156, 107-110, for a comparison with John Foxe's *Acts and Monuments*, or 'Book of Martyrs'.

8. D.N.B., XX, 67.

9. D.N.B., XX, 69, 67.

10. Seaver, *Puritan Lectureships*, 149.

11. *D.N.B.*, XX, 69.

12. *D.N.B.*, XX, 70.

13. *Ibid.*

14. *Ibid.*

15. [Archibald Alexander], *A History of the Westminster Assembly of Divines* (Philadelphia: Presbyterian Board of Publication, 1841), 247.

16. J.A. Carr, *The Life and Times of James Ussher, Archbishop of Armagh* (London: Wells Gardner, Darton and Co., 1895), 338.

17. Robert S. Paul, *The Assembly of the Lord* (Edinburgh: T. & T. Clark, 1985), 85 n.43.

18. Philip Schaff, *The Creeds of Christendom*, 6th ed. (New York and London: Harper & Brothers, 1877, 1919), I, 733.

19. Paul, *The Assembly of the Lord*, 105 n.10; *D.N.B.*, VI, 1142.

20. *D.N.B.*, VI, 1140.

21. *D.N.B.*, VI, 1141. She died in 1637 (VI, 1143).

22. *D.N.B.*, VI, 1141.

23. William Haller, *The Rise of Puritanism* (New York, Evanston, and London: Harper & Row, 1938), 101-102.

24. *D.N.B.*, VI, 1141; [Alexander], *History*, 246.

25. Mitchell, *Westminster Assembly*, 121.

26. Cf. Mitchell, *Westminster Assembly*, 151-159, for some excerpts of Featley's speeches.

27. *D.N.B.*, VI, 1142.

28. *Ibid.*

29. Quoted in [Alexander], *History*, 247-248.

Chapter 4

The Erastians

The Erastian view that church discipline should be exercised only with the approval of the civil authorities had support from a small minority of the Westminster divines. Not surprisingly, however, this view had significant support in Parliament. Among those appointed to the Assembly from the House of Commons, the following – in addition to John Selden – held Erastian views: John Glynn, Bulstrode Whitlocke, Oliver St. John, Sir Benjamin Rudyard, John Maynard, Sir John Evelyn, Sir Arthur Haselrig, Robert Reynolds, Sir John Cooke and Nathaniel Fiennes. Those appointed from the House of Commons leaning in the opposite direction would include Francis Rous, Edmund Prideaux and Zouch Tate.

John Selden (December 16, 1584-November 30, 1654)

Sentiment for Erastianism was strong in Parliament. The English Reformation had begun with King Henry VIII declaring that the monarch, rather than the Pope, was supreme head of the church in England. It was also natural that significant laymen, having battled what they viewed as abuses by Bishops, would not want to see discipline in the national church controlled by Presbyterian ministers and elders. The leader for this Erastian sentiment in the House of Commons was the renowned lawyer and legal, classical, and orientalist scholar, John Selden, who was also the leading lay member of the Westminster Assembly.

Although the lay commissioners from Scotland, such as Archibald Johnston and John Maitland, were present at the Assembly as ruling elders representing the church, the lay members from Parliament were present explicitly as laymen. Selden commented in his posthumously published *Table Talk*:

> There must be some laymen in the Synod to overlook the clergy, lest they spoil the civil work, just as when the good woman puts a cat into the milkhouse to kill a mouse she sends her maid to look after the cat, lest the cat should eat up the milk.[1]

Since he himself was an expert in both Jewish and classical antiquity, Selden could challenge the ministers and the theologians of the Assembly on their own ground. His fellow lay member of the Assembly from the House of Commons, Bulstrode Whitlocke, remarked:

> Sometimes when they had cited a text of scripture to prove their assertion, Selden would tell them 'Perhaps in your little pocket Bibles with gilt leaves' (which they would often pull out and read) 'the translation may be thus, but the Greek or the Hebrew signifies thus and thus,' and so would totally subdue them.[2]

William Haller comments concerning this story of the role of Selden at the Assembly:

> Needless to say, not all of Selden's ministerial colleagues were as unlearned as this story implies, but all shared the same embarrassment of having to carry on their discussions in the presence of one who, though not of their cloth, was recognized to be one of the most learned

scholars of the age on all matters it most concerned them to know. Historian, lawyer, and member of Parliament, he was, besides, more experienced than they in the ways of men in deliberative assemblies. He had long been acquainted with the clerical mind, and he observed the unguarded pretensions of the Westminster divines with an amused detachment which no doubt often put them at his mercy in debate. He was not above taking pleasure, as [John] Aubrey says, in being a thorn in their sides, in using his knowledge to baffle and his wit to vex them.[3]

Actually, accounts of the Assembly make it appear that Selden frequently offered his parliamentary skills to clarify issues and help move the debate along.[4] His main concern, however, was to counteract any form of church government by divine right and particularly to prevent the church, without the state, from having the final right of excommunication.

His major speech on the subject came on February 20, 1644, when he argued, with much learned reference to rabbinical material, that the term *ecclesia*, or 'church', in Matthew 18:15-17 should be understood as referring to a Jewish *civil* court, and hence the text could not be understood as a reference to excommunication by a church court. On the next day George Gillespie, the young Scottish commissioner, gave his response:

By seven distinct arguments [Gillespie] proved that the whole subject was of a spiritual nature, not within the cognizance of civil courts; and he proved also, that the Church of the Jews had and exercised the power of spiritual censures. The effect of Gillespie's speech was so great as to astonish and confound Selden himself, who made no attempt to reply ....[5]

Selden continued to participate in the debates of the Assembly, but when the subject of discipline became the focus of discussion in 1645 and 1646, he seems to have left the cause in the hands of his Erastian colleagues, Thomas Coleman and John Lightfoot, and concentrated his efforts on similar debates in the House of Commons.[6]

Selden's views are well summarized by Jonathan R. Ziskind:

Among the questions the Assembly had to deal with was whether there was a form of church government prescribed in the Bible (and hence by God), and if so, what was its relationship to the secular order. The answer that the Erastians would give to the first question is 'No' and to the second they would say that whatever the form, it would be subordinate to secular authority. Noting Christianity's origins in Judaism, Selden and his fellow Erastians could point to ancient Jewish practices contemporary with early Christianity as models for a Christian nation, especially one that had broken with the papacy and had not yet fully defined in the political context the nature of its Christianity. These ancient models showed that in the Jewish state there was no separate ecclesiastical jurisdiction, and there could be no excommunication unless allowed by secular authority. Selden was, therefore, more concerned about the *basis* of church government rather than its form, and in Erastian terms, supported by rabbinic practices, this meant that the final authority in religious matters should be Parliament.[7]

Selden once said: 'Whether is the church or the scripture judge of religion? In truth neither, but the state.'[8] Such a position naturally had its appeal to Parliament, but it makes one wonder how Selden was able to subscribe to the Solemn League and Covenant for conformity to the church government of Scotland.[9] In fact at one point Selden upset not only the Scots but even Lightfoot, 'by arguing that in English law the right of ordaining was still in the hands of the bishops acting in association with their presbyters, and that the Solemn League and Covenant provided no excuse for ignoring the laws of the land'.[10] Ziskind adds: 'As far as Selden was concerned, the kind of separation of spiritual and temporal matters that the Presbyterians were seeking was not attainable or advisable.'[11]

Selden's convictions were produced by years of extensive study, the result of which was 'an impressive list of works (twenty-seven titles in all) on various aspects of British legal history, classics, jurisprudence, comparative law and Jewish law'.[12] His works on Jewish law were reprinted on the Continent in his lifetime.

Their author's familiarity with rabbinical literature was such as has been acquired by few non-Israelite scholars; and many details of oriental civilization and antiquities were certainly brought to the knowledge of Europeans for the first time in them.[13]

Born on December 16, 1584 at Salvington, Sussex, Selden went from Chichester free school to Hart Hall, Oxford on October 24, 1600, but left without graduating to enter Clifford Inn in 1602 for the study of law. He was admitted to the Inner Temple in May, 1604, and called to the bar on June 14, 1612. Although he practised law, his main interest was the study of the history of constitutional law, and he was aided in this by the patronage of Henry Grey, ninth Earl of Kent, and by access to the library of Sir Robert Bruce Cotton.

In 1621 he entered upon his political career, supporting the legal basis of the House of Commons' protestation of the right of free debate over against the King. Elected to Parliament in 1623, 1626 and 1628, he continued to stand for the liberty of the subject on the basis of English common law. But on March 4, 1629 he and eight other Members of Parliament were haled before the Privy Council and imprisoned. Selden was not liberated until May 1631 and was unconditionally discharged only in October 1634. Elected to the Long Parliament for the University of Oxford in November 1640, he opposed the crown on the question of ship-money, but also opposed the abolition of Episcopacy. In 1642 the King offered him high office to induce him to leave London and join the court in York, but he declined. As Clarendon later said, 'He was in years and of a tender constitution; he had for many years enjoyed his ease which he loved; was rich, and would not have made a journey to York or have lain out of his own bed for any preferment.'[14]

A confirmed bachelor, Selden did manage to live in style. After the death of the Earl of Kent in 1639 the Dowager Countess allowed him to reside in her town mansion, called the Carmelite or White Friars, near to the Temple, which he spoke of as '*Museum meum Carmeliticum*': 'It contained his Greek marbles, his Chinese map and compass, his curiosities in crystal, marble, and pearl, his cabinets and cases, all indicated by letters, and, above all, his incomparable library.'[15] With the execution of the King in January 1649 and the ascendancy of Oliver Cromwell, Selden removed himself from public life. ' "The wisest way for men in these times is to say nothing" was a maxim of his, on which he seems to have rigorously acted (*Table Talk*, Peace).'[16]

According to Aubrey, Selden was 'very tall – I guess six foot high – sharp, oval face, head not very big, long nose inclining to one side,' with grey eyes, full and prominent.[17]

Selden died at Carmelite House on November 30, 1654 and was buried in the Temple Church, with judges and many persons of distinction in attendance. His friend Archbishop Ussher preached at the funeral. It is reported that near the end he had said that

> he could not recollect any passage out of those infinite books and manuscripts he was master of, wherein he could rest his soul, save out of the Holy Scriptures; wherein the most remarkable passage that lay most upon his spirit was Titus ii, 11, 12, 13, 14, 15.[18]

Those who have studied Selden's life and work carefully conclude that 'he was a genuine believer in Christianity as a religion having a divine origin'[19] and that he 'believed in divine revelation and accepted the Bible as the word of God'.[20] Yet his latitudinarian views, his 'cynical mode of speaking on the questions which were so keenly debated in his time,'[21] his irony, 'the weapon of men who know too much', all helped to pave the way for the less theistic atmosphere of the eighteenth century: 'Listening to the Westminster divines, he was confirmed in the same rational, critical, skeptical attitude which had been previously fixed in his mind by his brush with their rivals and former oppressors.'[22]

Thomas Coleman (1598 - c. March 23, 1646)

Of the clergymen at the Westminster Assembly Thomas Coleman was the most outspoken in favor of the Erastian position. Not only did he find himself in a small minority in this regard, but twice he so offended the majority in his expression of his views that he was reprimanded by the Assembly.

Once was when he gave one of the Fast Day sermons before the House of Commons on July 30, 1645 in which he spoke against a vote the Assembly had recently taken. Even though many in the House of Commons were sympathetic with his Erastian sentiments, while he was asked to have his sermon printed, he was not given the customary official thanks.[23] Coleman subsequently apologized to the Assembly, saying that the reports of his sermon were not altogether accurate, and he promised not to have it printed.

The second was when it was reported, on February 12, 1646, that he had said 'that the Covenant was made use of to beat all with', or words to that effect. He was protesting the addition of the words 'according to our Solemn Covenant' to a petition to Parliament. On the next day, by a vote of 26 to 1, the Assembly declared that the statement was scandalous, and a further vote added the words 'both to the Parliament and Assembly'.[24]

There is a touch of irony in the disfavor that Coleman gained with the Scots and the majority of the Assembly, for at the beginning he was an enthusiastic champion of the Solemn League and Covenant. Born in 1598 in Oxford, he entered Magdalen Hall in 1615 and received the B.A. in 1618 and the M.A. in 1621. His studies in Hebrew were so proficient that he became known as 'Rabbi Coleman'. He was rector of Blyton, Lincolnshire from 1623 to 1645, but in 1642 he was driven by the King's army from his parish to London, where he was assigned the sequestered rectory of St. Peter's Church, Cornhill.[25] His vigorous preaching style may have attracted attention, for he was invited to preach one of the Fast Day sermons before the Commons on August 30, 1643, in the early stages of the Assembly, and then again he was the single preacher on September 29, 1643, on the occasion of subscribing to the Solemn League and Covenant by 445 individuals, including noblemen, knights, and gentry, officers and soldiers, Scotsmen in London, and additional divines, besides Assembly members who had taken the oath on the 25th.[26] On the former occasion he had preached:

> If a stranger aske, what newes in England? what shall be our return, what shall we say? What? Why, the best news that ever was, God hath established Sion, and the poore of his people are confident in her; Oh, here is a change of late, religion is here setled in purity, and peace; here is a ground work laid to erect the Kingdom of Jesus Christ upon, that the gates of hell shall never prevail against it; God hath established Sion, and as for his people, there is a new world with them .... [27]

After the latter occasion Coleman commented:

> The day when this Covenant was subscribed was a day of contentment and joy. The honorable gentry accounted it their freedom to be bound to God, the men of war accounted it their honor to be pressed for this service, our brethren of Scotland esteemed it a happiness and a further act of pacification. Our reverend divines deserve not to be last either in praise or performance.[28]

But this enthusiasm had become a bit more reflective by the time he preached one of the monthly Fast Day sermons before the House of Commons on July 30, 1645. This was the occasion when he offended the Assembly by concluding his sermon with four points of application, contrary to the Assembly's own position, as to the best way to achieve unity of the church: 1. Establish as few things by divine right as can well be; 2. Let all precepts, held out as divine institutions, have clear Scriptures; 3. Lay no more burden of government upon the shoulders of ministers than Christ hath plainly laid upon them; and 4. A Christian magistrate, as a Christian magistrate, is a governor in the church.[29] This plainly Erastian approach especially upset the Scots, and the first chance to respond came when George Gillespie preached before the House of Lords on August 27. When his sermon was printed, Gillespie appended to it a pamphlet of nine leaves entitled *A Brotherly Examination of some Passages of Mr. Coleman's late printed Sermon* (it had been printed, contrary to Coleman's promise to the Assembly, but in accord with Parliament's request). Coleman responded on November 1 with *A Brotherly Examination Re-examined*; Gillespie replied on November 13 with *Nihil Respondes* (Thou answerest nothing). Coleman shot back on January 9, 1646 with *Male Dicis Maledicis* (Thou Indeed Speakest Amiss), and Gillespie further responded on January 24 with *Male Audis* (Thou Hearest Amiss).[30]

Thus a literary exchange of some six months set the stage for Coleman's final debate on the floor of the Assembly. He wished to dispute the proposition that church government was 'distinct from the civil magistrate'. Starting on March 9, 1646 and continuing to the 17th, Coleman sought to maintain that such passages as Matthew 18 and 1 Corinthians 5 did not provide a basis for excommunication by the church. On March 17, 'after a full debate', the Assembly resolved that his argument about Matthew 18 had 'been answered'. The next day Coleman was absent, and on the 19th word came that he was not well. Visitors reported on the 20th that he was 'very ill', but he hoped that the debate could be continued upon his return.[31]

On the 30th, however, the members of the Assembly were attending his funeral. Robert Baillie, rather uncharitably, wrote on April 3 to his cousin in the Netherlands: 'God has stricken Coleman with death; he fell ill in an ague, and after four or five dayes expired. It's not good to stand in Christ's way.'[32]

Thomas Fuller said of Coleman 'that he was a pious and learned man, equally averse to presbytery and prelacy'.[33] Yet he could say that 'doubtless many materials of Prelacy must of necessity be retained as absolutely necessary,'[34] and he could also see the Presbyterian position as expedient.[35] His main concern was the Erastian point:

> I know no such distinction of government Ecclesiastical and Civill, in the sense I take Government for the corrective part thereof. All ecclesiastical (improperly called) government being meerly doctrinall: the corrective or punitive part being civill or temporall.[36]

It was a position concerning church discipline that had sympathy in Parliament, but which would not prevail in the Assembly.

John Lightfoot (March 29, 1602 - December 6, 1675)

The remaining Erastian in the Westminster Assembly was the renowned Biblical scholar John Lightfoot. After Thomas Coleman's funeral Lightfoot carried on the debate 'more languidly'[37] into April of 1646. A more profound thinker, he spoke more cautiously on this subject, not finding in Scripture a clear distinction between ecclesiastical and civil government. For him the 'binding and loosing' of Matthew 18 referred more to the effect of teaching than of discipline. The civil magistrate could be the Lord's instrument for correction. He believed the arguments of the majority to be 'not convincing'.[38]

Lightfoot was frequently willing to be a minority of one in the Assembly, as he brought to bear on the discussions his penetrating but sometimes unusual interpretations of Scripture. His knowledge of textual criticism, of rabbinical material, and of the interconnectedness of the Bible itself was employed, sometimes persuasively, but many times in ways that appeared to the majority to be eccentric.[39] His primary concern seems to have been to have the church settled in a way that would make sound biblical truth available to the people. In a sermon preached before the House of Commons on August 27, 1645 he urged a new translation of the Bible:

> And certainly it would not be the least advantage that you might do to the three nations, if not the greatest, if they, by your care and means, might come to understand the proper and genuine reading of the Scripture, by an exact, vigorous, and lively translation. I hope, (I say it again) you will find some time, to set a-foot so needful a work.[40]

And this was only one generation after the appearance in 1611 of the Authorized Version of King James I. In an earlier Fast Day sermon, on March 29, 1643, Lightfoot had spoken vehemently against the publishing of the Apocrypha between the Old and New Testaments: 'It is not a little to be admired [i.e., wondered at], how this *Apocrypha* could ever get such a place in the hearts, and in the Bibles of the primitive times, as to come to sit in the very centre of them both.' He describes this intertestamental literature as the 'wretched Apocrypha, and this patchery of human invention'.[41] It was probably Lightfoot's zeal for biblical scholarship rather than for any particular ecclesiastical party that enabled him to retain his livings in 1662, when pressure to conform to the Anglican Book of Common Prayer caused many others to be ejected from their positions.[42]

One of the main contributions of Lightfoot to our knowledge of the Westminster Assembly is the record he kept in his *Journal of the Proceedings of the Assembly of Divines*, which covers the debates from July 1, 1643 to December 31, 1644. This gives his personal account and must be supplemented by the letters of Robert Baillie and the notes of George Gillespie as well as the official Minutes, but for some sessions when the Minutes are missing, they give us our only reliable information.[43] His journal reveals him to be clearly opposed to the Independents and favorable toward Presbyterianism.[44] He may even have engaged in strategizing with the Scots.[45] Repeatedly, Lightfoot's recording of the Assembly's slow pace reveals his own sense of urgency. He was frustrated with Cornelius Burgess's scruples over the Solemn League and Covenant, with the Independents' delaying tactics, and finally with the Presbyterians' own hesitancy to allow the civil government to establish their system of polity. Since Lightfoot did not believe in a form of church government by divine right, there was for him no need

THE KING JAMES BIBLE

When James VI of Scotland became James I of England after the death of Queen Elizabeth I in 1603, he was greeted on his way south by English Puritans bearing the Millenary Petition, purportedly conveying the desires of one thousand ministers to be relieved from certain rituals of the Church of England that they regarded as not supported by Scripture. King James therefore called the Hampton Court conference of 1604, where the Puritans were represented by such learned and moderate leaders as John Reynolds and Lawrence Chaderton. It was here that King James said, "Presbytery agreeth as well with monarchy as God with the devil," and "No bishop, no King." Out of this conference did come, however, agreement to produce a new translation of the Bible. Six groups of scholars were established - two at Oxford, two at Cambridge, and two at Westminster - to work independently on different parts of the Scriptures. The 50-some scholars were instructed to use the "Bishops' Bible" of 1568 as a basis, but to consult all earlier English versions, including the Catholic Douai version and the Geneva Bible favored by the Puritans. The result was the Authorized Version of 1611, commonly known as the "King James Bible." Despite its general acceptance and acknowledged beautiful cadences, many Puritans still preferred the Geneva Bible, particularly for its Calvinistic marginal notes.

for further discussion.[46] Playing a major role on the Assembly's committee for examining ministerial candidates, he seems to have been primarily concerned to see the church's pulpits filled with sound preachers.[47]

The son of Thomas Lightfoot, curate of Stoke-upon-Trent and subsequently rector of Uttoxeter from 1622 until his death on July 21, 1658, Lightfoot was born on March 29, 1602 at Stoke, attended school at Congleton, Cheshire, and entered Christ's College, Cambridge in June 1617. Having excelled in classical scholarship and oratory, he received his B.A. in 1621 and then spent two years as assistant in a school in Repton, Derbyshire. Ordained in 1623, he became curate of Norton-in-Hales, Shropshire, where he made the acquaintance of Sir Rowland Cotton, whose knowledge of Hebrew embarrassed him into dedicated study of that language: 'He was greatly ashamed to be baffled by a country gentleman as he confessed he frequently was, especially in a branch of learning which belonged to his profession.'[48]

Having taken his M.A. in 1624, he followed Cotton to London, with plans for possible study abroad. In 1626, however, he was called to be rector of Stone in Staffordshire, where he remained two years, marrying on May 21, 1628, Joyce, daughter of William Crompton of Stone Park and widow of George Copwood, who bore him four sons and two daughters before her death in 1656. (He later married Anne, widow of Austin Brograve; she died in 1666.)

In 1628 he moved to Hornsey, Middlesex in order to have ready access to the rabbinical materials in the library of Sion College. Here he produced his first work, *Erubhim, or Miscellanies, Christian and Judaical*, dedicated to his patron, Sir Robert Cotton. In 1630 he was presented by Cotton to the rectory of Ashley, Staffordshire, where he ministered in exemplary fashion for the next twelve years:

> That he might be secure from interruption, he purchased an adjoining field, where, in the midst of a garden, he erected a small building containing three rooms, his study, parlour, and bed-chamber. In this retirement he devoted to his studies, all the time which could be spared from his parochial duties; and not content in passing the day in study here, he often remained there through the night, although his parsonage was near at hand.[49]

In 1642, however, Lightfoot resigned this seemingly ideal position in Ashley in favor of his younger brother Josiah and moved to London, where, early in 1643, he became Lecturer on Sundays at St. Bartholomew's by the Exchange.[50] In 1644 he received the rectory of Great (or Much) Munden, Hertfordshire, and his journal of the Assembly indicates several times when he had to be absent to attend to pastoral duties there.[51]

He published in 1644 the first part of his *Harmony of the iv Evangelists among themselves and with the Old Testament*. The second and third parts would follow in 1647 and 1650. During the time of the Assembly he also published works on Genesis, Exodus, Acts, and the Temple. He became most famous for a series of volumes entitled *Horae Hebraicae et Talmudicae*, editions of which were published in Cambridge, London, Paris, Amsterdam, and Leipzig in his lifetime and then posthumously. An edition in English was published in four volumes in 1859.[52] Archibald Alexander could say in the nineteenth century:

> That the learning of Dr. Lightfoot was profound and extensive, is a thing so fully established by his writings, and so well known through the Christian world, that it would be superfluous to say any thing on the subject. In all departments of Biblical learning, he was richly furnished; but in Hebrew and rabbinical learning, it is doubtful whether he had a superior in the world.[53]

In November 1650 he was appointed Master of St. Catherine Hall, Cambridge, in succession to Dr. William Spurstowe, who had been ejected. In 1652 Cambridge conferred on him the D.D., and in 1654 he became Vice-Chancellor of the University. At the Restoration he offered to resign his Mastership to Spurstowe, but this was declined, and the Archbishop of Canterbury, in recognition of Lightfoot's learning, confirmed him in both the Mastership and his living. He participated in the Savoy Conference of 1661, siding with the Presbyterians. 'When the Act of Uniformity came into force in 1662 he complied with it, though he is said to have been not very scrupulous in fulfilling its provisions.'[54] On January 22, 1668 he was appointed a prebend at Ely. It was there he died on December 6, 1675 after catching a violent cold, accompanied with fever, on a journey from Cambridge: 'The malady affected principally his head, and was aggravated by a few glasses of claret, which he was persuaded to drink − a beverage to which he was entirely unaccustomed ....'[55]

A portrait of Lightfoot is in the hall of St. Catherine's College, Cambridge. He was, according to an account:

of a ruddy, but mild countenance; of a good stature, and well proportioned. He was in manner grave, but easy of access; affable and courteous, and very communicative to all inquirers; plain, unaffected, and gentlemanly. In the company of ingenious and learned men, he was free and unrestrained in conversation; but if he happened to fall into the company of rude and profligate men, he showed his disapprobation of their conversation, by keeping entire silence. On returning from a journey, he did not visit his family, until he had retired to his study, to offer thanksgivings to God. Temperate and abstemious in diet, he abstained altogether from wine, and drank only water or small beer, which he chose to use, when new. As to food, he cheerfully partook of whatever was set before him, never expressing any fastidious dislikes, but praising God for the supply of his temporal wants. This systematic temperance had given him a sound and healthy constitution, so that even in an advanced age, he was able to pursue his studies without intermission.[56]

Notes

1. Quoted in S.W. Carruthers, *The Everyday Work of the Westminster Assembly* (Philadelphia: Presbyterian Historical Societies of America and of England, 1943), 22.

2. Quoted in *Ibid.*, 46.

3. William Haller, *Liberty and Reformation in the Puritan Revolution* (New York and London: Columbia U. Press, 1955), 230-231.

4. Cf. Robert S. Paul, *The Assembly of the Lord* (Edinburgh: T. & T. Clark, 1985), 237 n.63, 283, 291 and n.86.

5. William M. Hetherington, *History of the Westminster Assembly of Divines* (Edmonton, Alberta: Still Waters Revival Books, 1993, reprint of 3rd ed., 1856), 240; cf. John Richard de Witt, *Jus Divinum* (Kampen: J.H. Kok, 1969), 177, and Paul, *The Assembly of the Lord*, 269.

6. Cf. Hetherington, *History*, 247-248; DeWitt, *Jus Divinum*, 179, 195; Paul, *Assembly of the Lord*, 494, 498.

7. Jonathan R. Ziskind, 'Introduction' to *John Selden on Jewish Marriage Law* (Leiden, New York, Kobenhavn, and Kola: E.J. Brill, 1991), 10.

8. de Witt, *Jus Divinum*, 216, quoting from Selden's *Table Talk*.

9. Cf. de Witt, *Jus Divinum*, 50.

10. Paul, *Assembly of the Lord*, 223.

11. Ziskind, 'Introduction', 13.

12. *Ibid.*

13. *Dictionary of National Biography*, eds. Leslie Stephen and Sidney Lee, 22 vols. (London: Oxford U. Press, 1921-22), XVII, 1157.

14. Quoted in *D.N.B.*, XVII, 1154.

15. *D.N.B.*, XVII, 1158.

16. *D.N.B.*, XVII, 1155.

17. Quoted in *D.N.B.*, XVII, 1160.

18. Quoted in S.W. Singer, 'Biographical Preface', lxvii, in *The Table-Talk of John Selden*, 2nd ed. (London: John Russell Smith, 1856).

19.*D.N.B.*, XVII, 1160.

20. Ziskind, 'Introduction', 14.

21. *D.N.B.*, XVII, 1160.

22. Haller, *Liberty and Reformation*, 232, 234.

23. James Reid, *Memoirs of the Westminster Divines*, 2 vols. in 1 (Edinburgh and Carlisle, Pa: Banner of Truth, 1982, reprint of edition of 1811 and 1815), I, 241.

24. Carruthers, *Everyday Work*, 179.

25. Larry Jackson Holley, "The Divines of the Westminster Assembly" (New Haven: Yale U. Ph.D. diss., 1979), 294; Reid, *Memoirs*, I, 237; Alexander F. Mitchell, *The Westminster Assembly*, 2nd ed. (Philadelphia: Presbyterian Board of Publication, 1897), 304;
de Witt, *Jus Divinum*, 197.

26. John F. Wilson, *Pulpit in Parliament* (Princeton, N.J.: Princeton U. Press, 1969), 73.

27. Quoted in *Ibid.*, 190.

28. Mitchell, *Westminster Assembly*, 172-173.

29. Cf. Hetherington, *History*, 289-290, and Reid, *Memoirs*, I, 241-243, for more of the substance of Coleman's sermon.

30. Cf. Reid, *Memoirs*, I, 243-246; Hetherington, *History*, 291-291; de Witt, *Jus Divinum*, 197 n.106.

31. Carruthers, *Everyday Work*, 179; Mitchell, *Westminster Assembly*, 331-332. Cf. DeWitt, *Jus Divinum*, 198-200, for the content of Coleman's arguments.

32. Quoted in Paul, *Assembly of the Lord*, 515.

33. Quoted in [Archibald Alexander], *History of the Westminster Assembly* (Philadelphia: Presbyterian Board of Publication, 1841), 237.

34. Quoted in de Witt, *Jus Divinum*, 55.

35. Paul, *Assembly of the Lord*, 119-120.

36. Quoted in de Witt, *Jus Divinum*, 216.William M. Lamont, *Godly Rule: Politics and Religion, 1603-60* (London: Macmillan and New York: St Martin's Press, 1969), 115, says: 'Thomas Coleman is a seriously undervalued figure; his role in the Erastian controversies is a crucial one.'

37. Mitchell, *Westminster Assembly*, 332.

38. de Witt, *Jus Divinum*, 201, 198. Cf. Reid, *Memoirs*, II, 66, 68; Paul, *Assembly of the Lord*, 359, 492 n.1.

39. Reid, *Memoirs*, II, 59-63, provides many examples.

40. Quoted in Reid, *Memoirs*, II, 65.

41. Quoted in Reid, *Memoirs*, II, 63, 64.

42. Cf. [Archibald Alexander], *History of the Westminster Assembly* (Philadelphia: Presbyterian Board of Publication, 1641), 327-328; de Witt, *Jus Divinum*, 51.

43. Paul, *Assembly of the Lord*, 74 and n.6, 208 and n.48, 251-252 and n.15.

44. *Ibid.*, 218 n.1, 240 n.76, 309, 333-334, 344, 514.

45. *Ibid.*, 223-224, 225 n.27: Lightfoot 'supported presbyterian order as a practical way of meeting the need for a national church and more ministers, and of combating the sects'.

46. Paul, *Assembly of the Lord*, 93 and n.75, 138 n.18, 255, 261, and especially 333-334; Reid, *Memoirs*, II, 65; Carruthers, *Everyday Work*, 123, 173.

47. Carruthers, *Everyday Work*, 148, 159-160.

48. Reid, *Memoirs*, II, 56. Biographical details are found in *D.N.B.*, XI, 1108-1110 and in Holley, 'Divines,' 322-323.

49. [Alexander], *History*, 324. Alexander's account of Lightfoot's life is extracted from the Preface to the 13-volume edition of Lightfoot's works, edited by John Rogers Pitman and published in London 1822-25. Volume XIII contains his *Journal of the Proceedings of the Assembly of Divines*.

50. Tai Lui, *Puritan London* (Newark, Del.: U of Delaware Press, 1986), 131, 151 and n.15.

51. Carruthers, *Everyday Work*, 78; Paul, *Assembly of the Lord*, 218, 239 (250), 324 n.64, 345 n.175 (360), 392 n.13, 422 n.159.

52. In a 1979 reprint of this edition by Baker Book House of Grand Rapids, Michigan, R. Laird Harris says in the Introduction: 'Lightfoot's commentary should be compared with the *Kommenter zum Neuen Testament* by Strack and Billerbeck [6 vols., 1922-1961]. This extensive German commentary is the only other work that attempts fully to use the Talmud and related Jewish material in elucidating the New Testament. Strack-Billerbeck is more extensive than Lightfoot, includes the whole New Testament, and is more recent. But the Talmud has not changed since Lightfoot's day, though obviously Talmud studies have advanced. Lightfoot's comments on the New Testament text and his use of the Talmud reflect his theologically conservative stance, however, and of course Lightfoot is in English' (p.iv).

53. [Alexander], *History*, 332.

54. *D.N.B.*, XI, 1109.

55. [Alexander], *History*, 328.

56. *Ibid.*, 329-330.

Chapter 5

The Independents

Those Puritans favoring an Independent or Congregational church polity had become a self-conscious party even before the beginning of the Westminster Assembly. Their leadership in the Assembly was provided by the 'Five Dissenting Brethren' who are described in this chapter. William Carter and William Greenhill joined them in signing the 'Reasons' for their declining to bring to the Assembly their model of church government. Also giving them at least occasional support in the Assembly were Joseph Caryl, Peter Sterry, John Green, and John Phillips, the one Westminster divine to have exercised ministry in New England. Of the members of the House of Commons appointed to the Assembly, Sir Henry Vane, Jr., Sir John Evelyn, Sir Arthur Haselrig and Nathaniel Fiennes were Independents; most of the others favored Presbyterianism.

Thomas Goodwin (October 5, 1600-February 23, 1680)

Thomas Goodwin made 357 speeches in the debates of the Assembly from August 4, 1643 to November 15, 1644, more than any other member and twice as many as all but six of the other members of the Assembly.[1] On October 15, 1644 he was called to order for speaking too long.[2] He was indeed the main spokesman for the Independents in the Assembly who became known as the 'five dissenting brethren' for their resistance to the Presbyterian majority. All five had helped to pastor Congregational churches in the Netherlands, and most of them would become leaders of the prevalent Independent churches during the Protectorate of Oliver Cromwell. With the same convictions on church polity as Cromwell, Goodwin's influence tended to rise as the Puritan army had success and Cromwell's influence gained in Parliament. Following the Assembly Goodwin was one of Cromwell's main ministerial advisers and, along with John Owen, Joseph Caryl, Peter Sterry and two others, attended the Lord Protector at his deathbed.

In the Assembly he was respected for both his learning and his godliness, which are reflected in his own diary's account of his conversion. Born at Rollesby, Norfolk on October 5, 1600, he entered Christ's College, Cambridge on August 25, 1613. Having begun to weep over his sins at the age of six, he learned to fear the pains of hell at seven. Still only in his early teens at Cambridge, he heard Richard Sibbes preach at Trinity Church and relished the reading of Calvin's *Institutes*: 'Oh how sweet was the reading of some parts of that book to me! How pleasing was the delivery of truths in a solid manner then to me!' At fourteen he took communion at Easter and rejoiced in the comfort of salvation. At the next communion, however, he being the smallest of the students in his College, his tutor spotted him and sent him out, supposing him not suitably prepared. Discouraged by this, he went into a spiritual decline for several years, until a funeral sermon in the autumn of 1620 moved him to what he perceived to be genuine repentance and faith. He says that before this time, 'God was to me as a wayfaring Man, who came and dwelt for a Night and made me Religious for a Fit but then departed from me ....'

'In a great Frost you shall see where the Sun shines hot, the Ice drips, and the Snow melts, and the Earth grows slabby; but 'tis a particular Thaw, only where the Sun shines, not a general Thaw of all things that are frozen.' Natural reason had so far enabled him to discover his 'grosser Acts against Knowledg,' but the light now suddenly vouch-safed him 'gave discovery of my Heart in all my Sinnings, carried me down to see the Inwards of my Belly (as Solomon speaks) and searched the lower Rooms of my Heart, as it were with candles'. What he saw there was, of course, sin, the innate propensity of all flesh to evil, the original corruption of man's nature. It was, he said, 'as if I had in the heat of Summer lookt down into the Filth of a Dungeon, where by a clear Light and a piercing Eye I discern'd Millions of crawling living things in the midst of that Sink and liquid Corruption.' Thus suddenly his sins came before him and would not be put out of mind. He was in the hands of a greater power than himself or any man, a power, however, which revealed to him thus suddenly the hell within in order as suddenly to save him from it. God 'saith of and to my Soul, Yea live, yea live I say.'[3]

This personal experience of the Lord's grace, which he took to be the difference between the natural conscience, though enlightened, and the motions of the heaven-born soul under the influence of the Holy Spirit, colored his preaching and ministry afterwards. He received his B.A. in 1617, moved to Catherine Hall in 1619 where he became a Fellow in the next year, and received his M.A. in 1620. Having come under the influence of the preaching of John Preston, some of whose sermons he helped later to publish, he eventually succeeded him as Lecturer at Trinity Church in Cambridge in 1628.[4] This appointment was not without opposition from Bishop Buckeridge of Ely:

The bishop wished to exact from Goodwin a promise that he would never preach on any of the controverted points of theology. Goodwin replied, that so many of the doctrines of Christianity were contro-verted, that if he were to follow this rule, there would be very little left to preach about; and that he was persuaded the king did not mean to lay him under an interdict from confuting the error of popery.[5]

Named vicar of Trinity Church in 1632, it was here that he became an effective preacher, at first aiming at conviction of sin, to alarm the conscience and wound the heart, but increasingly emphasizing the sweet comforts of the knowledge of Christ, free justification through his righteousness, and the glories of the gospel of grace. Richard Sibbes had advised him, 'Young man, if you ever would do good, you must preach the gospel, and the free grace of God in Christ Jesus.'[6]

In June of 1633 Goodwin, Philip Nye and John Davenport gathered in London to meet John Cotton, who was on his way to New England. Their aim was to persuade him to conform to the 'indifferent' ceremonies of the English church, but instead he persuaded them that his Congregational views were Scriptural.[7] In 1634 Goodwin resigned his vicarage in favor of Sibbes and left the University, unable in good conscience to conform to the High Church innovations of Archbishop Laud. In 1638 he married Elizabeth Prescott in London, where he probably was serving as a Congregational preacher.

By 1639 the vigilance of Laud made his position untenable, and he moved to the Netherlands to serve the Independent English church at Arnhem. This church of substantial and middle-class English exiles had been established in 1638 under the leadership of John Archer, who was assisted by Goodwin and Philip Nye as teachers from 1639 to 1641. It was a church open to certain innovations, such practices as anointing the sick with oil, laying on hands for healing, solo singing, 'prophesying' (the congregation having opportunity to ask questions after the

THOMAS GOODWIN

sermons), and the holy kiss being at least discussed if not actually implemented.[8] There was also millenarian teaching, Goodwin being the likely preacher of *Glimpse of Sions Glory*, a fast sermon based on Revelation 19:6 preached at one of the Netherlands churches and published anonymously in London in 1641.[9] At some point Goodwin, Nye, and two elders from Arnhem held a 'solemne assembly' with the English Independent church at Rotterdam, where the pastor, John Ward, opposed by William Bridge and others on the issue of prophesying, had been deposed in January 1639 and replaced by Jeremiah Burroughes. After this 'Synod of Rotterdam,' Ward was restored in the summer of 1641, the congregation concluding it had been hasty and both sides confessing their sins.[10] This incident was later cited in the *Apologeticall Narration* of the dissenting brethren as an example of how Independent churches could make use of a synod for advice and consultation.[11]

Soon after the Long Parliament opened in November 1640 Goodwin returned to London and gathered an Independent congregation in the parish of St. Dunstan's-in-the-East.[12] It is also reported that he held several lectureships in London during the course of the Westminster Assembly, including St. Christopher in 1644-1645, St. Michael Crooked Lane in 1646-1648, and Allhallows Lombard Street in late 1648.[13] In the Assembly he was respected for both his piety and his scholarship, but it was also recognized that he was the chief spokesman for a minority position that was going to employ stalling tactics:

> ... although it was apparent that in any test of strength in the assembly the Independents would be voted down, it was also apparent that the recommendations of the Presbyterian majority were not likely to be adopted by parliament without question or amendment, and the less likely the longer decision could be delayed.[14]

In this situation the five dissenting brethren, in January 1644, made a direct appeal to Parliament and put it before the public in print in *An Apologeticall Narration*, setting forth their Independent or Congregational polity. William Haller comments:

> More important, however, than anything said in *An Apologeticall Narration* was the fact that it was said at just this juncture in print. Goodwin and his associates thus carried their case from the assembly to parliament and into the forum of public discussion and by so doing

set the example for all opponents of theocracy to do the same. Godly
divines in the Jerusalem Chamber at Westminster might go on debating
as long as they like and finally produce a directory of worship and
confession of faith for the Scots to take home with them.[15]

Goodwin and the Independents did continue to debate through most of
1644, but by the early part of 1645 they withdrew from the Assembly
to spend the next six months putting their views in writing. They sought
for toleration, but they and the majority in the Assembly were not even
able to achieve an accommodation. The Independent position would
prevail after 1649, with the ascendancy of Oliver Cromwell.

Goodwin enjoyed the esteem of Cromwell. On November 2, 1649
he was appointed a chaplain to the council of state and given lodgings
in Whitehall. On January 8, 1650 he was named President of Magdalen
College, Oxford, where he preached regularly at St. Mary's and held a
weekly meeting, on Independent church principles, of which Stephen
Charnock and Theophilus Gale were members. John Howe when a
student there, though of Presbyterian principles, was admitted by
Goodwin 'upon catholic terms'.[16] On August 14, 1650 Goodwin was
appointed to a committee (including John Milton) to make an inventory
of the records of the Westminster Assembly.[17] Thomas Goodwin, Jr.
(1650?-1716?) informs us in his 'Memoir of Thomas Goodwin, D.D.,
Composed Out of His Own Papers and Memoirs, by His Son' that at the
Assembly his father 'took a brief account of every day's transactions,
of which I have fourteen or fifteen volumes, wrote with his own hand'.[18]
Apparently these were lost, which is unfortunate since our other
sources of information on the Assembly – Robert Baillie, George
Gillespie, John Lightfoot, and the official minute-takers – all wrote
from a Presbyterian perspective.

In 1658 Goodwin and John Owen persuaded Cromwell to sponsor
a conference at the Savoy Palace to enable the Congregational Churches
in England to produce a statement of their doctrine and polity. Although
the Protector died on September 3, representatives of over a hundred
Independent churches including Goodwin, John Owen, Philip Nye,
William Bridge, Joseph Caryl and William Greenhill met for eleven or
twelve days from October 12 at the Savoy. 'They adopted, with a few
verbal alterations, the doctrinal definitions of the Westminster confession, reconstructing only the part relating to church government.'[19]

With the Restoration in 1660 Goodwin was deprived of his office at

Oxford. He took several members of his church to London and founded an Independent congregation in Fetter Lane. In the great fire of 1666, he lost more than half of his library, but his books of divinity were remarkably spared. He died on February 23, 1680 and was buried in Bunhill Fields. During his brief final illness he said:

> I am going to the Three Persons, with whom I have had communion. They have taken me, I did not take them. I shall be changed in the twinkling of an eye. All my lusts and corruptions I shall be rid of, which I could not be here. These croaking toads will fall off in a moment.

Reflecting on Hebrews 11, he remarked: 'Christ cannot love better than he doth. I think I cannot love Christ better than I do. I am swallowed up in God.'[20] Thus, to the end, Goodwin maintained in his experience what he had taught concerning assurance. J. I. Packer describes Goodwin's teaching on assurance:

> 'It is a new conversion,' says Goodwin; 'it will make a man differ from himself in what he was before in that manner almost as conversion doth before he was converted. There is a new edition of all a man's graces.' This sounds startling, but Goodwin means what he says, and works the idea out. Assurance, he tells us, increases faith (faith 'receives a new degree'); and this invigoration of faith results in a new release of energy at every point in one's Christian life.[21]

His portrait shows his face, 'with its strong hooked nose and curling locks', under two double skullcaps.[22] This garb may account for his nickname among students at Oxford, 'Dr. Nine Caps', – or, Robert Paul surmises, that may come from 'the carefully itemized and somewhat prolix style of his theological writing'.[23] Goodwin came across to some as gloomy and austere. Addison in the *Spectator* for September 26, 1712 told how Dr. Goodwin, 'with half-a-dozen night-caps on his head and religious horror in his countenance', terrified a student being examined at Oxford by asking him in a sepulchral voice, 'Are you prepared for death?'[24]

Dr. Edmund Calamy, grandson of one of the Presbyterian leaders in the Assembly, said of Goodwin that 'he was a very considerable scholar, and an eminent divine; and had a very happy faculty in descanting upon Scripture so as to bring forth surprising remarks, which yet generally tended to illustration'.[25] He began to publish

OLIVER CROMWELL (1599-1658)

Man of action and a devout Puritan, Oliver Cromwell through his military victories had a profound effect on the course of the Westminster Assembly. Primarily concerned for liberty of conscience, he strengthened the influence of the Independents in the Assembly and in Parliament. The New Model Army became a counter-balance to the influence of the Scots and the Presbyterians.

Cromwell was born at Huntingdon in 1599 and entered Sidney Sussex College, Cambridge in 1616. He was elected to the House of Commons for Huntingdon in 1628 and again for Cambridge in 1640 and thereafter played a major role in the Long Parliament. His well-trained New Model

Army gained the victories at Marston Moor on July 2, 1644 and at Naseby on June 14, 1645. After his defeat of the Scottish Royalists at Preston on August 17, 1648, his Colonel Thomas Pride purged the Parliament of its Presbyterian members on December 6. The trial of Charles I began on January 20, 1649, and the King was beheaded on the 30th. Having put down Royalist insurrections in Wales, Ireland, and Scotland, with victories at Dunbar on September 3, 1650 and at Worcester on the same date in 1651, he dissolved the "Rump" of the Long Parliament on April 20, 1653 and became the Protector on December 16 of that year.

Advocating general toleration, he nevertheless set up a committee of Triers for the purpose of expelling from the churches unfit ministers. His closest religious advisers were Independents such as John Owen, Thomas Goodwin, Philip Nye, Joseph Caryl, and Peter Sterry, some of whom attended him at the approach of his death, which occurred on September 3, 1658, the anniversary of two of his greatest military victories.

A firm believer in divine providence as a guide in his military and political affairs, he was skeptical of religious dogmatism. In 1650 he protested to the Church of Scotland's General Assembly: 'Is it therefore infallibly agreeable to the Word of God, all that you say? I beseech you, in the bowels of Christ, think it possible you may be mistaken.'

sermons in 1636 which became bestsellers, but these were almost lost to posterity:

> His portmanteau which contained them was cut off from his horse, in the darkness of the night, by a thief, just opposite to St. Andrew's Church-yard in Holborn. The clerk, or sexton, coming on the morning of the Lord's day, to ring the bell, found a bundle of papers lying at the root of a large tree. These were Mr. Goodwin's evangelical sermons, which were only known to be his by some other papers which contained his name and that of a bookseller, who was his particular friend. The papers were all carried to this man, and so they were preserved to edify God's people for generations to come.[26]

Goodwin was invited by John Cotton in 1647 to go to New England and had actually put a part of his library on board ship when he decided against it. Cotton's grandson in America, Cotton Mather, would later write:

> If you would see sound doctrine, the works of an Owen have it for you. You have a Goodwin who will place you among the children of light, and will give you the marrow of the doctrine which is according to godliness. He often soars like an eagle; perhaps, you would have been content, if sometimes a little more concisely.[27]

Philip Nye (c.1596 - September 1672)

On February 21, 1644 the Jerusalem Chamber was packed, not only with members of the Assembly, but also with members of both Houses of Parliament. On the previous day John Selden had challenged the relevancy of 1 Corinthians 5 and Matthew 18 to ecclesiastical discipline, and at the beginning of this day George Gillespie would make his famous answer. Also on the previous day Philip Nye, next to Thomas Goodwin the most frequent speaker for the Independents,[28] had warned of the danger to the civil government of an established Presbyterian polity, but he had been ruled out of order. Now, seeing an opportunity to make this point in the presence of so many from Parliament, he raised the issue again. John Lightfoot reported on Nye's speech in his *Journal*:

> Where two vast bodies are of equal amplitude, if they disagree it is nought; if they agree, it will be worse, one will closely be working

against another. And here he read something out of Mr. *Rutherford's*
preface upon his assertion of the Scotch government, and would have
fetched something out of it: when it was sharply prohibited, and he
cried out of, as disorderly and dangerous; and Mr. *Henderson* cried out
that he spake like Sanballat, Tobiah, or Symmachus: and Mr. *Sedgwick*
wished that he might be excluded out of the Assembly: and here was
great heat, and it was put to the question, and voted that he had spoken
against order.[29]

Nye's point was that a national Presbyterian Church established *jure
divino* could become as powerful as the civil government and hence
threaten the state. In saying this, however, he was derogating the
Church of Scotland and indeed the church government in every land
where the Reformed faith was established.[30] The Scot Robert Baillie
reported, 'We were all highly offended with him. The Assembly voted
him to have spoken against the order; which was the highest of their
censures.' But then he added: 'God who brings good out of evil, made
that miscarriage of Nye a mean to do him some good; for, ever since,
we find him, in all things, the most accommodating man in the
company.'[31]

Up until that time Nye was recognized as the tactical leader of the
Independents, whose goal was to achieve toleration for their type of
Congregational church government and whose means to that end was
to delay as much as possible in the Assembly until there would be
sufficient support for their position in Parliament. He was acknowledged to be shrewd and was distrusted as something of a schemer.[32]

Born about 1596, Nye entered Brasenose College, Oxford on July
21, 1615, removed a year later to Magdalen Hall, and received the B.A.
on April 24, 1619 and the M.A. on May 9, 1622. It was from a Puritan
tutor at Magdalen Hall that he gained his distinctive religious sentiments.[33] He began preaching in 1620 and received the curacy of the
London parishes of Allhallows, Staining on October 9, 1627 and of St.
Michael's, Cornhill in 1630. By 1633, following a meeting with John
Cotton,[34] his nonconformity led him to withdraw to the Netherlands,
where he was associated with John Archer and Thomas Goodwin in the
English Independent church at Arnhem from 1639 to 1640 or 1641.[35]
Upon his return to England after the opening of the Long Parliament he
was active in Hull, Yorkshire and became vicar of Kimbolton,
Huntingdonshire, in both of which places he organized Independent
churches by the summer of 1643.[36] Around 1641 Nye had signed an

agreement with Edmund Calamy, a leader of the London divines of Presbyterian sentiment, that neither Independents nor Presbyterians would preach or publish against the other's view until they were sure to be rid of Episcopacy.[37]

It was at this sort of negotiation that Nye excelled. As a member of the Westminster Assembly, he was sent in July 1643 with Stephen Marshall (whose second daughter would marry Nye's second son, John), under the leadership of Sir Henry Vane, Jr., to consummate the terms for the Solemn League and Covenant in Scotland. Here Henry Vane, probably with Nye's advice, bargained to include the words 'according to the Word of God' along with in conformity with the 'example of the best reformed churches.'[38] With this opening for Independent convictions Nye became an advocate for the Solemn League and Covenant. He was one of the speakers along with Alexander Henderson at St. Margaret's, Westminster when the Covenant was subscribed by the Assembly and Parliament on September 25.[39] By January 1644, however, he and Thomas Goodwin had produced *An Apologeticall Narration*, signed also by Sidrach Simpson, Jeremiah Burroughes and William Bridge, expressing their dissent from the Presbyterian majority in the Assembly.[40] To show Nye's shift, the Presbyterians later, in January 1646, reprinted his St. Margaret's address.[41]

Nye was particularly astute with regard to matters of worship. He wrote the preface to the Assembly's Directory for the Public Worship of God, a piece considered 'a very able document'.[42] In the controversy between set forms and extemporaneous prayers he said, 'I plead for neither, but for *studied* prayers.'[43] He had some peculiar views:

> as, that the minister in preaching, should have his head covered, and the people uncovered, because he then acts as their teacher; but in administering the Lord's Supper, he should be uncovered, and the people covered, as he there acts as their servant.

Favoring the Lord's Supper every Sunday, he 'was opposed to the communicants coming to the communion table in successive companies; but thought, that while some sat at the table, others might be around it'.[44] He was very rigorous with regard to admission to the Lord's Table. Richard Baxter later observed that at Acton, Middlesex, where Nye succeeded Daniel Featley as rector on September 30, 1643, and then was followed by another Congregatonal minister, 'there remained but two Women in all the Town, and Parish, whom they had admitted to the Sacrament'.[45] In addition to his Acton rectory he held several lectureships in London and was one of the seven divines appointed to give the daily 7:30-8 o'clock morning lecture at Westminster Abbey during the course of the Assembly.[46]

Nye was one of the commissioners to treat with Charles I on the Isle of Wight in December 1647, and he continued to be one of the ministerial leaders in the time of Oliver Cromwell, serving as a 'Trier' in 1654 and an 'Ejector' for Middlesex in the same year. Also in 1654 he moved from Acton to St. Bartholomew, Exchange in London, and in 1658 he was one of the leaders at the Savoy Conference that endorsed the Westminster Confession with a few Independent modifications.[47] In 1653 he had made common cause with the Presbyterian clergy of London against the Fifth Monarchy men.[48]

With the Restoration Nye lost all his preferments and escaped exclusion from the general indemnity only on condition of never again holding civil or ecclesiastical office; thus he was the most harshly treated of all the Westminster divines.[49] He left London, but returned after the fire in 1666. With the indulgence of 1672 he ministered to an Independent church in Cutters' Hall, Cloak Lane, Queen Street. He died in September 1672 and was buried in St. Michael's, Cornhill. Robert Paul, sympathetic to the Independents, calls Nye an enigma[50] and summarizes his character as follows:

Philip Nye was an ecclesiastical statesman, and he was extremely able. At worst he exercised the same kind of duplicity (but with more ability) as those ranged against him; at best he practiced a political realism without which the principle of religious toleration might have been swept from seventeenth-century England. He liked to be at the center of direction and effective power, and perhaps it was the ability which he exercised, together with his readiness to stay in the shadows while remaining at the center, which caused him to be so much feared and disliked outside the ranks of his own party.[51]

Jeremiah Burroughes (c.1599 - November 13, 1646)

With the achievement of peace between England and Scotland the Long Parliament declared a day of thanksgiving on September 7, 1641 and invited the Presbyterian Stephen Marshall and the Independent Jeremiah Burroughes to preach. As an exile returned from the Netherlands, Burroughes in his sermon *Sions Joy*, based on Isaiah 66:10, declared:

> Now we are come and find peace and mercy here, the voice of joy and gladnesse, your houses, armes, bosomes, hearts are opened to entertaine us. We scarce thought we should ever have seene our Country, but behold we are with our Honorable Senators and Worthyes of our Land called by them to rejoyce with them, and to prayse our God in the great Congregation: oh! who is like unto thee, O Lord.[52]

His enthusiasm stemmed not only from the contrast of the present with the past, but also from his expectations for the future. He says to Parliament assembled at Lincoln's Inn:

> You have the advantage of the time, for this is the time for God to doe great things for his Churches; time was when God stirred up his servants to stand against the wayes of *Antichrist*, only to give testimony to his truth ... but *now* God calls you to appeare against him, and his waies; At this time God intends to ruine him. You come at the time of his downfall, when he is falling ....[53]

It was appropriate that at this early stage of the Puritan reform Burroughes should be linked with Marshall, for he was the most conciliatory of the Independents. Richard Baxter was later to say that if all the Episcopalians had been like Archbishop Ussher, all the Presbyterians like Stephen Marshall, and all the Independents like Jeremiah Burroughes, then 'the breaches of the church would soon have been healed'.[54]

Burroughes was born about 1599 and entered Emmanuel College, Cambridge in 1617. He received his B.A. in 1621 and M.A. in 1624. He assisted Edmund Calamy as minister in Bury St. Edmunds, Suffolk from about 1627 to 1631, when he became rector in Twitshall, Norfolk.[55] He was suspended, however, for not observing the 1636 injunctions of Bishop Wren of Norwich and especially for not reading the 'Book of Sports'. He was sheltered for some months by the Earl of Warwick, but moved to the Netherlands in 1637 upon the invitation of the English congregation in Rotterdam to become its Teacher.[56] When John Ward was deposed as Pastor, Burroughes replaced him in January 1639, and William Bridge continued as Teacher, the Rotterdam church thereafter being known as 'the Burroughes-Bridge church'.[57]

In 1641 he returned to England, becoming Lecturer at Stepney and St. Giles, Cripplegate, two of the largest congregations in London.[58] Although not gathering a congregation of his own, he also lectured at St. Michael, Cornhill and St. Mildred, Bread Street.[59] Preaching at Stepney at 7 a.m. on Sundays, he drew such large crowds that Hugh Peter, when speaking there, referred to him as the 'morning star' and William Greenhill, the afternoon preacher, as the 'evening star' of Stepney.[60] His preaching avoided fancy style: 'His great aim was to guide his hearers in the way to heaven; and accordingly, plainness and persuasion were the chief objects of his attention.'[61] His own advice to the hearers of sermons was this:

> Remember, you come to tender up your homage to God, to sit at God's feet .... Many times you will say, Come, let us hear such a man preach; Oh no, let us go and hear Christ preach, for it doth concern the ministers of God that they preach not themselves, but that Christ should preach through them: so it concerns you that hear ... to come to hear Jesus Christ.[62]

JEREMIAH BURROUGHES

Several of his sermons had a premillenarian cast: it was not clear when the millennial kingdom of Christ would come, yet 'God by his strange kind of workings among us, doth seem as if he were hastening of the time, as if it were at hand'.[63] The anonymous sermon *Glimpse of Sion's Glory*, probably by Thomas Goodwin but sometimes ascribed to Burroughes, even predicted Christ's second coming as early as 1650 or possibly in 1695.[64]

The main contribution of Burroughes to the Westminster Assembly was his clearly and moderately setting forth of the Independents' position. He served on the Committee for Accommodation that was revived in November 1645 to consider the question of toleration. When this failed, Burroughes was selected to speak for the Independents at the Committee's last meeting on March 9, 1646. He declared:

> that if their congregations might not be exempted from the coercive power of the classes; if they might not have liberty to govern themselves in their own way, as long as they behaved peaceably towards the civil magistrate; they were resolved to suffer or go to some other place of the world, where they might enjoy their liberty. But while men think that there is no way of peace but by forcing all to be of the same mind ..., while they think the civil sword is an ordinance of God to determine all controversies of divinity, and that it must needs be attended with fines and imprisonment to the disobedient; while they apprehend that there is no medium between a strict uniformity, and a general confusion of all things; while these sentiments prevail, there must be a base subjection of men's consciences to slavery, a suppression of much truth, and great disturbances in the Christian world.[65]

These sentiments were to be published in *A Vindication of Mr. Burroughs against Mr. Edwards his foule Aspersions in his spreading Gangraena, and his angry Antiapologia*, in 1646. This was the year when Burroughes died after falling off his horse and, after two weeks, succumbing to a fever on November 13, leaving a widow. Richard Baxter's later comment reflects both the importance of Burroughes to the Independent cause and also Baxter's appreciation of Burroughes' moderate spirit: 'Mr. *Burroughs* being dead, Dr. *John Owen* arose, not of the same Spirit, to fill up his place; by whom and Mr. *Philip Nye's* Policie the Flames were encreased, our wounds kept open, and carried on as if there had been none but they considerable in the World.'[66] The respect his Independent allies had for Burroughes is shown by the

publishing of his major works in 1657 by Thomas Goodwin, Philip
Nye, William Bridge, Sidrach Simpson, William Greenhill and others.[67]

Among his works were *An Exposition with Practical Observations
on the Prophecy of Hosea*, in 4 volumes, down to chapter 13, verse 11;
Irenicum, or *Heart-Divisions Opened*; *Gospel-Worship*; *A Treatise of
the Evil of Evils; or The Exceeding Sinfulness of Sin*; *A Vindication of
Mr. Burroughs against Mr. Edwards*; and several others, mostly
sermons. *The Rare Jewel of Christian Contentment*, first published in
1648, has been reprinted as recently as 1987 by the Banner of Truth
Trust.

William Bridge (c.1600 - March 12, 1671)

At a crucial point in the 'Grand Debate' on church government,
February 16, 1644, William Bridge 'set down the clearest statement of
Congregational ecclesiology to appear in the debates to that point.
Indeed, he had to, for time was rapidly running out'. In what was
'clearly an important speech', he declared 'what he regarded as the
proper New Testament ecclesiology':

> 'The government according to the mind of God and his word revealed,
> is this:
>
> 'That every particular congregation consisting of elders and breth-
> ren, should have entire and full power of jurisdiction within them-
> selves, Mat. xviii. 15-17.'
>
> This gave him the opportunity to expound the Congregational
> interpretation of this passage – the church mentioned here has power
> to declare the highest form of church censure and it is in the particular
> congregation. Against Selden and his friends Bridge insisted that it is
> a spiritual and not a civil court that is referred to in Matthew 18, and
> against the Presbyterians he declared that it is a Christian and not a
> Jewish church. Possibly against Episcopalians, he also insisted that the
> word 'church' here does not mean a particular bishop.[68]

Robert S. Paul describes how the Presbyterians responded with speeches
by George Gillespie and Stephen Marshall, the latter particularly
pointing out the practical current difficulty in England of dealing with
errant congregations. He comments on how close the two factions
really were in their understanding of the local church.[69] It was Bridge's
clarity that allowed them to come at least this close to agreement.

William Bridge, like the other leading Independents in the Assembly, was another who had experienced exile in the Netherlands, and he would suffer loss again in the ejection of Nonconforming ministers at the time of the Restoration. In the meantime he would become one of the main Puritan influences in East Anglia. Born in Cambridgeshire about 1600, he entered Emmanuel College, Cambridge in 1619, receiving his B.A. in 1623, and his M.A. in 1626, and becoming a Fellow of the College for several years. From 1630 to 1632 he held a lectureship in St. Peter's parish, London, and in 1631 he was also appointed to a lectureship in Colchester, Essex, which he held for only a short time. In 1633 he received a Friday lectureship at St. George's Tombland, Norwich, and in 1636 he became Rector of St. Peter's, Hungate, Norwich.[70]

In Norwich, Bridge was suspended for not conforming to the injunctions of Bishop Matthew Wren. He stayed in the city after his suspension, but when Bishop Wren actually excommunicated him and the writ was issued to apprehend him, he decided to move to the

WILLIAM BRIDGE

Netherlands. In Archbishop Laud's annual report to the King for 1636, he said, 'Mr. *Bridge* of *Norwich* rather than he will conform, hath left his Lecture and two Cures, and is gone into *Holland*.' Charles I wrote in the margin: 'Let him go: We are well rid of him.'[71] Clearly, Bridge was recognized as a force to be reckoned with. Earlier, when a delegation from Colchester had requested that Bridge be their lecturer, Laud had replied angrily, 'When you want one, you must first go to Dr. Gouge and to Dr. Sibbes, and then you come to me: I scorn to be so used. I'll never have him to lecture in my diocese.'[72]

Bridge settled in Rotterdam, where Hugh Peter, William Ames and John Davenport had pastored an English congregation founded in 1619. He and John Ward were invited to be ministers in 1636 and, renouncing their Episcopal ordination, they ordained each other in Independent fashion. In 1638 Sidrach Simpson arrived, renouncing his ordination, but joining the congregation only as a private member. This may account for his support of 'prophesying' ('that the people on the Lords dayes should have liberty after the Sermons ended, to put doubts and questions to the Ministers'). Bridge opposed this practice, except possibly on a weekday. Ward took Simpson's side, and this led to the congregation's deposing him in January 1639 and appointing Jeremiah Burroughes in his place. Simpson withdrew to form a second English Reformed Church in Rotterdam. Eventually, Thomas Goodwin, Philip Nye and John Archer came from the church in Arnhem to settle the dispute in a 'synod' and to restore Ward to the ministry in the summer of 1641.[73] It has been suggested that, while Goodwin and Nye had been persuaded of Independent views by John Cotton before arriving in the Netherlands, there is no evidence that Bridge, Burroughes, or Simpson was yet inclined to this position, but their experience in the Dutch context convinced them.[74] It was also suggested by Thomas Edwards that the divisions in Rotterdam may have contributed to the premature death of Bridge's first wife, Susannah. Upon his return to England he subsequently married Margaret, the widow of John Arnold, merchant and bailiff of Great Yarmouth, Norfolk.[75]

Whatever else was the consequence of Bridge's Dutch experience, he came back a fully persuaded Independent. In a radical sermon entitled *Babylons Downfall* preached to Parliament, probably on April 4, 1641, he rejected both the English and Scottish forms of church government and called instead for 'God's form'.[76] His several sermons before Parliament over the years of the Westminster Assembly challenged the governmental leaders to push the Reformation further than it had been carried in other lands.[77] His preaching did not relinquish the apocalyptic cast that characterized so many sermons in 1641 at the beginning of the Long Parliament.[78]

Bridge returned to the Rotterdam church for a brief time in 1642, but then settled in England, forming Independent churches in Norwich in 1642 and Yarmouth in 1644 which continue to the present.[79] After the death of Jeremiah Burroughes, he succeeded him as morning lecturer at Stepney in December 1646.[80] He remained active in London into the Protectorate, attending the Savoy Conference in 1658, but his main ministry was in Great Yarmouth, Norfolk, where his preaching and leadership exercised great influence among the Puritans of East Anglia. Locked out of St. Nicholas's Church in Yarmouth on November 18, 1661, he moved to Clapham, near London, and preached in, if he did not found, the 'Independent Meeting' there. In 1663 he left London, having been nearly arrested at a conventicle. From 1666 it was possible for him again to preach in Yarmouth, and it was reported that in March 1668 'the people flock in such numbers to hear him that by 7 a.m. there is no room to be got'. He died on March 12, 1671.[81]

Bridge was known for his diligence: 'A very hard Student, and rose at Four a Clock in the Morning Winter and Summer, and continu'd in his Study till Eleven.'[82] Geoffrey F. Nuttall comments, 'Few were more cautious and conservative in their piety than William Bridge ...' and records a contemporary testimony: 'To my best remembrance I never saw nor enjoyed more of the presence and glory of God in any Assembly (setting the Ministry of Mr. Bridge of Yarmouth aside) than I have done in your Assemblies.'[83] His publications were mainly sermons. His *A Lifting Up for the Downcast*, reprinted by Banner of Truth as recently as 1979, is a series of thirteen sermons on Psalm 42:11, first published in 1649.

Sidrach Simpson (c.1600 - April 18, 1655)

According to James Reid, Sidrach Simpson 'was accounted a meek and quiet Divine of considerable learning, of great piety and devotion, and a celebrated preacher'.[84] Alexander Gordon termed him 'an extreme advocate for liberty of conscience.'[85] Of the 'Five Dissenting Brethren' he had spoken the least in the Assembly's debates, and perhaps this is why he was given the unhappy assignment of finally reporting for the

Independents on October 13, 1645 the reasons why their Committee of Dissenting Brethren 'did not think fit to bring in their model government' long awaited by the Assembly. Robert Baillie described the reaction:

> We were in a long expectation of a modell from the Independents; but yesterday, after seven months waiting, they have scorned us. The Assemblie haveing put them to it, to make a report of their diligence, they gave us a sheet or two of injurious reasons why they would not give us any declaration of their tenets. We have appointed a committee to answer that lybell.[86]

Born about 1600, probably in Lincolnshire, Sidrach Simpson entered Emmanuel College, Cambridge in 1616, but later moved to Queen's College, where he took his B.A. in 1622 and his M.A. in 1625. Ordained in 1623, he became curate from 1629 to 1638 of St. Margaret's, New Fish Street, London, where he also held a lectureship. It was here that he gained a reputation as a preacher.[87] Summoned before the ecclesiastical authorities in 1635, he at first agreed to conform, but eventually finding his position intolerable, he emigrated to the Netherlands in 1638.

In the Rotterdam English congregation pastored by John Ward and William Bridge, Simpson renounced his Episcopal ordination and joined as a private member.[88] A contemporary described his testimony upon joining the church:

> ... two things were required of him, a profession of his faith, and a confession of his experience of the grace of God wrought in him .... for a whole hour he poured out his soul into our bosom, and we as heartily embraced him in the bosom of the church ....[89]

But soon after his arrival Simpson took issue with some of the church's practices. According to Thomas Edwards's *Antapologia*:

> he stood for the ordinance of prophesying to be exercised in that Church, that the people on the Lords dayes should have liberty after the Sermons ended, to put doubts and questions to the Ministers, & c. and he was troubled at a ruling Elder in that Church brought in by Mr. *Bridge* (which belike had more power and bore more sway than himselfe).[90]

As a result of this controversy Simpson left the church, without letters of dismissal, and with the help of a certain Mrs. White formed a new church in Rotterdam, which at the beginning had five members.[91] This completely voluntary church, without government support, flourished, attracting those who approved of 'prophesying', and increasing while Bridge's church declined. Simpson took as an associate Joseph Symonds; hence this congregation became known as the 'Simpson-Symonds church' in contrast to the 'Burroughes-Bridge church' when, by January 1639, Jeremiah Burroughes had replaced John Ward.[92]

Although the division between the Rotterdam churches had been sharp, once the leaders were back in England, basking in the hopes surrounding the Long Parliament, they were able to make common cause. Simpson resumed his lectureship at St. Margaret's, Fish Street and added one at St. Anne, Blackfriars in 1641. At both churches he preached his Congregational convictions, and Bridge, Burroughes, Thomas Goodwin and Philip Nye welcomed him as an ally in the Westminster Assembly. In 1644 he defended their views in *The Anatomist Anatomized*, a response to Alexander Forbes's attack, *The Anatomie of Independence*. He signed the *Apologeticall Narration* produced by Goodwin and Nye and consistently stood with the Independents as one of the 'Five Dissenting Brethren' throughout the Westminster Assembly.[93]

In 1650 he was appointed Master of Pembroke Hall, Cambridge in place of Richard Vines, and he was associated with Nye and Goodwin along with Joseph Caryl and the rising leader John Owen in a number of ecclesiastical projects under Oliver Cromwell in the 1650s.[94] In 1653 he became Rector of St. Bartholomew, Exchange, in London, where he faced some of the difficulties of combining a parish church with a congregation formed on Independent principles. The parishioners complained, 'Wee weare not willinge to take the tithes because hee refused to administer the Sacrament and to crissen children except wee would bee joyned in communion with his church.' Geoffrey Nuttall says this described the double difficulty Congregational ministers faced elsewhere:

> They were unwilling to administer the sacraments to all their parishioners indiscriminately; and the parishioners were unwilling to support them with the payment of tithes, which in any case many Congregational men were uneasy about accepting.[95]

In his Commencement address at Cambridge in 1653 Simpson preached against some of the extreme views of the Fifth Monarchy Men, and he cooperated with John Owen and Thomas Goodwin at Oxford and Philip Nye in the City of London in opposition to the Fifth Monarchy Men's resistance of a national church.[96] Nevertheless, his preaching of something against Cromwell's government led to his being imprisoned briefly in Windsor Castle and being prohibited from preaching within ten miles of London.[97] This may have been either the result or the cause of a depression he suffered in the last year of his life:

> In his last sickness, he laboured under spiritual darkness, and some melancholy apprehensions. In such circumstances, some of his friends and brethren assembled at his house, with a view to assist him by their prayers. Their labours were not in vain in the Lord; for in the evening, when they took their leave of him, he thanked them, and said, 'He was now satisfied in his soul,' and lifting up his hands toward heaven, cried out, *'He is come, He is come,'* and he died that night ....[98]

The date of his death was April 18, 1655. He had a wife, Isabella, and a son, Sidrach Simpson, D.D. (died in 1704), who was educated at Oxford after his father's death and was for forty years Rector of Stoke Newington and a high churchman.[99] A son-in-law, Cuthbert Sydenham (died 1654), was a Congregational lecturer at St. Nicholas's, Newcastle-upon-Tyne.[100]

Notes

1. Wayne R. Spear, 'Covenanted Uniformity in Religion: The Influence of the Scottish Commissioners upon the Ecclesiology of the Westminster Assembly.' (University of Pittsburgh Ph. D. diss., 1976), 362.

2. S.W. Carruthers, *The Everyday Work of the Westminster Assembly* (Philadelphia: Presbyterian Historical Societies of America and of England, 1943), 58.

3. William Haller, *The Rise of Puritanism* (New York, Evanston, and London: Harper & Row, 1938), 77.

4. *Ibid.*, 167, 168, 136; James Reid, *Memoirs of the Westminster Divines,* 2 vols. in 1 (Edinburgh and Carlisle, Pa.: Banner of Truth, 1982, reprint of edition of 1811 and 1815), I, 331; Robert S. Paul, *An Apologeticall Narration* (Philadelphia and Boston: United Church Press, 1963), 83.

5. [Archibald Alexander], *A History of the Westminster Assembly* (Philadelphia: Presbyterian Board of Publication, 1841), 276.

6. *Ibid.*, 276.

7. Paul, *Apologeticall Narration*, 84; Geoffrey F. Nuttall, *Visible Saints: The Congregational Way, 1640-1660* (Oxford: Basil Blackwell, 1957), 15-16; Paul S. Seaver, *The Puritan Lectureships* (Stanford, Cal.: Stanford U. Press, 1970), 241.

8. Keith L. Sprunger, *Dutch Puritanism: A History of English and Scottish Churches of the Netherlands in the Sixteenth and Seventeenth Centuries* (Leiden: E.J. Brill, 1982), 226-230.

9. *Ibid.*, 229-230. John F. Wilson, 'A Glimpse of Syons Glory,' *Church History XXXI* (1962): 66-73, argues for Goodwin as the preacher/author, and this is supported by A.R. Dallison in Peter Toon, ed., *Puritans, the Millennium and the Future of Israel: Puritan Eschatology* (Cambridge & London: James Clarke & Co. Ltd., 1970), 131-136. Paul Christianson, *Reformers and Babylon: English Apocalyptic Visions from the Reformation to the Eve of the Civil War* (Toronto, Buffalo, and London: U. of Toronto Press, 1978), 212-219, 251-252, argues for Jeremiah Burroughes as the preacher/author.

10. Sprunger, *Dutch Puritanism*, 169-170, 228.

11. *Ibid.* Sidrach Simpson was also involved in the Rotterdam church, in support of prophesying.

12. Philip Schaff reported in 1877 that Goodwin's Congregational church in London 'continues to this day, and has recently (under the pastorate of Dr. Joseph Parker) erected the City Temple with a memorial tablet to Goodwin in the vestibule' (*Creeds of Christendom*, 6th ed., New York and London: Harper & Brothers, I, 742, n.3).

13. Tai Liu, *Puritan London* (Newark, Del.: U of Delaware Press, 1986), 121 n.38, 106, 111, 112; Paul S. Seaver, *The Puritan Lectureships* (Stanford, Cal.: Stanford U. Press, 1970), 281.

14. William Haller, *Liberty and Reformation in the Puritan Revolution* (New York and London: Columbia U. Press, 1955), 116.

15. *Ibid.*, 117.

16. *Dictionary of National Biography,* eds. Leslie Stephen and Sidney Lee, 22 vols. (London: Oxford U. Press, 1921-22), VIII, 149.

17. *D.N.B.*, VIII, 149.

18. In *The Works of Thomas Goodwin, D.D.* (Edinburgh: James Nichol, 1861), II, lxxiii; cf. [Alexander], *History*, 278, and Reid, *Memoirs*, I, 337. This son was born to Goodwin's second wife, Mary Hammond (whom he married in 1649 when she was only 16), and became a Nonconformist minister.

19. *D.N.B.*, VIII, 149; cf. Paul, *Apologeticall Narration*, 88, and A.G. Matthews, *Calamy Revised* (Oxford: Clarendon Press, 1934), 228.

20. [Alexander], *History*, 279.

21. J.I. Packer, *A Quest for Godliness: The Puritan Vision of the Christian Life* (Wheaton, Ill.: Crossway Books, 1990), 182-183. Packer also describes Goodwin's peculiar teachings on the sealing of the Holy Spirit in Ephesians 1:13, and explains his preference for John Owen's view, on pages 186-189.

22. *D.N.B.*, VIII, 149.

23. Paul, *Apologeticall Narration*, 89.

24. Schaff, *Creeds of Christendom*, I, 743 n.1; *D.N.B.*, VIII, 149.

25. Reid, *Memoirs*, I, 340.

26. [Alexander], *History*, 277.

27. Reid, *Memoirs*, I, 341.

28. Spear, 'Covenanted Uniformity,' 362.

29. Quoted in Robert S. Paul, *Assembly of the Lord* (Edinburgh: T. & T. Clark, 1985), 271.

30. Reid, *Memoirs*, II, 90-91, quotes Robert Baillie's account at some length. This scene is also described in Alexander F. Mitchell, *Westminster Assembly*, 2nd ed. (Philadelphia: Presbyterian Board of Publication, 1897), 169-170; William Beveridge, *A Short History of the Westminster Assembly*, rev. ed. J. Ligon Duncan III (Greenville, S.C.: Reformed Academic Press, 1993), 62-63; J.R. de Witt, *Jus Divinum* (Kampen: J.H. Kok, 1969), 112-114; and Paul, *Assembly of the Lord*, 271-275, who says that Nye's speech 'from the point of view of his party must have been regarded as disastrous.'

This dramatic scene is the basis for the famous painting of the Westminster Assembly by John Rogers Herbert, executed about 1848 (cf. *Journal of the Presbyterian Historical Society*, XXI, Nos. 2 and 3 [June and September, 1943], 111-113, Frontispiece and opposite page). William Hetherington, *History of the Westminster Assembly of Divines* (Edmonton, Alberta: Still Waters Revival Books, 1993 reprint of 3rd ed. of 1856), 410-413, takes strong issue with the glorification of Nye as a hero of liberty of conscience and argues the opposite. The romantic painting includes several figures who would not have been present, including Richard Baxter, John Milton, John Owen, Daniel Featley, and probably Oliver Cromwell. It also fails to include several significant members of the Assembly, such as Thomas Coleman, Robert Harris, Charles Herle, John Ley, Herbert Palmer, Lazarus Seaman, Thomas Temple and Thomas Young.

31. Quoted in Reid, *Memoirs*, II, 90-91, Cf. Beveridge, *Short History*, 63.

32. Paul, *Apologeticall Narration*, 89 n.31, 90; Carruthers, *Everyday Work*, 2; Tai Liu, *Discord in Zion: The Puritan Divines and the Puritan Revolution,* 1640-1660 (The Hague: Martinus Nijhoff, 1973), 24, refers to him as 'surely the master mind of the Independents in Puritan Politics'.

33. [Alexander], *History*, 349.

34. Seaver, *Puritan Lectureships*, 241.

35. Sprunger, *Dutch Puritanism*, 227 and n.79, 230 and n.95. Nuttall, *Visible Saints*, 7 n.1, suggests an influence upon Nye of the Dutch theologian Gisbertus Voetius, who in turn was influenced in a Congregational direction by William Ames.

36. *D.N.B.*, XIV, 725; Liu, *Puritan London*, 106; Nuttall, *Visible Saints*, 33 and n.4.

37. Liu, *Discord in Zion*, 9.

38. Paul, *Apologeticall Narration*, 72-73, 91-92.

39. John F. Wilson, *Pulpit in Parliament* (Princeton, N.J.: Princeton U. Press, 1969), 72-73; Haller, *Liberty and Reformation*, 109-110; Mitchell, *Westminster Assembly,* 168-169.

40. Paul, *Apologeticall Narration*, 96.

41. George Yule, *Puritans in Politics: The Religious Legislation of the Long Parliament, 1640-1647* (Appleford, Oxfordshire: Sutton Courtenay Press, 1981), 166, says: 'Nye, though an expert wriggler, was hoist on his own petard.'

42. *D.N.B.*, XIV, 725.

43. Mitchell, *Westminster Assembly*, 236.

44. [Alexander], *History*, 350; cf. Reid, *Memoirs*, II, 91.

45. Quoted in Nuttall, *Visible Saints*, 137.

46. Seaver, *Puritan Lectureships*, 269-270; Wilson, *Pulpit in Parliament*, 16.

47. Paul, *Apologeticall Narration*, 93-95.

48. Lui, *Discord in Zion*, 126.

49. Hetherington, *History*, 410.

50. Paul, *Apologeticall Narration*, 89.

51. *Ibid.*, 96-97.

52. Quoted in Keith L. Sprunger, *The Learned Doctor William Ames: Dutch Backgrounds of English and American Puritanism* (Urbana, Chicago, London: U. of Illinois Press, 1972), 250; cf. Sprunger, *Dutch Puritanism*, 378, and Wilson, *Pulpit in Parliament*, 52-53.

53. Quoted in Liu, *Discord in Zion,* 18.

54. Paul, *Apologeticall Narration*, 106, 108; *D.N.B.*, III, 446.

55. Larry Jackson Holley, 'The Divines of the Wesminster Assembly' (New Haven: Yale U. Ph.D. diss., 1979), 287; *D.N.B.*, III, 445.

56. Paul, *Apologeticall Narration*, 104-105.

57. Sprunger, *Dutch Puritanism*, 169.

58. Holley, 'Divines', 287-288; Reid, *Memoirs,* I, 156.

59. Liu, *Puritan London*, 106.

60. Paul, *Apologeticall Narration*, 105; Reid, *Memoirs,* I, 157.

61. Reid, *Memoirs*, I, 157.

62. Quoted from *Gospel-Worship* in Iain H. Murray, 'The Directory for Public Worship,' in *To Glorify and Enjoy God: A Commemoration of the 350th Anniversary of the Westminster Assembly*, eds. John L. Carson and David W. Hall (Edinburgh and Carlisle, Pa.: Banner of Truth, 1994), 184.

63. Quoted in Liu, *Discord,* 46-47.

64. Sprunger, *Dutch Puritanism*, 332. Paul Christianson, *Reformers in Babylon,* 251-252, 212-219, argues for Burroughes as author.

65. Quoted in Paul, *Apologeticall Narration*, 107. Cf. also Liu, *Discord*, 49, and Paul, *Assembly of the Lord*, 480-481, n.51 for quotations from Burroughes' *A Vindication*. A selection from his *Irenicum*, or *Heart-Divisions Opened*, can be found in Iain H. Murray, ed., *The Reformation of the Church: A Collection of Reformed and Puritan Documents on Church Issues* (Edinburgh and Carlisle, Pa.: Banner of Truth, 1965), 325-340.

66. Quoted in Paul, *Apologeticall Narrative,* 109. Cf. de Witt, *Jus Divinum*, 164-165, n.87.

67. Paul, *Apologeticall Narration*, 108 and n.100; Nuttall, *Visible Saints*, 14.

68. Paul, *Assembly of the Lord*, 262-264.

69. *Ibid.,* 264.

70. Holley, 'Divines', 284; *D.N.B.*, II, 1223.

71. Reid, *Memoirs*, I. 139; cf. Seaver, *Puritan Lectureships,* 371-372, n.49, and Sprunger, *The Learned Dr. William Ames,* 212.

72. Seaver, *Puritan Lectureships,* 256.

73. Sprunger, *Dutch Puritanism*, 163, 168-170.

74. Yule, *Puritans in Politics,* 95-96. Cf. Sprunger, *Dutch Puritanism*, 172.

75. Paul, *Apologeticall Narration,* 99 and n.68; *D.N.B.*, II, 1224.

76. Wilson, *Pulpit in Parliament,* 46-47; cf. Liu, *Discord,* 15-16. Wilson, 277-278, discusses the dating of this sermon. He also points out that Hugh Trevor-Roper mistook an even more radical sermon by Walter Bridges in February 1643 as one by William Bridge (68 and n.41).

77. Wilson, *Pulpit in Parliament,* 75 and 179, 92-93 and 182.

78. Liu, *Discord*, 59.

79. Sprunger, *Dutch Puritanism*, 171, 172; Paul, *Apologeticall Narration*, 101 and n.74.

80. *Calamy Revised*, ed. A.G. Matthews (Oxford: Clarendon Press, 1934), 74.

81. *D.N.B.*, II, 1223; *Calamy Revised*, 74.

82. *Calamy Revised,* 74.

83. Nuttall, *Visible Saints*, 165.

84. Reid, *Memoirs*, II, 147.

85. *D.N.B..*, XVIII, 277.

86. Quoted in John Richard de Witt, *Jus Divinum*, 155; cf. Paul, *Assembly of the Lord,* 479-480.

87. Holley, 'Divines', 343; *D.N.B.*, XVIII, 277; Paul, *Apologeticall Narration*, 98.

88. Sprunger, *Dutch Puritanism*, 169.

89. Quoted in Nuttall, *Visible Saints*, 111.

90. Quoted in Paul, *Apologeticall Narration*, 99.

91. Paul, *Apologeticall Narration*, 99.

92. Sprunger, *Dutch Puritanism*, 169; *D.N.B.*, XVIII, 277; Paul, *Apologeticall Narration*, 99.

93. Paul, *Apologeticall Narration*, 100.

94. Nuttall, *Visible Saints*, 14; Paul, *Apologeticall Narration*, 101.

95. Nuttall, *Visible Saints,* 134-135, 22.

96. Liu, *Discord,* 127, 100.

97. *D.N.B.*, XVIII, 278; Nuttall, *Visible Saints*, 12; Paul, *Apologeticall Narration,* 101.

98. Reid, *Memoirs*, II, 147.

99. *D.N.B.*, XVIII, 278.

100. Nuttall, *Visible Saints*, 24.

Chapter 6

The Scots

After the acceptance of the Solemn League and Covenant in September 1643 the Westminster Assembly was greatly influenced by the Scottish commissioners, who, though not voting members of the Assembly, were free to participate in all committees and to engage in the debates on the floor. In addition to the four ministers and two ruling elders described in this chapter, Scottish ministers Robert Douglas of Edinburgh (who never sat) and Robert Blair of St. Andrews were appointed to the Assembly and also ruling elders John, Earl of Cassilis (who never sat); Robert Meldrum; John, Earl of Loudon; Sir Charles Erskine; John, Lord Balmerino; Archibald, Marquis of Argyll; and George Winrham of Libberton.

Alexander Henderson (1583 - August 19, 1646)

When the Scottish Commissioners arrived at Westminster in September of 1643 to seal the agreement of the Solemn League and Covenant and to carry out its provisions for a uniformity of religion in the realms of England, Wales, Scotland and Ireland, the clear leader of the delegation was Alexander Henderson. In his sixtieth year, he was among the senior members of the Assembly, and within three years he would depart this life (one of more than a dozen of the Westminster Divines who would die in the course of the Assembly's work), having devoted his final nine years to the cause of reformation.

Henderson came as the main drafter of the Solemn League and Covenant and as the Moderator of the just-concluded General Assembly of the Church of Scotland. Indeed, he had also been Moderator of the General Assemblies of 1638 and 1641 and the main drafter of the National Covenant of 1638 which had drawn the line on behalf of preserving the Protestant Reformation over against the imposition of Laudian ceremonies and hierarchy.

He had not always held such Presbyterian views, but had at first conformed to the Episcopacy prevailing in Scotland in the days of King James I. Born in the parish of Creich in Fife, he entered the University of St. Andrews in December 1599. Achieving his M.A. in 1603, he became a Regent or Quaestor in the Faculty of Arts and taught philosophy there for eight years. In 1611 he was licensed as a preacher, and in December 1613 or January 1614 he was presented to the parish of Leuchars, a village six miles northeast of St. Andrews. The County of Fife being among the most hostile to the Bishops, the parishioners nailed up the church doors on the day of his ordination. As a result, the ordaining party had to climb in through a window and carry out Henderson's ordination in an empty church.

Sometime between June 1615 and July 1616, however, Henderson heard that the renowned Robert Bruce was to preach in the nearby church of Fergan. To avoid notice, Henderson took a seat in a dark corner of the church. When Bruce proceeded to preach from John 10:1, 'Verily, verily, I say unto you, he that entereth not by the door into the sheepfold, but climbeth up some other way, the same is a thief and a robber,' Henderson was convicted and converted to Christ and, after subsequent study, to the Presbyterian position.

By the time of the crisis in Scotland over the imposition of a new Book of Canons in 1635 and a new Liturgy in 1636, after two decades of Reformed ministry in Leuchars, Henderson was marked out for leadership. Samuel Rutherford wrote to him on March 9, 1637: '... ye are the talk of the north and south.... Let us pray for one another. He who hath made you a chosen arrow in His quiver, hide you in the hollow of His hand.' Marcus Loane comments:

> Rutherford knew, as others knew, that Henderson combined a clear mind with a firm grasp of affairs. He was known as a man with a high-minded sense of courtesy in debate and a clear-sighted gift for promptitude in action. He was quiet and grave in manner, but he spoke with fluent ease and authority. He had always excelled as a spontaneous speaker, yet his utterances were so clear and rounded that they always seemed to suggest full and careful preparation.[1]

Henderson, as one of three in the Presbytery of St. Andrews to refuse to use the new Liturgy in August of 1637, was the first man of note to resist episcopal authority in this regard, and his appeal to the Privy Council made his case a test case for the whole Church of Scotland.

ALEXANDER HENDERSON

The Solemn League and Covenant

The document that provided the official basis for the Confession of
Faith, Catechisms, Directory for the Public Worship of God, and Form
of Presbyterial Church Government produced by the Westminster Assembly was The Solemn League and Covenant negotiated in the late
summer of 1643 between the English Commissioners appointed by
Parliament – among them Sir Henry Vane the Younger and Stephen
Marshall and Philip Nye for the Westminster Assembly – and representatives of both the Scottish General Assembly and the Scottish Parliament. Robert Baillie, who was one of the negotiators for the Scots,
said that the English wanted mainly a civil league while the Scots wanted
mainly a religious covenant. The need of the English Parliamentary
forces at the time was military assistance in the field against the Cavalier Army of Charles I. The aim of the Scots was the securing of Reformed doctrine and Presbyterian church government in Scotland and
the achievement of uniformity of religion in the two realms. After the
document was drafted by Alexander Henderson, evidently with the help
of Archibald Johnston of Warriston, Sir Henry Vane introduced the word
'League' into the title to emphasize the civil aspect and also achieved
the addition of the words 'according to the Word of God' with regard to
the reformation of religion. This was viewed by the Independents as a
counter-balance to 'the example of the best reformed churches,' which
suggested that the existing Presbyterian system in Scotland (and on the
Continent) would be a sufficient model. After some slight modifications, and some misgivings about forsaking a moderate Episcopacy, the
English Parliament and the Westminster Assembly subscribed to the
Solemn League and Covenant in late September 1643. Its first article
declared:

That we shall sincerely, really and constantly, through the grace of God,
endeavour in our several places and callings, the preservation of the
reformed religion in the Church of Scotland, in doctrine, worship, discipline and government, against our common enemies; the reformation
of religion in the kingdoms of England and Ireland, according to the
Word of God and the example of the best reformed churches; and we
shall endeavour to bring the churches of God in the three kingdoms to
the nearest conjunction and uniformity in religion, confessing of faith,
form of church government, directory for worship, and catechising, that
we and our posterity after us may, as brethren, live in faith and love, and
the Lord may delight to dwell in the midst of us.

When King Charles I and the Privy Council refused to make any concessions, a supplication gained the support of more than two hundred parishes. This was followed by a petition of complaint against the Bishops which was subscribed in October 'by thirty-eight nobles, several hundred ministers, gentlemen without number, and all the Burghs in Scotland except Aberdeen.'[2]

By early 1638 it was clear that Scotland must either submit to the King or prepare to go to war. On February 23 Henderson proposed a National Covenant, and he and Archibald Johnston were designated to draft such a document, which they did on the model of the Covenant of 1581. On February 28 the barons and nobles and leading ministers of Scotland gathered at Greyfriars Church in Edinburgh to sign it, many with tears. On the next day the people of Edinburgh signed it, and on March 1 copies were sent to every shire and parish.

Henderson then took steps to restore the General Assembly and to have a National Parliament summoned. When the General Assembly met in Glasgow in November, he was elected Moderator. The key issue was the trial of the Bishops, and when the King's Commissioner protested, dissolved the Assembly in the name of the King, and retired, Henderson led the Assembly to remain for a full month, proceeding to the trial and censure of the Bishops, six of whom were deposed and the other eight deposed and excommunicated. On December 13 Henderson preached to the Assembly on Psalm 110:1 and, as Moderator, pronounced the censures of deposition and excommunication.

Although Henderson preferred to stay in the quiet of Leuchars, the General Assembly resolved that he be moved to Edinburgh, and on January 10, 1639 he was installed as minister of the Cathedral Church of St. Giles. In the various stages of negotiation that led up to war, he was one of the main Scottish diplomats. King Charles was sufficiently attracted to him to grant him several private interviews, hearing his appeal for the abolition of Episcopacy in Scotland and for financial subsidies for the Scottish universities (Henderson became Rector of the University of Edinburgh in January of 1641) from the revenues of the Scottish Bishoprics. These requests were denied, but when the King visited Scotland in August of 1641, he appointed Henderson his chaplain, hearing him pray and preach morning and evening on Tuesdays. (Henderson also rebuked the King for playing golf on the Sabbath.) Having understood Charles to be committed to a Presbyterian uniformity of England and Scotland, Henderson had proposed to the General Assembly in July of 1641 (of which he was, for a second time, the Moderator) a Confession of Faith, a Catechism, and a Directory for Church Government and Worship, to become binding for both Scotland and England.

When war broke out in England between King and Parliament in August of 1642, Henderson sought at first to maintain neutrality. A year later it was clear that the King was opposed to Presbyterian uniformity, and so Henderson, Moderator of the General Assembly for a third time, was open to the request of the Parliamentary Commission of Sir Harry Vane, Philip Nye and Stephen Marshall to send a delegation to the Westminster Assembly. Once again, Henderson and Warriston were called upon to draft the terms of the Solemn League and Covenant for participation in reform of the English church in exchange for Scottish military aid.

In the Westminster Assembly Henderson played a leading role, preaching on the occasion of the subscribing of the Solemn League and Covenant by the House of Lords, the House of Commons, and the Divines on September 25, 1643 and preaching before the House of Commons in December 1643 and before the House of Lords in July 1644. Archibald Alexander describes his role:

> In the Westminster Assembly of Divines, Mr. Henderson acted a very conspicuous part; and perhaps no one in that body had a greater influence on its acts and decisions. When the members grew warm in debate, he endeavored to reconcile them, and had a happy art of removing difficulties which hindered the agreement of brethren.[3]

His vision for uniformity in religion in Scotland and England was, however, not to be realized. As Marcus Loane comments:

> Henderson's genius had shown its true instinct in the National Covenant at a grave hour in his own north country; it was in line with the tradition and sentiment of Scotland, and it bound the nation as one man to meet a pressing danger. But his ideal for one uniform religion in both Kingdoms as now proposed in the Solemn League and Covenant was less sure in instinct. Time was to prove that it did not fit in with the history and character of England, and the best that can be said is that it was a splendid vision.[4]

His dying effort was spent in last-gasp negotiations with the King, who by the spring of 1646, his military cause lost, had fled north and placed himself in the protection of the Scottish army at Newcastle-on-Tyne. With Charles expressing a desire to confer with him, Henderson journeyed north from London, reaching Newcastle on May 26. Into July they exchanged five papers on whether Episcopacy was of divine institution, but the King could not be dissuaded. Henderson's health had been precarious since 1641, and exhaustion from his labors brought him to his death in Edinburgh on August 19, 1646. 'As no man whom Scotland ever produced was more universally esteemed,' says Alexander, 'so his death was greatly lamented.'[5]

Henderson has been generally acclaimed for his sagacity and his modesty. Rather than seeking leadership, he tended to shy away from it until placed in a position of responsibility. But he always responded to duty and his sense of the Lord's cause, even when his strength was failing. When required to be in Edinburgh, where he was always unhealthy, he sought removal also because his voice was not strong enough to fill any church in the city.[6]

Six original portraits of him in Scotland show him 'to have been short and slight in stature, perhaps less than middle height but well formed, with small shapely hands and thoughtful features.... they reveal a face full of courage and calm benevolence.'[7] He had neither wife nor child. He reflected on his own rise from obscurity and the quietness and contemplation that he preferred:

> When...I begin to remember...how men are brought to act the things which they never determined, nor so much as dreamed of before: the words of the Prophet Jeremiah came to my remembrance: 'O Lord, I know that the way of man is not in himself; it is not in man that walketh, to direct his steps.'[8]

Samuel Rutherford (1600 - March 29, 1661)

J.D. Douglas says of Samuel Rutherford: '...this most complex and colourful character of all Scottish theologians quite eludes satisfying description.'[9] A beloved pastor whose letters of spiritual counsel are still of benefit and a scholar whose Latin works gained him an international reputation, he was capable of partisan polemic strong enough to sever fellowship with those who had been godly allies. In his own view, like his predecessor of the previous century, John Knox, he was simply loyal to King Jesus.

Born in the village of Nisbet, three or four miles from the town of

Jedburgh, Rutherford became a student at the University of Edinburgh in 1617. Receiving his M.A. there in 1621, he was appointed in 1623 as Regent of Humanity, a tutor in Latin studies. But in 1625 he was forced to resign for an alleged moral misdemeanor. This may have led to his conversion, for his letters indicate that he entered into a saving experience of Christ only as an adult, and he frequently bemoans and counsels against wasted youth.

In 1627 he was licensed as a preacher and called to the church of Anwoth near Kirkcudbright in Galloway. For nine years there Rutherford labored diligently among his people to help them know Jesus Christ. During this time his first wife, Eupham, died in 1630, his two children died, and also in 1635 his mother who had come to live with them. Marcus Loane comments: 'Rutherford's ministry while in Anwoth was a noble approach to the splendid ideal of Baxter's *Reformed Pastor* or Herbert's *Country Parson.*'[10] Of his preaching, one of his correspondents, Marion McNaught, wrote: 'I go to Anwoth so often because, though other ministers show me the majesty of God and the plague of my own heart, Mr. Samuel does both these things, but he also shows me, as no other minister ever does, the loveliness of Christ.'[11]

The ecclesiastical strife of the times is shown in Rutherford's being summoned before the Court of High Commission, deprived of his

pastoral office, forbidden to preach anywhere in Scotland, and confined within the town of Aberdeen in July of 1636. This came as a result of his publishing a book against Arminianism, *Exercitationes Apologeticae pro Divina Gratia,* an attack on Archbishop Laud's position. As Rutherford said, 'My newly printed book against Arminians was one challenge; not lording the prelates was another.'[12]

At Aberdeen, a center of Arminian and Episcopal sentiments, he was received

SAMUEL RUTHERFORD

coldly, though eventually his innocence gained sympathy. During his eighteen months there, from August or September, 1636 to February, 1638, he showed skill in some disputations with the University scholars, but mainly he wrote letters to his former parishioners, both high and low, and to others; more than half of his published letters come from 1637, and two-thirds from Aberdeen.

When the National Covenant was signed, the time was ripe for him to risk returning to Anwoth. The famous General Assembly of Glasgow in November of 1638, however, appointed him to St. Andrews to fill the Chair of Divinity at St. Mary's College. He would teach there from 1639 until his death in 1661, except for his four years at the Westminster Assembly 1643-1647, serving also as colleague of Robert Blair in the church of St. Andrews. St. Mary's College had been reorganized sixty years earlier, with Andrew Melville as Principal 1580-1607, and was the main theological school of Scotland. There William Guthrie was one of his students, and also Robert McWard, who went with him to London as his amanuensis at the Westminster Assembly.

Rutherford arrived in London with fellow commissioner Robert Baillie on November 17, 1643, Alexander Henderson and George Gillespie having already travelled south in August. He was to stay until November 1647, the longest of the Scottish Commissioners, Henderson having left in May 1646, Baillie later that year, and Gillespie in July 1647. Rutherford had a special friendship with Gillespie, who was born in 1613 and had come to Kenmure Castle in Galloway as a tutor during the last years of Rutherford's ministry at Anwoth. They had made a covenant one day at the castle to pray for each other and to write to each other on the life of God in their souls.[13]

Not only did Rutherford play a major role in the debates of the Assembly, but he also published five books during those years. His *Lex Rex* was written and published in 1644 and made quite a sensational impact on the Assembly and London in its argument for civil liberty versus absolute monarchy. He also wrote *The Due Right of Presbyteries* (largely against the arguments of the Independents) in 1644, and this was followed by *The Trial and Triumph of Faith* (1645), *The Divine Right of Church Government and Excommunication* (1646 – against Erastianism) and *Christ Dying and Drawing Sinners to Himself* (1647). In 1648 he published *A Survey of the Spiritual Antichrist* (against Antinomianism) and in 1649 *A Free Disputation against Pretended Liberty of Conscience.*

Upon his return to St. Andrews he was appointed Principal of St. Mary's College and in 1651 Rector of the University, having declined appointments in the Netherlands (including the Chair of Divinity at Utrecht where Voetius was) and at Edinburgh. Married a second time in 1640 to Jean McMath, he had two children die while he was in London, but they had five more after 1647, though only a daughter, Agnes, survived with his wife after his death.

The 1650s were marked by ecclesiastical strife, related to Scottish loyalty to Charles II and the Resolutions of 1650, against which Rutherford and the more extreme Covenanters offered a Protest. Protesters and Resolutioners were so divided that Rutherford would not even speak with his former colleague Robert Blair, who was also joined by such as Robert Baillie and David Dickson. He and Blair were

'Resolutioners' and 'Protesters'

Some of the Scottish Commissioners to the Westminster Assembly found themselves on opposite sides of a dispute in the Church of Scotland in the 1650s. Following the defeat of the Scottish army by Oliver Cromwell at Dunbar on September 3, 1650, the Church of Scotland was divided over the proper response. One side, including Robert Douglas and Robert Baillie, supported the Public Resolutions of December 1650 which raised an army behind Charles II, hence they were known as 'Resolutioners'. The other side, including Samuel Rutherford, James Guthrie, and Archibald Johnston of Warriston, supported a Remonstrance complaining against the admission of Charles II to the Covenants and presented a Protestation when twenty-two ministers were barred from election to the 1651 General Assembly, hence they were known as 'Protesters'. The Resolutioners, fearing some of the Sectarianism of Cromwell's England, viewed the Protesters as treasonable. The Protesters regarded the Resolutioners as naive with regard to Charles II's commitment to the Covenants and feared a return to Episcopacy. In 1653 both sides prepared separate General Assemblies although the English army prevented either from being held. Both sides appealed for support in England from some of their former colleagues in the Westminster Assembly. Although basically agreed in doctrine, the two sides were fiercely opposed in policy, with the result that there was no effective resistance to Episcopacy after the Restoration in 1660. The Protesters were eventually proven correct in their estimation of the character of Charles II, whose Act Rescissory of 1661 undid all of the acts of the Long Parliament, including the work of the Westminster Assembly.

reconciled before his death, by which time Dickson admitted that Rutherford had been right.

Charles II was restored in 1660, and persecution began in 1661. The Earl of Argyll would be beheaded on May 27, 1661 and James Guthrie hanged on June 1. Rutherford's *Lex Rex* was ordered burned, and he was summoned by the Committee of Estates, but ill health prevented him. Deposed from the ministry and dismissed from his Chair at St. Andrews, he faced a higher tribunal. Before he died on March 27, he sent the message, 'Tell them ... I behove to answer my first summons, and ere your day come, I will be where few kings and great folk come.'[14]

Taylor Innes described Rutherford as 'St. Thomas and St. Francis under one hood.'[15] James Walker compared him to Bernard of Clairvaux.[16] Alexander Whyte says, '... the greatest speculative freedom and theological breadth met in Rutherford with the greatest ecclesiastical hardness and narrowness.'[17] He further comments:

> In all my acquaintance with literature I do not know any author who has two books under his name so unlike one another, two books that are such a contrast to one another, as *Lex Rex* and the *Letters*. ... There is as much emotion in the multiplication table as there is in *Lex Rex*; and then, on the other hand, the *Letters* have no other fault but this, that they are overcharged with emotion.[18]

Rutherford once told David Dickson, 'I am made of extremes.'[19] Marcus Loane says, 'He was armed with a tremendous power of rebuke, and he had scant mercy on men who sinned against the light.' He combined this with such memorable aphorisms as these from his sermons and letters: 'Lovely in the womb, the Ancient of Days became young for me,' 'Prayer is like God's file to stir a rusty heart,' 'A good conscience is a good soft well-made bed,' and 'The world loves nothing worse than sorrow for sin.'[20]

In 1857 Anne R. Cousin, wife of Rev. William Cousin, minister of the Free Church of Melrose, wrote a poem 'The Sands of Time Are Sinking,' based on the *Letters* and last words of Rutherford, which has become a well-known hymn. The last three of the nineteen stanzas are as follows:

The Bride eyes not her garment
    But her dear Bridegroom's face;
I will not gaze at glory,
    But on my King of Grace –

Not at the crown He gifteth,
    But on His pierce'd hand:
The Lamb is all the glory
    Of Immanuel's land.

I have borne scorn and hatred,
    I have borne wrong and shame,
Earth's proud ones have reproach'd me,
    For Christ's thrice blessed name: –
Where God His seal set fairest
    They've stamp'd their foulest brand;
But judgment shines like noonday
    In Immanuel's land.

They've summoned me before them,
    But there I may not come, –
My Lord says, 'Come up hither,'
    My Lord says, 'Welcome Home!'
My kingly King, at His white throne,
    My presence doth command,
Where glory – glory dwelleth
    In Immanuel's land. [21]

Robert Baillie (April 30, 1602 - late August, 1662)

Although the quietest of the Scottish delegation in public debate, Robert Baillie may have been the most influential through his private diplomacy, and he may have become most influential also in the subsequent interpretation of the Assembly through his *Letters and Journals*, one of the three main sources for information about the Assembly's discussions and actions apart from the official minutes.

A.F. Mitchell remarks that Baillie 'has embalmed in graphic narrative both their serious debates and their lighter gossip ....'[22] J.R. de Witt comments: 'His accurate and highly individual reporting as an eye witness is an exceedingly valuable historical source.'[23] He also points out that Baillie did not mince words, as in his report of the Erastian Thomas Coleman's death: '... he fell in ane ague, and after four or five days expired. It's not good to stand in Christ's way.'[24] de Witt makes it clear that Baillie was not reporting as an objective observer:

Robert Baillie must be used with great care as a witness to the divisions in the Assembly. His outbursts upon any given occasion should be read in terms of what provoked him to them. He wrote 'letters' descriptive of the Assembly and its members, and they are just that – not dispassionate treatises in which he weighs the evidence and disinterestedly assesses the issues of the day. These letters of his show him to have been anything but a spectator: he was involved, deeply and personally involved in the events of which he was witness. Hence, friends who seemed to agree with him in one debate, and were described in his agreeable and gossipy correspondence as so doing, might very well be out of favour in the next.[25]

The part that Baillie played at the Assembly was that of behind-the-scenes negotiator for the Scottish interest of religious uniformity. H.M.B. Reid characterizes him as the brains behind such leaders of the Scottish church as Alexander Henderson, David Dickson and Robert Douglas, and describes him as the 'coach' always at Henderson's elbow at Westminster. 'He played among the clerics the same part as Johnston of Warriston did among the laics.'[26]

In his diplomatic capacity Baillie was constantly in correspondence with his cousin William Spang in the Netherlands and with various Reformed leaders on the Continent. Mitchell says:

Baillie restlessly wrote ... to friends on the Continent to send testimonies or arguments in favor of the Scottish views to influence the Assembly and the Parliament, and sadly disappointed the good man was when the testimonies did not in every point come up to his expectations. He busied himself also in organizing opposition in the city to the measures of the Parliament, and was still more sadly disappointed when this piece of artillery 'played nip-shot.'[27]

William Beveridge describes Baillie as 'the Nye of the Scottish Commissioners: he had an undue fondness for little matters of diplomacy – schemes, it has been pointed out, which were peculiarly transparent.' He furnishes an example of Baillie's method of operation:

Now and then, however, in committee God would open his mouth, to use his own expressive phrase, as, for instance, on one occasion when he spoke 'somewhat to his own contentment.' It so happened that the Directory for Public Worship was under discussion before a subcommittee in the end of 1643, and Goodwin had 'assayed to turn all upside downs, to reason against all directories.' Despite Baillie's 'good, new, extemporall answers,' Goodwin would not be satisfied; so adds Baillie, 'For the help of this evile, we thought it best to speak with him in private; so we invited him to dinner, and spent an afternoon with him very sweetlie' (*Letters*, ii, 123).[28]

There can be no question of the tirelessness of Baillie's efforts. Mitchell says, 'Hard had the good man labored, wire pulling and letter writing ....'[29] Robert S. Paul comments: 'In each subject in which he involved himself, Baillie became a well-informed expert. He made himself very knowledgeable about the earlier history of the relationships between the Church of England and the Church of Scotland ....'[30]

ROBERT BAILLIE

Baillie was born on April 30, 1602 in Glasgow, and much of his life was associated with that city. He attended Glasgow University, receiving his M.A. in 1620 and completing his divinity studies there in 1623. In 1625 he became a teaching regent there, a post that he held for six years before his ordination and charge to pastor the church at Kilwinning, where he served, with certain interludes, from 1631 to 1642. He married Lilias Fleming on July 12, 1632, who bore him five children, two of whom died in infancy. Although Rutherford and Gillespie had their wives and children with them for at least part of the time in London,[31] Baillie was separated from his family for sixteen months until he returned to Scotland to report to the General Assembly in January of 1645 and for another twenty-one months before his final departure from the Assembly on December 25, 1646.[32] His wife died on June 7, 1653, and he married again on October 1, 1656 to Helen Strang, adding a daughter the next year, as well as Helen's son by a previous marriage, to his household.

At the great reforming General Assembly of 1638 in Glasgow Baillie had shown both his moderation and independency of mind. All but a small minority were caught up with the cause of deposing the Bishops. Thus when the question of whether Episcopacy itself was abjured by the Confession of Faith of 1580 was put to a vote, Baillie was the lone dissenter:

> ... according to the express words of the Assembly 1580, 1581, Episcopacy was to be distinguished: Episcopacy as used and taken in the Church of Scotland, I thought to be removed; yea, that it was a Popish error, against scripture and antiquity, and so then abjured; but Episcopacy *simpliciter* such as was in the ancient church, and in our church during Knox's days, in the persons of the Superintendents, it was, for many reasons, to be removed, but not abjured in our Confession of Faith.[33]

Baillie's loyalty to the monarch is manifested in his becoming the leader of the Resolutioners in Glasgow in the 1650s. At one point, he wrote to Simeon Ashe of the London clergy to counteract a letter of January 1657 from Samuel Rutherford on behalf of the Scottish Protesters.[34]

When the Restoration occurred, Baillie was optimistic about the return of Charles II, with whom he had had dealings in 1649. But he feared the return of Episcopacy. When the Act Rescissory of April 1661 undid all the work of the Second Reformation, he believed the King had been misled by his advisers. These included his former colleague at Westminster the Earl of Lauderdale, who once had termed Baillie 'the little Monk of Kilwinning'.[35] When he died sometime after the 18th of August, 1662, some felt it was of a broken heart. F. N. McCoy says: 'He had lived to see the work of the Second Reformation destroyed by the prince for whose safety and return he had prayed throughout the Cromwellian years. He had lived beyond his time.'[36]

Appointed as professor of divinity at the Glasgow College in 1642, shortly before going to the Westminster Assembly, Baillie's scholarship was manifested in his years of service there. One of his specialties was Oriental languages, and he is said to have been competent in thirteen languages. His Latin style was regarded as pure and elegant, his *magnum opus,* published posthumously in Amsterdam in 1663, being entitled *Operis Historici et Chronologici,* representing his lectures in church history.[37] During the last year and a half of his life Baillie served as Principal of Glasgow College, most of his energies being spent on the school's financial burdens, in a position that he had not sought or desired. 'I was never desireous of any place but one,' that of teaching the first-year students in divinity.[38]

George Gillespie (January 21, 1613 - December 16, 1648)

The youngest of the Scottish Commissioners, and one of only a handful of those who played a significant role at the Assembly who were still in their thirties when it began, George Gillespie would die at only thirty-five in December of 1648, when the business was still being finished up at Westminster. He has been compared to a meteor in its sudden dazzling brilliance and then its soon setting.[39] He played a crucial role in the debates concerning church government, arguing strenuously for Presbyterianism by divine right and for the church's right to exercise discipline.

Gillespie first came to public attention through his anonymous publication of *The English Popish Ceremonies, obtruded upon the Church of Scotland* in 1637. Educated at the University of St. Andrews, he subscribed the National Covenant in 1638 as minister of Wemyss in the Presbytery of Kirkcaldy. That same year, only twenty-five years of age, he preached at the General Assembly in Glasgow. He became minister of Greyfriars Church in Edinburgh in 1642 and in the following year was chosen as one of the four Scottish ministers to attend the Westminster Assembly.

Legends have tended to develop around Gillespie's role at the Assembly, and while there is evidence to refute their accuracy, they nevertheless testify to the godly character of the Assembly and of Gillespie's contribution. Although Gillespie had departed for Scotland in July of 1647, when the debates on the Larger Catechism were still going on and those on the Shorter Catechism had not yet begun,[40] one story has the Assembly stymied in its producing an answer to the question, 'What is God?' Supposedly Gillespie was called upon to pray, and he began, 'O God, thou who art a spirit, infinite, eternal, and unchangeable in thy being, wisdom, power, holiness, justice, goodness, and truth ...,' thus producing the Catechism's famous answer.

Another story makes vivid Gillespie's role in the debate with the Erastians over the power of excommunication. The learned John Selden, Member of Parliament as well as of the Assembly and the great classical scholar of the age, gave an impressive speech, with display of rabbinical lore, 'to demonstrate that Matthew 18:15-17, the passage under dispute, contained no warrant for ecclesiastical jurisdiction, but concerned the ordinary practice of the Jews in their common civil courts.' J.D. Douglas describes the situation:

Even the most erudite and able of the divines present were in no hurry to encounter such a formidable opponent. Samuel Rutherford, the story goes, turned to Gillespie and said: 'Rise, George, rise up, man, and defend the right of the Lord Jesus Christ to govern by His own laws, the Church which He hath purchased with His own blood.' With every appearance of reluctance Gillespie rose, gave first a summary of the previous speech, stripping it of all its cumbrous learning and reducing it to simple language. Then steadily, point by point, he completely refuted it, proving that the passage in question could not be interpreted or explained away to mean a mere reference to a civil court, and that the Jews both possessed and exercised the right of spiritual censures. The effect of Gillespie's speech was so great as not only to convince the Assembly, but also to astonish and confound Selden himself, to whom Gillespie was a veritable *enfant terrible*. The Erastian leader is reported to have exclaimed in bitter mortification: 'That young man, by this single speech has swept away the learning and the labour of ten years of my life.'[41]

What we do know is that Gillespie was a main respondent to Selden's speech, but it was on the next day and there were others who responded as well.[42] What perhaps gives us a most accurate indication of Gillespie's ability and character is the account concerning one of his speeches, that he apparently was taking detailed notes of an opponent's address to which he was preparing to reply. After he had responded most persuasively, those sitting next to him, upon looking in his notebook, found nothing of the speech written but only these expressions, in Latin: 'Lord, send light', 'Lord, give assistance', 'Lord, defend thine own cause.'[43] In 1646 Gillespie published his chief work, *Aaron's Rod Blossoming; Or, The Divine Ordinance of Church-Government Vindicated,* a response to the Erastian position which went unanswered in his time. Gillespie's

GEORGE GILLESPIE

notes on the Assembly also provide us with one of the main sources of information along with those of Lightfoot, Baillie's *Letters and Journals*, and the official minutes.

After he returned from London, Gillespie was elected by the town council to the High Church of Edinburgh in 1647 and was chosen Moderator of the General Assembly in Edinburgh on July 12, 1648. He was assigned additional responsibilities, but soon fell ill and was clearly dying of tuberculosis. His older colleague Samuel Rutherford wrote from St. Andrews on September 27, 1648: 'Be not heavy: the life of faith is now called for; doing was never reckoned in your account; though Christ in and by you hath done more than by twenty, yea, an hundred grey-haired and godly pastors. Believing now is your last. Look to that word, Galatians 2:20.'[44] By December 17 Gillespie had died. Twelve years after his death the Restoration Parliament, in early 1661, brought his tombstone from the churchyard and had it 'solemnly broken' with a hammer by the public hangman at the Cross of Kirkcaldy.[45] But the work of the Westminster Assembly had been adopted by the Scottish Church, eventually to be passed on to its spiritual posterity.

Archibald Johnston, Lord Warriston
(March, 1611 - July 22, 1663)

Still in his thirties during the Westminster Assembly, Archibald Johnston of Warriston, 'the Lawyer of the Covenant,'[46] had already demonstrated his gifts and his commitment to the cause of the Second Reformation. Born in March of 1611, son of an Edinburgh merchant, he graduated from the University of Glasgow, studied in France, and then became an advocate in Edinburgh in 1633. His wife, Helen Hay, daughter of a judge, Lord Foresterseat, would bear him thirteen children.

With Alexander Henderson, the young Johnston drew up the National Covenant of 1638, and he read it out in a clear and distinct voice before the signing at Greyfriars Church. He served as Clerk and Secretary of the Central Table of the 'Four Tables' that carried on negotiations with the Privy Council. At the Glasgow General Assembly of 1638, he was elected Clerk and served ably in that capacity, rediscovering the lost records of the church from 1560 to 1590. Robert Baillie described him as 'a Nonsuch for a Clerk'.[47]

Johnston represented the Scots in the negotiations with Charles I in the first Bishops' War of 1639, and when it came time to prepare the Solemn League and Covenant in 1643, he and Henderson were the drafters. J. R. de Witt points out that, although Baillie reports that Henderson was the main author, Johnston's *Diary* for 1650-1654 records that the first draft was from his hand.[48] Whatever the exact relationship, Johnston was to be closely associated with the leader of the Scottish Church through the last eight years of Henderson's life. 'Canny, lynx-eyed lawyer' was Thomas Carlyle's description, 'full of fire, of heavy energy and gloom: a very notable character.'[49]

As one of the four ruling elders appointed to represent the Scottish Church at the Westminster Assembly, Johnston as a lawyer did much of the negotiating with the lawyers of Parliament. He made one very notable speech to the Assembly, however, on May 1, 1646, after the House of Commons had charged the Assembly for breach of privilege in its petition of March 23 asserting the divine institution of ecclesiastical censures in the hands of church officers. In his response Lord Warriston emphasized the sovereignty of Christ over his church: '... that Christ lives and reigns alone over and in his Church, and will have all done therein according to his word and will, and that he has given no supreme headship over his Church *to any pope, king, or parliament whatsoever*.' Over against the Erastianism of Parliament the lawyer stressed the limits of the civil authority with regard to the church: 'Christ's throne is highest, and his priviledge supreme as only head and king of his Church, albeit kings and magistrates may be members in it .... Is it so small a thing to have the sworde that they must have the keyes also?'[50]

After his return to Scotland at the end of 1646 Johnston sought to save Charles I from execution, but was not among those who favored support of his son. He accepted office from Oliver Cromwell, first as one of the seven judges appointed to superintend administration of the law in Scotland and then, in 1657, as Lord Clerk Register of Scotland. In part he took these appointments out of the financial need of his burgeoning household. D. Stevenson says that throughout his career he 'displayed a fecklessness in financial matters based on the belief that as he was devoting himself to serving God's cause, God would provide for him, an attitude that led to repeated problems.'[51] These appointments, as well as so much of his previous career, would make him a target for Charles II's punishment after the Restoration.

On July 14, 1660 a warrant was issued for his arrest, but he escaped to the Continent. In Hamburg he became seriously ill. After two years of wandering in Germany and the Low Countries, he ventured into France to meet his wife. The spies of Charles II apprehended him in Rouen, and Louis XIV extradited him to England. In January 1663 he was confined within the Tower of London and remained there six months until transferred to the Tolbooth in Edinburgh. Now a feeble invalid, his family appealed for delay in his execution. The Scottish Parliament was inclined to be compassionate, but not the Bishops or his former colleague at the Westminster Assembly, the Earl of Lauderdale. On July 22, having regained sufficient sense and voice to make a final speech to a crowd of spectators, Johnston was hanged at Mercat Cross on a scaffold directly opposite the windows of his house in Edinburgh.

Various estimates have been made of Johnston's character. Some see in his diary of the 1630s indications of manic-depressive mood swings. Early in his education he had considered preparing to be a minister but decided that his temperament was unsuitable; he wrote that he could not endure the burden of more souls than his own. On the other hand, he was able to tell a friend, on the night before his execution, that not once, for a long period, had he known a doubt regarding his salvation.[52] Perhaps the soundest estimate comes from the historian Bishop Gilbert Burnet, his nephew who knew him personally, but who was from a completely different ecclesiastical party. He described Johnston as:

> a man of great application, could sleep seldom above three hours in the twenty-four: he had studied the law carefully, and had a great quickness of thought, with an extraordinary memory. He went into very high notions of lengthened devotions, in which he continued many hours a day. He would often pray in his family two hours at time, and had an unexhausted copiousness that way. He was a deep enthusiast, for what thought soever struck his fancy during those effusions, he looked on it as an answer of prayer, and was wholly determined by it. He looked on the covenant as the setting Christ on his throne, and so was out of measure zealous in it; and he had an unrelenting severity of temper against all that opposed it. He had no regard to the raising himself or his family, though he had thirteen children; but presbytery was to him more than all the world.[53]

John Maitland, Second Earl and First Duke of Lauderdale
(1616 - August 20 or 24, 1682)

Another of the ruling-elder Commissioners sent to the Assembly from Scotland in 1643 was John, Lord Maitland, soon to become the Earl of Lauderdale and after the Restoration the Duke of Lauderdale. As Charles II's Secretary of State for Scotland, he would eventually become a severe persecutor of the Covenanters. But that could not be foreseen as he helped to draft the Solemn League and Covenant and participated in the Assembly.

He was twenty-seven years old at the time. Robert Baillie commented, 'I profess the very great sufficiencies and happiness of good Maitland, – a youth that brings, by his noble carriage, credit to our nation and help to our cause.' His role, like that of Lord Warriston, was to be mainly among the members of Parliament. Baillie remarked that 'the best here makes very much of him,' and later, in 1645, he said that there is 'no living man fitter to doe Scotland service against the plotting Independents, which for the time has a great hand in the State.'[54]

In December of 1647 he negotiated the Engagement with Charles I on the Isle of Wight. This provided Charles with a Scottish army in exchange for a commitment to establish Presbyterianism in England for a period of three years. Cromwell defeated this army at Preston in August of 1648, and the King was executed in January of 1649. Lauderdale continued to serve the Royalist cause, and after the Battle of Worcester he was imprisoned in London from 1651 to 1660.

Although he seems always to have preferred Presbyterianism to Episcopacy, with the Restoration he became the closest ally of Charles II. 'There was nobody who enjoyed such intimacy with Charles, and nobody who kept the friendship unshaken through so long a period.'[55] He remained in London from 1660 to 1667, and from that date until late in 1680 he was the real ruler of Scotland. After the Covenanter uprisings of 1666 he was able to persuade the King to seek reconciliation through the Indulgences of 1669 and 1672. When these measures failed to secure the peace, Lauderdale pursued more repressive measures, including the 'Highland Host' of 1678, an army of several thousand allowed to pillage the Covenanter territories of the southwest.

An able scholar, Lauderdale could converse in Latin, Italian, French, and even in Hebrew, and he was knowledgeable in the Greek and Latin classics and in ancient and modern history. At the same time he was comfortable with the sensuality of Charles II's court. Smellie claims:

His vices were notorious. It was difficult for him to speak without an oath or a lie. A frequent exercise of his humor was to make puns on the verses of Scripture, or to mimic the accents and gestures of the Covenanting preachers to whom he had listened in his more honourable youth.[56]

How should we account for such a turnabout? Some have thought that he was a conscious hypocrite, involved in a long drawn-out imposture in his youth. Smellie suggests another possibility: 'John Maitland may have deceived himself as well as his brethren in the camp of the Covenant. Shrewd and sagacious men have sometimes misread their own souls, and he may have been of their fellowship.'[57] However that may be, Lauderdale's attachment to Charles II and his actions following the Restoration appear to confirm Smellie's judgment: 'His King and himself – these were Lauderdale's deities, the Great Twin Brethren; and they occupied thrones of equal dignity.'[58]

Richard Baxter wrote to Lauderdale around 1670 warning him of his soul's danger: 'God forbid that you should lose in prosperity that which you gained in adversity! and that He Who was near you in prison should be put far from you in a Court! If our hearts once say to Him, *Depart from us*, it's a sad prognostick that we may hear from Him at last, *Depart from Me*.' Baxter's books had been among those that Lauderdale had read while in prison, taking notes on them and earnestly commending them to his kinsman, the Earl of Balcarres.[59]

Robert Baillie, a few months before his death, had written to Lauderdale, his admired colleague at the Westminster Assembly:

My Lord, you ar the nobleman in the world I love best and esteem most. I think I may say and writ to you what I lyk. If you have gone with your heart to forsak your Covenant, to countenance the Reintroduction of bishops and books, and strengthening the King by your advyse in thes things, I think you a prime transgressor and liable among the first to answer to God for that grit sin, and opening a door which in hast will no be closit, for persecution of a multitud of the best persons and most loyal subjects that ar in the thrie dominions.[60]

Baillie died in August of 1662. In August of 1682 Lauderdale died, after twenty years of fulfilment of Baillie's sad prophecy.

Notes

1. Marcus L. Loane, *Makers of Puritan History* (Grand Rapids: Baker, 1961, 1980), 28.

2. *Ibid.*, 31.

3. [Archibald Alexander], *A History of the Westminster Assembly of Divines ... and Biographical Sketches of Its Most Conspicuous Members* (Philadelphia: Presbyterian Board of Publication, 1841), 299.

4. Loane, *Makers,* 47-48.

5. [Alexander], *A History*, 301.

6. *Ibid.*, 297.

7. Loane, *Makers,* 49.

8. [Alexander], *A History*, 302.

9. J.D. Douglas, *Light in the North: The Story of the Scottish Covenanters* (Grand Rapids: Eerdmans, 1964), 48.

10. Loane, *Makers*, 70.

11. Alexander Whyte, *Samuel Rutherford and Some of His Correspondents* (Edinburgh and London: Oliphant, Anderson and Ferrier, 1894), 26-27.

12. Loane, *Makers*, 70.

13. Whyte, *Samuel Rutherford*, 152.

14. Loane, *Makers*, 101.

15. *Ibid.*, 97.

16. James Walker, *The Theology and Theologians of Scotland,* 2nd ed., revised (Edinburgh: T.& T. Clark, 1888), 13.

17. Whyte, *Samuel Rutherford,* 11.

18. *Ibid.,* 13.

19. Loane, *Makers,* 89.

20. *Ibid.*, 92, 93.

21. *Letters of Samuel Rutherford, With a Sketch of his Life and Biographical Notices of His Correspondents by the Rev. Andrew A. Bonar* (Edinburgh: Banner of Truth, 1984), 744.

22. Alexander F. Mitchell, *The Westminster Assembly: Its History and Standards,* 2nd ed., revised (Philadelphia: Presbyterian Board of Publication, 1897), 129.

23. John Richard de Witt, *Jus Divinum: The Westminster Assembly and the Divine Right of Church Government* (Kampen: J.H. Kok, 1969), 18 n.33.

24. *Ibid.*, 200 and n.118.

25. *Ibid.*, 29.

26. H.M.B. Reid, *The Divinity Professors in the University of Glasgow, 1640-1930* (Glasgow: Maclehose, Jackson and Co., 1923), 120-121.

27. Mitchell, *Westminster Assembly*, 292.

28. William Beveridge, *A Short History of the Westminster Assembly*, rev. and ed. J. Ligon Duncan III (Greenville, S.C.: Reformed Academic Press, 1993), 42, 43-44.

29. Mitchell, *Westminster Assembly*, 312.

30. Robert S. Paul, *The Assembly of the Lord* (Edinburgh: T.& T. Clark, 1985), 442 n.19.

31. Florence Nina McCoy, *Robert Baillie and the Second Scots Reformation*

(Berkeley, Los Angeles, London: U. of California Press, 1974), 110.

32. *Ibid.*, 98-100, 101, 110. Most of the details of Baillie's life are to be found in this work.

33. *Ibid.*, 57.

34. *Ibid.*, 190.

35. *Ibid.*, 217-218, 27 n.32.

36. *Ibid.*, 219.

37. Reid, *Divinity Professors,* 104-105.

38. McCoy, *Robert Baillie*, 208-211.

39. William M. Hetherington, *History of the Westminster Assembly of Divines,* reprint of 3rd ed. (Edmonton, Alberta: Still Waters, 1993), 146.

40. Mitchell, *Westminster Assembly,* 440-441. It is still possible that Gillespie's legendary prayer occurred in the Committee's preparation of the catechisms.

41. Douglas, *Light in the North*, 41, citing Robert Wodrow, *Analecta* (1834), III, 110. Gillespie's biographer, Alexander Gordon, in the *Dictionary of National Biography* calls the statement ascribed to Selden 'incredible'.

42. Mitchell, *Westminster Assembly*, 297 and n.1, referring to 'that far-famed single combat between Selden and Gillespie ... around which later Scottish tradition has thrown such a halo.'

43. James Reid, *Memoirs of the Westminster Divines*, 2 vols. in 1, (Edinburgh: Banner of Truth, 1982), II, 282.

44. *Ibid.*

45. Douglas, *Light in the North*, 48.

46. Alexander Smellie, *Men of the Covenant*, 11 ed. (London: Banner of Truth, 1962), 131.

47. *Ibid.*, 133-134.

48. de Witt, *Jus Divinum*, 47 n.143.

49. Smellie, *Men of the Covenant,* 133.

50. Mitchell, *Westminster Assembly*, 325, 327. The entire speech, slightly abridged, appears on 323-328.

51. D. Stevenson, 'Johnston, (Sir) Archibald (Lord Warriston),' in *Dictionary of Scottish Church History and Theology*, ed. Nigel M. de S. Cameron *et al.*(Downers Grove, Ill.: InterVarsity Press, 1993).

52. Smellie, *Men of the Covenant,* 139.

53. de Witt, *Jus Divinum*, 211-212, citing Gilbert Burnet, *History of His Own Time* (Oxford, ed. 1833), I, 49-50.

54. Beveridge, *Short History*, 42.

55. Smellie, *Men of the Covenant*, 187.

56. *Ibid.*, 189, 191.

57. *Ibid.*, 187.

58. *Ibid.*, 188.

59. *Ibid.*, 190.

60. *Ibid.*

Chapter 7

Noted Preachers

The Puritans strongly believed in preaching. Salvation came through faith, faith came through hearing of the word, and, as the Apostle Paul said in Romans 10, how shall they hear except there be a preacher? All of the Westminster divines were preachers of the word, but those whose gifts were especially recognized can be determined by their invitations to preach to Parliament or to the Assembly itself on the regular monthly Fast Days or other special occasions of humiliation or thanksgiving. The Long Parliament, by February of 1642, established the practice of a public Fast Day on the last Wednesday of each month. Typically two preachers would address the House of Commons at St. Margaret's, Westminster. By October 1644 the House of Lords would also have two preachers, in Westminster Abbey, on these occasions. Sometimes the two Houses would meet together, along with the Assembly, at Lincoln's Inn. A Puritan Fast Day might include not only two hour-long sermons, but also a pair of two-hour-long prayers and other worship activities constituting a nine-hour service, presumably with some breaks for the sake of leaders and people alike!

In addition to the seven Westminster divines described in this chapter, the following were also renowned preachers: Edmund Calamy, Edmund Staunton, William Gouge, Thomas Goodwin, Jeremiah Burroughes, William Bridge and Robert Harris. Of almost equal recognition were Charles Herle, Edward Reynolds, William Greenhill, Simeon Ashe, Thomas Case and Matthew Newcomen. Also worthy of mention are Samuel Rutherford, Alexander Henderson, Cornelius Burgess, Herbert Palmer, Daniel Featley, Thomas Coleman, Philip Nye, Thomas Gataker, Anthony Tuckney, William Spurstowe and Lazarus Seaman. If Geneva in the 1550s offered one the choice of hearing a sermon from John Calvin or from John Knox, clearly London in the 1640s afforded an abundance of opportunities for hearing the word effectively preached.

Stephen Marshall (c.1594 - November 19, 1655)

Stephen Marshall was the favorite preacher of the Long Parliament. According to Thomas Fuller:

> He was their *Trumpet*, by whom they *sounded* their solemn *Fasts*, preaching more *publick Sermons* on that occasion, than any *foure* of his Function. In their *Sickness* he was their *Confessor*, in their *Assembly* their *Councellour*, in their *Treaties* their *Chaplain*, in their *Disputations* their *Champion*.[1]

During the course of the Westminster Assembly he preached eight times before the Houses of Parliament on the regular monthly Fast Days, plus three times before the monthly system was established, and he was enlisted to preach on ten other special occasions, as well as at the funeral of his patron John Pym. He also preached two more times to the Rump Parliament in 1649 and 1653. Of these twenty-four sermons, sixteen were printed. No one else matched this record.[2]

Not only was Marshall the foremost preacher among the Westminster divines, but he was also a leading activist among the English Presbyterians. Clarendon would later say, 'And without doubt, the Archbishop of Canterbury had never so great an influence upon the councils at court, as Mr. Marshall and Dr. Burgess had upon the Houses of Parliament.'[3] Trevor-Roper, with only one misleading statement, otherwise describes him accurately:

> In the Long Parliament he would emerge as the inseparable political and spiritual ally of Pym, the interpreter of Pym's policy after Pym's death. At every stage of the revolution we can see him. Now he is thumping his pulpit on great occasions; now he is meeting with Pym, Hampden and Harley to prepare parliamentary tactics; now he is bustling through Westminster Hall to push voters into the Parliament before the division; now he is retiring, exhausted, to recuperate in the well-appointed house of his good friend 'my noble Lord of Warwick'. Later he would be the Parliament's envoy to Scotland, its chaplain with the captive King; he would pass unscathed from Presbyterianism to Independency; and if he always appeared as the spokesman for the winning side, his changes can be explained by one consistent aim, which was also the aim of Pym: to preserve the unity of opposition against royal and clerical reaction.[4]

Marshall did not move from Presbyterianism to Independency, as we shall see, but his political realism did lead him to cooperate with Oliver Cromwell, the Army, and the Independents when he perceived this as the necessary way to maintain the Puritan-Parliamentary cause. He was a Presbyterian of the English sort who sometimes puzzled his Scottish allies.

Stephen Marshall was born about 1594 at Godmanchester, Huntingdonshire, son of a poor glover. As a boy he had to glean in the fields. He entered Cambridge on April 1, 1615 and, enrolled in Emmanuel College, received the B.A. in 1618, the M.A. in 1622, and later the B.D. in 1629. In 1618 he became lecturer at Wethersfield, Essex after the death, on April 21, of the famous Puritan preacher there, Richard Rogers. In 1625 he became Vicar of Finchingfield, Essex, just

FAMILY TIES

It is not surprising that the membership of the Westminster Assembly should reveal family relationships within the English Puritan movement. Sometimes, however, these crossed over the line between Independents and Presbyterians. Edmund Calamy's first wife, Mary Snelling, came from the family of the Independent theologian William Ames's wife. Matthew Newcomen was Calamy's brother-in-law by virtue of being married to a sister of Mary Snelling. (John Phillips, a member of the Assembly, was a brother-in-law of Dr. Ames.) Independent leader Philip Nye's son was married to a daughter of Stephen Marshall. (Henry Nye, who was appointed to the Assembly but died before it convened, was either Philip Nye's brother or his father.) Anthony Tuckney was a cousin of Congregationalist John Cotton's first wife, Elizabeth Horrocks. Tuckney also married, as his second wife, the widow of Thomas Hill, Mary Willford. After her death he married, as his third wife, the widow of William Spurstowe.

John White was husband of a sister of Cornelius Burgess. Archibald Johnston of Warriston was a "kinsman" of Robert Baillie. Henry Wilkinson Sr. and Jr., both members of the Assembly, were father and son. Francis Rous, a Parliamentary member of the Assembly, was step-brother of Parliamentary leader John Pym. Obadiah Sedgwick was father-in-law of later Puritan leader Thomas Manton. Robert Harris was married to a sister of Puritan preacher William Whately, and Henry Scudder, another member of the Assembly, was married to a sister of Whately's wife. William Gouge's mother was a sister of Samuel and Ezekiel Culverwell, and two of her sisters married Lawrence Chaderton and William Whitaker, thus making Gouge the nephew of four notable Puritan preachers and scholars.

a couple of miles from Wethersfield. In 1636 he was reported to the ecclesiastical authorities for 'irregularities and want of conformity,' and in March 1637 Sir Nathaniel Brent described him to Archbishop Laud as

> a dangerous person, but exceeding cunning. No man doubteth but that he hath an inconformable heart, but externally he observeth all .... He governeth the consciences of all the rich puritans in those parts and in many places far remote, and is grown very rich.[5]

He had become a client of Robert Rich, second Earl of Warwick and Lord-Lieutenant of Essex, and in the first quarter of 1640 he spoke on behalf of Warwick's candidates for Parliament throughout Essex.

Marshall was scheduled to preach on the first Fast Day of the Short Parliament, but it was dissolved on May 5, 1640 before this could take place. When the Long Parliament was opened in November 1640, Marshall and Cornelius Burgess were the preachers on that momentous first Fast Day on November 17.[6] He would preach again on September 7, 1641 (with Jeremiah Burroughes) and then again on December 22, 1641 (with Edmund Calamy). What further brought him to national attention, however, was the response to Bishop Joseph Hall's claims for the divine right of Episcopacy produced by Marshall with Edmund Calamy, Thomas Young, Matthew Newcomen and William Spurstowe under the name 'Smectymnuus', taken from their initials. In a literary exchange running through 1641, with three pieces written on each side, the third in support of the Smectymnuans from John Milton in 1642, Marshall and his colleagues set the stage for the abolition of Episcopacy. The five Smectymnuans would all support Presbyterianism in the Westminster Assembly.[7]

It was for his preaching, though, that Marshall was primarily known. James Reid says: 'His sermons which have been printed abound with striking comparisons, and pointed appeals to the hearers ....'[8] Much of his effectiveness apparently resided in his personal delivery. Alexander Gordon comments:

> His sermons, denuded of the preacher's living passion, often have the effect of uncouth rhapsodies. His funeral sermon for Pym (December 1643) made an indelible impression, and is the finest extant specimen of his pulpit eloquence as well as of his 'feeling and discernment'.... His ordinary preaching is described as plain and homely, seasoned with 'odd country phrases' and 'very taking with a country auditory.'

Gordon concludes: '... he was listened to because no man could rival his power of translating the dominant sentiment of his party into the language of irresistible appeal.'[9]

His most famous sermon was *Meroz Cursed,* based on Judges 5:23 where Deborah in her victory song pronounces a curse on the Israelite city in Naphtali that would not come to the aid of the Lord's people. It was preached before Parliament at the first of the regular monthly Fast Days, on February 23, 1642, and was a stirring call to arms that left royalists like Clarendon outraged. Trevor-Roper calls it 'the first of a long series of incendiary sermons which, from now on, scandalized royalists and moderate men alike.'[10] It found favor with the majority of his hearers as a call to commitment to the Parliamentary cause, for by his own account, 'he afterwards preached it, up and down the country, sixty times, and it was several times printed.'[11]

The freedom to preach was revolutionary, and the preaching itself had revolutionary consequences. After the first Fast Day sermons of Marshall and Cornelius Burgess, Thomas Knyvett wrote home to a friend in Norfolk on November 24, 1640, 'Now reformation goes on again as hot as a toast. If thou didst but hear what sermons are preached to Parliament men, thou wouldst bless thyself.' Paul Seaver comments: 'In effect, from the opening of the Long Parliament those Puritans who commanded London pulpits were for the first time free to preach without fear of episcopal censure.'[12] William Haller adds: 'The fixing of the custom of regular fast days, with special services at St. Margaret's for the House of Commons, gave the preachers recognition and responsibility such as they had never known.'[13]

When apocalyptic themes were combined with this new freedom of preaching, the effect could indeed be revolutionary. On June 15, 1643 Marshall preached from Revelation 15:2-4:

> He used the imagery of the Apocalypse in order once more to bring the struggle of parliament against the king and the prelates into line with the legend of the true church beset by Antichrist and of Christ's expected advent and triumph. He would have his hearers see themselves again in the most valid and compelling of perspectives. The great stream of history, directed by God from eternity to eternity, having reached its present point, would inevitably go on, and they were called to be the agents and actors of its next advance.[14]

While not as extreme as some others, Marshall had commended the

millenarian writings of Joseph Mede,[15] and the Scot Robert Baillie was
to comment on the English clergy, '... the most of the chiefe divines
here, not only Independents, but others, such as Twiss, Marshall,
Palmer, and many more, are express Chiliasts.'[16] John F. Wilson draws
out the possible implications of such preaching:

> ... even such relatively moderate sentiments as those articulated by the
> equivocal Marshall testify that the apocalypticism and millenarianism
> which were clearly present in some of the preaching to the Long
> Parliament worked toward revolutionary ends, whether or not they
> were directly intended to do so. Stated very simply, whereas prophetic
> and reformist puritans sought merely to make the times intelligible,
> another strain within Puritanism labored to interpret the times accord-
> ing to a calculus which required their basic transformation. That latter
> rhetoric, in effect if not intent, was basically disruptive of all acknowl-
> edged authority.[17]

It is clear that neither Parliament nor Marshall himself perceived the
imminent kingdom of Christ as undermining all other legitimate
authority. Early in 1642, Parliament, overriding a petition from the
church in Finchingfield to retain his services, recommended that the
people of the parish of St. Margaret's, Westminster appoint Marshall
as a regular lecturer.[18] On February 28, 1644 he was appointed one of
the seven daily lecturers at Westminster Abbey.[19] It is true that
Marshall preached to the House of Lords on January 31, 1649, the day
after the execution of Charles I, thus condoning that act,[20] but his
associate Giles Firmin tells us that he was 'so troubled about the king's
death' that on Sunday, January 28, he interceded with the heads of the
army, 'and had it not been for one whom I will not name, who was very
opposite and unmovable, he would have persuaded Cromwell to save
the king. This is truth.'[21] Preaching before the Barebones Parliament in
November 1653, he spoke in favor of tithes to support a national
ministry.[22] Marshall was not one for overthrowing all authority.

In the Assembly's debates over church polity Marshall moved
gradually to a *jure divino* Presbyterian position,[23] but as Robert Baillie
observed, he was seeking a 'middle way of his own'. At the beginning
of the Assembly he was commissioned, with Philip Nye, to accompany
Sir Henry Vane Jr. to Scotland, where they negotiated the Solemn
League and Covenant on August 17, 1643 for uniformity with the
Scottish Church. He was concerned, however, to find a way that would
avoid a breach with the Independents, granting local congregations

some powers of discipline and ordination, though not without involvement with presbytery.[24] In December of 1643 he had drafted a pamphlet, *Certane considerations to Disswade Men From Further Gathering of Churches in this present juncture of Time,* and persuaded several leading men of the Assembly and also of the Independents to endorse it, in order to wait to see what polity the Assembly would decide on. But this counsel of patience was not followed by the 'Five Dissenting Brethren,' who produced their *Apologeticall Narration* in January 1644, appealing the Congregational cause directly to Parliament and the public.[25] In the summer of 1647, when the Army, having seized the King, threatened the City of London, it 'was Stephen Marshall, who once again, in a moment of crisis, emerged as the politician of the hour'.

> Like other men who were neither Cromwellians nor radicals, Marshall believed that, at that moment, the unity of Parliament and Army was all-important and that the alternative would be confusion leading to unconditional royal reaction. So, in these last days of July, he flung himself into action. He made a party in the Westminster Assembly, worked on the aldermen of the City, darted to and fro between Lords, Commons and Army headquarters, and finally, with seventeen supporters in the Assembly, presented a petition to Parliament and City offering to make their peace with the Army. His efforts were successful. The City militia offered no resistance, and the Army entered London without a struggle. When all was over, the defeated party recognized Marshall as the chief architect of their ruin. 'In that nick of time,' wrote Baillie, when 'one stout look more' would have established Presbyterianism for ever, it was Mr. Marshall, 'the main instrument' of the Solemn League and Covenant, who, with 'his seventeen servants of the Synod ... put presently in the Army's power both Parliament, City and nation ...' [26]

Marshall maintained his Presbyterian convictions to his deathbed, but he was able to co-operate with Cromwell and the increasingly prevalent Independents. He was among a group of Presbyterians, Independents and Baptists with whom Cromwell consulted for the sake of reconciliation and peace in October and November 1653, with some of whom he was appointed 'Triers' by Cromwell on March 20, 1654.[27] Perhaps it helped that one of his daughters had married John Nye, one of the sons of Independent leader Philip Nye.[28]

Marshall's broad and accommodating spirit is shown also in the manner in which the Assembly's Directory for Worship was drawn up. As chairman of the committee responsible for doing the preliminary work, he

> presented the general reasons for a Directory and the criteria adopted by his committee – to find a mean between a completely fixed liturgy and a form of worship in which everyone would be 'left to his own will.'[29]

As Alexander Mitchell described it:

> In other words, those who conducted the ordinary services were not directly prohibited from turning the materials furnished to them into an unvarying form of prayer, keeping as near to the words of the Directory as they could; but at the same time they were not only not restricted or counseled to do so, but they were counseled and encouraged to do something more, according to their ability and opportunities.[30]

This spirit has continued in Presbyterian worship to the present day.

Marshall himself felt great freedom in prayer and sometimes prayed at great length in public. When he and Joseph Caryl were chaplains to the commissioners treating with the King at Newcastle in 1646, they were at the dinner table with Charles, and Marshall 'put himself more forward than was meet to say grace; and, while he was long in forming his chaps, as the manner was among the saints, and making ugly faces, his Majesty said grace himself, and was fallen to his meat, and had eaten up some part of his dinner, before Marshall had ended the blessing....'[31]

In 1651 Marshall had left Finchingfield to become town preacher at Ipswich at St. Mary's at the Quay. He died of consumption on November 19, 1655 and was buried in Westminster Abbey. On September 14, 1661, however, by royal warrant of Charles II, his remains were taken up and cast into a pit in St. Margaret's churchyard. He had married, about 1629, a rich widow, Elizabeth, daughter of Robert Castell of East Hatley, Cambridgeshire, and they had a son and six daughters. He was described as 'of middle height, swarthy, and broad shouldered, rolling his eyes in conversation; not fixing them on those he addressed; his gait was "shackling", and he had no polish.' It is said that he was an indulgent father, allowing his daughters to dress in unpuritanical fashion. He could jest, and 'he frequently read himself asleep with a playbook or romance'.[32]

Richard Baxter regarded him 'a sober and worthy man' and said that if all the Bishops had been of the same spirit as Archbishop Ussher, the Independents like Jeremiah Burroughes, and the Presbyterians like Stephen Marshall, the divisions of the church would soon have been healed.[33]

Not long before his death Marshall said, 'I cannot say, as one did, I have not so lived that I should now be afraid to die; but this I can say, I have so *learned Christ,* that I am not afraid to die.'[34]

Joseph Caryl (1602 or 1603 - March 10, 1673)

Next to Stephen Marshall, Joseph Caryl preached most often at the Fast Days and other special occasions during the Long Parliament and the Westminster Assembly. John F. Wilson summarizes:

> He delivered his initial sermon to parliament at the third monthly fast (April 27, 1642). He preached next at a Covenant-taking ceremony in October 1643. Thereafter he participated in many of the monthly fasts of the lower house and became a favorite choice as preacher for extraordinary humiliations and thanksgivings, too. He graced the Lords regular fasts once or twice. Of some fourteen sermons he gave between 1640 and 1649, one-half were published. Caryl also preached frequently to the Rump, participating in some six special humiliations of that body.[35]

His sermon before both Houses of Parliament on the occasion of the taking of the Covenant by all who would willingly present themselves shows his commitment to the Puritan understanding of a biblical covenant. Entitled *The Nature, Solemnity, Grounds, Property, and Benefits, of a Sacred Covenant*, his sermon defines a covenant as a 'solemne compact or agreement betweene two chosen parties or more, whereby with mutual, free, and full consent they binde themselves upon select conditions, tending to the glory of God and their common good.' As Wilson points out, for Caryl and his associates the Solemn League and Covenant would make possible

> the drawing of distinctions between different sorts of men and in this way facilitate separation of the precious from the malignant and the vile. It would help 'congregate' the 'homogeneall' in uniting the Kingdom and would bring together 'sincere' Christians in diverse lands with God. Above all, the Covenant promised to create a holy and happy people.[36]

Other samples of his preaching exhibit a Puritan style of analysing a text or topic and of making direct appeal and application. Speaking of what constitutes a good work, he mentions three things: 1. That the work may be good, we must be sure that the matter of it be good. 2. The aim, or the end, of the work must be good, and chiefly the glory of God. 3. The principle or spring of the work must be good. Unless the principles be good, the work is not good. As the tree is, such is the fruit that grows upon it. Hence see the necessity of regeneration. You must be God's workmanship before you can do God's work. As we are grafted into Christ, he changes the branch. Being planted into Christ, by the power of the Spirit, we are then made like him; and then we bring forth fruits of righteousness, which are to the glory of God *by him*. That is, by virtue of union with Christ, of implantation and ingrafture into Christ. They are from a principle of life in Christ, and from a principle of love unto Christ.[37]

Caryl was born of genteel parents in London in 1602 or 1603 and entered Exeter College, Oxford in 1621, receiving his B.A. in 1625 and his M.A. in 1627. Upon ordination he first served in the vicinity of Oxford or as curate of Battersea, Surrey.[38] From 1632 to '47 he was preacher to Lincoln's Inn, where many of the prominent people of

London would hear him. In 1645 he was appointed minister of the Church of St. Magnus, near London Bridge. Not only did he serve in the Westminster Assembly, but he was also appointed by Parliament to serve as a chaplain, along with Stephen Marshall, to the Commissioners sent to treat with the King at Newcastle to arrange terms of peace early in 1647. In 1650 he and John Owen were designated by Oliver Cromwell to accompany him into Scotland. With the Restoration he was ejected from the church of St. Magnus by the Act of Uniformity of

JOSEPH CARYL

1662. He was able to remain in London, however, and gathered a congregation in the vicinity of London Bridge which numbered one hundred and thirty-six communicant members when he died on March 10, 1673.

Caryl is most famous for his commentary on Job. It first appeared in twelve volumes, quarto sized, published between 1644 and 1666. Then it was published in 1676-1677 in two large folio volumes. Cotton Mather in his *Student and Preacher* placed this commentary in a very high class:

> How happy should we have been, ... if a Caryl on Job, a Greenhill on Ezekiel, a Burroughs on Hosea, an Owen on the Hebrews, a Manton on James, and a Jenkins on Jude, were accompanied with others like them on the rest of the sacred pandects.[39]

Caryl steadily taught through the Book of Job for the better part of three decades because he felt that the account of Job's afflictions bore 'the image of these times and presents us with a resemblance of the past, present, and (much hoped for) future condition of this nation.'[40] Archibald Alexander said of Caryl's commentary:

> Though this work possesses great merit, its enormous size has been a great obstruction to its usefulness .... It has been wittily said, that this book is a good exercise of that patience which the book of Job was intended to inculcate and exemplify.[41]

Joseph Caryl did not play a major role in the debates of the Westminster Assembly; however, we do find him entering the discussions of church government on the side of the Independents.[42] In his Fast Day sermon of April 17, 1642 Caryl claimed that the test of government, discipline and worship 'cannot be made by that which is usually called Antiquity: But by that which transcends all humane Antiquity, Customes, Councels, and Traditions (though all those may contribute some help) *The Word of God*.'[43] Tai Liu sees in this sermon and in Caryl's Fast Day sermon of May 28, 1645 subtle opposition to a national Presbyterian establishment.[44] Caryl was one of the six ministers, including Thomas Goodwin, John Owen and Peter Sterry, present at the deathbed of Oliver Cromwell.[45] He was also a participant in the Savoy Conference of 1658.[46] Tai Liu comments on his pastorate of St. Magnus, which had previously been pastored by Cornelius Burgess:

Yet it appears that the general religious attitude of the parish was a moderate one, neither strongly Presbyterian nor extremely Independent. And Caryl himself was a moderate, or perhaps even a conservative, Independent; as such, he was probably the only Independent divine who ever participated in the Presbyterian church government in the City of London.[47]

After Caryl's death in 1673 his congregation chose John Owen as successor, merging with the congregation on Leadenhall Street which Owen pastored. Subsequent ministers of this church would be David Clarkson and Isaac Watts, for whom they built a new meeting-house in Bury Street, near St. Mary Axe.[48]

When Caryl was ejected from the parish church of St. Magnus in 1662, he preached his farewell sermon from Revelation 3:4, Christ's words to the church in Sardis: 'And they shall walk with me in white; for they are worthy.' His concluding words were:

> It shall be the desire and prayer of my heart that, if I should have no more opportunities among you, as you have been stirred up to obtain this *white robe of grace*, you and I may meet in *glory*, where we shall never part. That is the best of all. That is the answer of all our prayers; and that is the issue of all our working. Then shall we have as much *joy* as we can hold for ever.[49]

Obadiah Sedgwick (c.1600 - early January 1658)

Obadiah Sedgwick is classed by John F. Wilson in the small group of preachers second only to Stephen Marshall in popularity for the Fast Days and other special occasions before Parliament and the Westminster Assembly. He says:

> Sedgwick preached at the May fast to Commons in 1642, early in the series. Although he appeared once more in the sequence and several times in the Lords regular fasts, he made his basic contribution to the program on extraordinary occasions, delivering sermons to nine or ten of them between 1643 and the early fall of 1648.

Five of these fourteen sermons were published.[50] Robert M. Norris describes him as one of the Assembly's 'liveliest and most colorful preachers.'[51] It was reported that 'it was usual with him, especially in hot weather, to unbutton his doublet in the pulpit, that his breath might be the longer, and his voice more audible ....'[52]

Born about 1600, he was the son of Joseph Sedgwick, Vicar of St. Peter's, Marlborough, Wiltshire. He entered Queen's College, Oxford on June 18, 1619, but then transferred to Magdalen Hall, where he received the B.A. on May 5, 1620 and the M.A. on January 28, 1623. He became chaplain to Horatio, Baron Vere of Tilbury, whom he accompanied to the Netherlands. Returning to Oxford, he received the B.D. on January 16, 1630. During this period he may have served as a contact between Lord Vere and the Puritan John Davenport, whom he likely knew at Magdalen Hall, Oxford, for the provision of Puritan preachers for London.[53] Sedgwick became curate and lecturer at St. Mildred's, Bread Street, London in 1630, but his nonconformity caused him to be censured and suspended by Bishop Juxon in 1637, 'the only London lecturer among those censured by Juxon in 1637 "as their faults deserved."'[54] On July 6, 1639, however, he was presented by Robert Rich, second Earl of Warwick, to the vicarage of Coggeshall, Essex, where he succeeded the famous Puritan John Dod. With the opening of the Long Parliament he regained the lectureship at St. Mildred's and used that pulpit to oppose Episcopacy.[55]

Sedgwick's Fast Day sermon on May 25, 1642, *England's preservation*, was based on Jeremiah 4:3, 'For thus saith the Lord to the Men of Judah and Jerusalem, Break up your fallow ground, and sow not among thorns.' From this text, in typical Puritan 'plain style' form, he developed two doctrines: 'the breaking up of sinfull hearts, is a singular meanes to prevent the breaking downe of a sinfull Nation' and 'all penetentiall and reforming works must be so managed and acted that it may not prove a vaine and fruitlesse worke, but may come to be a successfull and profitible work.'[56]

His concern for the maintenance of order and the authority and unity of the church led him to oppose toleration of diverse viewpoints. In his Thanksgiving sermon, preached on April 9, 1644, he declared, 'I had rather my particular opinion were buried in the dust, and my private interest were laid in the grave, than at this time to pursue either one or the other, to the hazard of a Kingdome, or of all the Churches of Christ.'[57] On October 22, 1644, in *An arke against a deluge*, he told the House of Commons they should abhor

of the mentioning, yea of the very thought of tolerating all opinions in the church. This was such a monstrous prodigy, such an intolerable way of confusion, such a mocking of the people of God. To whom we have all solemnly encouraged our utmost for unity in doctrine and uniformity in discipline, such a speedy grave for the kingdom and church that mischief itself could not easily dig the like.[58]

When Philip Nye, on February 21, 1644, made his appeal for liberty of conscience against the dangers of established Presbyterianism, Sedgwick was sufficiently shocked to desire that Nye be expelled from the Assembly.[59]

Obadiah Sedgwick was so respected and trusted by the Assembly that he was one of the three preachers, along with Thomas Hill and Stephen Marshall, on December 18, 1644, when both Houses met together in Lincoln's Inn chapel, with the public excluded, when the 'Self-Denying' ordinance was under consideration.[60] He was appointed to the expanded committee of nineteen to work on the Confession of Faith, and he was also assigned to the committee of twenty to give answer to the Independents' 'Reasons'.[61]

For a short time after December 13, 1645 he held the rectory of St. Andrew's Holborn, but before May 1646 he was appointed to the rectory of St. Paul's, Covent Garden and resigned Coggeshall, where John Owen succeeded him on August 18. He was a member of the eleventh London classis in the Presbyterian system established by Parliament, but he also was one of the commission of Triers, to examine candidates for the ministry, under Oliver Cromwell in March 1654. He was invited to preach to the Rump Parliament in April 1651.[62]

With his health failing, Sedgwick resigned St. Paul's in 1656, being succeeded by his son-in-law, Thomas Manton.[63] As a man of property, lord of the manor of Ashmansworth, Hampshire, he retired to Marlborough, where he died at the beginning of January 1658 and was buried near his father in the church of Ogbourne St. Andrew, Wiltshire.[64]

Richard Vines (c.1600 - February 4, 1656)

Richard Vines is placed by John F. Wilson with Joseph Caryl and Obadiah Sedgwick in the group of preachers second only to Stephen Marshall in their frequency of preaching by appointment of Parliament for the Fast Days and other special occasions:

Vines first contributed to the program of exhorting the Long Parliament in the fall of 1642. He preached a second and a third time to monthly fasts for Commons and once to one of the Lords regular humiliations. Like Sedgwick, however, he did the bulk of his additional preaching at extraordinary occasions, seven in all. Vines also preached at the funeral for Essex in 1646. As late as June 1648 he was still active in the fast program.[65]

Not only was he one of the great preachers in the Assembly, but he was also one of the leaders in the debates among the English Presbyterians, so that he was termed 'our English Luther.'[66] He was ninth in number of speeches in the debates on church government, after George Gillespie and before William Gouge.[67]

Vines rose to fame by virtue of his powerful preaching, which eventually caused him to be much in demand. Born about 1600 at Blaston, Leicestershire, he received the B.A. from Magdalene College, Cambridge in 1622 and the M.A. in 1627. Around 1624 he became schoolmaster at Hinckley, Leicestershire, and he continued to live there when he became Rector of nearby Weddington, Warwickshire on March 11, 1628 and also of the neighboring Caldecote on June 10, 1630. These churches were only half a mile apart, so he could preach at one in the morning and at the other in the afternoon, or at one on one Sunday and at the other on the next.[68] In the early 1630s he was persuaded by friends to become lecturer at Nuneaton, Warwickshire, a market town just seven miles from Coventry. Here he attracted many hearers, including those of the gentry and other ministers. When the Civil War began, he was forced, after August, 1642, to take refuge in Coventry, but here too he was able with other ministers to set up a daily lectureship.

Having preached a Fast Day sermon before the House of Commons on November 30, 1642 and being appointed to the Westminster Assembly in June 1643, he was placed in the London rectory of St. Clement Danes, where Robert Devereux, third Earl of Essex, was one of his parishioners. He served there from 1643 to 1645 and also held office as Master of the Temple between 1644 and 1647.[69] In April and June 1644 he was called to the vicarage of St. Michael's, Coventry, but then on June 27 he was appointed by the Earl of Manchester to be Master of Pembroke Hall, Cambridge. For reasons that are not entirely clear Vines did not want to accept the academic appointment and sought the counsel of the Assembly. It is an indication of his importance that the Assembly spent a good deal of time, over several months, helping him to decide to serve at Cambridge rather than Coventry while continuing to be present in Westminster.[70] His reputation did much to repair the College, attracting scholars, and he proved himself an effective administrator.

After the execution of Charles I on January 30, 1649 he refused the Engagement of allegiance to the existing government, without a King or House of Lords, and so was replaced as Master of Pembroke Hall by Sidrach Simpson in October 1650. The parishioners of St. Lawrence Jewry in London immediately called him to be their minister, and he was also chosen to be one of the weekday lecturers at St. Michael's Cornhill. St. Lawrence Jewry had 'perhaps the richest endowments for lectureships in seventeenth-century London' and thus was able to have a series of prominent preachers there, including Anthony Burgess, Christopher Love and Edward Reynolds as well as Richard Vines.[71]

Vines's preaching style tended to be bombastic. Thomas Fuller describes him as a workmanlike preacher, using 'strong stitches'.[72] John F. Wilson says of his November 30, 1642 Fast Day sermon, *Calebs Integrity in Following the Lord Fully*, that he

> espoused the conventional puritan criterion of faithfulness to a Hebraic God and inveighed against 'murmuring and disaffected Israelites' who might, for example, begrudge financial support for the parliamentary forces.[73]

At the funeral for the Earl of Essex, to which all of the Assembly was invited on October 21, 1646, Vines said concerning his patron and friend:

> Such as were for reformation and groaned under pressure in religion he took by the hand, and they him. Such as were patriots, and would stand up for common liberties, he took by the hand, and they him. And so he became the bond or knot of both, as the axle-tree of the world, upon which both the poles do move.[74]

Primarily a preacher, Vines disclosed that at least part of his reservation about accepting the academic appointment to Cambridge was that if he could not exercise his ministry 'his gifts will rust'.[75]

Vines was also an able scholar. He had excelled in Greek and devoted much of his study to the doctrine of justification. Published posthumously in 1657, *A Treatise of the Right Institution, Administration, and Receiving of the Lord's Supper* represented twenty sermons he had preached at St. Lawrence Jewry.[76] In the early stages of the

Assembly he supported the view, along with William Twisse and Thomas Gataker, that it was only the suffering or *passive* obedience of Christ that was imputed to the believer, whereas Daniel Featley supported the view of Archbishop Ussher in the Irish Articles that Christ's *active* obedience or fulfilling of the law was also imputed to the believer and was necessary for eternal life.[77] Throughout the Assembly's debates one finds Vines offering careful and helpful distinctions. When it was debated whether the office of ruling elder was instituted by the Word of God, Vines distinguished between the terms 'instituted' and 'warranted':

> ... Vines pointed out that there was 'a difference betwixt a word of institution and warrant. The powers that be are ordained of God. If I say that Justices of peace are warrantable by the word of God it is true; if I say instituted, it is not true.'[78]

To avoid offence to those not ready to accept Presbyterianism by divine right, he distinguished between 'may be' and 'must be', in order to provide accommodation for the Independents within a Presbyterian establishment: 'So that *must be* will make each side condemn other, but *may be* will make each side bear with other.'[79]

Although inclined to Presbyterianism from the beginning of the Assembly, Vines was at first, like Herbert Palmer, not convinced of the Scriptural mandate for the office of ruling elder.[80] As the debates progressed, he like Palmer became persuaded and strongly advocated Presbyterianism.[81] He still defended the position, however, that only preaching elders should ordain,[82] and he continued to have reservations about whether the sole power to ordain lay with presbyteries.[83] His positions seem to have been influenced by a strong streak of practical realism. It was he who made the motion to have two catechisms, a larger and a shorter, rather than just one.[84]

He was aware of the state of the ordinary people. In April 1644, preaching to the Lord Mayor and Aldermen of London, he complained of the kind of person he termed a nomad or walker,

> 'who will not endure to sit at the feet of a constant godly ministry' but who 'wanders away the Sabbath by peeping in at Church-dores, and taking essay of a sentence or two, and then if there be no *scratch* for his *itch, lambit & fugit*, he is gone.'[85]

Alarmed at the multiplicity of sectarian views, he preached to the
House of Commons on March 10, 1647:

> I would I might intreat, nay press it upon those that are called pure
> Independents that they would zealously and sincerely declare against
> doctrinal errors and heresies of these days that such pernicious opin-
> ions may not shelter themselves under their name or wing.[86]

Vines did strive to reach agreement with the Independents, but as he
said in March 1644, 'I feare we are like men upon the welch mountains
[who] toutch hands at tope & [are] 2 miles asunder at bottome [.]'[87]
Later on, he cooperated with the Independents against the Fifth
Monarchy Men[88] and served as a local assistant, for London, to
Cromwell's 'Triers'.

About a year before his death he was afflicted with acute headaches,
and his sight so diminished that he could not read the largest print and
glasses would not help. He persevered in preaching although his voice
became very low. A few days before his death, when he was preaching,

> a rude fellow cried aloud to him, 'Lift up your voice, for I cannot hear
> you': to whom Mr. Vines replied, 'Lift up your ears, for I can speak no
> louder.'[89]

He died on February 4, 1656 and was buried in the church of St.
Lawrence Jewry, with Thomas Jacombe preaching the funeral sermon.
He had married, while at Hinckley, Katherine, daughter of Humphrey
Adderlay, patron of the church at Weddington.

Jeremiah Whitaker (1599 - June 1, 1654)

Jeremiah Whitaker preached before Parliament and the Assembly
seven times between late 1642 and March 1648, putting him just
beneath Joseph Caryl, Obadiah Sedgwick and Richard Vines in such
appearances.[90] Deeply loved and widely respected, he suffered from a
variety of physical afflictions that often made it difficult for him to
enter the pulpit, but he persevered in his preaching and became the
object of many heartfelt prayers before his painful death.

Whitaker was born in 1599 at Wakefield, Yorkshire. He seems to
have been an early convert, for as a boy he would travel eight or ten
miles with other religiously disposed people to hear a sermon. He

would take copious notes in order to share with others what he had heard. From an early age he wanted to enter the ministry, even though his father sought to dissuade him.[91] He entered Sidney Sussex College, Cambridge in 1616, about the same time as Oliver Cromwell. In 1620 he received his B.A., and from 1623 to 1629 he served as a schoolmaster at Oakham, Rutland. In 1630 he became Rector of Strelton, Rutland, just six miles from Oakham, where he continued to provide a weekly lecture while he preached twice on Sundays at Strelton.[92]

In the 1630s Whitaker had some trouble with the authorities for refusing to read the Book of Sports. In 1640 he informed his Bishop that he could not in good conscience contribute in support of the war against the Scots, but without his knowledge one of his neighbors paid for him. Upon coming to London in 1643 for the Westminster Assembly, he was appointed Rector of St. Mary Magdalen, Bermondsey in Southwark. His gifts for preaching were recognized by his selection as one of the seven lecturers to conduct the daily early-morning services at Westminster Abbey. He typically preached four times a week while in London; twice in Southwark, once in Westminster, and once at Christ Church, Newgate, and he later added two lectures quarterly at St. Michael's, Cornhill, besides his preaching to Parliament on special occasions.[93] When Nottingham parishioners petitioned Parliament for Whitaker's services as their minister, the Assembly decided on October 28, 1644 'that Mr. Whitaker shall be continued here,' apparently finding his contributions too valuable to lose.[94]

In the midst of the controversy over Erastianism, Stephen Marshall and Jeremiah Whitaker were invited to preach for a special Fast Day before a combined gathering of the House of Lords, House of Commons, and members of the Assembly on January 14, 1646. In his sermon, *The Danger of Greatness: Or, Uzziah's Exaltation and Destruction,* based on 2 Chronicles 26:15-16, Whitaker said, 'To sober spirits, some things seem more clear, others more disputable.'

But he then elaborated those things which he asserted were above dispute. 'It is,' he said, 'a sin against the Gospel to revile and scorn those who labour in the Word and doctrine,' a sound warning to the Erastian parliamentarians. 'Elders,' he went on, 'have a peculiar charge and special trust committed to them.' 'Christ's end is that the purity of Ordinances may be exalted, that profaneness might be suppressed.' Then he concluded with words of gentle warning against schism, 'Christ's end is that mutual love may be increased' and this was why God gave officers in his church 'that the whole body might by fitly joined together'. It was an able performance for the occasion, bolstering up the petitioners and their supporters, making their opponents uncertain and yet creating a reconciling atmosphere.[95]

Not only did he defend the prerogatives of the clergy, but in the Assembly's debates on whether congregations or presbyteries had the power of ordination, he showed concern for maintaining the quality of standards for the clergy in opting for presbyteries.[96] Although he may not have seen the details of Presbyterianism as by divine right,[97] in the 1650s he was a member of the Tenth Classis of the Presbyterian London Province,[98] and he had a chief hand in composing the *Defence of the Gospel Ministry* published in 1654 by the Provincial Synod of London. According to Daniel Neal, 'No man was more beloved by the Presbyterian ministers of London than Mr. Whitaker.'[99]

Thomas Fuller in describing Whitaker's character emphasized his humility and charity:

> He conversed most familiarly with the poorest Christians, even with babes in Christ; and was very communicative, 'like a tree loaden with fruit, bowing down its branches to all who desired to ease it of the burden thereof.'[100]

James Reid says:

> Sometimes upon special occasions, he gave away all the money that he had in the house. He frequently gave twenty shillings to a poor saint .... By his last *will*, he gave twenty pounds to the godly poor of his own parish.[101]

But the most remarkable thing about Whitaker was how he handled his physical afflictions. From his youth he had been bothered with various diseases, but in the last several years of this life he was 'much distressed with the painful distempers of gout and stone.' His discomfort was apparent:

> He sometimes went upon crutches unto his own congregation. Yea, once he adventured to preach at Michael's Cornhill, when he was scarce able to get into the pulpit, and his friends with much difficulty helped him out of the church homeward.

Yet once in the pulpit, he could preach without distraction; he often said, 'If I could but preach, I should be much better.'[102] But sometimes this was not possible. In a letter to Oliver Cromwell, preserved in the British Museum, Whitaker asks to be excused for not attending in person to present a book to the Lord Protector, 'being confined to my chamber under extreme tormenting paines of the stone, which forceth me to cry and moane night and day.'[103]

From the beginning of November 1653 his pains from kidney stones were so great that he was confined to his bed or his room for the final seven months of his life.[104] After his death on June 1 the doctors opened his body and found both kidneys full of ulcers,

> and one of them swelled to an extraordinary bigness, through the abundance of purulent matter in it; and on the neck of his bladder was found a stone, about an inch and a half long, and one inch broad, weighing above two ounces, when first taken out; and also an ulcer which was gangrened, judged to be the cause of his death. All other parts of his body were found upon examination firm and sound.[105]

Through the final stages of his afflictions Simeon Ashe, a fellow London minister and member of the Westminster Assembly and Whitaker's bosom-friend, accompanied him with comfort. He told in his funeral sermon how Whitaker in the racking pain of his last sickness 'did roar many times till his throat was dry, but none ever heard him speak one word in the way of murmuring, or discontentment, on account of God's afflicting providence.'[106] It was reported that he 'had such a tender feeling for his friends, that when his pains threatened to come with great violence he entreated them to withdraw from him, that they might not be distressed with his roarings.'[107]

When asked how he was doing, Whitaker would often reply, 'The bush always burning, but not consumed. Though my pains be too great for the strength of nature, yet they are not above the support of grace.'[108] During the last week of his life the pains became more sharp and more frequent, returning every half-hour, then every quarter-hour, then two or three times in a quarter-hour, until his strength was exhausted. Simeon Ashe, who was with him through most of the last day,

> laying his hand upon Mr. Whitaker's cold hand, covered with a clammy sweat, took his last farewell of him with a sore heart. Upon his departure, the last words, wherewith he addressed him were: 'Brother, I thank you, I pray God bless you, and I bless God for you.'[109]

That day was spent in concentrated prayer for Whitaker at St. Peter's, Cornhill, where Matthew Newcomen preached from John 11:3-4, 'Lord, behold, he whom thou lovest is sick,' and William Jenkyn preached from Luke 23:28, 'Weep not for me.' That evening of June 1, 1654, he died, his final prayer request to Ashe being answered: 'Do not complain, but bless God for me, and entreat him to open the prison-door.'[110]

London minister and Westminster divine Edmund Calamy summarized his former colleague's testimony in a preface to the printed version of Ashe's funeral sermon:

> Such as were best acquainted with him reckoned, that it was disputable, whether he preached more by the heavenliness of his doctrine, or by the holiness of his life. But they conclude, that it is certain, he preached as effectually by his sickness and death, as by either his doctrine or his life.[111]

Among several who wrote elegies for Whitaker was Westminster divine Edward Reynolds of Oxford:

> Great preacher of thy heavenly Father's will,
> Thy tongue did many ears with manna fill.
> Thy life out-preach'd thy tongue, O blessed strife!
> Thy sickness the best sermon of thy life.[112]

While at Oakham Whitaker had married Chephtzibah, daughter of William Peachey, a Puritan minister of Oakham, and she bore him four sons and three daughters. One son, William Whitaker (1629-1672), studied at Emmanuel College, Cambridge and became a minister, succeeding his father at St. Mary Magdalene, Bermondsey.[113]

Thomas Hill (c.1602 - December 18, 1653)

After the Fast Day sermons by Thomas Hill and Herbert Palmer on August 13, 1644 Robert Baillie reported to Scotland that they had preached to Parliament 'two of the most Scottish and free sermons that ever I heard any where.' He said:

> ... these two good men laid well about them, and charged publicke and parliamentarie sins strictlie on the backs of the guilty; among the rest, their neglect to settle religion according to the Covenant, and to sett up Ordination, which lay so long in their hands.[114]

Hill had preached previously on such occasions on July 27, 1642 to the House of Commons and on July 21, 1643, to a joint gathering of Commons and Lords and he seems to have become a particularly favorite choice late in 1644, preaching to the House of Lords on November 27 and to a special joint gathering on December 18.[115]

Hill was born at Kington, Worcestershire at an unknown date, but probably around 1602. He entered Emmanuel College, Cambridge in 1618 and received his B.A. in 1622 and his M.A. in 1626. He lived for a time with his friend John Cotton in Boston, Lincolnshire 'for the more happy seasoning of his spirit'.[116] Returning to Cambridge, he was elected a Fellow of Emmanuel College and, being ordained in 1629, he began preaching in the parish of St. Andrew's, Cambridge. In 1633 he received his B.D. and also became Rector of Titchmarsh, Northamptonshire. By this time he had gained a reputation not only for his effective tutoring, but also for preaching that was 'plain, powerful, spiritual, frequent and laborious'. In 1635 it was reported to the authorities that he had not yet read the Book of Sports to his congregation and that people from all over the county were flocking to hear him.[117] At some point he made the acquaintance of the household of Robert Rich, Earl of Warwick, for he married the governess of the Earl's daughter, Mary Willford, who after Hill's death would marry his widowed friend, Anthony Tuckney.[118]

Before the beginning of the Westminster Assembly Hill was one of those appointed by the House of Lords in the spring of 1643 to serve on the committee under Archbishop of York John Williams to consider various 'innovations' in religion.[119] No doubt his Fast Day sermon of July 27, 1642 had helped to get him this appointment. In his sermon *The Trade of Truth Advanced* he had challenged the House of Commons: 'Would you have a flourishing Kingdome, advance the Kingdome of Christ in it. Let the State maintaine Religion, and Religion will blesse the State.'[120] His message took on an evangelistic, even a missionary, cast:

> Improve your power to help forward the word of truth, that it may run and be glorified throughout the land: 1st, Provide that every congregation may have an able trumpet of truth; 2d, especially that great towns may have lectures – markets of truth; 3d, afford any faithful Paul and Barnabas encouragement, yea power, if Sergius Paulus desire to hear the word of God, to go and preach, though Elymas the sorcerer should be unwilling. Such ambulatory exercises have brought both light and

heat into dark and cold corners; 4th, What if there be some evangelical itinerant preachers sent abroad upon a public stock to enlighten dark countries?[121]

After military defeats suffered by the Parliamentary forces in the west, Hill preached on July 21, 1643 *The Militant Church Triumphant over the Dragon*: 'Never say, because the *event* is *uncertaine*, therefore it is not best to appeare for Christ and his cause.' With the Solemn League and Covenant soon to be negotiated with the Scots, Hill assured Parliament that 'the time may come when *Christs true hearted souldiers in England* may be vindicated, justified, and honoured as much as they are disgraced.'[122]

On February 28, 1644 Hill was designated as one of the seven daily preachers at the early morning services at Westminster Abbey. He also

FAST DAYS

During the time that the Westminster Assembly was meeting, Parliament held regular Fast Days on the last Wednesday of every month. Dr. Edmund Calamy (grandson of the member of the Assembly by that name) later described the way in which John Howe conducted a Puritan Fast Day:

> It was upon these occasions his common way to begin about nine in the morning with prayer for about a quarter of an hour in which he begged a blessing on the work of the day: and afterwards read and expounded a chapter or psalm in which he spent three-quarters of an hour. Then [he] prayed for about an hour, preached for another hour and prayed for about half an hour. After this he retired and took some little refreshment for about a quarter of an hour more (the people singing all the while) and then came again into the pulpit and prayed for another hour and gave them another sermon of about an hour's length, and so concluded the service of the day at about four of the clock in the evening with about half an hour or more in prayer.

The seven hours of such a service included about three and a quarter hours of prayer and two and three-quarters hours of preaching. The Parliamentary Fast Days likewise tended to have even more prayer than preaching, sometimes with two one-hour sermons and two prayers of two hours length apiece.

preached regularly on Sundays at St. Martin's-in-the-Fields.[123] Following the 'most Scottish and free sermons' that he and Herbert Palmer
delivered on the joint Day of Humiliation in August, Hill preached on
November 27, 1644 *The Right Separation Encouraged* and called for
a spiritual separation from that which is false in doctrine, worship, and
government, but acknowledged that only 'the Church Triumphant in
Heaven' was absolutely perfect and that there could be no perfect
reformation in this world.[124] At the critical juncture when the Self-
Denying Ordinance was under consideration, it was Thomas Hill,
Obadiah Sedgwick and Stephen Marshall who preached 'for eight or
ten hours' before Lords and Commons in Lincoln's Inn chapel on the
Special Fast Day of December 18, 1644.[125]

Hill's ministry, however, extended beyond the Assembly. In February 1645 he was elected Master of Emmanuel College, Cambridge, but
on April 11 he exchanged this for the Mastership of Trinity College. For
two years he served as Vice-Chancellor of the University, and in 1646
he took the degree of D.D.[126] During his remaining years he continued
very active in preaching:

> Beside his preaching in the University, he set up a lecture every
> Sabbath morning, in one church in the town, which was performed only
> by himself, and cheerfully frequented both by many scholars and
> inhabitants of the town; and one lecture in another church, every Lord's
> day in the afternoon, in which he did bear at least, the fourth part of the
> burden; and both *gratis*. He also preached occasionally in several
> adjacent towns and villages.[127]

Hill's evangelistic zeal inspired a corresponding zeal in his converts.
John Machin, later to become a Nonconformist minister ejected in
1662, entered Cambridge in 1646 'without any view to the ministry';
however, he

> had a gracious change effected in him, chiefly by the preaching of Dr.
> Hill; and that of Dr. Arrowsmith was much to his comfort and
> edification. No sooner did he find this blessed change in his heart, than
> his friends found it by his letters; by which together with his exemplary
> conversation afterward, he was the means of converting his three
> sisters, and there was room to hope, both his parents ....[128]

Although Hill's strong Calvinism made him unpopular with some of the Fellows of Trinity College, he was nevertheless an effective tutor. When his friend and former colleague of the Westminster Assembly, Anthony Tuckney, delivered his funeral sermon in 1653, he testified that Hill

> had been a diligent and successful tutor of very many pupils 'and divers of them of quality who have proved great blessings both in Church and Commonwealth.' Like his colleagues he was an exponent of Calvinist doctrine: in Tuckney's words he firmly adhered to 'the good old doctrine of the Church of England, that which in this our University our famous [William] Whitaker, [William] Perkins, [John] Davenant, [Samuel] Ward and others maintained in their time.[129]

He was 'no friend to Arminianism'. James Reid reports that Hill used to lay his hand upon his breast and say, 'Every true Christian has something here, that will frame an argument against Arminianism.'[130]

Thomas Hill's final illness was 'a long continued quartan ague'. Anthony Tuckney comforted and guided his soul at the end:

> To Dr. Tuckney, about half an hour before his departure, who made inquiry respecting the settlement of his outward estate, and of his inward peace, he readily, and without any hesitation, answered, *Through the mercy of God in Christ, his peace was made, and that he quietly rested in it.* Then, with tranquillity, he suddenly departed, Dec. 18th 1653, in an advanced age, very much lamented by his acquaintance and brethren.[131]

John Arrowsmith (March 29, 1602 - February 1659)

In the 'crisis of the Assembly' in April 1646, the House of Commons charged the Divines with breach of privilege. This was because of their petitioning against the House's Erastian ordinance to set up parliamentary commissions to which cases of church discipline could be appealed, and had presented to the Assembly nine queries concerning divine-right church government. The Assembly's immediate decision, following the charge, was to call a special day of fasting for May 6, 1646. Daniel Cawdry and John Arrowsmith were assigned to preach. Arrowsmith's sermon, based on Isaiah 9:6, was particularly memorable and appropriate to this crucial situation.

'The work of this day is not to make a fence,' he said, 'but to dig a well, and to build a tower of confidence, and that's the use I shall make of this; therefore it will go well with his Church; Christ is such a King as is able to subdue all his enemies.' Referring to the Messiah's title of 'Wonderful,' he acknowledged the previous accomplishments of the Long Parliament: 'wonders of providence; we may look to those as much as ... any people under heaven .... Which of us could have expected such Acts of Parliament, Ordinances of Parliament, such deliverances .... We expect more wonders still ....' With regard to Christ as 'Counsellor,' he said: 'Be exhorted to look to Him for counsel in the great business now before us, the work of every day .... If ever we needed counsel, we need it now, therefore take heed of leaning to our own understandings.' Expounding on Christ as 'Prince of Peace,' he said:

> Dearest brethren, whom I love in my heart, if Christ be Prince of Peace, how is [it] that we are such men of commotion; do we not preach the gospel of peace? .... Our reputation goes very low with all the sectaries in the kingdom .... If you would have your reputation grow, you must agree.

Then he concluded:

> I will tell you what rules I have set myself to walk by. 1. Take heed of voting against light. 2. Take heed of voting without light; let every one be fully persuaded; he hath to subscribe with a trembling hand. 3. Take heed of refusing to bring thy judgment to light by thy vote .... Take a short view of the royal titles of Christ together.[132]

Thus were the Divines prepared, by reminder of the Kingship of Christ, for the next two months' work of answering the queries before proceeding to the completion of the Confession of Faith and the Catechisms.

John Arrowsmith was born near Newcastle-on-Tyne, Northumberland (some sources say at Gateshead, Durham, across the Tyne) on March 29, 1602, the same day and perhaps at the very same hour as John Lightfoot. He entered St. John's College, Cambridge in 1616 and received his B.A. in 1620 and his M.A. in 1623.[133] In 1623 he also became a Fellow of St. Catherine Hall, Cambridge, where Richard Sibbes would be Master from 1626 to 1635. During the years 1626 to

1642 the Fellows of St. Catherine Hall were virtually all Puritans, including subsequent members of the Westminster Assembly Thomas Goodwin, Andrew Perne, William Spurstowe and William Strong as well as John Arrowsmith.[134] In 1631 he was married and also became Vicar of St. Nicholas Chapel in King's Lynn, Norfolk. At some time in his youth he was shot in the eye by an arrow and as a result had a glass eye, but this disability did not hinder his studies, as he received the B.D. in 1633.[135]

On April 25, 1642 Arrowsmith was chosen one of the two Norfolk clergy to be consulted on church affairs. On January 25, 1643 he was one of the preachers to the House of Commons on the monthly Fast Day when terms of peace were being discussed with the King at Oxford. His sermon, based on Leviticus 25:25, 'I shall bring a sword upon you, that shall avenge the quarrel of my covenant,' pointed out that civil war was not to be unexpected when God's covenant was neglected, and he summoned his hearers to new obedience.[136] Arrowsmith preached to the Assembly on a Special Fast Day for the Army on May 17, 1644. His sermon this time was based on Haggai 2:4-5, 'Yet now, be strong, O Zerubbabel, saith the Lord ...', with the outline composed of three 'triplicities': of persons – the magistrates under Zerubbabel, the ministers under Joshua, and the people; of duties – be strong, work, fear not; and of encouragements – precept, prayer, and promise. In his application he said:

> ... they should be humbled because they had fallen short; let each man say, like Pharaoh's butler, 'I remember my own fault this day.' It was an act of spiritual fortitude to subdue passions; differences occurred, but 'the people of God, though they differ, it is but like the shaking of boughs of a tree in a storm, they are united in one root; the sons of Belial are like a heap of chaff, scattered in the storm, never to meet again.' Yet 'bitter contentions are dolorous,' and dangerous also because they 'hinder the discerning of truth and retaining of joy.'

Arrowsmith challenged the Assembly not only to unity, but also to hard work:

> ... they were called of God, who is ever active, to an honourable work. But there was much yet to do, and 'except you go on, you lose all you have done.' Much had been done in pulling down, less in building up; God levelled the mountains in Zerubbabel's way, He could do the same for the Parliament.

He concluded by reminding his hearers that God had done wonders and would do more if they trusted him and by calling for a spirit of charity and a spirit of prayer.[137]

Arrowsmith would preach before the House of Commons again on January 27, 1647, as well as during the 'crisis of the Assembly' on May 6, 1646, but his remaining contribution would be chiefly as a scholar. The Earl of Manchester had ejected five heads of Colleges at Cambridge for gross scandals and now sought on March 15, 1644, the Assembly's permission to replace them with John Arrowsmith, Herbert Palmer, Richard Vines, Lazarus Seaman, and Thomas Young. The Assembly acquiesced in these appointments when assured the reforms in the University could be accomplished without depriving the Assembly of the services of these men.[138] Arrowsmith was made Master of St. John's College and also received his D.D. in 1644. In 1647 he became Vice-Chancellor of Cambridge University and in 1651 Regius Professor of Divinity at Cambridge. In 1653, after the death of Thomas Hill, he became Master of Trinity College.[139]

At the Assembly Arrowsmith was called upon to translate communications to foreign churches into Latin.[140] In 1645 he obtained the rectory of St. Martin's, Ironmonger Lane, where he would be succeeded by John Wallis in 1649, and he was a member of the Sixth London Classis when the Presbyterian form of government was set up.[141] He also preached at St. Pancras, Soper Lane in 1646-1647.[142] In 1654 he was appointed to the national commission of 'Triers' for the examination of candidates for ministry.[143] It has been suggested that Arrowsmith may have been the main shaper of the Shorter Catechism, but Alexander Mitchell rejects that opinion and emphasizes the role of John Wallis, and others give credit to Anthony Tuckney.[144] Other than his sermons, Arrowsmith's chief publication was *A Chain of Principles*, published in 1659. Archibald Alexander comments:

> ... he commenced writing an elaborate work, of the nature of a body of divinity. It was entitled, 'A Chain of Principles,' in thirty distinct 'aphorisms', which he intended to illustrate by exercitations, under each; but sickness and death interposed, so that no more than six out of the thirty were ever finished. These have been published, and give occasion for regret that the whole was not completed.[145]

James Reid remarks, 'This is a book of real worth; and it is strange that it has not been oftener printed. It will amply repay the trouble of a perusal.'[146] Cotton Mather says in his *Student and Preacher*, 'Everything of an Arrowsmith is admirable' and puts him in a class as a scholar with John Lightfoot, John Selden, Thomas Gataker, William Greenhill, William Twisse, Edward Reynolds and John Wallis.[147]

Arrowsmith died in February 1659, being buried on the 24th of that month. He was clearly respected as both a preacher and a scholar by the Assembly, which he repeatedly summoned to unity and diligence in its work.

Notes

1. Quoted in William Haller, *Liberty and Reformation in the Puritan Revolution* (New York and London: Columbia U. Press, 1955), 36; cf. James Reid, *Memoirs of the Westminster Divines*, 2 vols. in 1 (Edinburgh and Carlisle, Pa.: Banner of Truth, 1982 reprint of 1811 and 1815 edition), II, 73.

2. John F. Wilson, *Pulpit in Parliament* (Princeton, N.J.: Princeton U. Press, 1969), 109-110, 87.

3. Quoted in Reid, *Memoirs*, II, 73.

4. H.R. Trevor-Roper, *The Crisis of the Seventeenth Century: Religion, the Reformation and Social Change* (New York and Evanston, Ill.: Harper & Row, 1968), 297-298. Trevor-Roper says 'There is no adequate biography of Marshall, whose importance, at least as the spokesman for policy, seems to me greater than has been allowed' (298 n.1).

5. *Dictionary of National Biography*, eds. Leslie Stephen and Sidney Lee, 22 vols. (London: Oxford U. Press, 1921-22), XII, 1128; Larry Jackson Holley, 'The Divines of the Westminster Assembly' (New Haven: Yale U. Ph.D. diss,. 1979), 325.

6. Wilson, *Pulpit in Parliament,* 36-37.

7. Robert S. Paul, *Assembly of the Lord,* (Edinburgh: T. & T. Clark, 1985), 119; Haller, *Liberty and Reformation*, 34-35.

8. Reid, *Memoirs*, II, 79.

9. *D.N.B.*, XII, 1131.

10. Trevor-Roper, *Crisis,* 307-308; cf. Wilson, *Pulpit in Parliament*, 63-64, and Haller, *Liberty and Reformation*, 69.

11. Trevor-Roper, *Crisis*, 307; cf. *D.N.B.*, XII, 1131. Extracts from the sermon are to be found in George Yule, *Puritans in Politics* (Appleford, Oxfordshire: Sutton Courtenay Press, 1981), 297-304.

12. Paul S.Seaver, *Puritan Lectureships* (Stanford, Cal.: Stanford U. Press, 1970), 268.

13. Haller, *Liberty and Reformation*, 68.

14. *Ibid.*, 101.

15. Wilson, *Pulpit in Parliament*, 221.

16. Quoted in Paul, *Assembly of the Lord,* 394 n.24.

17. Wilson, *Pulpit in Parliament*, 233-234.

18. *D.N.B.*, XII, 1129; Haller, *Liberty and Reformation,* 67.

19. Wilson, *Pulpit in Parliament*, 16.

20. Trevor-Roper, *Crisis,* 337; Wilson, *Pulpit in Parliament*, 95. This sermon was not published, so we do not know what he preached.

21. Quoted in *D.N.B.*, XII, 1130.

22. Tai Liu, *Discord in Zion* (The Hague: Martinus Nijhoff, 1973), 128-129.

23. *D.N.B.*, XII, 1130; George Yule, *Puritans in Politics*, 150; John Richard de Witt, *Jus Divinum* (Kampen: J.H. Kok, 1969), 149 and n.32, 223-224.

24. Yule, *Puritans in Politics*, 139-140.

25. Haller, *Liberty and Reformation*, 116; de Witt, *Jus Divinum*, 87.

26. Trevor-Roper, *Crisis,* 327-328.

27. Liu, *Discord,* 133; *D.N.B.*, XII, 1131.

28. Liu, *Discord,* 128. Marshall was not Philip Nye's father-in-law, as many modern sources have it.

29. Paul, *Assembly of the Lord*, 364.

30. Alexander F. Mitchell, *The Westminster Assembly: Its History and Standards*, 2nd ed. (Philadelphia: Presbyterian Board of Publication, 1897), 240-241.

31. Reid, *Memoirs,* II, 78, quoting the antagonistic Anthony a' Wood.

32. *D.N.B.*, XII, 1131. Eliza Vaughan, *Stephen Marshall, A Forgotten Essex Puritan* (London: Arnold Fairbairns & Co., 1907), 15-16, 121, refers to Marshall's wife as Susanna Castell.

33. Reid, *Memoirs*, II, 81.

34. *Ibid.*, II, 80.

35. Wilson, *Pulpit in Parliament*, 111.

36. *Ibid.*, 171.

37. From a paraphrase in Reid, *Memoirs*, I, 199-200.

38. Larry Jackson Holley, 'The Divines of the Westminster Assembly,' 290; *Calamy Revised*, ed. A.G. Matthews (Oxford: Clarendon Press, 1934), 103; Reid, *Memoirs*, I, 193.

39. Reid, *Memoirs*, I, 202-203; cf. *D.N.B.*, III, 1163.

40. Quoted in Holley, 'Divines,' 290.

41. [Archibald Alexander], *A History of the Westminster Assembly of Divines* (Philadelphia: Presbyterian Board of Publication, 1841), 226-227. An abridged one-volume version was published in 1959 by Sovereign Grace Publishers of Evansville, Indiana.

42. Paul, *Assembly of the Lord*, 250 n.9.

43. Quoted in Wilson, *Pulpit in Parliament*, 209.

44. Liu, *Discord*, 33-34, 48-49.

45. Robert S. Paul, *An Apologeticall Narration* (Philadelphia and Boston: United Church Press, 1963), 88 n.29.

46. [Alexander], *History,* 225-226.

47. Tai Liu, *Puritan London* (Newark, Del.: U. of Delaware Press, 1986), 112.

48. Reid, *Memoirs,* I, 199; Geoffrey F. Nuttall, *Visible Saints* (Oxford: Basil Blackwood, 1957), 17 n.2; *D.N.B.*, III, 1163.

49. Quoted in Reid, *Memoirs*, I, 197. A fine portrait of Caryl appears in his *The*

Nature and Principles of Love, as the end of the Commandment, published posthumously in London in 1673 (I, 203).

50. Wilson, *Pulpit in Parliament*, 111.

51. Robert M. Norris, 'The Preaching of the Assembly,' in *To Glorify and Enjoy God*, ed. John L. Carson and David W. Hall (Edinburgh and Carlisle, Pa. : Banner of Truth, 1994), 74.

52. Reid, *Memoirs*, II, 142.

53. Seaver, *Puritan Lectureships*, 324 n.109.

54. *Ibid.*, 260.

55. *D.N.B.*, XVII, 1121.

56. Wilson, *Pulpit in Parliament*, 157-158.

57. Quoted in Paul, *Assembly of the Lord*, 226 n.28.

58. Quoted in Yule, *Puritans in Politics*, 139-140.

59. Paul, *Assembly of the Lord*, 271; de Witt, *Jus Divinum*, 113.

60. Trevor-Roper, *Crisis*, 320.

61. Paul, *Assembly of the Lord*, 399 and n.48; 427 and n.190.

62. *D.N.B.*, XVII, 1121; Liu, *Discord*, 142 and n.86; 78.

63. *D.N.B.*, XVII, 1121; Nuttall, *Visible Saints*, 136 n.5.

64. *D.N.B.*, XVII, 1121-1122.

65. Wilson, *Pulpit in Parliament*, 112.

66. *D.N.B.*, XX, 370; Reid, *Memoirs*, II, 193.

67. Wayne R. Spear, 'Covenanted Uniformity in Religion' (Pittsburgh: U. of Pittsburgh Ph.D. diss., 1976), 362.

68. Holley, 'Divines,' 355; *D.N.B.*, XX, 369.

69. Wilson, *Pulpit in Parliament*, 112; S.W. Carruthers, *The Everyday Work of the Westminster Assembly* (Philadelphia: Presbyterian Historical Societies of America and England, 1943), 178.

70. Carruthers, *Everyday Work*, 143, 176-178.

71. Liu, *Puritan London*, 77.

72. *D.N.B.*, XX, 370.

73. Wilson, *Pulpit in Parliament*, 67.

74. Quoted in Carruthers, *Everyday Work*, 185.

75. Carruthers, *Everyday Work*, 176-177.

76. [Alexander], *History*, 394.

77. Mitchell, *Westminster Assembly*, 154.

78. de Witt, *Jus Divinum*, 83-84.

79. *Ibid.*, 105; cf. Paul, *Assembly of the Lord*, 249.

80. de Witt, *Jus Divinum*, 79; Paul, *Assembly of the Lord*, 164, 166 n.132.

81. Paul, *Assembly of the Lord*, 241 n.78, 344.

82. *Ibid.*, 217.

83. *Ibid.*, 351-352.

84. *Ibid.*, 519.

85. Quoted in Haller, *Liberty and Reformation*, 165-166. Cf. Liu, *Discord*, 43-44.

86. Quoted in Yule, *Puritans in Politics*, 223. Cf. Liu *Discord*, 45.

87. Quoted in Paul, *Assembly of the Lord*, 305-306.

88. Liu, *Discord*, 131-132 n.47.

89. Reid, *Memoirs*, II, 196.

90. Wilson, *Pulpit in Parliament*, 113.

91. Reid, *Memoirs*, II, 216-217.

92. *Ibid.*, II, 218; Holley, 'Divines', 360; cf. *D.N.B.*, XXI, 16. Antonia Fraser, *Cromwell, Our Chief of Men* (London: Mandarin, 1993, 1973), 19-20, provides an interesting description of Sidney Sussex College in 1616-17 when Oliver Cromwell was there.

93. Reid, *Memoirs*, II, 219-220; Wilson, *Pulpit in Parliament*, 16; Seaver, *Puritan Lectureships*, 270.

94. Carruthers, *Everyday Work*, 184, 163.

95. Yule, *Puritans in Politics*, 169-170.

96. Paul, *Assembly of the Lord*, 351.

97. *Ibid.*, 424.

98. Liu, *Puritan London*, 85.

99. Quoted in Reid, *Memoirs*, II, 221.

100. Quoted in Reid, *Memoirs*, II, 222.

101. Reid, *Memoirs*, II, 222.

102. *Ibid.*, II, 224, 225.

103. *D.N.B.*, XXI, 17.

104. Reid, *Memoirs*, II, 225.

105. *Ibid.*, II, 238-239.

106. *Ibid.*, II, 228. William Haller, *The Rise of Puritanism* (New York, Evanston, and London: Harper & Row, 1957), 108.

107. Reid, *Memoirs*, II, 236.

108. *Ibid.*, II, 229.

109. *Ibid.*, II, 236, 238.

110. *Ibid.*, II, 238, 237.

111. *Ibid.*, II, 236.

112. *Ibid.*, II, 245.

113. *Ibid.*, II, 218; *D.N.B.*, XXI, 17; *Calamy Revised*, 524.

114. Paul, *Assembly of the Lord*, 395; cf. Carruthers, *Everyday Work*, 74, 127; Haller, *Liberty and Reformation*, 125.

115. Wilson, *Pulpit in Parliament*, 240, 241, 244.

116. Holley, 'Divines', 317. Cf. *D.N.B.*, IX, 874.

117. J.T. Cliffe, *The Puritan Gentry: The Great Puritan Families of Early Stuart England* (London, Boston, Melbourne, and Henley: Routledge & Kegan Paul, 1984), 180.

118. *D.N.B.*, IX, 874.

119. Paul, *Assembly of the Lord*, 64 and n.37.

120. Quoted in Wilson, *Pulpit in Parliament*, 173.

121. Quoted in Mitchell, *Westminster Assembly*, 102-103, n.1.

122. Liu, *Discord*, 23-24.

123. Wilson, *Pulpit in Parliament*, 16; Seaver, *Puritan Lectureships*, 269-270; *D.N.B.*, IX, 874.

124. Liu, *Discord*, 23-24.

125.Trevor-Roper, *Crisis*, 320-321.

126. Carruthers, *Everyday Work*, 143, 183; *D.N.B.*, IX, 874.

127. Reid, *Memoirs*, II, 38.

128. *Ibid.*, II, 41.

129. Cliffe, *Puritan Gentry*, 93.

130. Reid, *Memoirs,* II, 40.

131. *Ibid.*, II, 39.

132. From the scribe's notes in *Minutes of the Westminster Assembly*, ed. Alexander F. Mitchell and John Struthers (Edmonton, Alberta: Still Waters Revival Books, 1991 reprint of 1874 ed.), 464-467. Cf. de Witt, *Jus Divinum*, 214-215; Carruthers, *Everyday Work*, 72; Yule, *Puritans in Politics,* 188-189; Mitchell, *Westminster Assembly*, 322.

133. Holley, 'Divines', 282; cf. *D.N.B.*, I, 596.

134. Cliffe, *Puritan Gentry*, 100-101.

135. Holley, 'Divines', 282; Reid, *Memoirs,* I, 107.

136. Cf. Liu, *Discord*, 22; Trevor-Roper, *Crisis*, 310-311; Wilson, *Pulpit in Parliament*, 68, 81, 204-205.

137. Carruthers, *Everyday Work,* 66-67.

138. *Ibid.*, 142-143.

139. *D.N.B.*, I, 597; Reid, *Memoirs*, I, 107-108.

140. Reid, *Memoirs*, I, 107; Carruthers, *Everyday Work*, 37-38.

141. *D.N.B.*, I, 597; Liu, *Puritan London,* 75, 73-74.

142. Liu, *Puritan London*, 87, 117.

143. Liu, *Discord,* 142 and n.86; cf. 112 and n.112.

144. Mitchell, *Westminster Assembly,* 442-443, n.1; cf. 428.

145. [Alexander], *History*, 190.

146. Reid, *Memoirs*, I, 113.

147. *Ibid.*

Chapter 8

Notable Scholars

The divines of the Westminster Assembly typically had both their Bachelor of Arts and Master of Arts degrees from either Oxford or Cambridge. Not uncommonly they served as Fellows in the Colleges of those Universities. About half continued their studies to obtain the Bachelor of Divinity and approximately a quarter to obtain the Doctor of Divinity degree. To acquire a B.D. one normally had to be a Master of Arts of seven years' standing, performing in the divinity disputations, in addition serving as respondent once and as opponent once in two disputations. Then, within a year, one delivered a Latin sermon to the clergy of the University at Oxford, or at Cambridge preached three sermons, one in Latin to the clergy of the University, one in English in the University Church, and another in English at Paul's Cross in London. For the D.D., one had to be a B.D. of four years' standing, deliver six lectures on any part of Scripture or three lectures on one of the Epistles, take part in disputations and preach as for the B.D. The obtaining of a D.D., therefore, or becoming Master of a College, was a mark of distinguished scholarship.

In addition to the ten scholars of the Assembly described in this chapter, the following members were also recognized for their scholarship. John Selden, William Twisse, D.D., Samuel Rutherford, and John Lightfoot, D.D. gained international reputations. Thomas Goodwin, D.D., John Arrowsmith, D.D., Richard Vines and Thomas Hill, D.D. were also highly acclaimed academicians. Cornelius Burgess, D.D., Herbert Palmer, William Gouge, D.D., Daniel Featley, D.D., George Gillespie, Alexander Henderson, Robert Baillie, Lazarus Seaman, D.D. and Matthew Newcomen, D.D. were also notable scholars.

Thomas Gataker (September 4, 1574 - July 27, 1654)

Thomas Gataker was the friend of James Ussher and John Selden, 'and after them was accounted the most learned man then in England,' says Alexander F. Mitchell. 'He was distinguished by the quaint richness of his style and the argumentative power of his controversial works.'[1] In the Westminster Assembly's debates on church government in 1643-1644 he was the eleventh most active participant, just behind William Gouge and before Samuel Rutherford in number of speeches.[2] Nearly in his seventieth year when the Assembly began, he was among the oldest of the members and, except for Henry Wilkinson, Sr., he may have been the oldest active participant.[3] He had published thirty-one works by July 1643, making him the most prolific of the Westminster divines, and his eventual total would be forty-eight.[4]

Gataker was born on September 4, 1574 in the rectory house of St. Edmund's Lombard Street, London, where his father, Thomas Gatacre (the son changed the spelling 'to prevent miscalling'), had become the minister two years earlier, having been ordained by Bishop Edmund Grindal in 1568 after conversion from Roman Catholicism through the testimony of Protestant confessors under Mary Tudor.[5] The younger Thomas entered St. John's College, Cambridge in 1590 and received his B.A. in 1594 and M.A. in 1597. He excelled in Greek and Hebrew and also made a close friendship with fellow student Richard Stock, who became a Puritan preacher (and the childhood rector of John Milton at All Hallow's, Bread Street). In 1596 Gataker was nominated one of the first Fellows of the new Sidney Sussex College, but since the building was still under construction, he served as tutor and chaplain in the household of William Ayloffe of Braxted, Essex. Having been ordained, he came into residence at Sidney Sussex College in 1599. The building being still incomplete, he shared his rooms with another Fellow, William Bradshaw, another Puritan who became a long-time friend. Gataker participated briefly in a plan to provide preachers for neglected parishes around Cambridge, serving on Sundays at Everton, Bedfordshire, where the vicar was reported to be one hundred and thirty years old![6]

For reasons that are unclear Gataker moved to London around the end of 1600 and became tutor in the family of Sir William Cooke at Charing Cross. He preached occasionally at St. Martin's-in-the-Fields, where an old manservant was heard to remark that 'he was a prettie pert boy, but he made a reasonable good sermon'.[7] His sermons appealed as well to some of the upper classes, who secured for him the lectureship at Lincoln's Inn in 1601. Here he remained until 1611, proceeding to the B.D. in 1603. Since the Society of Lincoln's Inn required him to preach only in term time, he spent vacations at Sir William Cooke's country seat in Northamptonshire.[8] When he arrived at Lincoln's Inn, the only Sunday lecture was at seven in the morning, most of the rest of the day being spent by the barristers in conference with their clients.

> But Gataker soon convinced them that it was as evil to conduct business on the Sabbath as to farm. He then moved the morning lecture to a later hour and the Wednesday lecture to Sunday afternoon. A more nearly Puritan Sabbath was henceforth observed.[9]

Gataker's contact with young noblemen at Lincoln's Inn was recognized as an opportunity for extensive Christian influence. When dedicating one of his books to John Hobart, the son of Sir Henry Hobart, the Lord Chief Justice of the Common Pleas and owner of the Blickling estate in Norfolk, he told him:

> those who were 'more eminent than ordinary, either for place or parentage' could draw many others on. 'In the ranke it hath pleased God to range your Worship whose religious cariage therefore shall not onely benefit your selfe but may pricke on and encourage others, both at home and abroad.'[10]

Gataker refused in 1609, and subsequently, to proceed to the D.D., partly for economic reasons, 'and also because, like Cato the censor, he would rather have people ask why he had no statue than why he had one.'[11] James Montague, Master of Sidney Sussex College, had come to London to offer him a chair in Hebrew, and preferments were offered in Shropshire and in Kent, but he declined all of these. In 1611 he accepted the rectory of Rotherhithe, Surrey, near to London Bridge, in response to Richard Stock's urgings because the alternative was an unworthy candidate. Despite appeals to continue his lectureship at Lincoln's Inn, he maintained his scruples against pluralities, saying he thought one cure of souls was enough for any man, and resigned to take up the pastorate across the Thames in Southwark.[12] He would remain as Rector of Rotherhithe the rest of his life, some forty-three years. Having married before 1611, he conducted an active pastoral ministry, his Friday catechetical lectures for children being crowded. He also opened his house to students preparing for ministry. His friend Simeon Ashe said that 'his house was a private semminary for divers young Gentlemen of the Nation, and more forreigners did resort to him and sojourn with him, to receive from him advice and advancement in their studies.' One of his assistants in this ministry was his later colleague at the Westminster Assembly, Thomas Young.[13]

In 1620 he spent the month from July 13 to August 14 traveling in the Netherlands, where he preached in the English church at Middleburgh, debated with some Roman Catholic priests in Flanders, and came away with an appreciation of the robust Protestantism of the Dutch.[14] Meanwhile he had begun to bring his scholarly gifts into the public arena. He corresponded with James Ussher in 1616 concerning some manuscripts he possessed of Robert Grosseteste, the thirteenth century Bishop of Lincoln, and they exchanged more letters in 1617 and 1621.[15] Gataker's first publication appeared in 1619, a pamphlet on *The Nature and Use of Lots* in which he sought to show that lots 'in games for mere amusement, were not in themselves sinful, but that lots of *divination*, or to ascertain the will of God, in matters of importance, were now unlawful.'[16] In 1624 he published *A Discourse of Transubstantiation*, in which he sought to demonstrate that this Roman Catholic teaching was 'against Scripture, Nature, Sense, Reason, Religion, the judgment of the Ancients, and the Faith of our Ancestors.'[17]

Several of Gataker's publications of the 1620s and '30s exhibit his practical insights gained from pastoral ministry. *A Wife in Deed,* based on Proverbs 18:22, was preached at the wedding of Sir Robert Harley to his third wife, Brilliana Conway, in July 1623. *A Good Wife God's Gift* was based on Proverbs 19:14. He also published *Eleazer's Prayer; A Marriage Sermon* and *Marriage Duties*. Everett Emerson comments:

> Among the authors referred to in the marginal gloss of *A Good Wife God's Gift* are Petronius, Ovid, Sophocles, Galen, Menander, Hesiod, Aeschylus, Plutarch and Erasmus as well as Lipsius, many Fathers, schoolmen, and Protestant theologians. Most of the quotations, one of Gataker's admirers explains, were provided from memory. In this sermon, as well as in three other marriage sermons, one detects more than reading. As William Haller has observed, there is in them 'something of the quality of personal confession,' revealing 'the joys and sorrows of the godly lover's heart.' Since Gataker outlived four wives, he had reason to know what he was talking about in his marriage sermons.[18]

Gataker's first wife, the widow of William Cupp or Cupper whom Gataker had married shortly before 1611, died in childbirth, leaving a son, Thomas, who died before his father. His second wife, a daughter of the Rev. Charles Pinner and cousin of Sir Nicholas Crisp also died in childbirth, leaving a son, Charles (c.1614-1680), who received the B.A. from Sidney Sussex College, Cambridge and the M.A. from Pembroke College, Oxford and became Rector of Hoggeston, Buckinghamshire and edited some of his father's posthumous publications. His third wife, a sister of Sir George and Sir John Farwell, died of consumption, leaving a daughter, who married one Draper and survived her father. In 1628 he married his fourth wife, a citizen's widow who died in 1652. Not only did he lose four wives, but three of his children died before he did.[19] J.I. Packer tells of Gataker's criticism of some saint's method of choosing a wife:

> Gataker knew a man who 'would test any woman on whom he had cast his roving eye ... by asking her, in sermon time, where the minister's text was. If she not only told him the text, but offered him her Bible, she was the woman who was to be his wife.' To Gataker this seemed both irreverent and asinine, and it is hard to quarrel with his verdict.[20]

In 1627 Gataker preached the funeral sermon for Richard Stock, and the virtues he saw in his friend were no doubt the ones he upheld for himself:

> He was not 'like the hand on the highway that pointeth others the way, but never walks therein itself.' 'He was none of those that say and do not; but as he taught so he wrought.' He delivered himself in the pulpit 'with clear method, sound proof, choice words, fit phrases, pregnant similitudes, plentiful illustrations, pithy perswasions, powerfull enforcements, allegations of antiquity, and variety of good literature, that both the learned might receive satisfaction from him, and the very meanest and dullest might also reap benefit by him.' ... 'Many famous lights in Gods Church and faithfull Ministers of the Word do profess to have lighted their candles at his Lampe.'[21]

The minister's life and preaching must be consistent with each other. A man must preach first to himself:

> A man might, conceded Thomas Gataker, 'be like ... a stonegutter (saith Augustine) that conveigheth water into a garden, but receiveth no

benefit thereby itselfe; ... or like to the baptisme water (saith Gregory), that helps men to Heaven ward, and goeth after downe to the sinke itselfe.'[22]

During the 1630s Gataker seems to have been left undisturbed by the ecclesiastical authorities. This was not because of any lack of antagonism to Arminianism on his part, for he expressed his concerns about the trends at Court and at St. Paul's Cross to his friend Samuel Ward, Master of Sidney Sussex College, in February 1631.[23] A more likely explanation is his connections with influential friends. He later wrote that

> Sir Henry Hobart, the celebrated judge, gave him the title of his chaplain, 'being but a titular matter, requiring no constant attendance, onelie a visit now and then and a Sermon sometime upon some special occasions, the rather that by his power and countenance I might sit the more quietlie and exercise my Ministerie more freelie.'[24]

On April 19, 1640 Gataker began to expound Romans 3:28 concerning the doctrine of justification. In the early stages of the Westminster Assembly he found himself aligned with William Twisse and Richard Vines in support of the concept that Christ's sufferings and death, or passive obedience, alone are imputed to the believer, whereas Daniel Featley contended for the idea that both Christ's passive obedience and his active obedience, or fulfillment of the law, are necessary to be imputed to the believer for eternal life. When Featley's arguments proved persuasive to the Assembly, Gataker was content merely to see the word 'whole' removed from the revised version of Article XI of the Thirty-Nine Articles, 'his *whole* obedience and satisfaction being by God imputed to us,' and to have Chapter XI of the Westminster Confession read 'by imputing the obedience and satisfaction of Christ unto them,' and he refrained from publishing his exposition of Romans 3:28. His son, Charles, however, published his discourses in 1670 as *An Antidote against Errour concerning Justification.*[25]

Like several others of the older generation at the Assembly, Gataker was able at first to give only qualified acceptance of the Covenant, not being able to forswear all forms of Episcopacy in the church.[26] He described himself as in favor of what was called 'moderated Episcopacy, denying the distinction of that order from that of Presbyters, divesting the Prelates of their baronies and seats in the House of Lords, and abolishing the rest of the hierarchy.'[27] He at first opposed the office of ruling elder, but eventually identified with the Presbyterians in the Assembly. In 1653 he said: 'So of the *Presbyterian Discipline* say I, It can not be other than some very needful and useful thing, that such creatures as these do so eagerly oppose.'[28]

After the first two years of the Assembly Gataker's health forced him to curtail his activities. The Minutes show him among the sick who were visited on August 5, 1645 and April 14, June 12, and September 14, 1646.[29] He had been subject to excruciating headaches ever since childhood, and in 1642 he had nearly died from a violent colic. Further illness occurred in 1645, and then when he recovered and resumed some of his pastoral duties, a vessel in one of his lungs burst, 'which was followed by frequent alarming discharges of blood.'[30] In his illness Gataker was still able to write. One of his main contributions was his commentary on Isaiah, Jeremiah, and Lamentations for the *Annotations upon all the books of the Old and New Testament* (1645, 1651, 1657), sometimes called the 'English Annotations' or the 'Assembly's Annotations' or 'Westminster Annotations' although not an official product of the Assembly, but produced by a committee appointed by Parliament that included several members of the Assembly.[31] On April 14, 1646 the Assembly was presented with Gataker's book *A Mistake or Misconstruction Removed* against the Antinomians and John Saltmarsh in particular. After Saltmarsh responded with *Shadows flying away*, Gataker presented to the Assembly on September 14 his reply, *Shadows without Substance; or, Pretended New Light.*[32] In 1652 he would publish *Antinomianism Discovered and Confuted*, in which he was concerned to refute the contention 'that God doth not, will not, cannot, in these times see any sin, in any of his justified children.'[33]

In the midst of the Assembly's discussions he found time to write a Latin work on the name Jehovah, *De Nomine Tetragrammato Dissertatio* (1645), in which he inclines to 'Jahveh,' but is content to retain the traditional 'Jehovah' as preferable to the substituted word 'Lord.'[34] He also published a book on diphthongs in 1646, arguing against the possibility of two vowels being combined in one syllable.[35] In 1648 he published *De Novi Testamenti Stylo Dissertatio* on the style of the New Testament, in which he was

> one of the first in Britain to write in defence of the opinion then much questioned, but now generally received, that the Greek of the New

Testament was of a different character from that of the classical authors, and by its many Hebraisms gave unmistakable evidence of the nationality and training of the writers.[36]

Archbishop Ussher showed great respect for this work, commending it to a colleague in Paris.[37] His most lasting classical contribution was his 1652 edition of the Meditations of the Stoic Emperor Marcus Aurelius (Antoninus), which has been termed 'the earliest edition ... of any classical writer published in England with original annotations.'[38] In his final years Gataker also wrote works in support of infant baptism and against astrology.[39]

Gataker's scholarship contributed much to the Assembly's interpretation of Scripture. 'Sir, we dare not allegorize the Scriptures,' he said, 'where the letter of it yields us a clear and proper sense.'[40] He employed the analogy of faith in interpreting unclear passages. Refuting an Antinomian interpretation of a passage, he said that 'this cannot be the meaning of the place, because it evidently crosseth the main tenor of the story and the truth of God's Word.' He commented: 'The whole doctrine of faith is to be received, that is contained in holy Writ; and that collation of Scripture with Scripture may afford much light unto places more obscure.'[41] Gataker could also appreciate the aesthetic aspects of Scripture:

> Among the rest of Psalms, some of them are about which the Holy Ghost's pleasure was that the penmen thereof should take more pains than usual, and more art than ordinary should be showed, in the framing and contriving of them: and where he useth more art, we may well expect more excellence.[42]

For proof of a doctrine or institution, such as the office of teacher as distinct from pastor, he required a clear Scripture passage: 'Matters of speciall Institution are stars of the first magnitude. They must not be drawne out of some obscure places.'[43] He agreed to the Scottish way of having communicants seated at the Lord's Table if it could be done conveniently, but he did not think there was 'any necessity in the thing'.[44]

He strongly opposed the trial and execution of King Charles I, and his criticisms of the civil and ecclesiastical governments in the 1650s led to suspicion and withholding of tithes by some of his parishioners.[45] In 1654 a fever caused him to ask his dear friend and colleague from the

Assembly, Simeon Ashe, to prepare his funeral sermon. The day before his death he summoned his son, his sister and his daughter, to each of whom he delivered a dying charge.[46] He died on July 27.

In the epistle to the Presbyterian ministers of London appended to his funeral sermon, *Gray Hayres Crowned with Grace*, based on Proverbs 16:31, Simeon Ashe said that the death of Gataker 'may well minde us of the deaths of many more of our brethren, whose hearts, heads and hands, went along with us in the setting up and exercising of the Presbyterian government in our respective Congregations, with mutual Assistance, Classical and Provinciall, both for the Ordination of Ministers, and the more pure administration of the Sacraments.' Although 'much contempt is cast upon us ... as an inconsiderable number,' Ashe insisted that there still were 'three score Presbyterian Ministers within the precincts of our Province, who preach profitably, did live godly, who are not tainted with the erroneous tenets either of the Arminians, Antinomians or Anabaptists.'[47]

Gataker was buried in his church of Rotherhithe, but no stone marks his grave. He never allowed his portrait to be painted or engraved. He was described as 'of a middle stature, of a thin body, of a lively countenance, and of a fresh complexion.'[48] Something of the quality of his mind and soul appear in a poem he composed shortly before his death:

> I thirst for thirstiness;
> I weep for tears;
> Well pleased I am to be displeased thus;
> The only thing I fear is want of fear;
> Suspecting I am not suspicious.
>
> I cannot choose but live, because I die;
> And, when I am not dead, how glad am I:
> Yet, when I am thus glad for sense of pain,
> And careful am, lest I should careless be;
> Then do I grieve for being glad again,
> And fear lest carelessness take care from me.
>
> Amid these restless thoughts this rest I find,
> For those who rest not here, there's rest behind.[49]

Robert Harris (1581 - December 1 or 11, 1658)

When Sir Anthony Cope, Member of Parliament, sought to fill the vacancy in the church of Hanwell, Oxfordshire with Robert Harris in 1607, Archbishop Richard Bancroft was not going to make it easy for another Puritan to succeed the ejected John Dod. He first said that Harris must be examined by his most learned chaplain, who upon sufficient examination reported him to be 'moderately learned'. Unsatisfied, the Archbishop committed Harris to William Barlow, Bishop of Rochester (and later to be a translator of the Authorized Version), a man of great wit and learning, who was glad for the opportunity to conduct the further examination. He covered divinity, then other branches of learning, and finally the Greek language: 'They Greeked it till they were both run aground for want of words, upon which they burst into a fit of laughter, and so gave it over.'[50] Harris served as pastor at Hanwell for the next thirty-five years.

Harris served faithfully in the Westminster Assembly and then was appointed President of Trinity College, Oxford on April 12, 1648, at which time he received the degree of D.D. It is said that in the Assembly he heard all and said little.[51] He was, however, one of the seven English divines most influential in preparing the Confession of Faith along with Edward Reynolds, Cornelius Burgess, Thomas Temple, Charles Herle, Joshua Hoyle and Thomas Gataker.[52] This important role makes his life and theological development of special interest.

Born in 1581 to a large family of modest means in Broad Campden, Gloucestershire, Harris did not receive the best schooling before entering Magdalen Hall, Oxford on June 10, 1597, but his tutor there, a Mr. Goffe or Gough, encouraged him spiritually while instructing him in philosophy. Eventually Harris instructed Goffe in Greek and Hebrew, and they read together Calvin's *Institutes*. Harris received the B.A. on June 5, 1600 and decided to pursue the ministry rather than the law which was his original intention.[53]

He preached his first sermon in 1604 at Chipping-Campden, where he had attended school. Upon his arrival at the church, there was no Bible to be found from which he could read his text. Even in the greater town there was not one to be obtained. Finally, in the house of the vicar of the parish one was located although it had not been seen for some months. Harris preached from Romans 10:1, 'Brethren, my heart's desire and prayer to God for Israel is, that they might be saved.' His sermon was so well received that his friends sought to persuade him that he needed no further education. He returned to Oxford, however, only to be thwarted by the plague, which had closed down the University. A Mr. Doyly invited Harris to stay in his home near Oxford, and there he met the Rector of Chiselhampton, Mr. Pries, who was in a weak condition and needed assistance in his church. Harris's effective preaching there brought him to the attention of Mr. Doyly's brother-in-law, Sir Anthony Cope, who secured his appointment to the church in Hanwell in 1607.[54]

Although the congregation at Hanwell was still loyal to John Dod, who had been their pastor for twenty years, Dod helped to get the younger Harris established there.[55] It also helped that at about the same time two contemporaries of Harris were appointed to churches within a couple of miles of Hanwell, William Whately at Banbury and Henry Scudder (who would also become a member of the Westminster Assembly) at Drayton. The three young ministers met together weekly to translate and analyse a chapter of the Bible, and eventually Harris married Whately's sister and Scudder married Whately's wife's sister, Elizabeth Hunt.[56] Harris's wife suffered a long and difficult illness upon the birth of their first child, and late in life experienced mental disorder and spiritual torment although she had lived a devout life and managed a large household well with Harris for about fifty years.[57]

Harris continued his studies, receiving the B.D. from Oxford on May 5, 1614. His reputation as a preacher apparently spread, for he preached at St. Lawrence Jewry in London in the summer of 1619,[58] gave a sermon at Paul's Cross in 1622,[59] served as Lecturer at St. Saviour's in Southwark from September 1623 to January 1625, and was invited to be Lecturer at St. Mary Aldermanbury when the Archbishop put a stop to it, his being Lecturer at St. Saviour's.[60] On February 18, 1629 he preached for a Fast Day to the House of Commons.[61] From 1629 to 1631 he preached every other week at Stratford-upon-Avon, and crowds came to hear him.[62] The Long Parliament invited him to preach on the monthly Fast Day, May 25, 1642.[63]

When the first battle of the Civil War took place on Sunday, October 23, 1642, the Battle of Edgehill, just a few miles from Hanwell, Harris held his customary services without being aware of it: '... the wind being contrary, he did not hear the least noise of it until the public exercises of the day were over; nor could he believe the report of the battle till soldiers, besmeared with blood, came to make it known.'[64]

Royalist troops were quartered in his home, and some of those abused him with derogatory names and swearing. The latter he could not tolerate, and so he preached on James 5:12, 'But above all things, my brethren, swear not.' This was so offensive that they threatened to shoot him if he should preach upon that text again. When he preached on the same verse again the next Sunday, 'he observed a soldier preparing his firelock, as if he designed to shoot; but Mr. Harris went on without fear, apprehending that the soldier intended only to disturb him, and he finished his discourse without interruption.'[65] Eventually his property was burned and his and his family's safety was sufficiently endangered that they fled to London.

While serving in the Assembly, he ministered at St. Botolph's, Bishopsgate and continued to preach to other audiences, such as the London City Council on April 7, 1645, where he encouraged order and mercy to the poor.[66] Of Harris's preaching, Samuel Clarke the biographer said that he

> could so cook his meat that he could make it relish to every pallate: He could dress a plain discourse, so as that all sorts should be delighted with it. He could preach with a learned plainness, and had learned to conceal his Art. He had clear Notions of high Mysteries, and proper language to make them stoop to the meanest capacity.[67]

Sermons, he said, should not be divinity lectures.[68] He complained that

> some preachers spent too much time insisting upon doctrinal points and too little upon applications, 'wherein ... a Sermons excellency doth consist.' He for his part 'contrived the Uses first,' and 'did often handle the same Texts, and the same Points, and yet still would pen new Applications.'[69]

He said of the Bible that 'we must be careful to read it, hear it, lodge it in our hearts, apply it close to our consciences, and then it will heal our hearts.'[70]

With regard to the Westminster Confession's doctrine of predestination, Harris was an infralapsarian, emphasizing that unbelievers were responsible for their own condemnation.[71] Committed to the doctrine of election, he also declared that God's Fatherhood was universal in some sense:

> God's adversaries are in some way his own. He is a piece of a Father to them also. For he is *a common Father by office* to all, *a special Father*

by adoption to saints, *a singular Father by nature* to Christ. A Prince, besides his particular relation to his children, is *pater patriae*, ... and is good to all, though with a difference. So here, though Christ hath purchased a peculiar people to himself, to the purpose of salvation, yet others taste of this his goodness.[72]

Harris had a very practical approach to the covenant of grace, emphasizing the personal application of the doctrine:

When Noah looked outward into the flood he saw 'nothing but feare and death.' And when he looked inward 'there were no neighbours but Bears and Lyons, and other beasts.' But Noah had his Ark, 'a pledge of God's care.' And so too 'stands our case,' for 'looke wee inward into our selves, there's nothing but guilt, sin, death, rottennesse, corruptions crawling in every roome in the soule; looke we outward ... there's nothing before our eyes but confusion and destruction, every place is a sea.' But we too have a pledge and, Harris added, 'for such as are already enrolled within the covenant ... there is not onely a possibility, but a certainty too of their blessedness.'[73]

He stressed that a troubled soul should make use of the means of grace available in the church:

Especially apply your selves to the communion of the Saints: A dead coale, put to live coales, will take fire from them, which it would never do lying in the dead heape: so here ... sort your selves with such as are godly, and frequent the ordinances ... that you may have part in the new covenant.[74]

He saw assurance of salvation as a matter of degree, something to be desired, but not necessarily complete in every believer: 'There be Christians of all ages and of all sizes in Gods family,' meaning that 'all Gods children have some assurance, though all have not alike.'[75]

In characteristic Puritan fashion Harris kept a spiritual diary for the sake of self-examination. He would write down 'the evidences which he found in himself, on account of which he hoped to reach heaven.' Usually these were propositions from Scripture or syllogisms that contributed to his own assurance.[76] The way such a spiritual diary functioned in place of the confessional for Puritans is illustrated by Harris's pastoral care of Elizabeth Wilkinson. This young woman had become concerned about her soul at the age of twelve, being assailed by atheistical doubts. These were relieved by reading Calvin's *Insti-*

tutes, but then she despaired that she had committed the sin against the Holy Ghost. She was helped by reading Henry Scudder's *Christians Daily Walk* and by Christian fellowship.

> The upshot of her struggle was that she wrote out a 'particular account of Gods gracious dealing' toward her and sent it to Robert Harris, then Master of Trinity, Oxford, begging him to admit her to communion. He granted her request; she entered upon the life of a saint, kept a diary, and when she died [in 1654], the story of her spiritual progress was published by Edmund Staunton, the preacher chosen to pronounce the sermon at her funeral.[77]

Harris spent the last ten years of his life as President of Trinity College, Oxford and as Rector of Garsington, near Oxford. He preached regularly on Sundays at Garsington and once a week at All Soul's College, also preaching in turn at the University in English and in Latin.[78] He died on December 1 or 11, 1658, at seventy-seven years of age.[79] One of his sayings was 'That a preacher has three books to study: the *Bible, himself*, and the *people. –* That preaching to the people was but one part of the pastor's duty: he was to live and die in them, as well as for, and with them.'[80] Robert Harris exemplified the Puritan preacher/pastor/theologian.

MILLENNIAL VIEWS

The Westminster Standards are generally viewed as amillennial in their eschatology, mainly because – especially in the Larger Catechism – a general resurrection is presupposed. Several of the Westminster divines, however, were premillennial. After his arrival from Scotland, Robert Baillie wrote on June 7, 1644 that 'the most of the chiefe divines here, not only Independents, but others, such as Twiss, Marshall, Palmer, and many more, are express Chiliasts'. Thomas Goodwin, Philip Nye, Jeremiah Burroughes and William Bridge were premillennial Independents, and the American Congregationalist John Cotton was postmillennial. Baillie devoted a whole chapter of his 1645 work *A Dissuasive from the Errours of the Time* to an argument that 'The Thousand Yeares of Christ his visible Raigne upon Earth is against Scripture.' William Gouge and John Lightfoot specifically opposed such millennial views in sermons before Parliament, the latter dealing with Revelation 20. James Ussher, John Selden and Lightfoot espoused the view that the thousand years of Revelation 20 ended with the coming to the papacy of Gregory VII in 1073.

Thomas Young (1587 - November 28, 1655)

In 1639 Thomas Young published, anonymously and in Latin, *Dies Dominica*, or as it was translated under Richard Baxter's auspices in 1672, *The Lords-Day ... A Succinct Narration Compiled out of the Testimonies of H. Scripture and the Reverend Ancient Fathers*. William Haller comments:

> But *Dies Dominica* was something more than a treatise of the learned on the sabbath. Behind his Latin erudition and his elaborate pseudonym, the author took advantage of his party's resentment at royal encouragement of Sunday sports in order to put forth a reasoned statement of the Puritan conception of the church. He begins, as we should expect, with preaching rather than with government. 'For,' he declares in his preface, 'so long as a door is open to hear Gods Word,' godliness will flourish, faith abound, and charity not wax cold.

Young thus was expressing an essential Puritan tenet and anticipating much of the work of the Westminster Assembly. Haller continues:

> By the time he gets to Book II, he declares that the title of bishop in the ancient church comprehended both bishops and presbyters and that the principal office of both was to preach. Indeed, 'the Bishops' work was especially to interpret the Holy Scriptures, when the Church gathered together.' So he goes on to present a Puritan statement, well buttressed by ancient learning, of the general Protestant view of the history of the church and of the relation of the church, the church fathers, councils, and historians, to the scriptures.[81]

Thomas Young was a Scot, born in 1587 in Luncarty, Perthshire, son of William Young, minister of the parishes of Luncarty and Redgorton and one of those who signed the protest of July 11, 1606 against the introduction of Episcopacy into Scotland. After attending the grammar school in Perth, Thomas entered St. Leonard's College in the University of St. Andrews, where he obtained the M.A. in July 1606.[82] Probably gaining his further theological education in Germany, he settled in London in 1612 or soon after, supporting himself by teaching and assisting Puritan ministers, including Thomas Gataker at Rotherhithe in Southwark.[83] About 1618 he was engaged by the father of John Milton to supervise the education of the nine-year-old boy. Young was his tutor for two years before Milton entered St. Paul's School in 1620, and Milton seven years later thanked him in a Latin poem for introducing him to classical poetry and expressed admiration for Young as a preacher and pastor.[84] On March 25, 1625 Milton wrote to his former teacher, telling him that he considers him 'in the light of a father,' perhaps indicating that Young had brought him to faith in Christ.[85]

In 1622 Young became chaplain to the English merchants resident in Hamburg, apparently – according to Milton's poetic expressions – forced into exile from England by the prelates.[86] Young returned in 1628, being presented on March 27 with the vicarage of St. Peter and St. Mary in Stowmarket, Suffolk. Here he served until the Westminster Assembly and renewed his friendship with the young poet.[87] After the publication of *Dies Dominica*, in 1639, Young was involved with Stephen Marshall, Edmund Calamy, Matthew Newcomen and William Spurstowe (all future members of the Assembly) in the production of responses to Bishop Joseph Hall's *Humble Remonstrance* defending Episcopacy. These responses were published in 1641-1642 under the name 'Smectymnuus', an anagram composed of their initials, Thomas Young being the 'ty'. Young was the eldest of the five contributors, and he is regarded as the ringleader. There is plausibility to this since Smectymnuus repeats much of the argument of *Dies Dominica*. Haller comments:

> That Young had the principal hand in compiling Smectymnuus' *Answer*, which is little more than a brief summary of *Dies Dominica*, to Hall's *Humble Remonstrance* is a likely inference, for which there is no definite proof .... [Robert] Baillie tells us that [Alexander] Henderson, addressing the General Assembly at Edinburgh on July 29, 1641, alluded to Young as the author of the 'Synctymnias for the most part,' but Henderson may have exaggerated the importance of the fellow-Scot he had found in the front rank of London preachers.[88]

After the Westminster Assembly was under way, Young was one of the preachers to the House of Commons on the monthly Fast Day, February 28, 1644. Entitled *Hopes Incouragement Pointed At*, his sermon was based on Psalm 31:24 and challenged the members of Parliament as 'publicke persons sharing in that *legislative* power, which hath influence upon the whole kingdome' to make no laws contrary to religion and piety. Referring to the Roman Emperor Valentinian's making a law allowing two wives so that he could marry his lover, Young said, '... how inconsistent his Law was with the Law of God, I need not speake.'[89] William Haller believes that Young included this specific illustration as an allusion to Milton's *Doctrine and Discipline of Divorce*, the second edition of which had recently appeared.[90] He believes that Young, 'surely, must have tried to argue his former pupil out of his errors before undertaking to warn parliament against "digamy".' He supposes that Milton must have been disappointed that his former fellow reformers did not take his divorce tracts seriously enough to respond to them constructively:

> Why the men of the pulpit held off so long we can only speculate. Conceivably, they held back out of consideration for a friend in error. Conceivably, too, they attached less importance to John Milton's ideas than John Milton did or than we do, and they took them up only when and as it suited their own polemic occasions. Unquestionably, they had at the time much else to think about.[91]

This last assessment was certainly true of Young. At the Assembly he was one of the few Church of England ministers who was a convinced Presbyterian from the start.[92] On May 6, 1644 he reported for a committee including Herbert Palmer and Lazarus Seaman that achieved a compromise concerning the role and number of ruling elders in a congregation:

> ... For officers in a single congregation there ought to be one at least, both to labour in the word and doctrine, and to rule; it is also requisite that there be others to join in government; and likewise it is requisite that there be others to take special care of the poor; the number of each of which is to be proportioned according to the condition of the congregation.
> This he, Mr. Palmer, and Mr. Seaman had agreed on, contriving it so that the first part, *ought to be*, might be held forth an institution, the other part, *requisite*, might be held forth as prudential conveniency for ruling elders in a congregation; for Mr. Seaman holds that there is *jus divinum* for ruling elders, but not *jus divinum* that there should be an elder in each congregation.[93]

With regard to the qualifications of ministers, Young commented on the double situation of many vacant charges and many candidates for ministry and was desirous that these candidates be allowed to preach.[94] On the other hand there was concern that they have an adequate command of Greek. Young said, that much depended on the place to which the man was designated; to which [William] Price replied, 'We may think the place obscure, yet it may have knowing people therein,' and emphasized the need to conflict with popish ideas. Then Young, much concerned about the right decision, suggested that knowledge of Greek, though perhaps not to a high standard, was necessary ....[95]

Young was on a sub-committee to do the preliminary work on the Directory of Worship, and he was asked to draw up the part dealing with the reading of Scripture and the singing of Psalms – not an inappropriate assignment for one born a Scot.[96] Young also showed himself to be among the closest to the Scottish position on Erastianism by following up George Gillespie's famous response to John Selden on February 21, 1644.[97] He was one of the select group of thirteen appointed to the 'Grand Committee' to oversee treaty obligations to the Scots.[98] He also served on several other important committees of the Assembly.[99]

While in London he was appointed to be preacher at St. James's, Duke Place, in succession to Herbert Palmer, and on March 15, 1644 the Earl of Manchester, as Chancellor of Cambridge University, appointed him Master of Jesus College. Although this was apparently against Young's will, he was installed on April 12, 1644.[100] In 1650, unable to support the Engagement in support of the republican government, he was deprived of his Mastership and appears to have lived the rest of his days in retirement at Stowmarket. He died there on November 28, 1655 at sixty-eight years of age. He was buried in the parish church beside his wife, Rebecca Manister, who had died in April 1651.[101] Their son Roger received the M.A. from Jesus College, Cambridge in 1653, was ordained by the 4th London Classis, May 24, 1654, and served as Curate of St. Nicholas, Ipswich before being ejected in 1662 and then later conforming.[102]

Joshua Hoyle (c.1590 - December 6, 1654)

Joshua Hoyle served on the various committees to prepare the Westminster Confession of Faith; according to the analysis of Jack B. Rogers, he was among the seven divines most responsible for producing the Confession, along with Edward Reynolds, Cornelius Burgess, Thomas Temple, Charles Herle, Thomas Gataker and Robert Harris.[103] Hoyle was the fifteenth most active participant in the debates on church government, behind Edmund Calamy and before Thomas Temple.[104]

He was also the only Irish divine of the Assembly.[105] Perhaps because he represented Ireland, he was chosen along with the Prolocutor to welcome the Scottish commissioners to the Assembly on September 15, 1643. He thought that the church of God united could face 'the worst concurrence of our worst brethren':

> Churches, he said, that have come through the smoke of popery are the purest churches; and the purest have prospered the best. Scotland was an instance; 'had we done as our brethren about us had, we had not had this occasion.' They needed not to say, 'Come over to Macedonia and help us'; they might say with David, 'You are come to us to help us; our hearts are knit to yours.'[106]

Hoyle was born around 1590 at Sowerby, near Halifax, Yorkshire and was educated at Magdalen College, Oxford. Invited to Ireland, probably by relatives, he became a Fellow of Trinity College, Dublin in 1609, received his D.D., and became professor of divinity there.[107] He labored there for thirty-two years, concentrating first on scholastic theology and then focusing on the study of Scripture. Lecturing daily as professor of divinity and preaching three times on most Sundays, he expounded the whole Bible in fifteen years and then covered the majority of it again in the next ten years.[108] He also spent eight years in answering the arguments of Cardinal Robert Bellarmine on the seven sacraments and followed that with further response to Bellarmine's writings.[109] In 1634 he attended the Convocation held in Dublin.

When the Irish rebellion broke out in October 1641, with the slaughter of Protestant English and Scottish men, women and children, Hoyle took refuge in London, where he became Vicar of Stepney. Some in the parish found his preaching to be 'too scholastical' and no doubt favored the sermons of the two lecturers at Stepney, Jeremiah Burroughes and William Greenhill. The House of Commons in February 1643 ordered the Provost and Fellows of Eton to bestow on Hoyle the parsonage of Sturminster-Marshall, Dorsetshire. At the trial of Archbishop William Laud he gave evidence against Laud as to his policy as Chancellor of the University of Dublin.[110]

In the Assembly Hoyle's scholarly gifts were employed in the drafting and translation from Latin of letters to the Dutch churches.[111] He chaired the committee dealing with vacant fellowships at some of the Colleges.[112] He served on the 'Grand Committee' for dealing with treaty obligations to the Scots.[113] He also served on the committee appointed in November 1644 to consider the 'Reasons' submitted by the Dissenting Brethren.[114] Hoyle originally was not convinced of the office of ruling elder, but he eventually supported Presbyterianism.[115]

In 1648 Hoyle was appointed Master of University College, Oxford and Regius Professor of Divinity. Like the several other Westminster divines appointed to Masterships of Colleges at Oxford or Cambridge, Hoyle's aim was 'to restore and confirm, not to revolutionize'. Just as John Arrowsmith recalled the tradition of John Davenant at Cambridge, so Hoyle 'devoted a large part of his inaugural lecture at Oxford to the earnest commendation of Bishop [William] Prideaux,' who had resisted much of the program of Laud at Oxford.[116]

Hoyle's scholarship was highly regarded by his predecessor at the University of Dublin, Archbishop James Ussher.[117] Dr. Edmund Calamy summarized: '... Dr. Hoyle was a member of great esteem and honour in the Assembly of Divines, as a master of all the ancient learning of the Greek and Latin fathers, and one who reigned both in his chair and in the pulpit.'[118] Hoyle died on December 6, 1654 and was buried in the old chapel of University College, Oxford.

Thomas Temple (c.1601 - 1661)

Thomas Temple was one of the seven scholars of the Westminster Assembly most responsible for the preparation of the Confession of Faith, according to Jack B. Rogers's analysis, along with Edward Reynolds, Cornelius Burgess, Charles Herle, Joshua Hoyle, Thomas Gataker and Robert Harris.[119] He was also the sixteenth most frequent speaker in the debates on church government, behind Hoyle and before George Walker.[120] He apparently chaired the Third Committee of the three working committees into which the entire Assembly was divided since he regularly reported for it.[121] S.W Carruthers, in describing the committee of Herbert Palmer, Richard Vines and Temple appointed to deal with Cornelius Burgess's difficulties in regard to the Solemn League and Covenant, refers to them as 'three very wise and brotherly men'.[122] Robert S. Paul, in describing their appointment as a committee to communicate to the House of Commons the Assembly's concerns about Antinomianism, calls Palmer, Burgess, Thomas Gataker and Temple 'four of the most respected leaders among the Assembly's conservative majority'.[123]

One of the reasons why Thomas Temple was a good choice to be a mediator between the Assembly and Parliament is that he was from the landed aristocracy, and his older brother, Sir John Temple, was a member of the House of Commons in 1646-1647.[124] The second son of Sir William Temple, Thomas Temple was born about 1601.[125] His father, from a prominent family in Warwickshire, was a Fellow of King's College, Cambridge, where he was a tutor in logic and became 'the most active champion' of the philosophy of Petrus Ramus in England. William Temple was closely associated with Sir Philip Sidney, who died in his arms on October 17, 1586. He also served several officers of Queen Elizabeth's government, in 1594 joining the household of Robert Devereux, second Earl of Essex, whom he apparently accompanied to Ireland in 1599 and 1600 after being elected to Parliament in 1597. On November 14, 1609 he was made Provost of Trinity College, Dublin at the urgent request of James Ussher. There he was an effective administrator and also defied Archbishop Abbott's requirement that he should wear a surplice in chapel, since he was a layman. Knighted on May 4, 1622, Sir William possessed much land in Ireland. His wife, Martha, was daughter of Robert Harrison of a prominent Derbyshire family.[126]

From such a background, Thomas Temple entered Trinity College, Dublin in 1615 and received his B.A. in 1620 and M.A. in 1623. He became a Fellow of Trinity College in 1620 and probably served there until March 6, 1627 when he became Rector of Old Ross parish in the Irish diocese of Ferns, Wexfordshire.[127] He apparently resided in Lincoln College, Oxford from about 1628 to around 1634, receiving his D.D. there in 1639. He became Vicar of Battersea, Surrey in the vicinity of London in 1634.[128]

He evidently achieved a reputation as a Puritan preacher, for he was invited to preach to the House of Commons on the monthly Fast Day of October 26, 1642. His sermon, based on Psalm 2:6, was entitled *Christ's Government In and Over His People* and urged the abolishing of Episcopacy.[129] He preached to the House of Lords a year later on the occasion of their taking the Covenant on October 15, 1643.[130] He preached to the Lords again on October 22, 1644 for the extraordinary humiliation on behalf of the Parliamentary armies.[131] He also preached to the Commons on September 24, 1645, to a joint gathering of both Houses of Parliament on August 31, 1647, and to the Lords on December 27, 1648.[132]

Temple's role in the Assembly shows him to have been a very

cautious, careful and businesslike member. He questioned whether the Assembly had warrant to report its progress to the Scottish General Assembly, and he wanted every word of such a report to be carefully weighed.[133] He urged that the Assembly's business proceed with dispatch, moving that they no longer set apart one day a week 'for our own private employments'. He said, 'One cause of our slow proceeding is our inconstancy; let us go through with whatsoever we undertake.'[134] Concerned for accurate record-keeping, he at one point 'aspersed' the scribe for 'not setting down his name' as present.[135] He cautioned that candidates for the ministry should not be admitted without full academic qualifications 'except in cases of necessity'.[136]

He played an important role in the effort to identify the sins of the Assembly, of the armies, of the people, and of Parliament in September 1644, and then made the motion that sent this action back to committee, in effect killing it before the extraordinary humiliation of October.[137] He made a lengthy speech concerning the keys of church government, arguing against the Independents that power was given by Christ to the Apostles, not to the community of the faithful.[138] Along with such conservatives as Charles Herle, Cornelius Burgess, Lazarus Seaman, Herbert Palmer, Edmund Calamy and John White, he preferred to restrict the public reading of the Scriptures to the clergy, whereas Stephen Marshall and the Scots wanted more latitude.[139]

Concerning the administration of the Lord's Supper, Temple resisted the Independents' desire to restrict admission: '... you put it under the power of every particular man to put a whole parish from the sacrament.'[140] He was one of the few that Robert Baillie recognized from the beginning of the Assembly as supporting Scottish discipline,[141] yet he at first opposed the office of ruling elder.[142] Not belonging to any faction, he sometimes sided with the Independents. At one point he engaged in a long debate with John Lightfoot, opposing the idea that the number of converts in Jerusalem in the book of Acts meant that the church there was a presbytery.[143] Perhaps because of his ability to think for himself, he was assigned to the 'sub-committee of Agreements' to work out with the Independents the broad areas of agreement and specific points of difference.[144] Temple also served on the 'Grand Committee' for dealing with the treaty obligations with the Scots and on several other important committees, including the committee to prepare the petition to Parliament in March 1646 concerning the divine right of church censures.[145]

In 1648 Temple joined with other Presbyterian ministers of London in opposing the trial of Charles I,[146] but not much is known about his activities after the Westminster Assembly. What is known is that he purchased an estate of 750 acres in County Westmeath, Ireland. He died in 1661, leaving two daughters by his wife, Anne, who was of a Reading family. He was buried in the Church of St. Lawrence, Reading.[147]

Anthony Tuckney (September 1599 - February 1670)

Anthony Tuckney, Matthew Newcomen, Jeremiah Whitaker and John Arrowsmith 'played the largest supporting roles' to the seven Westminster divines who, according to Jack B. Rogers's analysis, were primarily responsible for preparation of the Confession of Faith.[148] The committee that did the final work on the Shorter Catechism, from October 19, 1646 to November 25, 1647, was chaired by Tuckney and included Stephen Marshall and John Ward with the help of Samuel Rutherford. William Carruthers concludes: 'It is to these four men, and especially to the convener, Mr. Tuckney, that we owe the production of the Shorter Catechism.'[149] Anthony Tuckney is also credited with contributing the wording for the very full exposition of the Ten Commandments in the Larger Catechism.[150] Discussing Tuckney along with his Westminster and Cambridge colleague John Arrowsmith, Alexander F. Mitchell says that these Professors of Divinity 'were not only clever college tutors, but, as several of their published works clearly indicate, men of high scholarship and considerable mental breadth, and force of character.'[151]

Tuckney was born at Kirton, three miles south of Boston in Lincolnshire, where his father William Tuckney was Vicar. He was baptized on September 22, 1599. On June 4, 1613 he was admitted to Emmanuel College, Cambridge and received the B.A. in 1617 and the M.A. in 1620. He served for a time as household chaplain to Theophilus Clinton, fourth Earl of Lincoln. Elected a Fellow of Emmanuel College in 1619, he established himself as a distinguished tutor, Benjamin Whichcote being among his pupils. He gained the B.D. in 1627, and on October 2, 1629 he was elected 'town preacher', or lecturer, at Boston, where his cousin's husband, John Cotton, was Vicar of St. Botolph's, the largest parish church in England.[152] When Cotton resigned in order to emigrate to America, Tuckney was chosen to succeed him on July 22, 1633. In 1635 he founded a library in a room over the church porch, contributing many books to it. He ministered faithfully to his parishioners during the plague of 1637.

His personal life was not without grief in Boston, for his first wife, Mary, was buried there October 26, 1633, and his second wife, Elizabeth, bore him a son, John, who was baptized December 3, 1635 and died in 1636. They would later have a son, Jonathan, born December 13, 1638, who would receive his arts degrees from St. John's College, Cambridge and be elected a Fellow there in 1657 before being ejected for Nonconformity after the Restoration. There was also a daughter, Mary, who in 1652 married John Whitlock, later a Nonconforming minister. After Elizabeth's death Tuckney married Mary (Willford), the widow of his Westminster and Cambridge colleague Thomas Hill, who had died on December 18, 1653. When Mary also died, he married on September 30, 1668 his fourth wife, Sarah, the widow of another Westminster and Cambridge colleague, William Spurstowe.[153]

When appointed to the Westminster Assembly, he moved his

OTHER THEOLOGICAL DIFFERENCES IN THE ASSEMBLY

The Westminster divines were generally good Calvinists, but they were able to allow for differences in areas that were deemed secondary. Besides the millennial question, they allowed for differences of opinion on such matters as the logical order of the decrees of God, leaving room for supralapsarians as well as infralapsarians. One of the interesting debates in the summer of 1643 pertained to the question of the imputation of Christ's active obedience, as well as his passive obedience, to the believer in justification. Daniel Featley, echoing Archbishop James Ussher, argued for the imputation of Christ's active obedience. Ranged against him were such figures as William Twisse, Thomas Gataker and Richard Vines, who contended that it was Christ's passive obedience alone that was imputed to the believer for justification. Such formidable theologians succeeded in getting the term '*whole* obedience' removed from the phrase 'imputing the obedience and satisfaction of Christ unto them' in Chapter XI of the Westminster Confession, but the imputation of Christ's active obedience was thus included; and in the Savoy Declaration, under John Owen's influence, it would be sharpened into 'Christ's active obedience unto the whole law, and passive obedience in his death for their whole and sole righteousness'. The Westminster divines, in such controversies, sought to be clear and faithful to Scriptural language, yet to allow for shades of difference within a generic Calvinism.

family to London. Although he would not reside in Boston again, the church desired him to retain the vicarage; however, he transferred the salary to the curate in charge. In London he received the rectory of St. Michael-le-Querne, Cheapside. At the Assembly he was one of those who was gradually persuaded of Presbyterianism from a moderate Episcopacy.[154] He served actively, participating on many committees, including the one to deal with Antinomianism, the 'Grand Committee' for dealing with treaty obligations to the Scots, the committee to prepare the Directory for Ordination (for which some special negotiations with the House of Commons were necessary), the committee to consider the 'Reasons' given by the Independents, and several other committees.[155] As already mentioned, he played a major role in producing the Confession of Faith and the Larger and Shorter Catechisms.

On April 11, 1645 the Assembly approved Tuckney's appointment as Master of Emmanuel College, and he then spent some months each year in Cambridge. In the push to finish the Shorter Catechism in the autumn of 1647, the University gave him a leave of absence to finish that important work.[156] In 1648, the dogmatic work of the Assembly being completed, he moved his family to Cambridge, resigning his London rectory. That year he served as Vice-Chancellor of the University, and in 1649 he received the D.D. From September to November 1651 occurred his 'memorable correspondence' with Benjamin Whichcote, 'in whose preaching he noted "a vein of doctrine" which made him uneasy, as tending to rationalism.'[157] Whichcote, his former pupil, was Vice-Chancellor of Cambridge in 1650-51, and was a leader of the Cambridge Platonists. Tuckney's four letters to him were published with responses in Whichcote's *Moral and Religious Aphorisms*. On June 3, 1653 Tuckney became Master of St. John's College in place of John Arrowsmith, and he again acted as Vice-Chancellor of the University that year. He became Regius Professor of Divinity and, as such, also Rector of Somersham, Huntingdonshire. Although not self-assertive (Richard Baxter termed him 'over humble') Tuckney proved a strong administrator of St. John's College. Dr. Edmund Calamy said that he showed 'more courage in opposing orders sent by the higher powers in those times than any of the heads of the university, nay, more than all of them'. There was a tradition at St. John's that Tuckney, in elections of Fellows, 'was determined to choose none but scholars, adding very wisely, they may deceive me in their godliness, they cannot in their scholarship.'[158]

Tuckney continued to be active as a churchman. While Rector of St. Michael-le-Querne he was a member of the Presbyterian Fifth London Classis.[159] In March 1654 he was appointed one of Cromwell's 'Triers' for the examination of candidates for ministry.[160] He corresponded with John Cotton in New England, being concerned for the conversion of the Indians there and raising contributions at the University for the propagation of the gospel in America.[161]

Tuckney was himself a notable preacher. He gave a Fast Day sermon before the House of Commons on August 30, 1643, based on Jeremiah 8:22 and entitled *The Balm of Gilead for the Wounds of England*.[162] He preached again before the House of Lords on April 28, 1647.[163] He also preached the funeral sermon of his colleague Thomas Hill on December 22, 1653, which was published as *Death Disarmed; and the Grave Swallowed up in Victory*, based on I Corinthians 15:55.[164] In the Assembly Tuckney had criticized the traditional Puritan style of preaching, opposing preaching 'by doctrine, reason, and use, as too strait for the variety of gifts, and occasion doth claim liberty.'[165] John H. Leith comments on Tuckney's preaching:

After Tuckney's death, forty of his sermons were published by his son. The sermons belie the criticisms that are sometimes made of the Westminster Confession. They are warm-hearted, practical, and strongly Biblical in character. Christian faith must be embodied in life. Propositions are never adequate statements of the faith. 'Logic Rules do not circumscribe God, nor should our reason.' '*Theologia* is not *scienta speculativa* but *practica*.' 'Divinity is an art of living.' In death all learning is lost. The notes of scholars may do others some good, but they do not help the dead.[166]

Tuckney's own death came only after some further sufferings. With the Restoration he was deprived of his positions at Cambridge although he was given a pension. In September 1661 he moved to London, occasionally preaching privately. When the plague struck in 1665, he was guest of Robert Pierrepont at Colwick Hall, near Nottingham, where he was for some months under house arrest for preaching as a nonconformist. Under the restrictions of the Five-Mile Act he moved about, to Oundle and Warrington in Northamptonshire and then, after his library was burned in the great fire of 1666, to Stockerston, Leicestershire and Tottenham, Middlesex before returning to London in 1669 in bad health. There he died in Spital Yard of jaundice and scurvy in February 1670, being buried on March 1 in the church of St. Andrew Undershaft.[167]

Anthony Tuckney's spirit is perhaps best shown in one of his letters to Benjamin Whichcote in which he saw the Westminster Standards as a guide to Scriptural truth and a guard against false teaching:

> In the Assembly I gave my vote with others, that the Confession of Faith, putt-out by Authorities, should not bee required to bee eyther sworne or subscribed too. Wee having bin burnt in the hand in that kind before: but so as not to be publically preached or written against; which is indeed contrarie to that liberty of prophesying which some call for; but, you say, you plead not for; though your second advice in your sermon seemed, in mine and other men's eyes, to look fullie that way ....[168]

Among Tuckney's other publications were a catechism (1628) for use at Emmanuel College, some verses in University collections (including an elegy on Cromwell), and his editions of *John Cotton on Ecclesiastes* (1654) and on *Canticles* (1655). Published posthumously by his son in 1679 was his *Praelectiones Theologicae; Theological Exercises and Lectures in the University*, in which there is a dissertation against propagating religion by the sword.

Edward Reynolds (November 1599 - July 28, 1676)

Edward Reynolds is one of the seven Westminster divines that Jack B. Rogers identifies as most responsible for producing the Confession of Faith. In fact Rogers singles him out as the person who provided continuity through the various committees that drafted the Confession:

> Edward Reynolds is the one person who was a member of all three committees for the Confession of Faith. He belonged to the original large committee [of nineteen, with four later additions] having been appointed on September 4, 1644. He was a member of the drafting committee [of seven divines]. And he was the first chosen for the committee [of three, with four later additions] for rewording and perfecting the Confession. Thus Reynolds is the one man who could be said to have provided continuity during the development of the Confession of Faith over a period of two years and three months.[169]

Rogers acknowledges that Cornelius Burgess, Thomas Temple, Charles

Herle, Joshua Hoyle, Thomas Gataker and Robert Harris played a role practically equal to that of Reynolds. He also acknowledges that Matthew Newcomen, Anthony Tuckney, Jeremiah Whitaker and John Arrowsmith and the four Scots, Alexander Henderson, Robert Baillie, George Gillespie and Samuel Rutherford, were major supporters in this work. It is ironic, however, that the one who seems to have contributed most to the Presbyterian doctrinal confession was the only Westminster divine to become a bishop after the Restoration and one of only four who were active in the Assembly who conformed.[170]

Son of Augustine Reynolds, described as a 'customer' of the port of Southampton, Edward Reynolds was born in November 1599 and attended Southampton grammar school. He entered Merton College, Oxford on January 26, 1616. There he excelled in Greek, receiving the B.A. on October 15, 1618, becoming a Fellow in 1619, and gaining the M.A. on July 10, 1624. In 1627 he preached a sermon at Merton College in which he took the side of John Prideaux against the Arminian Peter Heylin. In 1628 he was appointed one of the chaplains of King Charles I.[171] That year he also became one of the preachers at Lincoln's Inn as a successor to John Preston.[172] In 1631 he became Rector of Braunston, Northamptonshire, resigning his prominent preaching post at Lincoln's Inn.

When the Civil War began, he was recognized as a Calvinist who was also a moderate in church polity. Appointed to the Westminster Assembly, he began participation in the summer of 1643 but did not take the Covenant until March 1644. His moderation and concern for the unity of the church showed in his Fast Day sermon before the House of Commons on July 27, 1642, *Israels Petition in Time of Trouble*.[173] In another sermon published in 1642, *Eugenia's Tears for Great Brittaynes Distractions*, he sought to recall England from the Laudian innovations and divisions of the 1630s to her Reformation past.[174] In his summons to peace and conciliation he was an exception to most of the preaching of the time.[175] His nineteenth-century Anglican biographer comments:

> He was one of the very few *public* preachers, during the Usurpation, who did not carry the ever-varying events of the time into the pulpit. From strong political bias he was preserved both by principle and temper. Although living in an age when there was no choice but of extremes, he passed between them with as much caution as could have been expected from human infirmity.[176]

This spirit of moderation may account for the Assembly's selecting him, along with Herbert Palmer, to preach on the day of humiliation for its own business, October 8, 1645. He preached from Matthew 16:24, 'If any man will come after me, let him deny himself':

> In his concluding exhortation he exclaimed, 'Oh, that when the church is in a flame, any should come with a mind to serve their own turns by the common fire.' They should deny their opinions rather than hinder the peace of the church. 'A divided ministry is fomented by the episcopal interest; but whence is it that we still have a divided ministry?' 'When sheep push and run heads against one another, it is a foretoken of ill weather.' They must sacrifice their private affairs, for their friends expected haste, and their enemies derided their slowness; the eyes of the churches abroad were upon them.... 'Some men have excellent abilities of copious and fluent speaking ... a felicity which I so much the more honour and admire wherever I find it, by how much the greater my own inability of digesting or uttering mine own conceptions. Yet considering the necessity of hastening the work which we have before us, I humbly conceive it were fitter to speak as Aristotle than Cicero; concise arguments than copious orations.'[177]

BISHOP REYNOLDS

In the Assembly Reynolds was regarded as one of those who were supportive of the Scottish discipline from the beginning and who were soon persuaded of the Presbyterian position.[178] Although he did not speak much in the general debates, he played a very active part in committee work. He served on the 'Grand Committee' dealing with the treaty obligations to the Scots.[179] On September 4, 1644 he was among the ten men added to the nine-man committee on the Confession which had been appointed just fifteen days earlier.[180] He served on the committee to consider the 'Reasons' offered by the Independents and on the committee to respond to Parliament concerning the divine right of church government.[181] Time and again his moderation reached for accommodation between differing parties.[182] Alexander F. Mitchell suggests:

> Dr. Edward Reynolds was a divine 'eloquent, learned, cautious,' and that
> may have been the reason why the Assembly devolved on a committee of
> which he was convener the adjusting of those much-maligned sentences in
> their Confession regarding predestination and preterition.[183]

In 1647 Reynolds participated in the visitation of Oxford University. Having received the D.D. on April 12, in 1648 he became Vice-Chancellor of the University as well as Dean of Christ Church College. Toward the end of 1650 he was ejected from the deanery for refusing to take the Engagement in support of the new republican government. For a time he devoted his attention to supervising a reissue of the Confession of Faith.[184] In 1656 he was elected unanimously by the vestry of St. Lawrence Jewry to succeed the deceased Richard Vines as Vicar, so his voice was heard again in London. In that same year he preached to Parliament, urging

> all men who 'agree in the main fundamental Doctrines of truth and
> godliness, in the substantials of Faith, Worship and Obedience' to live in
> 'mutual love, toleration and forbearance of one another in differences
> which are not subversive unto faith and godliness'....[185]

Following the death of Oliver Cromwell on September 3, 1658, Reynolds became a leader of the Presbyterian clergy. He preached to Richard Cromwell's Parliament several times in 1659 and '60, counseling the suppression of radical opinions with the warning, 'who knows in combustible matters, and in dubious and discontented times, how great a flame a few such sparks may kindle?'[186] At the same time he called for mutual tolerance of differences on secondary issues when 'the foundation and necessary doctrines of law and gospel, of faith and worship and obedience are safe ....':

> If undue passions and exasperations happen, the Christian magistrate may interpose by his authority to forbid and moderate them. He may ... call colloquies wherein there may be a fraternal and amicable debate and composure of them. And if after all this, differences be not perfectly healed ... brethren must mutually bear with one another and pray for one another, and love one another; whereunto they have already attained they must walk by the same rule and mind the same things, and wherein they yet differ, wait humbly upon God to reveal his will unto them; *where one and the same straight road to heaven is kept, a small difference of paths does not hinder travelers from coming to the same inn at night.*[187]

When General George Monck was marching on London from the north, early in 1660, to put down the armies that had expelled Richard Cromwell's Rump Parliament, Reynolds 'led a group of sixty-two Presbyterian divines of London in issuing a public declaration, in which they condemned the sectarian groups for the dangerous state of religion and urged an understanding with the Anglicans.'[188]

It is in this context that Reynolds worked with the Convention Parliament of 1660 and with other Presbyterian leaders such as Edmund Calamy, Richard Baxter and Thomas Manton to restore the monarchy and to see the kind of moderate Episcopacy that Archbishop Ussher had earlier proposed established in the Church of England. With the Restoration, Calamy was offered the Bishopric of Lichfield and Coventry, Baxter that of Hereford, and Reynolds that of Norwich. After consultation with Baxter and Calamy, who declined, Reynolds accepted, expecting Charles II to keep to the agreements he had made and perhaps expecting that still others of the Presbyterians would be appointed, in both of which expectations he was disappointed.[189]

Richard Baxter later described Reynolds as 'a solid, honest man, but through mildness and excess of timorous reverence to great men, altogether unfit to contend with them ....'[190] Anthony à Wood, though claiming he had a hoarse voice, said, 'Dr. Reynolds was a person of excellent parts and endowments, of a very good wit, fancy and judgment, a great divine, and much esteemed by all parties for his preaching and florid style.' Daniel Neal said that 'he was reckoned one of the most eloquent pulpit men of his age, and a good old Puritan, who never concerned himself with the politics of the Court.'[191] Of the modern assessments of Reynolds, George Abernathy says:

> ... that branch of the Presbyterian party led by Edward Reynolds was ready to live in peace with the Anglicans. ... He was a true Puritan, and of the Puritans he had become less involved in controversy than any other .... Reynolds, in reference to most of the Presbyterians, stood at the extreme right of his party.[192]

Paul Seaver concludes:

> He pursued a moderate course at the Savoy Conference and was moderate thereafter in his treatment of dissenters. In an age of fierce partisanship his life presents rather an unheroic picture, but the popularity he enjoyed with his London vestrymen suggests that moderation in doctrine and action was regarded as a virtue by many of the laity.[193]

Interestingly, although Reynolds became a bishop, he stressed the role of the laity in critiquing their ministers' sermons.[194] As Bishop of Norwich for fifteen years, Reynolds was exceedingly gentle in his treatment of dissenters. Dr. Edmund Calamy, in his catalog of ejected ministers, 'has not advanced a single instance of oppression in the diocese of Norwich; on the contrary, in one or two instances where he has occasion to notice the bishop's conduct, he speaks of him with respect.'[195] Reynolds and other Presbyterian conformists like him 'became the progenitors of a Low Church party, remaining loyal to Puritan ideals and favouring the comprehension of Dissenters within the [Anglican] Church.'[196]

Reynolds had for many years 'suffered much by the stone and gravel.'[197] He had had to be absent from the Westminster Assembly on account of sickness from May-July 9, 1646.[198] After sustained illness he died on July 28, 1676 at the Palace, Norwich and was buried in the chapel, where there is a monument to his memory. His widow, Mary, most likely the daughter of John Harding, who had been President of Magdalen College, Oxford, went to live at Kingsthorpe, Northamptonshire with their son, Edward Reynolds (1629-1698), who was Archdeacon of Norfolk. She died on September 29, 1683, at the age of seventy-three.[199] Their youngest daughter, Elizabeth, married John Conant, a minister ejected in 1662, but who later conformed.

Among Reynolds' publications, *The Sinfulness of Sin* has been recently reprinted by Soli Deo Gloria publishers of Ligonier, Pennsylvania. The 1829 edition of his *Works* comprised six volumes. He provided the commentary on Ecclesiastes in the *English Annotations*. Philip Doddridge said that Edward Reynolds' works 'are most elaborate both in thought and expression. Few men are more happy in the choice of their similitudes. He was popular, affable, meek and humble, of great learning, and a frequent preacher.'[200]

Edmund Staunton (October 20, 1600 - July 14, 1671)

After the Westminster Assembly organized its entire membership of divines into three major working committees, the Second Committee chose as its chairman Dr. Edmund Staunton.[201] This no doubt represented respect for his scholarly attainments since he had gained the D.D. at Corpus Christi College, Oxford in 1634. In 1648 he would become President of Corpus Christi and serve in that capacity until 1660. He was equally recognized for his preaching and evident deep piety. Known as 'the searching preacher,' he was one of the seven chosen to lead the early morning daily exercises at Westminster Abbey, 'whereby many that lived in darkness and ignorance for many years together do now see the light of the gospel more clearly and plainly than ever ....'[202]

Staunton was born on October 20, 1600 at Woburn, Bedfordshire, a younger son of Francis (later to be Sir Francis) Staunton, who provided for his education. He entered Wadham College, Oxford on June 9, 1615, but transferred to Corpus Christi by October 4. While still an undergraduate, he was chosen a probationary Fellow before eighteen of his seniors in the College.[203] It was at this stage of his life that he experienced two nearly fatal incidents, one when a drunken surgeon was unable to open a vein to relieve his pleurisy and the other when, not being able to swim, he almost drowned when he went into the water alone to wash himself. His friend and later biographer, Richard Mayo, records what was in Staunton's diary:

> About the year 1620, I had many sad and serious thoughts concerning my spiritual and eternal state. Then upon the advice of Dr. Barcroft, I

bought Brinsley's *Watch*, the second part; where the sins against the Commandments are set down in order, and I fell upon the work of examination; wherein this seems remarkable, that, reading over the several sins there mentioned, my heart (such was the blindness and deceitfulness of it) cried not guilty of any one of them: Whereupon I began to suspect my heart, and calling upon God to enlighten mine eyes, and discover my sins to me, and then reading them over again, I judged myself guilty, very guilty, even of most of the sins there set down and enumerated.[204]

After gaining the B.A. in 1620 and the M.A. in 1623, Staunton was given the choice by his father of one of the three learned professions; lawyer, physician, or preacher. He chose the last, saying 'that he had for some time past inclined his studies that way, and that he esteemed the turning of souls to righteousness to be the most desireable work in the world ....'[205] His first preaching was as Sunday-afternoon lecturer at Witney, Oxfordshire for about six months. He was very acceptable to the people, who flocked to hear him, but not to the Rector, who increased the time for reading the service so that Staunton might have less time for preaching. On April 19, 1627 he became Rector of Bushey, Hertfordshire, where, as a minister of nearby Watford later reported, many persons 'acknowledged his ministry to be the means of their conversion'.[206]

About this time he married the daughter of a Mr. Scudamore of Watford, who bore him one daughter before her death. He subsequently married Mary, daughter of Richard Balthrop, Esq., who bore him many children, ten of whom evidently died in infancy or childhood, all of them being buried in one grave in Kingston-upon-Thames.[207] Two children survived: one son, Francis, became a draper in London, and another, Thomas, became an Anglican minister.[208]

It was at Kingston-upon-Thames, Surrey, that his pastoral ministry came to full fruition. The Rector there, Dr. Seaton, desired Staunton's valuable living at Bushey, and found some legal fault with his title at that church. After some legal negotiations an exchange was worked out, so that Staunton was officially established as Vicar of Kingston by February 14, 1633 although his ministry of about twenty years there probably began a few years earlier.[209] He preached twice on Sundays, catechized the young and the ignorant, taught from house to house, and set up a weekly lecture supplied by several eminent preachers in that part of England, only ten miles from London. His own earnest style of preaching and praying was particularly effective in working conversions:

> When preaching once at Warborough, near Oxford, one person of the congregation was so affected with his first prayer, that he ran to his own house (which was at a short distance), and told his wife, that she should make herself ready and come to church, for there was one in the pulpit who prayed like an angel, so as he never heard the like. The woman hastened away with her husband; and God so ordered, that this sermon proved a mean of her conversion, and she proved afterward a serious and eminent Christian.[210]

During the Westminster Assembly Staunton preached to the House of Commons on the Fast Day of April 24, 1644 a sermon entitled *Rupes Israelis; the Rock of Israel,* based on Deuteronomy 32:31.[211] On the crucial Fast Day of October 30, 1644, before the trial of Archbishop Laud, Staunton preached before the House of Lords on Psalm 106:30, *Phinehas's Zeal in Execution of Judgment: or a Divine Remedy for England's Misery,* the Lords having given the Assembly the right to choose the preachers for that day. The doctrines which he derived from his text, 'Then stood up Phinehas, and executed judgment: and so the plague was stayed,' were as follows:

> [1] The Magistrates due and regular execution of justice bindeth not up Gods hands from pouring out of his wrath upon his enemies, in wayes something strange and extraordinary.
> [2] When God hath work to do, he can finde out workmen, a Phinehas.
> [3 & 4] Execution of judgment, is Gods way to pacifie Gods wrath and to stay his judgements.[212]

Alexander Mitchell argues that this sermon was not referring specifically to Laud, but rather was like several of the following year, after Laud's execution on January 10, 1645, expressing the general principle that those who shed innocent blood can only atone for it by their own.[213] Hugh Trevor-Roper, however, makes a strong case for Staunton's being very conscious of the current situation, with the House of Lords serving as the Archbishop of Canterbury's judges. The preacher made reference to the City of London's petition for the blood of delinquents and concluded his sermon:

and now, could I lift up my voice as a trumpet, had I the shrill cry of an angel which might be heard from east to west, from north to south, in all the corners of the kingdom, my note should be *Execution of Justice, Execution of Justice, Execution of Justice!* That is God's way to pacify wrath: *Then stood up Phinehas and executed judgment, and so the plague was stayed.*[214]

Alexander Mitchell admits that, although the depth of feeling against Laud at the time was understandable 'when the memory of his rigor and cruelty was fresh, it will not be all but universally admitted to have been a blunder as well as a crime' to execute the old man who could no longer do any harm. He argues that 'more than almost any other single occurrence,' the execution of Laud hurt the Parliamentary cause and destroyed for a generation all hope of honorable compromise among the religious leaders on both sides.[215]

Edmund Staunton was but one of numerous voices uttering sentiments of judgment on that occasion, but his was a strong voice, and it carried influence in the Assembly on other issues. He began as one who was not yet fully persuaded of Presbyterianism, but as he brought in report after report from the Second Committee on such distinctive points as the ruling elder, the right of appeal to higher church courts, and the proper source of ordination, his own commitment to Presbyterianism seems to have become increasingly firm.[216] Consistent with his deep piety, Staunton desired that ordination should be conferred with fasting as well as prayer, but others objected, Lazarus Seaman pointing out that 'This will make the people say, that those who were not ordained with fasting were not rightly ordained.'[217]

When Cromwell's army purged Parliament of Presbyterians in December 1648 and prepared for the trial of the King in January, Staunton was one of the signers of *A Vindication of the Ministers in, and about London* opposing those actions.[218] He was, however, able to accept the Engagement in 1650, and on June 15, 1652 he was nominated by a committee of Parliament to be on the new Board of Visitors. He continued to serve as President of Corpus Christi College, Oxford, also preaching wherever he could.[219] One of his pupils in this time was Joseph Alleine, who became an effective minister in Taunton, Somersetshire, emulating Staunton in fervent piety and in sharp reproof of sin.[220]

With the Restoration, Staunton was ejected from his position at

Oxford on August 3, 1660. He went first to Rickmansworth, Hertfordshire, where he found some opportunity to preach. By the Act of
Uniformity of August 1662 he was silenced, but he still found places
to preach to a few in private homes, in St. Alban's and finally in the
village of Bovingden, Hertfordshire, all these places being northwest
of London, where, it is reported, he had been 'pastor of a celebrated
meeting house at Salters' Hall, which was built on purpose for him.'[221]

At Bovingden he was stricken with palsy, all on one side, on July 8,
1671. His speech began to fail him, but he could still utter such
expressions of faith as 'I know that my Redeemer liveth' for the next
few days. On July 10 he was deprived of any use of speech and 'lay four
days seemingly in a very comfortable condition, lifting up his eyes and
hands toward heaven, with a smiling and cheerful countenance.'
Shortly before death, when a minister prayed with him, 'he took the
minister by the hand, and held it fast, expressing his inward joy in God,
and thanks to him, by outward signs.'[222] He died on July 14, 1671.

Edmund Staunton was not only a scholar and a preacher, but a man
of prayer. His friend Richard Mayo, who was his Curate and then
successor at Kingston, said, 'He was the most praying Christian that
ever I was acquainted with.' He commonly wept in his prayers, in
public as well as private. He ordinarily conducted his prayers kneeling,
'even when he was almost overwhelmed by the multitude around him.'
He said that the 'humblest gesture, as well as spirit, became the duty of
prayer; and that he knew no way of wrestling with the Almighty, like
that of lying at his feet, and prostrating ourselves before him.'[223] His
publications, beside a few sermons, were *A Dialogue between a
Minister and a Stranger about Soul Affairs* and *A Treatise of Christian
Conference*, both published at the end of Richard Mayo's biography in
1671.[224]

William Spurstowe (c.1605-January or February 1666)

William Spurstowe, although slightly younger than the other academ-
ics of the Westminster Assembly, was another recognized scholar, who
was appointed Master of Catherine Hall, Cambridge in 1645 and
received the D.D. in 1649. He preached several times before Parliament
during the Assembly, but he is probably best known for his involvement in the production of the anti-Episcopal tracts under the name
Smectymnuus, along with Stephen Marshall, Edmund Calamy,

Thomas Young and Matthew Newcomen, the last three letters 'UUS' representing his initials.

Spurstowe was born around 1605, the son and heir of William Spurstowe, a London citizen and mercer who would later become a member of the Long Parliament.[225] He was admitted to Emmanuel College, Cambridge in 1623 and received the B.A. in 1627, but he moved to Catherine Hall, or St. Catherine's College, and received the M.A. in 1630, about which time he also became a Fellow there.[226] He served as Fellow at St. Catherine's from around 1630 to 1637, along with such other eventual members of the Assembly as Thomas Goodwin, John Arrowsmith, Andrew Perne and William Strong, under the Mastership of the Puritan Richard Sibbes and then of Ralph Brownrigg, later Bishop of Exeter, who was nominated for the Westminster Assembly but asked to be excused.[227] From this budding Puritan institution he accepted the call to the rectory of Great Hampden, Buckinghamshire, the church of the Parliamentary leader John Hampden. He was officially installed on June 30, 1638 but probably began his services there in August 1637.[228]

In 1641 the Smectymnuan tracts appeared in response to Bishop Joseph Hall's *Remonstrance* in defence of divine-right Episcopacy. The specific role of Spurstowe in producing these is not known, but it means that at the beginning of the Westminster Assembly he was among the English divines who most strongly favored Presbyterianism.[229] Shortly before the Assembly convened, he became Vicar of Hackney, Middlesex on May 3, 1643, replacing Calybute Downing, who had been nominated for the Assembly but died early in 1643.[230]

In the course of the Assembly Spurstowe preached before Parliament on four occasions. On July 21, 1643 he preached to a joint gathering of Lords and Commons for a special day of fasting and humiliation. John Hampden had been killed in battle on June 18, and the military campaign was not going well. Preaching from 1 Samuel 7:6, Spurstowe entitled his sermon *England's Pattern and Duty in its Monthly Fasts* and called for a passionate, rather than merely rational, sorrow: 'Did you not take this day to afflict your soules before God, as not knowing whether you might see any more the returne of your monthly Fasts, so exceedingly did the wrath of God hasten its progresse against you?'[231]

On November 5, 1644, the anniversary of the Gunpowder Plot of 1605, he preached to the House of Lords *England's eminent Judgments caused by the abuse of God's eminent Mercies*, based on Ezra 9:13, 14. Tai Liu describes how he

> admonished the House of Lords to show their zeal for reformation 'in suppressing of those monstrous births of opinions which every day multiply.' 'Let no religion,' he said in a moving, eloquent passage, 'which should be like the seamless coate of Christ, be like a beggars cloake, which hath a thousand patches in it.' Then using another biblical metaphor, Spurstowe continued, the Church which was 'the enclosed garden of Christ' must not be allowed, like a sluggard's field, to be overrun 'with so many noisome and poysonous weeds, which in a short time will eat out the very life and power of holiness.'[232]

Spurstowe also preached to the House of Commons on June 24, 1646 and to the House of Lords on August 25, 1647.[233] On October 30, 1653, when the Independents were looking for help against the Fifth Monarchy Men, he preached to the Lord Mayor and Aldermen of London *The Magistrate's Dignity and Duty*, based on Psalm 82:2, in which he recalled some of the anarchy produced by Anabaptists in Germany.[234]

In the Westminster Assembly itself Spurstowe seems not to have played a major role, perhaps because he was appointed Master of Catherine Hall, Cambridge on May 12, 1645 and had to attend to duties at the University.[235] He was on the committee to consider the 'Reasons' offered by the Independents.[236] He also was one of the clergy appointed as commissioners to confer with King Charles I in the Isle of Wight between September and November 1648.[237] Interestingly, along with Cornelius Burgess, Edmund Calamy and Stephen Marshall, he did not wish to share in the distribution of money made to the Assembly on April 7, 1645, 'being a man of independent fortune.'[238] He was among the signers of *A Vindication of the Ministers of the Gospel in, and about London* at the end of 1648 which opposed the anticipated trial and execution of the King.[239] As pastor of the church in Hackney, Middlesex, he was a member of the Presbyterian 8th Classis of London along with Thomas Manton. On July 10, 1656 he preached the funeral sermon of Lady Honor Vyner, who had been wife of Sir Thomas Vyner, Alderman (1646-65), Sheriff (1648-49) and Lord Mayor (1653-54) of London.[240]

Spurstowe had refused the 'Engagement' of allegiance to the government without King or House of Lords, and therefore he was deprived of his Mastership of St. Catherine's in March 1650. In

November it was given to John Lightfoot. At the Restoration, Lightfoot offered to resign the Mastership in Spurstowe's favor, but he declined.[241] In 1658-1660 he was very much involved with Edward Reynolds, Edmund Calamy, Simeon Ashe, Thomas Case, Thomas Manton and other Presbyterian ministers in seeking to serve the Parliament of Richard Cromwell.[242] He assisted in the negotiations with Charles II, going to Holland on May 11, 1660 with Reynolds, Calamy, Case and Manton.[243] He was one of nine or ten Presbyterians appointed Royal Chaplains, and he was one of only four of them who preached before Charles II.[244] In the discussions toward an accommodation of religious parties he was a commissioner to the Savoy Conference of April-July 1661. It was at Spurstowe's house in Hackney that Richard Baxter drafted the Presbyterian ministers' response to the Bishops' defence of the Book of Common Prayer, and most likely he was one of the 'brethren who,' Baxter said, 'read and consented to' his paper.[245]

When the Act of Uniformity took effect on August 24, 1662, Spurstowe resigned his living and retired at Hackney. In 1664 he visited Cambridge and was entertained at dinner in Catherine Hall. He died in late January or early February 1666, being buried at Hackney on February 8. His only child, William, had died at Hackney in March 1654 at the age of nine, with Simeon Ashe preaching the funeral sermon.[246] His widow, Sarah, on September 30, 1668 became the fourth wife of his thrice-widowed colleague from the Assembly and at Cambridge, Anthony Tuckney. Spurstowe founded six almshouses for six poor widows at Hackney which were endowed by his brother, Henry Spurstowe, a London merchant.[247] Besides his sermons and the Smectymnuus tracts, his publications included *The Wells of Salvation Opened; or a Treatise ... of the Gospel Promises* (1655, 1659), *The Spiritual Chymist; or, Six Decades of Divine Meditations* (1666), and *The Wiles of Satan* (1666). Edmund Calamy refers to his charity and the agreeableness of his conversation. Richard Baxter describes him as 'an ancient, calm, reverend minister'.[248]

John Wallis (November 23, 1616 - October 28, 1703)

As a young Puritan clergyman John Wallis served in the Westminster Assembly as an assistant to the two scribes, Henry Roborough and Adoniram Byfield, rather than as a voting member. His main fame came somewhat later as Savilian Professor of Geometry at Oxford University and in mathematical history 'as the greatest of Newton's English precursors'.[249] He also may have played a significant part in the final preparation of the Shorter Catechism, and he was 'probably one of the last surviving officials of the great Assembly,'[250] living into the early eighteenth century.

Wallis was born at Ashford, Kent on November 23, 1616, son of the Rev. John Wallis (1567-1622) who was minister there from 1602 until his death on November 30, 1622. In 1612 he had married as his second wife, Joanna, daughter of Henry and Mary Chapman of Godmersham, Kent, who bore him three daughters and two sons, John and Henry. Young John's education began at Ashford, but an outbreak of plague there in 1625 caused him to be removed to a private school at Ley Green near Tenterden, Kent, which was conducted by a Scot named James Moffat, or Mouat.[251] Before this school broke up in 1630, Wallis had manifested his brilliance in that he wrote and spoke Latin with facility and knew Greek, Hebrew, French, logic and music before being placed in the school at Felsted, Essex, where he continued his studies for two years. During the Christmas vacation of 1631 he was introduced by his younger brother Henry to the rules of arithmetic, at that time considered a mechanical subject, more suited to 'the business of traders, merchants, seamen, carpenters, surveyors of lands, and the like' than as a subject for academic study.[252]

At Christmas 1632 he was admitted to Emmanuel College, Cambridge, where his tutor was Anthony Burgess, later to be a member of the Westminster Assembly.[253] He became noted there as a dialectician, and his studies included ethics, physics, metaphysics, medicine and anatomy. He received the B.A. in 1637 and the M.A. in 1640. Ordained in 1640, he became chaplain to Sir Richard Darley at Buttercrambe, Yorkshire and then (1642-44) to Lady Mary Vere, widow of Sir Horatio Vere, sometimes at Castle Hedingham in Essex and sometimes in London. It was under Lady Vere's roof that he had his first experience of deciphering a letter in code, one that related to the capture of Chichester on December 27, 1642:

> ... a chaplain of Sir William Waller shewed me one evening just as we were sitting down to supper at Lady Vere's, as a curiosity, an intercepted letter written in cypher, and it was indeed, the first thing I had ever seen of this kind; and asked me, between jest and earnest, if I could

make any thing of it, and was surprised when I told him, perhaps I might. It was about ten o'clock when we rose from supper, and I withdrew from my chamber to consider of it. By the number of different characters in it, there being not more than 22 or 23, I judged it could be no more than a new alphabet; and before I went to bed I found it out; which was my first attempt upon decyphering.[254]

As a result of this experience he became useful to the Parliamentary party as an expert in the cryptological art, until then almost unknown.

On December 18, 1643 he was appointed by Parliament as 'amanuensis to be assistant to the scribes' at the Westminster Assembly, and he took his place there on December 20.[255] By November 1644 he was established as the minister of St. Gabriel, Fenchurch Street in London,[256] a living which he exchanged in 1649 for St. Martin, Ironmonger Lane, succeeding John Arrowsmith there.[257] In 1644 he was made a Fellow of Queen's College, Cambridge, where Herbert Palmer was Master, but he gave up this Fellowship when he married, on March 14, 1645, Susanna, daughter of John and Rachel Glyde of Northiam, Sussex, and settled in London. He was financially independent, his mother's death in 1643 having left him with a substantial estate in Kent.[258]

Although his official role at the Westminster Assembly was only secretarial, the Minutes show that he was specifically assigned to assist the committee doing the final preparation of the Shorter Catechism.[259] Because of this and because of his later publication of *A Brief and Easy Explanation of the Shorter Catechism*,[260] it has been supposed that his logical mind had much to do with the concise framing of the questions and answers.[261] Alexander F. Mitchell argues, largely on the basis of Wallis's relationship to Herbert Palmer, the original convener of the committee on the Shorter Catechism, that Wallis played a significant role:

> From first to last, it appears to me in its clear, condensed, and at time almost frigidly logical definitions, to give unmistakable evidence of its having passed through the alembic of Dr. Wallis, the great mathematician, the friend and *protege* of Palmer, the opponent of Hobbes and the Socinians, and probably the last survivor of those connected with the great Assembly who was not ashamed to speak of the benefit he had derived from its discussions during the preparation of its Confession and Catechisms, long after he had conformed to the Church of the Restoration.[262]

William Carruthers, however, plays down the role of John Wallis and gives more credit to Anthony Tuckney, Stephen Marshall, John Ward and Samuel Rutherford:

> It is to these four men, and especially to the convener, Mr. Tuckney, that we owe the production of the Shorter Catechism. I wish I could accept the suggestion of Dr. Mitchell that the Catechism has 'unmistakeable evidence of its having passed through the alembic of Dr. Wallis, the great mathematician'; but, unhappily, he was not instructed to attend the committee till the work was practically done, on the 9th November, an instruction which would not have been given were he already in attendance.[263]

The role of Tuckney and his final associates cannot be denied; however, Mitchell's thesis concerning the part of Palmer and Wallis should not be ruled out on the slim evidence of the sketchy Minutes.

Wallis was a member of the Presbyterian 6th London Classis, and he was among the signers of *A Vindication of the Ministers in, and about London* of late 1648 which opposed the Army's actions leading to the trial and execution of Charles I.[264] Nevertheless, Oliver Cromwell had great respect for him and in 1649 appointed him Savilian Professor of Geometry at Oxford, of which he was incorporated M.A. from Exeter College that year. On May 31, 1654 he received the D.D., and in 1658 he became Keeper of the Archives of the University of Oxford.

In the negotiations to bring back Charles II as King, Wallis was one of the nine or ten Presbyterians, along with Edward Reynolds, William Spurstowe, Edmund Calamy, Simeon Ashe, Thomas Case, Richard Baxter and others, to be appointed a Royal Chaplain.[265] At the crucial conference of October 22, 1660 at Edward Hyde's residence, Worcester House, between eight Bishops and the seven Presbyterians named above (except for Thomas Manton instead of Case), Wallis advised Baxter, the spokesman for the Presbyterians, to 'let the Bishops speak' first when Hyde introduced a proposal from Independents and Anabaptists to allow more general toleration. Both Presbyterians and Episcopalians recognized that this might allow toleration also for Roman Catholics, but Baxter spoke against it first and managed to offend the King and also damage the Presbyterian cause.[266]

When the Restoration was accomplished, Wallis was confirmed in his two positions at Oxford and was appointed one of the divines commissioned in 1661 to revise the Book of Common Prayer. Like

Edward Reynolds, who became Bishop of Norwich, he conformed and continued to serve in the Anglican Church, thus being among those former Presbyterians 'who became the progenitors of a Low Church party, remaining loyal to Puritan ideals and favouring the comprehension of Dissenters within the Church'.[267]

Wallis's scientific work had proceeded even during the Westminster Assembly. The war forced many of the leading thinkers to seek refuge in London, and there Robert Boyle began weekly meetings, after 1649 in Oxford as well as London, for reformers of scientific method. These meetings led in 1663 to the incorporation of the Royal Society, of which Wallis was one of the founders. Already in 1643 Wallis had published *Truth Tried; or Animadversions on the Lord Brooke's Treatise on the Nature of Truth*. In 1655 he published *Arithmetica Infinitorum*, 'the most stimulating mathematical work so far published in England. Newton read it with delight when an undergraduate, and derived immediately from it his binomial theorem.'[268] This work contained the beginnings of both differential and integral calculus, arrived at the value of 'pi' by interpolation, and brought scientific fame to its author. A treatise prefixed to the book, in which analysis was first applied to conic sections as curves of the second degree, led to a long, drawn-out controversy with Thomas Hobbes, which resulted in exposure of Hobbes's inability in geometry.

Wallis's *Commercium Epistolicum*, published in 1659, led to a challenge from Pierre de Fermat (1601-65), a French mathematician excelling in the theory of numbers (and creator of the famous 'last theorem') to answer a numerical question. Wallis solved the problem to the applause of the international mathematicians participating in the correspondence, and Fermat wrote, 'Now must Holland yield to England, and Paris to Oxford.'[269] One other example illustrates both his mathematical genius and prodigious memory:

> He often whiled away sleepless nights with exercises in mental arithmetic. On one occasion he extracted the square root of a number expressed by fifty-three figures, and dictated the result to twenty-seven places next morning to a stranger. It proved exact.

He also invented the symbol for infinity.[270]

One of his scientific pursuits had immediate social benefits. In 1652 he published *Grammatica Linguae Anglicanae*, or English grammar for foreigners, to which he appended *De Loquela*, a tract describing the various modes of producing articulated sounds. This led him to the invention of a method to teach deaf mutes to speak, and he succeeded in demonstrating this in the cases of two individuals with whom he worked.[271]

Wallis continued to apply his intellectual powers to theological issues. In 1650 he wrote a book criticizing Richard Baxter's controversial 1649 work, *Aphorisms of Justification and of the Covenant*.[272] Besides his work on the Shorter Catechism he also wrote in defence of the Trinity, of the Sabbath, and of infant baptism.[273] His collected mathematical works were published, with a dedication to William III, in three folio volumes in Oxford in 1693-1699. His theological writings were published in a single volume in 1691, and in 1791 his great grandson, William Wallis, published thirteen of his sermons with an account of his life.[274]

Wallis's wife of forty-two years, Susanna, died on March 17, 1687. Their only son, John, entered law in 1676. They also had two daughters. A full-length portrait was painted in 1701 by Godfrey Kneller for display in Oxford. Five other portraits are exhibited in such places as the National Portrait Gallery, the Royal Society, and the Uffizi Gallery in Florence.[275] A biographer wrote that Wallis was endowed with 'a hale and vigorous constitution of body, and a mind that was strong, serene, calm, and not soon ruffled and discomposed.'[276] Wallis wrote in 1697:

> It hath been my lot to live in a time wherein have been many and great changes and alterations. It hath been my endeavour all along to act by moderate principles, between the extremities on either hand, in a moderate compliance with the powers in being.[277]

He died at Oxford on October 28, 1703, aged eighty-six.

Notes

1. Alexander F. Mitchell, *The Westminster Assembly: Its History and Standards*, 2nd ed. (Philadelphia: Presbyterian Board of Publication, 1897), 125-126.
2. Wayne R. Spear, 'Covenanted Uniformity in Religion' (Pittsburgh: U. of Pittsburgh Ph.D. diss., 1976), 362.
3. Cf. Larry J. Holley, 'The Divines of the Westminster Assembly' (New Haven: Yale U. Ph.D. diss., 1979), 232. Holley (303) gives 1576 as the year of Gataker's

birth although other sources uniformly give September 4, 1574.

4. Holley, 'Divines', 303; James Reid, *Memoirs of the Westminster Divines*, 2 vols. in 1 (Edinburgh and Carlisle, Pa.: Banner of Truth, 1982 reprint of 1811 and 1815 ed.), I, 309-310; [Archibald Alexander], *A History of the Westminster Assembly of Divines* (Philadelphia: Presbyterian Board of Publication, 1841), 265-267.

5. *Dictionary of National Biography*, eds. Leslie Stephen and Sidney Lee, 22 vols. (London: Oxford U. Press, 1921-22), VII, 939, 938.

6. *D.N.B.*, VII, 939.

7. *Ibid.*

8. Holley, 'Divines', 304; *D.N.B.*, VII, 939.

9. Everett H. Emerson, *English Puritanism from John Hooper to John Milton* (Durham, N.C.: Duke U. Press, 1968), 200.

10. J.T. Cliffe, *The Puritan Gentry* (London, Boston, Melbourne, and Henley: Routledge and Kegan Paul, 1984), 9.

11. *D.N.B.*, VII, 939.

12. Holley, 'Divines', 304; Reid, *Memoirs*, I, 290, 291-292.

13. William Haller, *Liberty and Reformation in the Puritan Revolution* (New York and London: Columbia U. Press, 1955), 37. Cf. Reid, *Memoirs*, I, 304; Holley, 'Divines', 304-305; *D.N.B.*, VII, 939.

14. Reid, *Memoirs*, I, 295; Holley, 'Divines', 305; *D.N.B.*, VII, 939-940.

15. Reid, *Memoirs*, I, 293; [Alexander], *History*, 256.

16. [Alexander], *History*, 256; cf. Reid, *Memoirs*, I, 294, 295-296.

17. Reid, *Memoirs*, I, 296.

18. Emerson, *English Puritanism*, 201. *A Good Wife God's Gift* appears on pages 203-218. Cf. Jacqueline Eales, *Puritans and Roundheads* (Cambridge, New York, etc.: Cambridge U. Press, 1990), 15, 19, 62.

19. *D.N.B.*, VII, 940.

20. J.I. Packer, *A Quest for Godliness: The Puritan Vision of the Christian Life* (Wheaton, Ill.: Crossway Books, 1990), 268.

21. William Haller, *The Rise of Puritanism* (New York, Evanston, and London: Harper & Row, 1938), 291.

22. *Ibid.*, 115.

23. Cliffe, *Puritan Gentry*, 157.

24. *Ibid.*, 163.

25. Mitchell, *Westminster Assembly*, 154-160; Reid, *Memoirs*, I, 298, 299. C.F. Allison, *The Rise of Moralism* (London: S.P.C.K., 1966), 172-174, describes Gataker's position on justification as like that of Calvin, John Davenant and George Downame and opposed to the Antinomians on the one hand and to Richard Baxter's doctrine 'that our own works of faith and repentance are acceptable as the righteousness of justification.'

26. J.R. de Witt, *Jus Divinum: The Westminster Assembly and the Divine Right of Church Government* (Kampen: J.H. Kok, 1969), 50 and n.156.

27. Reid, *Memoirs*, I, 299-300.

28. de Witt, *Jus Divinum,* 25 n.56. Cf. Emerson, *English Puritanism*, 203; Robert S. Paul, *The Assembly of the Lord* (Edinburgh: T. & T. Clark, 1958), 119, 296-297.

29. *Minutes of the Westminster Assembly*, ed. Alexander F. Mitchell and John Struthers (Edmonton, Alberta: Still Waters Revival Books, 1991 reprint of 1874 edition, 118, 444, 243, 281; S.W. Carruthers, *The Everyday Work of the Assembly* (Philadelphia: The Presbyterian Historical Societies of America and of England, 1943), 181. In each case one of the two visitors to Gataker was Jeremiah Whitaker, who liked to joke about the Assembly's two *acres*, Gat*aker* and Whit*aker* (David Masson, *The Life of John Milton* [Gloucester, Mass. Peter Smith reprint, 1965], II, 522).

30. Reid, *Memoirs,* I, 292, 299, 300-301, 302; *D.N.B.*, VII, 939, 940.

31. Reid, *Memoirs*, I, 301-302, 311; *D.N.B.*, VII, 940. Assembly members John Ley did the Pentateuch and the four Gospels, William Gouge did Kings to Esther, Francis Taylor did Proverbs, Edward Reynolds did Ecclesiastes, and Daniel Featley did the Pauline Epistles (in part). Carruthers, *Everyday Work,* 192, claims that the references in the Assembly's Minutes for September 16, 17, 22, and 25, 1645 are to the *Dutch Annotations* 'ordered and appointed by the Synod of Dort, 1618.'

32. Carruthers, *Everyday Work,* 184. Cf. Reid, *Memoirs,* I, 311-312.

33. Allison, *Rise of Moralism*, 172-173.

34. *D.N.B.*, VII, 940; Reid, *Memoirs,* I, 301, 310.

35. Reid, *Memoirs*, I, 301, 311.

36. Mitchell, *Westminster Assembly*, 125. Cf. Reid, *Memoirs*, I, 303, 312-313.

37. Reid, *Memoirs,* I, 313.

38. Henry Hallam, quoted in Emerson, *English Puritanism*, 200. Cf. [Alexander], *History*, 261; *D.N.B.*, VII, 940; Reid, *Memoirs*, I, 303.

39. Reid, *Memoirs,* I, 303, 305.

40. Quoted in Leland Ryken, *Worldly Saints: The Puritans As They Really Were* (Grand Rapids, Mich: Zondervan, 1986), 145.

41. Ryken, *Worldly Saints,* 148, 253 n.69.

42. *Ibid.,* 150.

43. de Witt, *Jus Divinum*, 76.

44. Paul, *Assembly of the Lord,* 368.

45. Reid, *Memoirs,* I, 304.

46. *Ibid.,* I, 306, 307.

47. Tai Liu, *Puritan London* (Newark, Del.: U. of Delaware Press, 1986), 88-89.

48. Reid, *Memoirs*, I, 307-308.

49. Emerson, *English Puritanism,* 202; cf. Reid, *Memoirs*, I, 308.

50. *D.N.B.*, IX, 23; Reid, *Memoirs,* II, 12.

51. Reid, *Memoirs*, II, 15.

52. Jack Bartlett Rogers, *Scripture in the Westminster Confession* (Kampen: J.H. Kok, 1966), 174-176. Rogers's careful analysis concludes that the main supporters in this work were Matthew Newcomen, Anthony Tuckney, Jeremiah Whitaker and John Arrowsmith, along with the Scottish divines Alexander Henderson, Robert Baillie, George Gillespie and Samuel Rutherford. Cf. Mitchell, *Westminster Assembly,* 367-368.

53. *D.N.B.*, IX, 23; Holley, 'Divines', 314; Reid, *Memoirs*, II, 8-9.

54. *D.N.B.*, IX, 23; Holley, 'Divines', 314; Reid, *Memoirs,* II, 10-11.

55. Haller, *Rise of Puritanism*, 57.

56. Reid, *Memoirs*, II, 12-13; Holley, 'Divines', 340.

57. Reid, *Memoirs,* II, 13, 19.

58. Holley, 'Divines', 314; Paul S. Seaver, *Puritan Lectureships* (Stanford, Cal.: Stanford U. Press, 1970), 234.

59. Seaver, *Puritan Lectureships*, 57.

60. *Ibid.*, 135, 137-138, 272.

61. John F. Wilson, *Pulpit in Parliament* (Princeton, N.J.: Princeton U. Press, 1969), 35; Holley, 'Divines', 314.

62. Emerson, *English Puritanism*, 260; Holley, 'Divines', 314-315.

63. Wilson, *Pulpit in Parliament*, 65, 204.

64. Reid, *Memoirs*, II, 14.

65. *Ibid.*, II, 14-15.

66. George Yule, *Puritans in Politics* (Appleford, Oxfordshire: Sutton Courtenay Press, 1981), 167, 199 n.108 and 109.

67. Quoted in Haller, *Rise of Puritanism*, 132.

68. *Ibid.*, 129.

69. *Ibid.*, 135.

70. Quoted in Ryken, *Worldly Saints*, 153.

71. John von Rohr, *The Covenant of Grace in Puritan Thought* (Atlanta: Scholars Press, 1986), 41.

72. Quoted in Alexander F. Mitchell, 'Introduction,' lxiii, n.1, in *Minutes of the Westminster Assembly*, ed. Mitchell and Struthers. Cf. Mitchell, *Westminster Assembly*, 396 n.1.

73. Von Rohr, *Covenant of Grace,* 12, quoting from Harris's *The Way to True Happinesse* (1632), twenty-four sermons on the Beatitudes.

74. Von Rohr, *Covenant of Grace*, 57, quoting from Harris's *A Treatise of the New Covenant* (1632).

75. Von Rohr, *Covenant of Grace*, 156-157.

76. [Alexander], *History*, 307; Reid, *Memoirs*, II, 18-19.

77. Haller, *Rise of Puritanism*, 99.

78. Reid, *Memoirs*, II, 16; *D.N.B.*, IX, 23.

79. *D.N.B.*, IX, 23 has December 1; Reid, *Memoirs*, II, 22 has the 11th.

80. Reid, *Memoirs*, II, 23.

81. Haller, *Liberty and Reformation,* 38.

82. *D.N.B.*, XXI, 1307.

83. *Dictionary of Scottish Church History and Theology*, ed. Nigel M. de S. Cameron *et al.* (Downers Grove, Ill: InterVarsity Press, 1993), 903; *D.N.B.*, XXI, 1307.

84. Haller, *Rise of Puritanism*, 293.

85. *D.N.B.*, XXI, 1307; Emerson, *English Puritanism*, 279-280.

86. Haller, *Rise of Puritanism*, 294-295.

87. *D.N.B.*, XXI, 1307; Haller, *Liberty and Reformation*, 37.

88. Haller, *Liberty and Reformation*, 361-362 n.15. Cf. Paul, *Assembly of the Lord*,

119 n.48, for a list of all the Smectymnuus tracts.

89. Haller, *Liberty and Reformation*, 123. Cf. Wilson, *Pulpit in Parliament*, 77; Reid, *Memoirs*, II, 268.

90. Haller, *Liberty and Reformation*, 123-124.

91. *Ibid.*, 179. .

92. Cf. Paul, *Assembly of the Lord*, 144.

93. Paul, *Assembly of the Lord*, 345 n.174, quoting George Gillespie's *Notes*. Cf. de Witt, *Jus Divinum*, 125.

94. Carruthers, *Everyday Work*, 120.

95. *Ibid.*, 151.

96. Paul, *Assembly of the Lord*, 361-362; cf. Mitchell, *Westminster Assembly*. For his stance on the Lord's Supper, see Carruthers, *Everyday Work,* 153.

97. Paul, *Assembly of the Lord*, 270; Mitchell, *Westminster Assembly,* 297 n.1.

98. Paul, *Assembly of the Lord*, 243 and n.87.

99. *Ibid.*, 427-428 n.190; 432 n.215; 433 n.220.

100. *D.N.B.*, XXI, 1308; Carruthers, *Everyday Work*, 143.

101. *D.N.B.*, XXI, 1308.

102. *Calamy Revised*, 552.

103. Rogers, *Scripture in the Westminster Confession*, 176; cf. Mitchell, *Westminster Assembly*, 367-368; Paul, *Assembly of the Lord*, 399 and n.48.

104. Spear, 'Covenanted Uniformity', 362.

105. Philip Schaff, *Creeds of Christendom*, 3 vols., 6th ed. (New York and London: Harper & Brothers, 1877, 1919), I, 743. Thomas Temple was pastor of an Irish parish in the 1620s, but came to the Assembly from an English pastorate.

106. Carruthers, *Everyday Work*, 25.

107. Holley, 'Divines', 319; *D.N.B.*, X 134; Reid, *Memoirs*, II, 45.

108. Reid, *Memoirs*, II, 45; Holley, 'Divines', 319.

109. Reid, *Memoirs*, II, 46.

110. Holley, 'Divines', 320; *D.N.B.*, X, 134-135; Reid, *Memoirs*, II, 46-47.

111. Carruthers, *Everyday Work*, 36, 43.

112. *Ibid.*, 144.

113. Paul, *Assembly of the Lord*, 243 and n.87.

114. *Ibid.*, 427-428 n.190.

115. *Ibid.*, 166 n.132, 253, 327 and n.78.

116. Mitchell, *Westminster Assembly*, 355-356.

117. *D.N.B.*, X, 135; Reid, *Memoirs*, II, 48.

118. Reid, *Memoirs,* II, 47.

119. Rogers, *Scripture in the Westminster Confession*, 176. Cf. Mitchell, *Westminster Assembly*, 367; Paul, *Assembly of the Lord*, 399 and n.48.

120. Spear 'Covenanted Uniformity', 362.

121. *Ibid.,* 63; Paul, *Assembly of the Lord*, 80 n.27, 556; 140, 211, 316, 421; de Witt, *Jus Divinum*, 68.

122. Carruthers, *Everyday Work*, 175.

123. Paul, *Assembly of the Lord*, 84, 179.

124. *D.N.B.*, XIX, 514-515. Wilson, *Pulpit in Parliament*, 101 and n.2, assumes

only identical surnames in Sir John Temple's thanking Thomas Temple for his sermon to the joint session of Lords and Commons on August 31, 1647. Sir John Temple was also author of a history of the Irish rebellion which inflamed English sentiment against the Irish, but which modern scholarship has criticized for some of its claims (*D.N.B.*, XIX, 514).

125. Holley, 'Divines', 348, gives his birth date as c.1599; however, *D.N.B.*, XIX, 514, says his older brother, Sir John Temple, was born in 1600 in Ireland.

126. *D.N.B.*, XIX, 520-522.

127. Holley, 'Divines', 348; *D.N.B.*, XIX, 522.

128. Holley, 'Divines', 348. Reid, *Memoirs*, II, 182, says he 'settled first at Winwick in Northamptonshire' before going to Battersea, but perhaps this is a confusion with the rectorship he held, according to Holley, in Northamptonshire in 1657.

129. Wilson, *Pulpit in Parliament*, 66, 191-192; Reid, *Memoirs*, II, 182-183.

130. de Witt, *Jus Divinum*, 54.

131. Wilson, *Pulpit in Parliament*, 79.

132. *Ibid.*, 245, 249, 251.

133. Carruthers, *Everyday Work*, 29, 30.

134. *Ibid.*, 53, 50.

135. *Ibid.*, 52 and 61.

136. *Ibid.*, 151. For other examples of his cautious approach, cf. 129, 153, and 157; de Witt, *Jus Divinum*, 83; and Paul, *Assembly of the Lord*, 210.

137. Carruthers, *Everyday Work*, 80, 83.

138. Paul, *Assembly of the Lord*, 148; de Witt, *Jus Divinum*, 69.

139. Paul, *Assembly of the Lord*, 141, 365.

140. *Ibid.*, 154-155. Cf. Carruthers, *Everyday Work*, 153.

141. de Witt, *Jus Divinum*, 28.

142. Paul, *Assembly of the Lord*, 164, 166 n.132, 171.

143. *Ibid.*, 299, 281-282.

144. de Witt, *Jus Divinum*, 132, 161.

145. Paul, *Assembly of the Lord*, 243 n.87, 427-428, 433 n.220, 506.

146. Tai Liu, *Discord in Zion* (The Hague: Martinus Nijhoff, 1973), 162-163, 55.

147. *D.N.B.*, XIX, 522. Holley, 'Divines', 348, gives the date of his death as 1661, whereas *D.N.B.* says simply 'before 1671.'

148. Rogers, *Scripture in the Westminster Confession*, 176.

149. William Carruthers, 'Historical Account', revised, in S.W. Carruthers, *Three Centuries of the Westminster Shorter Catechism* (Fredericton; N.B.: U. of New Brunswick, 1957),5. Cf. Mitchell, *Westminster Assembly*, 438-439; Douglas F. Kelly, 'The Westminster Shorter Catechism', in John L. Carson and David W. Hall, eds., *To Glorify And Enjoy God* (Edinburgh and Carlisle, Pa.: Banner of Truth, 1994), 110-111.

150. *D.N.B.*, XIX, 1213; W. Robert Godfrey, 'The Westminster Larger Catechism', in Carson and Hall, eds., *To Glorify and Enjoy God*, 132-133.

151. Mitchell, *Westminster Assembly*, 126.

152. Halley, 'Divines', 209. For the biographical information on Tuckney, see

D.N.B., XIX, 1213-1214; *Calamy Revised*, 496; Holley, 'Divines', 349-350; Reid, *Memoirs*, II, 186-190. Cotton's first wife, Elizabeth Horrocks, who died in April 1631, was Tuckney's cousin (*D.N.B.*, XXII, 494; Larzer Ziff, *The Career of John Cotton* [Princeton, N.J.: Princeton U. Press, 1962], 65).

153. *Calamy Revisited*, 496; *D.N.B.*, XIX, 1214.

154. Paul, *Assembly of the Lord*, 119.

155. *Ibid.*, 180, 244 and n.90, 330, 395-396, 427 and n.190, 433 and n.220, 506.

156. Mitchell, *Westminster Assembly*, 438 and n.2. Cf. Reid, *Memoirs*, II, 187; Carruthers, *Everyday Work*, 143.

157. *D.N.B.*, XIX, 1214.

158. *Ibid.*; cf. Mitchell, *Westminster Assembly*, 355.

159. Liu, *Puritan London*, 65, 69.

160. Liu, *Discord in Zion*, 142 and n.86.

161. *D.N.B.*, XIX, 1214.

162. Wilson, *Pulpit in Parliament*, 154; Liu, *Discord*, 36.

163. Wilson, *Pulpit in Parliament*, 249.

164. Cliffe, *Puritan Gentry,* 93; Reid, *Memoirs*, II, 189.

165. Paul, *Assembly of the Lord*, 364.

166. John H. Leith, *Assembly at Westminster: Reformed Theology in the Making* (Richmond, Va.: John Knox Press, 1973), 46-47. Cf. Mitchell, *Westminster Assembly*, 395.

167. *D.N.B.*, XIX, 1214.

168. Leith, *Assembly at Westminster*, 103-104.

169. Rogers, *Scripture in the Westminster Confession*, 175-176.

170. The others were Richard Herrick, John Lightfoot (who seems to have escaped enforcement of the Act of Uniformity's provisions although accepting it), and John Wallis, who was not a voting member of the Assembly, but one of its scribes.

171. *D.N.B.*, XVI, 926.

172. Seaver, *Puritan Lectureships*, 287 and 372 n.64. Holley, 'Divines', 337, follows *D.N.B.* in having Reynolds preaching at Lincoln's Inn from 1622 to '31 and also being Vicar of All Saints, Northampton 1628-31.

173. Wilson, *Pulpit in Parliament*, 66, 185, 204; Liu, *Discord in Zion*, 36.

174. Paul Christianson, *Reformers and Babylon* (Toronto, Buffalo, and London: U. of Toronto Press, 1978), 183-184; Liu, *Discord*, 36.

175. Christianson, *Reformers and Babylon*, 234.

176. Alexander Chalmers, 'Memoirs of the Life of the Author', in *The Whole Works of the Right Rev. Edward Reynolds, D.D.*, 6 vols. (London: B. Holdsworth, 1826), I, lxx.

177. Carruthers, *Everyday Work*, 70. Extensive notes on this sermon appear in the *Minutes of the Westminster Assembly*, ed. Mitchell and Struthers, 135-142. The sermon was published in 1646 and appears in the 1826 edition of Reynolds' *Works*, IV, 318 ff.

178. de Witt, *Jus Divinum*, 28; Paul, *Assembly of the Lord*, 119.

179. Paul, *Assembly of the Lord*, 244 and n.90, 340 and n.154.

180. *Ibid.*, 399 and n.48.

181. *Ibid.*, 427-428 and n.190; 506.

182. Cf. *Ibid.*, 354, 431 n.212.

183. Mitchell, *Westminster Assembly*, 124-125. Cf. Benjamin B.Warfield, *The Westminster Assembly and Its Work* (Cherry Hill, N.J.: Mack Publishing Co., 1972 reprint), 122-147.

184. Cf. *D.N.B.*, XVI, 927; Reid, *Memoirs*, II, 129. For an account of the visitation of Oxford and its limited accomplishments, cf. Chalmers, 'Memoirs', in Reynolds, *Works,* I, xlv-xlviii.

185. George R. Abernathy, Jr., 'The English Presbyterians and the Stuart Restoration, 1648-1663', *Transactions of the American Philosophical Society*, New Series, 55, Part 2 (1965), 15, quoting from Reynolds' sermon *The Peace of Jerusalem*.

186. Liu, *Discord*, 157.

187. Quoted in Mitchell, *Westminster Assembly*, 214-215.

188. Liu, *Discord*, 157-158, referring to *A Seasonable Exhortation*.

189. Cf. C. Gordon Bolam, Jeremy Goring, *et al.*, *The English Presbyterians: From Elizabethan Puritanism to Modern Unitarianism* (Boston: Beacon Press, 1968), 74-76; Abernathy, 'The English Presbyterians', 74-78.

190. Quoted in Seaver, *Puritan Lectureships*, 287.

191. Both Wood and Neal are quoted in Reid, *Memoirs*, II, 130.

192. Abernathy, 'The English Presbyterians', 62-63.

193. Seaver, *Puritan Lectureships*, 287.

194. Ryken, *Worldly Saints*, 119.

195. Chalmers, 'Memoirs of the Life of the Author', in Reynolds, *Works*, I, lxvii.

196. Bolam and Goring, *English Presbyterians*, 84.

197. Chalmers, 'Memoirs', lxviii.

198. Carruthers, *Everyday Work*, 181.

199. Chalmers, 'Memoirs', lxix; *D.N.B.*, XVI, 927.

200. Chalmers, 'Memoirs', lxxi.

201. de Witt, *Jus Divinum*, 34; Paul, *Assembly of the Lord*, 80 and n.26, 555-556.

202. Carruthers, *Everyday Work*, 137, quoting from the Minutes of July 12, 1645. Carruthers and Seaver, *Puritan Lectureships*, 269, name Staunton with Stephen Marshall, Herbert Palmer, Philip Nye, Jeremiah Whitaker, and Thomas Hill. Wilson, *Pulpit in Parliament*, quoting the Minutes of February 28, 1644, includes Charles Herle.

203. Reid, *Memoirs*, II, 152; *D.N.B.* XVIII, 999.

204. Quoted in Reid, *Memoirs*, II, 153.

205. *Ibid.*, II, 154.

206. *Ibid.*, II, 155.

207. *Ibid.*, II, 157-158.

208. *Calamy Revised,* 461.

209. *Ibid.*, 460; Holley, 'Divines', 346; Reid, *Memoirs*, II, 156.

210. Reid, *Memoirs*, II, 156.

211. Wilson, *Pulpit in Parliament*, 179.

212. Quoted in *ibid.*, 160-161.

213. Mitchell, *Westminster Assembly*, 251.

214. H.R. Trevor-Roper, *The Crisis of the Seventeenth Century* (New York and Evanston: Harper & Row, 1968), 318.

215. Mitchell, *Westminster Assembly*, 252-253.

216. Paul, *Assembly of the Lord*, 119, 142, 166, 216, 222, 225, 252, 292-293, 353-354, 434; de Witt, *Jus Divinum*, 84.

217. Paul, *Assembly of the Lord*, 322 n.44.

218. Liu, *Discord in Zion*, 55, 162-163.

219. Reid, *Memoirs*, II, 159.

220. *Ibid.*, II, 161, 167.

221. *D.N.B.*, XVIII, 999.

222. Reid, *Memoirs*, II, 173.

223. *Ibid.*, II, 163-164.

224. *D.N.B.*, XVIII, 1000; Reid, *Memoirs*, II, 174.

225. *D.N.B.*, XVIII, 843; Holley, 'Divines', 345. Wilson, *Pulpit in Parliament*, 101 and n.2, indicates that Parliament's thanks to Spurstowe for his sermon on July 21, 1643 was communicated through William Spurstowe simply because of identical surnames.

226. Holley, 'Divines', 345.

227. Cliffe, *Puritan Gentry*, 100-101.

228. *D.N.B.*, XVIII, 843.

229. Paul, *Assembly of the Lord*, 119 and n.48; Haller, *Liberty and Reformation*, 34-36.

230. *D.N.B.*, XVIII, 843-844.

231. *Complete Prose Works of John Milton*, Vol. II, ed. Ernest Surlock (New Haven: Yale U. Press, and London: Oxford U. Press, 1959), 62. Cf. Paul, *Assembly of the Lord*, 84; Wilson, *Pulpit in Parliament*, 71-72.

232. Liu, *Discord in Zion*, 44. Cf. Haller, *Liberty and Reformation*, 132.

233. Wilson, *Pulpit in Parliament*, 88, 249.

234. Liu, *Discord in Zion*, 131-132 n.47.

235. Carruthers, *Everyday Work*, 181, indicates he was excused on May 1, 1646 'for a short time, to preach at Cambridge.'

236. Paul, *Assembly of the Lord*, 427-428, n.190.

237. *D.N.B.*, XVIII, 844.

238. Carruthers, *Everyday Work*, 62; *D.N.B.*, XVIII, 844.

239. Liu, *Discord*, 162-163.

240. Liu, *Puritan London*, 84, 62.

241. *D.N.B.*, XVIII, 844.

242. Abernathy, 'The English Presbyterians', 15; Liu, *Discord*, 158.

243. Abernathy, 'The English Presbyterians', 65.

244. *Ibid.*, 68; A.H.Drysdale, *History of the Presbyterians in England* (London: Publication Committee of the Presbyterian Church of England, 1889), 375 n.1.

245. *D.N.B.*, XVIII, 844; Reid, *Memoirs*, II, 150.

246. *D.N.B.*, XVIII, 844.

247. *Ibid.*; Reid, *Memoirs*, II, 150.

248. *D.N.B.*, XVIII, 844.

249. *D.N.B.*, XX, 601.

250. Mitchell, *Westminster Assembly*, 126-127.

251. Reid, *Memoirs*, II, 206, has 'Moffat'; *D.N.B.*, XX, 598, has 'Mouat'.

252. *D.N.B.*, XX, 598, quoting from a later statement by Wallis.

253. Reid, *Memoirs*, II, 207.

254. *Ibid.*, II, 208.

255. Carruthers, *Everyday Work*, 8, 45.

256. Liu, *Puritan London*, 109 and 121 n.40.

257. *Ibid.*, 75. Cf. *D.N.B.*, XX, 599.

258. *D.N.B.*, XX, 599.

259. *Minutes of the Westminster Assembly*, Mitchell and Struthers, eds., 483, 488.

260. Reid, *Memoirs*, II, 214, refers to an 8th edition published in 1659. Mitchell, *Westminster Assembly*, 427, refers to its original publication in 1648. Cf. S.W. Carruthers, *Three Centuries of the Westminster Shorter Catechism*, 120.

261. William Beveridge, *A Short History of the Westminster Assembly*, rev. and ed. by J. Ligon Duncan, III (Greenville, S.C.: Reformed Academic Press, 1993 reprint of 1904 ed.), 101.

262. Mitchell, *Westminster Assembly*, 442; cf. 422, 426-427, 438-439 and n.1.

263. W. Carruthers, 'Historical Account', rev. ed., in S.W. Carruthers, *Three Centuries of the Westminster Shorter Catechism*, 5.

264. Liu, *Puritan London*, 74; *Discord in Zion*, 163.

265. Abernathy, 'The English Presbyterians', 68.

266. *Ibid.*, 75.

267. Bolam, Goring, *et al.*, *The English Presbyterians*, 84.

268. *D.N.B.*, XX, 599.

269. Reid, *Memoirs*, II, 210-211; *D.N.B.*, XX, 599-600.

270. *D.N.B.*, XX, 601.

271. Reid, *Memoirs*, II, 212; *D.N.B.*, XX, 600.

272. Reid, *Memoirs*, II, 211; Allison, *The Rise of Moralism*, 154.

273. Reid, *Memoirs*, II, 210, 211, 213-214.

274. *D.N.B.*, XX, 601; Reid, *Memoirs*, II, 214.

275. *D.N.B.*, XX, 600-601.

276. Quoted in *D.N.B.*, XX, 601.

277. *D.N.B.*, XX, 601.

Chapter 9

London Clergy

The ministers in the City of London and its suburbs played a unique role in the period of the Civil War and the Puritan Republic because they could influence the people of their congregations whose public opinion could in turn have an influence upon Parliament. The seven clergymen described in this chapter exerted this sort of influence, conveying the work of the Westminster Assembly to the City through their preaching, their gatherings at Sion College (which became a center for Puritan and Presbyterian activity), and the Presbyterian Classes (presbyteries) and Provincial Assemblies of the greater London area.

In addition to the seven described in the chapter, other Westminster divines who were significant ministers in London include William Gouge (the patriarch of the London Clergy), Cornelius Burgess (a catalyst of Sion College), Edward Reynolds, Edmund Staunton, Stephen Marshall, Joseph Caryl, Obadiah Sedgwick, Richard Vines, Jeremiah Whitaker, John Arrowsmith, Anthony Tuckney, Thomas Gataker, Thomas Coleman, Thomas Goodwin, Philip Nye, Jeremiah Burroughes, Sidrach Simpson, Thomas Temple, William Spurstowe and John Wallis.

Many of these held Lectureships in London, the majority of them coming to London only after the beginning of the Long Parliament in November 1640. Along with the few who had been Puritan pastors in London prior to the 1640s, the Westminster divines soon filled numerous pulpits and made their presence felt for the further reformation of the church.

Edmund Calamy (February 1600 - October 29, 1666)

From the events leading up to the Westminster Assembly on through the outworking of the Assembly's actions in Revolutionary England, no single figure provided greater leadership for the Presbyterians than Edmund Calamy. As Archibald Alexander says:

> No minister of his time was more popular; and none had more energy and public spirit, together with a fearless boldness in declaring his sentiments, and going forward in the path which conscience directed. He may well be considered the leader of the Presbyterian party; their confidence in his courage, prudence, and integrity, was unbounded; and they manifested their estimation of his talents and address, by generally making him their chairman, at all their meetings.[1]

James Reid says: 'Mr. Calamy was well acquainted with the subjects appropriate to his profession: as a preacher, he was plain and practical; and he boldly avowed his sentiments on all necessary occasions.'[2] William Haller, comparing him to Stephen Marshall, the greatest preacher of the Assembly, says: 'Calamy, his colleague in the pulpit on several occasions, was, perhaps, among all the preachers, the next greatest favorite with parliament.'[3] Tai Liu says that

> ... Calamy commanded unparalleled prestige and exercised an irrefutable influence in the City of London during the revolutionary era. As his grandson would later say: 'No Minister in the City was more follow'd; nor hath there ever been a Week-day lecture so frequented as his; which was attended not only by his own Parish, but by Eminent Citizens, and many Persons of the Greatest Quality, and constantly for 20 years together; for there seldom were so few as 60 coaches.' Indeed it was often in Calamy's house in Aldermanbury that strategy and actions of the London Puritan brethren were planned ....[4]

Edmund Calamy was born in February 1600, the only son of a tradesman in Walbrook, London who came from the island of Guernsey where, according to family tradition, he was a Huguenot refugee from the coast of Normandy.[5] Young Edmund entered Pembroke Hall, Cambridge on July 4, 1616 and received the B.A. in 1620 and the M.A. in 1623.[6] His aversion to Arminianism prevented him from becoming a Fellow, in the English reaction to the Synod of Dort, but he was elected *Tanquam Socius*, an arrangement peculiar to Pembroke Hall that allowed him most of the privileges of a Fellow without any share in the government of the College.[7]

Nicholas Felton, Bishop of Ely, made him a chaplain of his household, permitting him to spend much time in study. During this stage of his life Calamy not only acquainted himself with the writings of Robert Bellarmine and Thomas Aquinas, but read over Augustine's works five times.[8] Bishop Felton presented him to the vicarage of St. Mary, Swaffham Prior, Cambridgeshire on March 6, 1626, but in the next year he resigned this position to become a Lecturer at Bury St. Edmunds, Suffolk. He would remain there for ten years, with Jeremiah Burroughes his colleague from around 1627 to 1631. The enforcement of Bishop Matthew Wren's articles of 1636 drove him from Bury, but Robert Rich, second Earl of Warwick, secured him a position at Rochford, Essex, where he served as Rector or Lecturer from November 9, 1637 until May 1639.[9] The marshes of Essex did not agree with him, however, and an illness left him with a chronic dizziness that prevented him from mounting a pulpit, so that he always afterward preached from the reading-desk.[10]

Calamy was elected on May 27, 1639 to the perpetual curacy of St. Mary Aldermanbury, London, a parish with a strongly Puritan tradition and with many prominent citizens in its membership.[11] It also paid its minister handsomely. From the beginning Calamy was given what was 'probably the highest annual stipend a London minister received so early in this period.'[12] It was from this base that Calamy became involved in the attack upon Episcopacy. From early in 1641 he joined with Cornelius Burgess, John White, Stephen Marshall, and various noblemen and lay leaders to plot their strategy.[13] When Bishop Joseph Hall published his defence of Episcopacy by divine right, Calamy joined with Stephen Marshall, Thomas Young, his brother-in-law Matthew Newcomen, and William Spurstowe to produce responses under the name 'Smectymnuus', an anagram of their initials. The full title of their first treatise reveals their subject matter: *An Answer to a Book entitled, An Humble Remonstrance; in which, the Original of Liturgy and Episcopacy is discussed: and Queries propounded concerning both. The Parity of Bishops and Presbyters in Scripture demonstrated. The occasion of their Imparity in Antiquity discovered. The Disparity of the Ancient and our Modern Bishops manifested. The Antiquity of Ruling Elders in the Church vindicated. The Prelatical Church bounded.*[14] Five years later Calamy wrote:

After my coming to *London* at the beginning of this Parliament I was one of those that did joyn in making *Smectymnuus*, which was the first deadly blow to *Episcopacy* in England of late years .... I was the first that openly before a *Committee* of *Parliament* did defend that our *Bishops* were not only not an *Order* distinct from *Presbyters*, but that in Scripture a Bishop and Presbyter were all one.[15]

It was towards the beginning of the Long Parliament that Calamy for the Presbyterians and Philip Nye for the Independents made an agreement at Calamy's house in Aldermanbury, 'That (for advancing of the publicke *cause* of a happy Reformation) neither side should Preach, Print, or dispute, or otherwise act against the other's way; And this to continue 'til both sides, in a full meeting, did declare the contrary.'[16] Presbyterians and Independents thus were aware of their differences before the Westminster Assembly, but were united in opposing Episcopacy.

On December 22, 1641 Calamy and Stephen Marshall preached before the House of Commons for a special Fast Day for the Irish crisis. Calamy's sermon, *Englands Looking-Glasse*, based on Jeremiah 18:7-10, developed four points that made Parliament's responsibility clear:

(1) 'That God hath an independent and illuminated Prerogative over all Kingdoms and Nations to build them, or destroy them as he pleaseth';
(2) 'Though God hath this absolute power over Kingdoms and Nations, yet he seldome useth this power, but first he gives warning';
(3) 'That Nationall turning from evill, will divert Nationall judgments, and procure Nationall blessings' (repentance he construed as 'Humiliation for sins past, Reformation for the time to come');
(4) 'That when God begins to build and plant a Nation; if that Nation do evill in Gods sight, God will unbuild, pluck up, and repent of the good he intended to do unto it.'

Along with other preachers Calamy urged Parliament to call a 'free Nationall Synod' for the sake of reform.[17]

When the system of regular monthly Fast Days was established, Calamy and Marshall were selected by the House of Commons to begin the series on February 23, 1642. Calamy's sermon, based on Ezekiel 36:32, was entitled *Gods free Mercy to England. Presented as a Pretious, and Powerful motive to Humiliation*. John F. Wilson refers to it as 'something of a classic exposition of puritan doctrine for the times.' Steering between Arminian moralism and Antinomian irresponsibility, it argues: 'That Nationall mercies come from free grace, not from free will; Not from mans goodnes, but Gods goodnes.'

'The contemplation of Gods free mercy to Nations and persons ought to be a mighty incentive, and a most effectuall argument to make them ashamed, ... ashamed for sin for the times past, and ashamed to sin for the time to come.' Repentance for the past and reform for the future, or change in attitude and change in action, were the available means of salvation. Sundered from each other, both were ineffectual and potentially heretical. Conjoined, they defined the religious practices appropriate to a people or a nation in explicit covenant with God.[18]

In another move to pave the way for cooperation between the London clergy and the Westminster Assembly, the Puritans gained control of Sion College in London. In April 1643 Andrew Janaway of All Hallows was elected President, and Calamy and Henry Roborough, who would be one of the two scribes for the Assembly, were elected Assistants. Calamy would serve as President in 1650.[19] On June 15, 1643, as the Assembly was about to get under way, Calamy preached to the House of Lords *The Nobleman's Pattern of true and real thankfulness*, from Joshua 24:15. He said, 'It is the duty of all men, but especially of such as are Joshuah's, such as are Rulers and Nobles, to ingage themselves and their Families to serve God resolutely, speedily, and publickely ....'[20]

SION COLLEGE

Sion College, the gathering place of Presbyterian clergy in London during the Westminster Assembly and in subsequent years, was founded by Thomas White (1550?-1624), who left £3,000 to purchase a building for a 'college' or a 'corporation' or guild of the clergy of London and its suburbs, with almshouses for twenty people attached. A library was added to the hall, chapel, and almshouses in London Wall. Its three main goals were to provide aid for the needy, to provide books for students, and to serve as a center for the London clergy to assemble. Members of the Westminster Assembly who served as President of Sion College were John Ley (1644), George Walker (1645), Cornelius Burgess (1647, 1648), William Gouge (1649), Edmund Calamy (1650), Lazarus Seaman (1651, 1652), and Edward Reynolds (1659).

In 1886 Sion College was moved to the Victorian Embankment and served primarily as a theological and historical library. Financial difficulties since the autumn of 1993 led to announcements in February and March of 1995 that the library of more than 100,000 books and 150 manuscripts might have to be sold.

In the Assembly itself Calamy was the fourteenth most active speaker in the debates on church government, just behind William Bridge in number of speeches recorded in the Minutes down to November 15, 1644 and ahead of Joshua Hoyle.[21] His role in the debates shows him arguing for distinctively Presbyterian positions from the beginning of the Assembly.[22] He served on the Grand Committee for the treaty obligations to the Scots.[23] He also served on the committee to consider the 'Reasons' offered by the Independents.[24] He and Stephen Marshall were entrusted with distribution of money paid by Parliament to the Assembly on January 3, 1644, and he, Marshall, Cornelius Burgess and William Spurstowe said that they did not wish to share in the distribution of April 7, 1645, evidently because of being better off than most of the divines.[25] Repeatedly in the discussions Calamy showed an awareness of actual situations in English parishes and a concern for the practical consequences of decisions made at the Assembly.[26]

From 1643 to 1648 he had as his assistant at St. Mary Aldermanbury his brother-in-law and fellow Smectymnuan, Matthew Newcomen,

EDMUND CALAMY

who was also a member of the Assembly.[27] Meanwhile, when the idea of toleration had been broached in Parliament, Calamy preached to the House of Commons on the special Fast Day of October 22, 1644 *England's Antidote against the Plague of Civil War*, based on Acts 17:30. In this sermon he said:

> If you do not labour according to your duty and according to your power, to suppress the errors and heresies that are spread in the Kingdom, all these errors are your errors .... You are Anabaptists and you are the Antinomians, and it is you that hold all religions are to be tolerated, even Judaism and Turkism.[28]

Just two months later, on December 25, 1644, Calamy preached to the House of Lords on the regular Fast Day *An Indictment against England because of her self-murdering Divisions; with an Exhortation to Concord*, based on Matthew 12:25. With the differences between Independents and Presbyterians in mind he said: 'Divisions, whether they be Ecclesiasticall, or Politicall, in Kingdomes, Cities, and Families, are infallible causes of ruine ....' He concluded that if England should perish in the Civil War, her epitaph could be written: 'Here lyeth a Nation that hath broken Covenant with God ....'[29] Incidentally, since the regular Fast Day fell on Christmas Day, Calamy expressed some Puritan sentiments on the superstition and profaneness connected with that day and opined that since Christmas could not be reformed, it should be dealt with as Hezekiah dealt with the bronze serpent.[30]

On January 14, 1646 Calamy preached to the Lord Mayor with the Sheriffs, Aldermen, and Common Council of London on the occasion of their renewing the Solemn League and Covenant. His text was 2 Timothy 3:3 and his title was *The Great Danger of Covenant-refusing, and Covenant-breaking*. He said that 'the famous City of London is become an Amsterdam, separation from our churches is countenanced, toleration is cried up, authority lieth asleep.'[31] This and other sermons, according to George Yule, 'stressed that settling the Presbyterian system, having no toleration and maintaining the Covenant were all of a piece, and thus helped the Council see the issue as a whole which was a powerful weapon against the Erastians.'[32] After this date Calamy seems not to have preached on the Parliamentary Fast Days. He was invited for June 24, July 29, and August 26, 1646, but asked to be excused on account of illness on the first date and declined the other invitations. Since he was previously enthusiastic about the monthly

Fast Days, either his illness continued or he had become disenchanted with the practice.[33]

Part of his disillusionment may have stemmed from an incident in his own parish. Henry Burton was permitted to hold a 'catechisticall lecture' on alternate Tuesdays at St. Mary Aldermanbury, and on September 23, 1645 he spoke out in favor of 'his congregationall way'. At the instigation of Calamy the churchwardens locked Burton out, and an exchange of pamphlets ensued: *The Door of Truth Opened* by Calamy and *Truth still Truth, though Shut Out of Doors* by Burton, both in 1645, and *A Just and Necessary Apology* (i.e. defence) by Calamy in 1646.[34] The kind of atmosphere that was increasingly developing in London in the late 1640s is described by Christopher Hill:

> In 1648 the General Baptist Edward Barber was invited by the parishioners of St. Benet Fink, London, to come to the parish church and add to what the minister (Edmund Calamy) should say, or contradict him if erroneous. Hanserd Knollys created several 'riots and tumults' by going around churches and speaking after the sermon. One can imagine the irritation this practice might cause when, as time went on, the parson himself became the main target of itinerant interrupters, professionally skilled hecklers, denouncing his self-righteousness and his greed in taking tithes.[35]

After the triumphant Army occupied London in the summer of 1647, Calamy 'openly denounced the latter in a sermon for the morning exercise at St. Michael Cornhill,' with the result that a pamphlet responded: 'When we come to hear you, we expected to be instructed in Divinity, and not to be corrupted in Civility; if we had a desire to learn the language of *Billingsgate*, we should not have gone to Michael Cornhill in London, especially when Mr. Calamy was the Teacher.'[36] Under these circumstances it is understandable that the English Puritan majority sided with the Scottish Presbyterians for reasons such as Robert S. Paul enumerates: 'fear of the growing sectarianism, determination to maintain an established state church, and a strong desire to maintain the status and authority of the clergy.'[37]

Calamy was a member of the Presbyterian 6th London Classis.[38] He was one of the signers of Cornelius Burgess's *A Vindication of the Ministers of the Gospel in, and about London* that opposed the Army's actions leading to the trial and eventual execution of the King.[39] Under the Protectorate he 'kept himself as private as he could,' but he was the main author in 1650 of *Vindication of the Presbyteriall-government*, reaching out to Independents, and in 1654 of *Jus divinum ministerii evangelici, or the divine right of the Gospel-ministry*, appealing to Episcopalians as well as to Independents.[40] Oliver Cromwell did consult with some of the London clergy, including Edmund Calamy, when he was contemplating expulsion of the Rump Parliament, probably in early April 1653. Calamy advised that it was both unlawful and impracticable that one man should assume the government of the country. Concerning its being unlawful Cromwell appealed to the safety of the nation as the supreme law. When asked why he thought it impracticable, Calamy said, 'Oh, it is against the voice of the nation; there will be nine in ten against you.' But Cromwell responded, 'Very well; but what if I should disarm the nine, and put the sword in the tenth man's hand, would not that do the business?'[41]

In the period following Oliver Cromwell's death on September 3, 1658 Calamy was involved with other Presbyterian ministers in support of Richard Cromwell and the restored Long Parliament, but when the government began to disintegrate, he worked for the restoration of monarchy.[42] He went to Holland with Edward Reynolds, William Spurstowe, Thomas Case and Thomas Manton to consult with Charles II, and their delegation was well received.[43] Along with all of the delegation plus John Wallis, Simeon Ashe, Richard Baxter and one or two others, he was appointed a Royal Chaplain.[44] On the one occasion when he preached before the King, August 12, 1660, Samuel Pepys commented in his *Diary* that he 'made a good sermon upon these words "To whom much is given of him much is required". He was very officious with his three reverences to the King, as others do.'[45]

At the crucial point of negotiations with the King's representatives and the Bishops, Calamy joined with Edward Reynolds in seeking to tone down some of Richard Baxter's response, but even so the Presbyterian exceptions were more than the Bishops would accept.[46] Offered the Bishoprics of Hereford, Norwich, and Lichfield and Coventry respectively, Baxter declined, Reynolds accepted, and Calamy hesitated and then declined.[47] J. I. Packer explains what was operative for Calamy at this juncture:

> ... these Puritan clergy were prevented from trying to stretch their consciences by the sense that the eyes of their own flocks – indeed, of all Englishmen – were upon them, and that they could not even appear to compromise principles for which they had stood in the past without discrediting both themselves, their calling, and their previous teaching.

Calamy records a contemporary comment which focuses their fear: 'had
the ministers conformed, people would have thought there was nothing in
religion.' It had become a question of credibility. The Puritan clergy held
that they should be ready to confirm what they had publicly maintained as
truth by suffering, if need be, rather than risk undermining their whole
previous ministry by what would look like time-serving abandonment of
principle.[48]

When it became clear that the King and his advisers were not going to
accommodate those who could not conform, Calamy did not hide his
feelings. On one occasion when General George Monck, who had
persuaded him and Simeon Ashe that the Long Parliament must be
dissolved, was present in his church, he had occasion in his sermon to
refer to filthy lucre:

> 'and why,' said he, 'is it called *filthy*, but because it makes men do base and
> *filthy* things? Some men,' said he, 'will betray three kingdoms for *filthy
> lucre's* sake.' Saying this, he threw his handkerchief, which he generally
> waved up and down while he was preaching, toward the General's pew.[49]

With the passage of the Act of Uniformity, knowing he would be
ejected, he preached his Farewell Sermon on August 17, 1662, a week
before the Act would take effect, on the text of 2 Samuel 24:14. James
Reid summarizes it:

> The chief design of it is to illustrate and improve this point, 'that sin brings
> persons and nations into great perplexities.' He observes, That beside
> many outward troubles, this brings a spiritual famine upon a land: a famine
> of the word.... Have not some of you *itching ears* who would fain have a
> preacher who would feed you with dainty phrases; and who begin not to
> care for a Minister that unrips your consciences, and speaks to your hearts:
> some who by often hearing sermons are become sermon proof? There is
> hardly any way to raise the price of the gospel-ministry, but the want of it
> .... Give glory to God by confessing and repenting of your sins, before
> darkness comes; and who knoweth but that may prevent that darkness.[50]

On the eve of the fateful day, August 24, St. Bartholomew's Day,
Simeon Ashe, who had been Sunday-afternoon Lecturer at St. Mary
Aldermanbury since 1651 and Calamy's assistant there until January
1655, 'went seasonably to Heaven at the very Time when he was cast
out of the Church.'[51] Calamy preached his funeral sermon on August

23, at St. Austin's Church on the text Isaiah 57:1, 'The righteous perisheth, and no man layeth it to heart: and merciful men are taken away, none considering that the righteous is taken away from the evil to come.'

After St. Bartholomew's Day Calamy continued to attend St. Mary Aldermanbury from which he had been ejected. On December 28 he was present as usual when the assigned preacher did not appear. Urged by the people, he entered the desk 'and preached with some warmth.'[52] His sermon was based on 1 Samuel 4:13, 'And when he came, lo, Eli sat upon a seat by the wayside watching; for his heart trembled for the ark of God.' It was later written out and published in the collections of farewell sermons as *Trembling for the Ark of God*. His fifth and final application was:

> The ark was called the ark of the covenant. Keep covenant with God, and God will preserve the ark. But if you break the covenant of the ark, the covenant made in baptism, and that covenant often renewed in the sacrament, if you break covenant, God will take away the ark.[53]

On January 6, 1663 Calamy was arrested and committed to Newgate Prison, the first of the nonconformists to be penalized for disobeying the Act of Conformity for preaching without permission. Many of Calamy's friends came to visit him in prison, their coaches jamming the traffic in Newgate Street. 'A certain Popish lady,' apparently the King's mistress, was detained by the jam and, inquiring as to its cause, learned from disturbed people standing by that 'a person much beloved and respected, was imprisoned there for a single sermon.' She immediately reported this to the King, whose express order set Calamy free, although the House of Commons said that the Act had not provided for longer restraint and took steps to tighten the regulations against toleration.[54]

Edmund Calamy lived to see the great fire of London of September 3, 1666. It is said to have overrun 373 acres within the City's walls, burning down 13,200 houses, 89 parish churches, besides chapels, leaving only eleven parishes within the walls still standing. Driven in a coach through the ashes and ruins as far as Enfield, Calamy was devastated by the sight. Heartbroken, he never again emerged from his room and died on October 29, 1666. He was buried on November 6 in the ruins of the church he had served for twenty-three years, 'as near to the place where his pulpit had stood as they could guess.'[55]

Calamy was the first of six Edmund Calamys and to avoid confusion is known as Edmund Calamy the Elder. His son Edmund Calamy the Younger (1635?-85) was one of three children of his first wife, Mary Snelling. He was educated at Sidney Sussex College, and Pembroke Hall, Cambridge, was ordained as a Presbyterian in 1653, was ejected from the rectory of Moreton, Essex in 1662, and attended his father in London until his death. Edmund Calamy the Elder's second wife was Anne Leaver, of the Lancashire Leavers, who bore him three sons, Benjamin, James, and John. The older two became ministers who conformed to the Church of England after the Restoration, but enjoyed cordial relations with their Nonconformist half-brother Edmund. Benjamin Calamy (1642-1686) gained the D.D. in 1680 and, as Vicar of St. Lawrence Jewry with St. Mary Magdalene, Milk Street annexed and a Prebendary of St. Paul's, was a prominent churchman.

Edmund Calamy the Younger had one son, Edmund Calamy (1671-1732), the great biographical historian of Nonconformity, often referred to as 'Dr. Calamy' since he received the D.D. from the University of Edinburgh upon a journey to Scotland in 1709. His eldest son, Edmund Calamy (1697?-1755), was a Dissenting minister who served on the Presbyterian Board, as did his son, Edmund Calamy (1743-1816), who became a barrister of Lincoln's Inn. His son, Edmund Calamy, the great-great-great-grandson of Edmund Calamy the Elder, died August 27, 1850 at the age of seventy. His younger brother, Michael Calamy, who occasionally preached for the Unitarians at Exeter and Topsham, died unmarried on January 3, 1876, aged 85, the last of a notable line.[56]

Simeon Ashe (c.1597 - August 20, 1662)

When the Parliamentary and Scottish armies turned the tide against the King's forces to win a great victory in the Battle of Marston Moor near York on July 2, 1644, a second battle was fought in London as to who deserved credit for the victory, David Lesley and the Scottish cavalry that arrived at a critical point or Oliver Cromwell who rallied the troops for a brilliant counter-attack. Robert Baillie wrote to fellow-Scot Robert Blair that the first reports gave a great boost to the Independents, 'makeing all believe, that Cromwell alone, with his unspeakablie valorous regiments, had done all that service; that the most of us fled; and who stayed, they fought so and so, as it might be.' Then came news with the Scottish version. 'Then we sent abroad our printed relations, and could lift up our face.'

> But within three dayes Mr. Ashe's relation was also printed, who gives us many good words, but gives much more to Cromwell than we are informed is his due. Let good Mr. Ashe know what is the use that generallie here is made of his relations; much I know beside his intention: even in plain terms, the Independents have done so brave service, yea, they [are] so strong and considerable a party, that they must not only be tollerate, but in nothing grieved, and no wayes to be provocked. It seems very necessare, that since none of yow of purpose, and ordinarlie, sends up relations and Mr. Ashe sends to the presse constant intelligence of your actions, which, for the man's known integrity, are every word believed, your proceedings have a great influence in all affairs here both of Church and State; I say, it seems needfull that all Mr. Ashe's letters which are sent hither to the presse, should be first seen and pondered by some of yow there.[57]

The 'good Mr. Ashe' whose integrity was well known was Simeon Ashe, a strong Presbyterian and member of the Westminster Assembly who was serving as a military chaplain with Edward Montagu, Earl of Manchester, one of the Parliamentary generals and also a member of the Assembly from the House of Lords. Ashe would become one of the major London Presbyterian ministers, would be a correspondent of Robert Baillie following the Assembly, and would continue to be an important liaison for the Assembly with the Earl of Manchester and with affairs in Parliament.

Not much is known about Simeon Ashe's family or background, although he was later 'a man of some property'.[58] Born probably about 1597, he entered Emmanuel College, Cambridge in 1613. Although there is no record of his having obtained degrees, he was ordained in October 1619.[59] His earliest ministry is unknown, but he became Vicar of Rugeley, Staffordshire in 1627. Here he made the acquaintance of fellow Puritans, such as John Ball whose treatise on the Covenant of Grace he later edited, and he was ejected from his living for refusing to read 'The Book of Sports' which promoted recreational activities on Sundays.[60] Sir John Burgoyne befriended him and allowed him liberty to preach at Wroxall, Warwickshire, a public chapel free from diocesan jurisdiction where the Burgoynes 'shelter'd many a Hunted Deer, both in the days of Queen Elizabeth and in the two succeeding Reigns.'[61] Ashe also ministered in Warwickshire under the protection of Lord

Brook,[62] but he came to London as a chaplain of the Earl of Manchester, preaching there as early as November 1639.[63]

In London he was a Lecturer at St. Bartholomew-Exchange in 1641 and 1642.[64] On March 15, 1642 the House of Commons, in response to a petition from the parishioners, recommended that he serve as Sunday-afternoon and Tuesday Lecturer at St. Bride's, a position he would hold until 1646.[65] He appears to have found opportunity to address public issues in his preaching. On January 4, 1642, when the King had sought to arrest five members of the Commons, he preached *A Support for the sinking Heart in times of distresse ... January 4th. Which was a day of great trouble and deepe danger in the City.*[66] On March 30, 1642 he was invited by the House of Commons, along with Cornelius Burgess, to preach for the second of the regular monthly Fast Days, Stephen Marshall and Edmund Calamy having opened the series in the previous month.[67] Based on Psalm 9:9, his sermon was entitled *The Best Refuge for the Most Oppressed.* In it he described the Bishops as great oppressors both in church and commonwealth, and he concluded, 'Great things have bin raised in our hearts by understanding you, your intention to call an Assembly of Divines,' and he added that 'we will daily pray for the directing and perfecting thereof.'[68] On May 17, 1642 Ashe also preached a sermon entitled *Good Courage Discovered, and Encouraged,* based on Psalm 31:24, to 'the Commanders of the Military Forces of the Renowned Citie of London.'[69] By this time he may already have been functioning as a military chaplain for Manchester's troops. He was present in that capacity when the war began at the Battle of Edgehill on October 23, 1642. There Ashe was one of the chaplains who 'rode up and down the army through the thickest dangers, and in much personal hazard, most faithfully and coura-geously exhorting and encouraging the soldiers to fight valiantly and not to fly.' It was also reported about that time that Ashe rebuked plunderers in Somserset and Dorset, and 'much appeased them, though abused for his pains.'[70]

Ashe was actually not among those originally nominated for the Westminster Assembly by the House of Commons, but replaced Josiah Shute who died before the Assembly began, by nomination of the House of Lords for Cardiganshire, Wales.[71] The influence of the Independents, according to Samuel Rutherford in his *Free Disputation Against Pretended Liberty of Conscience,* prevented the original nomi-nation of Ashe and William Rathband.[72] Ashe's role in the actual debates of the Assembly was limited, for when Manchester appealed for more military chaplains, the Assembly granted that Ashe and William Good could continue with him, being 'very willing, out of the apprehension of the necessity and difficulty of the work his Lordship is now about[,] to afford their best assistance to his Honour therein.'[73] As a result, Ashe was with Manchester not only for the Battle of Marston Moor in July, but also during a previous lull in the war for the Earl's visitation of Cambridge as Vice-Chancellor of the University. Ashe reported on this to the Assembly on March 15, 1644, indicating that many Arminian, non-preaching, or simply incompetent Masters and Fellows had been ejected and conveying Manchester's request that John Arrowsmith, Herbert Palmer, Richard Vines, Lazarus Seaman, and Thomas Young be appointed as Masters of various Colleges in their place.[74]

On February 26, 1645 Ashe was back in London preaching to the House of Lords from Isaiah 63:5 on *The Church Sinking, Saved by Christ*. In this sermon he deplored the divisions in the church.[75] On January 14, 1646 he preached along with Edmund Calamy to the Lord Mayor, Sheriffs, Aldermen and Common Council of London on the occasion of their renewing the Solemn League and Covenant. From Psalm 76:11, he preached on *Religious Covenanting Directed, and Covenant Keeping Persuaded* and 'urged that because others strove to bring in heresy and schism they must strive to maintain the Covenant and the brotherly union with the Scots, and expedite reformation.'[76] Ashe preached again to the House of Commons on the regular Fast Day of April 28, 1647 on *God's Incomparable Goodness unto Israel*, based on Psalm 73:1.[77] On February 23, 1648 he preached to the Commons on *Self-surrender unto God,* asking 'whether, witting, willing, deliberate covenant breaking can stand with a sincere self surrender unto God.'[78]

In March 1646, in the midst of the crisis of the Assembly over Parliament's effort to develop its own commissions for handling church discipline, Robert Baillie sought to make use of Ashe's relationship to the Earl of Manchester. Writing to Francis Roberts, he urged him to persuade Ashe to intercede with Manchester to get the offending parts of the bill killed in the House of Lords: 'If God help yow to keep on the City's zeale, more is like to happen in a week than hitherto in a year. Be diligent in this happie nick of time.'[79] By this time Ashe was the Sunday and Tuesday Lecturer at the well-to-do church, St. Michael

Bassishaw, where he would continue for six years, until 1652.[80] In 1651 he became Sunday-afternoon Lecturer and assistant to Edmund Calamy at St. Mary Aldermanbury.[81]

Ashe was one of the signers of *A Vindication of the Ministers of the Gospel in, and About London* that opposed the actions of the Army leading to the trial and execution of Charles I.[82] On August 22, 1651, along with Edmund Calamy and Thomas Manton, he stood with fellow-Presbyterian minister Christopher Love on the scaffold on Tower Hill before Love was beheaded for alleged conspiracy against Oliver Cromwell's government.[83] In 1654 he became practically the preacher of choice for Puritan funerals. In March he delivered the funeral sermon for William Spurstowe's only child, a nine-year-old boy, *Christ the Riches of the Gospel, and the Hope of Christians*, based on Colossians 1:27. On June 6 he preached *Living Loves betwixt Christ and Dying Christians*, based on John 11:11, 'Our friend Lazarus sleepeth,' at St. Mary Magdalene Bermondsey in Southwark for the funeral of his friend Jeremiah Whitaker after a long and agonizing illness.[84] On August 1 he preached the funeral sermon for another former Assembly colleague, Thomas Gataker, *Gray Hayres Crowned with Grace*, based on Proverbs 16:31.[85] In his epistle to the Presbyterian ministers of the Province of London annexed to the published version of this sermon Ashe wrote that the death of Gataker

> 'may well minde us of the deaths of many more of our brethren, whose hearts, heads and hands, went along with us in the setting up and exercising of the Presbyterian government in our respective Congregations, with mutual Assistance, Classical and Provinciall, both for the Ordination of Ministers, and the more pure administration of the Sacraments.' Although 'much contempt is cast upon us ... as an inconsiderable number,' Ashe insisted that there still were 'three score Presbyterian Ministers within the precincts of our Province, who preach profitably, did live godly, who are not tainted with the erroneous tenets either of the Arminians, Antinomians or Anabaptists.'[86]

On October 12, 1658 he preached the funeral sermon for the Countess of Manchester, third wife of his patron the Earl.[87]

On January 1, 1655 Ashe became Rector of St. Augustine's in London while continuing to be Lecturer at either St. Michael's or St. Peter, Cornhill.[88] From December 1655 to November 1658 he maintained correspondence with Robert Baillie in Scotland in which they shared their concerns over the views of Richard Baxter, who was emerging as the leader of Puritan unity. Ashe wrote in January 1656 that Baxter was 'doubtless a godly man, though tenacious in his mistakes. Mr. Burgess and Mr. Vines dealt with him to reduce him, but could not convince him to satisfaction.'[89]

In the brief regime of Richard Cromwell, Ashe was among the Presbyterian clergy appointed as commissioners for the approbation of ministers.[90] He was associated with the efforts of Edward Reynolds and Edmund Calamy to bring back the monarchy, and he was one of the nine or ten Presbyterians appointed Royal Chaplains by Charles II.[91] A. H. Drysdale describes their motivation in 1660:

> ... much the larger section of the London ministers, led by Calamy, Reynolds, Ashe, and Manton, *with the strong support of Baxter and others*, realizing the difficulties surrounding them, seemed much more disposed to accede at once, and frankly, to a combination of a modified Presbyterianism with a modified Episcopacy; seeking to save their essential principles, while willing to surrender much that was distinctive of outward Presbyterial organization and nomenclature.[92]

One can only imagine Ashe's disappointment when it turned out that Episcopacy would not be significantly modified in the Restoration. Had he lived, he would not have conformed, but 'he went seasonably to Heaven at the very Time when he was cast out of the Church,' dying on August 20, 1662 and buried on the eve of St. Bartholomew's Day.[93] In the funeral sermon Edmund Calamy described him

> as a man of great sincerity, humility, benevolence, prudence, and patience: as eminently diligent in preaching the glorious gospel of the grace of God in season and out of season, so as not to please the ear, but to wound the heart; seeking not the applause of men, but the salvation of souls: as singularly careful in visiting the sick: as excelling in prayer, and in maintaining great acquaintance and communion with God.[94]

Looking back over twenty-three years of association in London, Calamy said:

> I can freely and clearly profess, and that with a sad heart, that I and many others, have lost a real, wise, and godly friend, brother, and fellow-labourer in the Lord: the church hath lost an eminent member, and choice pillar: and this city hath lost an ancient, faithful, and painful minister ....

The ministerial excellencies of many ministers were collected and concentered in one Simeon Ashe. He was a Bezaleel in God's tabernacle, a master-builder, an old disciple, – a burning and a shining light; one whom many Ministers, and other good Christians called Father, insomuch that it was a common proverb in the City, Father Ash.[95]

Samuel Rutherford called him 'gracious and zealous Mr. Ashe'.[96]

Thomas Case (1598 - May 30, 1682)

Thomas Case was generally recognized as among the most vehement and outspoken of the Presbyterian ministers.[97] Thomas Coleman included him among what he termed 'Parliament-Pressing Ministers'.[98] Anthony à Wood called him a fire-brand.[99] James Reid says, 'It is readily allowed that he was quick and passionate; this seems indeed to have been his infirmity ....'[100] He was imprisoned for over five months in 1651 for being implicated in the conspiracy against Oliver Cromwell's government usually called the 'Christopher Love Plot'. He outlived all of the other active Members of the Assembly,[101] and it appears that he mellowed with age.

Case was perhaps the most ardent of the English Puritans for Presbyterianism from the start of the Assembly. When the Scottish delegation arrived in September 1643, the Prolocutor and Joshua Hoyle gave official greetings on the 15th, as assigned on the previous day. Then Case,

with an apology for his presumption in speaking, added a greeting. They had trodden the winepress alone, but 'Blessed be God that hath taken off from our lips all occasion of so sad a complaint this day.' He rejoiced that Scotland had sent them 'a noble Bezaleel, a reverend Paul, a learned Timothy' (Warriston, Henderson, and Gillespie).[102]

He preached a series of three sermons to persuade his hearers to support the Solemn League and Covenant. The first was preached on the Fast Day on September 27 at St. Lawrence Jury (not before Parliament), the second on Saturday evening the 30th at his own church, St. Mary Magdalene, Milk Street, and the third on Sunday morning, October 1, again in his own church, where the Covenant would be taken.[103] These sermons were published together under the title *The Quarrell of the Covenant, with the Pacification of the Quarrell* and were based on Leviticus 26:25 and Jeremiah 50:5. To allay fears of an automatic commitment to the existing Scottish system, Case said, '... we are not yet called to sware the *Observation* of any kinde of Government, that is, or shall be presented to us, but to *endeavour* the Reformation of Religion in *Doctrine, Worship, Discipline, and Government, According to the Word of God.*' He went on to say, '... by this Covenant *we* are bound no more to conform to *Scotland*, then *Scotland* to us: The *Astipulation* being Mutuall, and this Astipulation binding us not so much *one* to *another*, as *both* of us to the *Word*.'[104]

Thomas Case was born in 1598 in Boxley, Kent, the son of George Case, the Vicar there. He is said to have been converted when only six years old and to have conducted an active prayer life by the age of eight.[105] He was educated first at Canterbury, then at the Merchant Taylors' School in London, until financial difficulties caused him to be schooled at home by his father. He was able to enter Christ Church College, Oxford in 1616, obtaining his B.A. there on June 15, 1620 and his M.A. on June 26, 1623. He stayed at the University one or two more years, preaching in the vicinity of Oxford and then in Kent.[106] He was ordained in the Diocese of Norwich on September 24, 1626. His close friend Richard Heyrick, who was his contemporary at the Merchant Taylors' School and then at Oxford and who would also become a member of the Westminster Assembly, obtained the Rectory of North Repps, Norfolk, and Case became his Curate there. On January 4, 1629 he became Rector of Erpingham, just six miles away, where he continued to minister until about 1637. On March 24, 1631 he married Ann Potts at Itteringham, Norfolk.[107] She apparently died sometime before 1637, by which time he had experienced difficulties with Bishop Matthew Wren of Norwich and had joined Heyrick in Manchester, where the latter had become Warden of the Collegiate Church in 1635. He preached frequently at the chapel at Salford, newly erected by the Booth family, and at other chapels in the vicinity of Manchester. On August 8, 1637 he was married for a second time at Stockport, Cheshire, to Anne, daughter of Oswald Mosley of Ancoats, Manchester and widow of Robert Booth of Salford.[108] Case never had any children of his own, but he became a loving father to his second wife's children from her previous marriage.

Probably by April 1641 Case had moved to London, for two sermons of his, delivered to the Long Parliament, were published in that year. In the first sermon, based on Ezekiel 20:25, he called on the House of Commons to make laws for the good of both church and commonwealth according to God's laws. In the second, from Ezra 10:2-3, he urged a universal reform of all aspects of society: 'Oh if it might be reported in heaven that England is reformed – that such a drunkard, such a swearer, such a covetous man ... is become a new man.'[109] In 1641 Case became Lecturer, and in 1642 Rector, of St. Mary Magdalene, Milk Street, where he would remain until 1649, helping this church to become strongly Presbyterian.[110]

Case's prominence in London increased in 1642 as he added a Thursday Lectureship at St. Martin's-in-the-Fields on February 15 which he would keep until the Restoration,[111] and he also became Chaplain to Richard Gurney, Lord Mayor of London.[112] On the Fast Day of October 26 he was preaching to the House of Commons on *God's Rising, his Enemies' Scattering* from Psalm 68:1-2 when he received a note from Lord Wharton 'which permitted the preacher to make a dramatic announcement of the divine intervention at Edgehill.'[113] He would preach again to the House of Commons on April 9, 1644[114] and then again on August 22, 1645, when he would say boldly:

> You have by you a Treasury or Library of Parliamentary Sermons; in which you have many choice directions and encouragements in the Service to which God and the Kingdom hath called you. As you have heard them, hearken to them; as you have printed them, so consult with them: I presume you printed them for that end.[115]

He preached again to the Commons on February 19, 1646 and then to the Lords on March 25, 1646, a sermon entitled *Deliverance, Obstructions; or the Set-backs of Reformation*, based on Exodus 5:22-23. One can almost hear him shouting, 'for God's sake, my Lords, let us not have a *Reformation* that shall *need* a *Toleration*, much lesse that shall *enforce* it; to have *found* such a one, would have been grievous; but to *make* such a one, would be intolerable.'[116] He then confronted Parliament's Erastianism:

> Be tender of Christ's Prerogative. You are very jealous of your own priviliges; whoso toucheth them toucheth the apple of your eye: Do you think Jesus Christ will not be jealous of his own Prerogative? And oh, if you should do anything which the Parliament in heaven, that upper House (for I know you look upon yourselves as the nether House of Parliament) should vote a breach of Priviledge, a trespass upon the Prerogative Royal of the King of Saints, how would ye be able to answer it in the day of Accounts.[117]

He also preached to the House of Commons on May 26, 1647.

Case belonged to the Presbyterian 6th London Classis while at St. Mary Magdalene, Milk Street. It is from there that he launched the 'Morning Exercise', a series of services with prayers and sermons that developed into a veritable 'Body of Divinity' for Nonconformity as various preachers participated in several different locations around London down to 1690. These were published in six separate volumes in 1660, 1661, 1674, 1675, 1682, and 1690.[118] It all started during the Civil War when Case was receiving so many notes from parishioners of St. Mary Magdalene asking prayer for their relatives or friends in the Earl of Essex's army that he did not have time to read them or pray for them in the regular service. The result was a special seven-o'clock service for this particular purpose. James Reid describes its development:

> Mr. Case began it in his church at seven o'clock in the morning, and when it had continued there a month, it was removed by turns to other churches at a distance, for the accommodation of the several parts of the city, and was called the *Morning Exercise*. The service was performed by different ministers, with fervent prayer both for the public welfare and for particular cases, in the presence of a large auditory. When the heat of the war was over, it became a casuistical lecture, and was carried on by the most learned and eminent divines of those times till the Restoration of King Charles the Second.[119]

In 1648 Case spoke out strongly against the Independents both in the Army and in Parliament.[120] He was one of the signers of *A Vindication of the Ministers of the Gospel in, and about London* opposing the actions of the Army leading to the trial and execution of the King.[121] In June 1649 he was accused of praying publicly for Charles II, but the charges seem to have been dropped.[122] By refusing to take the 'Engagement' in 1649, he lost his position at Milk Street, but by this time Case was also a Lecturer at St. Mary, Aldermanbury and at St. Giles, Cripplegate.[123] In 1651 he was implicated in the Royalist conspiracy associated with the name of fellow Presbyterian minister Christopher Love. Oliver Cromwell's government in 1650 apprehended Thomas Coke, whose testimony claimed that as many as nine London ministers were involved.[124] On May 2, 1651 Case was among the first to be arrested, along with Love.[125] Love was executed on August 22. Case was imprisoned for about five months, his wife obtaining permission to lodge with him. He and his old friend Richard Heyrick were to be

brought to trial on September 30, but instead they were released by
October 16, Cromwell gradually releasing the remaining figures charged
with conspiracy after his victory over the forces of Charles II at the
Battle of Worcester on September 3.[126] While in prison Case wrote
Correction, Instruction: or, A Treatise of Afflictions, in which he said,
'Oh how amiable are the assemblies of the saints and the ordinances of
the Sabbath, when we are deprived of them.'[127]

Soon after his release from prison Case became Lecturer at the large
church of St. Giles-in-the-Field, beyond Holborn, and eventually its
Rector. In 1658 he was urging unity, and in March 1660 he was
included among Richard Cromwell's new commissioners for the
approbation of ministers.[128] In May 1660 he went with Edward Reynolds,
Edmund Calamy, William Spurstowe and Thomas Manton as part of
the Presbyterian delegation to Charles II in Holland. They were well
received, and Case was one of nine or ten Presbyterian ministers
appointed Royal Chaplains.[129] Case's impetuosity was manifested,
however, when

> on one occasion Case pressed in an 'unmannerly way' into Charles's
> presence and began to give him advice, [and] 'he was interrupted by the
> King, who said he did not remember that he had made him one of his
> council.'[130]

The mellower side of Thomas Case is shown in his *Mount Pisgah:
or, A Prospect of Heaven,* an exposition of 1 Thessalonians 4:13-18
published in 1670. The ten-year-old son of Sir Robert Booth, his second
wife's son, had died and also a similarly aged son of William and
Elizabeth Hawes, his second wife's daughter, and in the touching
dedicatory epistles prefixed to this work Case writes to Robert Booth,
Lord Chief Justice of Common Pleas in Ireland:

> As for me, I cannot long survive, having so often received in myself the
> sentence of death, 2 Cor. 1.9; I have lived already one full age of man, and
> am now in the third year of my labour and sorrow, Psa. xc.10, and it is little
> that I can do for God. I must decrease, but may you increase; yet pray for
> me, that I may live much in a little time; and that myself and your aged
> mother may, like those trees of God, Psa. xcii. 14, 15, bring forth more fruit
> in old age than in the beginning, to show that the Lord is upright, &c.[131]

Having been ejected from St. Giles-in-the-Fields, he preached his
farewell sermon there on August 17, 1662 on Revelation 2:5. After that

he remained in London, writing and preaching when he could. He was among the signers in 1676 of Richard Baxter's *The judgment of Nonconformists of the interest of reason in matters of religion*, an appeal for unity.[132] In August 1677, after the death of Richard Heyrick, he wrote an epitaph preserved in brass in the Collegiate Church of Manchester, commemorating his friend of sixty years.[133]

Having outlived all of the active voting members of the Westminster Assembly, he died on May 30, 1682, and was buried on June 3 at Christ Church, Newgate Street, London. Dr. Edmund Calamy, grandson of Case's friend and associate, described Case as 'one of a quick and warm spirit, an open plain-hearted man, a hearty lover of God, goodness, and all good men.' Richard Baxter called him 'an old faithful servant of God'.[134]

Lazarus Seaman (c.1607 - September 3, 1675)

Lazarus Seaman was invited at one time by a noble lady, whose family was contemplating converting to Roman Catholicism, to engage in a disputation with two Catholic priests on the subject of transubstantiation. According to William Jenkyn in his funeral sermon for Seaman, though the priests were two of the most able Romanist debaters available, they quickly were silenced by Seaman and yielded the field, and 'those persons who were popishly inclined stood amazed,' and thus Seaman 'was the instrument in preserving the whole family from a revolt, and in keeping them stedfast in the Protestant Religion'.[135] Jenkyn described him as 'almost ... an invincible disputant':

> He was a person of a *most deep, piercing*, and eagle-eyed judgment in all points of controversial divinity. He had few equals, if any superiors, in ability to decide and determine a dark and doubtful controversy. He could state a theological question with admirable clearness and acuteness, and knew how, in a controversy, to cleave, as we say, an hair.[136]

This hair-splitting ability stood him in good stead in the Westminster Assembly as he took on the likes of Thomas Goodwin and John Lightfoot in defending the Presbyterian positions against the Independents and the Erastians. Although he was among the youngest members of the Assembly,[137] being in his late thirties through the main debates, he was one of the most active speakers. He was second only to Thomas Goodwin in number of speeches in the debates on church government and well ahead of the third, Stephen Marshall.[138]

Lazarus Seaman was born around 1607 in the town of Leicester to parents who were poor. On July 4, 1623 he entered Emmanuel College, Cambridge and gained his B.A. in 1627 and M.A. in 1631. His economic situation forced him to leave Cambridge in order to be a school teacher, apparently in London. He was ordained a deacon on February 12, 1628, but apparently was never ordained a priest. He served as a Lecturer at St. Martin's, Ludgate in London, 1634-36, and became a chaplain to Algernon Percy, tenth Earl of Northumberland.[139] In 1638 he became Lecturer and Curate of All Hallows, Bread Street, where he eventually became Rector in 1643.[140]

In the Westminster Assembly he was 'one of the Independents' most intransigent opponents.'[141] He seems to have been a convinced Presbyterian from the start.[142] He supported the office of ruling elder, although he was willing to differ with the Scots on whether by divine right there should be one in each congregation.[143] As early as January 26, 1644 he was willing to argue 'that materially and *substantially there is a presbytery* in London.'[144] He could confront Thomas Goodwin in debate on Brownism, excommunication, and the whole doctrine of the church,[145] and yet he could also on occasion show sympathy for Goodwin's position.[146] He served on the committee for seeking an accommodation between the dissenting Independents and the majority Presbyterians, represented by him with Richard Vines and Herbert Palmer along with the Scots.[147] On September 30, 1644 he made a helpful speech in which he crystallized where Goodwin and the majority agreed, where there were still disagreements, and where Goodwin still had doubts.[148] On November 15 he was appointed to the committee of twenty to consider the 'Reasons' offered by the Independents.[149]

Seaman also played a leading role with regard to Erastianism. On April 3, 1646 he gave the main response to John Lightfoot's arguments.[150] The Assembly had earlier, on January 7, 1645, put him on a small committee to deal with the question of excommunication.[151] He also was placed on the important committee to handle the delicate communication with Parliament over church discipline on March 20, 1646.[152] He served as well on the committee on Antinomianism and showed himself fair to Peter Sterry who was accused of holding Antinomian views.[153] In his numerous activities in the Assembly he also served on the Grand Committee to deal with the treaty obligations to the Scots and chaired the committee to expedite the filling of vacant pulpits.[154] Robert Paul claims to see a common thread in Seaman's arguments: 'Lazarus Seaman and many in the Assembly like him, whatever their views on church polity, were determined to maintain the unique status and authority of the ordained ministry.'[155] He certainly did seek to maintain the authority of the clergy; however, it could be argued from the evidence of his participation in the Assembly that he emphasized even more the authority of Presbytery (including ruling elders) and the importance of keeping the Covenant.[156]

The Covenant was his emphasis in his sermon before the House of Commons on the Fast Day, September 25, 1644. Entitled *Solomon's Choice: or, A Precedent for Kings and Princes, and all who are in Authority* and based on 1 Kings 3:9, it concluded with Seaman's challenge that the Covenant was '*Holy, Just,* and *Good. Urge it, Renew it,* but above all, *Keep it.*'[157] Seaman preached to Parliament on four other occasions: to the House of Lords on September 5, 1645 for the special Humiliation for the Miseries of Scotland; to the Lords again on the regular monthly Fast Day on January 27, 1647; to the Commons on the regular Fast Day of December 29, 1647; and possibly to the Lords on the regular Fast Day of December 27, 1648. His sermon on January 27, 1647 was entitled *The Head of the Church, the Judge of the World: or, The Doctrine of the Day of Judgment briefly Opened and Applied,* based on Acts 17:30-31. It consisted mainly of six propositions:

(1) There would be a day of judgment.
(2) It was already set.
(3) The Judge had been appointed.
(4) It would be Jesus Christ.
(5) The world was to be judged by him.
(6) The judgment would take place according to the will of God in his righteousness.[158]

At this stage the Presbyterian preachers were not expecting to bring in the Kingdom: '"We doe and should pray daily, *Thy Kingdome come*", said Lazarus Seaman, but he added that it was vain to think that its coming was near or could be quickened. It was presumptuous even to desire it so.'[159] He blamed Parliament, however, for its lukewarmness in religion, 'neither so cold as by publique indulgence to tolerate all opinions, nor so hot as to suppresse one sect.'[160]

On March 15, 1644 the Earl of Manchester requested that the

Assembly allow five of its members, Seaman, John Arrowsmith, Herbert Palmer, Richard Vines and Thomas Young, to fill Masterships of Colleges at Cambridge. As a result Seaman served as Master of Peterhouse College from April 11, 1644 to August 3, 1660.[161] He performed the normal exercises to obtain the D.D. in 1649, defending with ability and force of argument the providence of God in disposing of political governments.[162] His scholarship was also shown when he was one of the four Presbyterians participating in the discussions of church government with Charles I on the Isle of Wight between September and November of 1648, and the King complimented him on his ability.[163] Especially gifted in the biblical languages, he customarily carried around with him a small Hebrew Bible without vowel points.[164]

Little is known about Seaman's family, except that his wife, Elizabeth, died during the Assembly, in 1648. At the time of his death in 1675 only one child, Elizabeth, was surviving. There was a son, Joseph, who was born around 1637, received the B.A. in 1655 and the M.A. in 1659 from Peterhouse, Cambridge, but was buried at All Hallows, Bread Street on November 8, 1661. Another son, Benjamin, was baptized there on November 8, 1638, but apparently died early.[165]

Seaman was a signer of *A Vindication of the Ministers of the Gospel in, and about London* opposing the actions of the Army leading to the trial and execution of King Charles I in January 1649.[166] He was a member of the Presbyterian First London Classis and played an active part in the London Provincial Assembly, serving as Moderator at its second meeting on November 8, 1647, and 'being the only founding member who also attended its very last session in 1660.'[167] He served as President of Sion College, the rallying point for the Presbyterian clergy of London, 1651-1653, a particularly difficult time at the beginning since Oliver Cromwell's government decided to quarter troops there on April 16, 1651.[168] In 1653 Seaman and Cornelius Burgess led the Presbyterians in making common cause with the Independents against the Fifth Monarchy Men.[169] In October 1653 he appeared with Burgess before the Committee for Tithes of the Barebones Parliament.[170] Meanwhile Seaman continued to be occupied at Cambridge, serving as Vice-Chancellor of the University 1653-1654.[171]

After the death of Oliver Cromwell on September 3, 1658, Seaman was among the Presbyterian ministers of London represented by Edward Reynolds in an address to the new Protector, Richard Cromwell, on October 11.[172] In September 1659 he was active in trying to unite

Presbyterians and Independents in an apparent attempt to ward off the restoration of the monarchy and Episcopacy.[173] Along with William Jenkyn and a few other Presbyterians he stood aloof from the negotiations of Reynolds, Edmund Calamy, and the majority of the Presbyterian leaders with Charles II, and he 'was looked upon as an uncompromising man, whom it was useless to tempt with offers of preferment.'[174]

With the Act of Uniformity he was ejected from All Hallows, Bread Street in August 1662, having already been replaced as Master of Peterhouse, Cambridge on August 3, 1660. His farewell sermon in London was based on Hebrews 12:20-21. In it he concluded:

> That the care of the Church is in the hands of Christ, – that all Providences respecting it, designed to exercise and to try it, must be borne with patience; approving what he orders, and doing whatever he commands; with a cheerful dependence upon the faithfulness of *the Great Shepherd of the Sheep, who being brought again from the dead*, lives for ever; and a firm reliance on God's Covenant.[175]

He preached in private to a congregation of his former parishioners, and then after the Great Fire of 1666 he preached publicly. After the Indulgence of 1672 he built a chapel in Meeting-house Yard, Silver Street and Wood Street, Holborn. In his latter days he became much interested in the prophetical writings of the Bible and produced some 'Notes on Revelation', which, however, were never published.[176]

Lazarus Seaman died in Warwick Court, Newgate Street on September 3, 1675 and was buried on the 7th in the chancel of All Hallows, Bread Street.[177] He left a significant library of 5,000 volumes, the first to be sold by auction in England.[178] William Jenkyn, longtime friend and fellow-Presbyterian minister in London, preached his funeral sermon on 2 Peter 1:15. He said that Seaman

> was an *ocean of Theology*, and that he had so thoroughly digested the whole body of divinity, that he could upon all occasions discourse upon any point without labour. He was a living body of Divinity, *and his tongue as the pen of a ready writer*. He was a person of great stability and steadiness in the truth. I am confident that he valued one truth of Christ, above all the wealth of both the Indies.[179]

Alexander Gordon says, 'Seaman was a man of much learning, noted as a casuist, charitable in disposition, and a model of prudent reserve.'[180]

Matthew Newcomen (c. 1610 - c. September 1, 1669)

The young preacher's text was Isaiah 62:6-7, 'I have set watchmen upon thy walls, O Jerusalem, which shall never hold their peace day nor night: ye that make mention of the Lord, keep not silence, and give him no rest, till he establish, and till he make Jerusalem a praise in the earth.' The occasion was a special Fast Day for both Houses of Parliament and the Westminster Assembly on July 7, 1643 as the Assembly was beginning its business. It had opened on Saturday, July 1 with a sermon by the Prolocutor, Dr. William Twisse, but then it had adjourned to the next Thursday, when it organized itself. Prior to actual business, though, would be a Friday of fasting and prayer and, of course, preaching, with Oliver Bowles, one of the oldest members of the Assembly, preaching in the morning on John 2:17, *Zeale for Gods House Quickened*, and Matthew Newcomen, one of the youngest members, preaching in the afternoon *Jerusalems Watch-Men, the Lords Remembrancers*. Newcomen revealed his own excitement at the prospect of the Assembly's discussions: 'Verily I have often from my heart wished that your greatest adversaries and traducers might be witnesses of your learned, grave, and pious debates, which were able to silence, not convert malignity itself.'[181] The Assembly was a long-awaited fulfilment of the desire for a church government 'according to the Word of God' and the 'effecting of a more neer and full union between us and the rest of the Reformed Churches.'[182] Indeed the whole world was anticipating what God would accomplish through the prayers and deliberations of the divines:

> Keep no silence, give the Lord no rest until He establish the House .... except the Lord build the house, reform the Church, it is to no purpose to go about to reform it .... I need not tell you how many eyes and expectations there are upon this Assembly .... What you pray for, contend for .... as you pray that God would establish his Church in peace, so labour to work out the Church's peace. And lastly, as you pray that God would make the Church a praise, so endeavor that also; endeavoring ... that all her ways may be ordered according to the rule of God's Word: that the Gospel may run and be glorified: that those two great illuminating ordinances of Preaching and Catechizing, which are as the greater and lesser lights of heaven, may have such liberty, encouragement, maintenance, that all the earth may be filled with the knowledge of the Lord.[183]

John F. Wilson says that Newcomen was 'apparently a last-minute replacement', and it is surprising that on such an auspicious occasion

Parliament would not have called upon one of their favorite veteran preachers, such as William Gouge, Cornelius Burgess, Stephen Marshall or Edmund Calamy.[184] Newcomen did have connections with these leaders, however, and had gained a measure of fame as one of the 'Smectymnuans' who had responded to Bishop Hall's defence of Episcopacy by divine right in 1641, and he had already preached to the House of Commons once before, in 1642.

Matthew Newcomen was born at Colchester, Essex about 1610, the second son of Stephen Newcomen, Vicar of St. Peter's, Colchester since 1600, who came from a long line of Newcomens of Saltfleetby, Lincolnshire. Matthew was educated under William Kempe at the Royal Grammar School of Colchester and on November 8, 1626 entered St. John's College, Cambridge, where he obtained the B.A. in 1630 and the M.A. in 1633. His older brother Thomas had preceded him at St. John's College by about four years and became a minister in Colchester with strong Royalist leanings, which made him the object of much abuse in Puritan Essex.[185] In contrast, Matthew, after serving as Curate of Messing, Essex in 1632, being ordained as a deacon, and then serving as Curate to Thomas Mott at Stoke-by-Nayland, Suffolk until 1636, was recommended to the Lectureship of Dedham, Essex, where the famous Puritan John Rogers had died on October 18, 1636.[186] His gifts were quite different from those of Rogers, who was

> a grave, severe, and solid divine. His great gift lay in the delivery of the solid matter which he had prepared with a peculiar gesture and elocution, so that few persons heard him without trembling at the word of God. He was indeed one of the most awakening preachers of the age.[187]

Newcomen, on the other hand, 'was much esteemed as a wit, and for his curious parts, which being afterwards sanctified by Divine grace fitted him for eminent service in the church'.[188] He would remain as Lecturer and Curate at Dedham until August 20, 1662 although he would be active as a London clergyman during the Assembly.[189] While at Dedham he may have produced a catechism.[190] In the summer of 1640, anticipating repression after the dissolving of the Short Parliament in May, he predicted that he might be silenced and urged his followers to read John Foxe's *Acts and Monuments* to fortify themselves against apostasy.[191]

In 1640 he married Hannah, daughter of Robert Snelling, member of Parliament for Ipswich 1614-1625, who was sister of Edmund

Calamy's first wife and widow of Gilbert Reyney (or Rany), Rector of
St. Mary's Stoke, Ipswich. They would have four sons and seven
daughters, but three boys and three girls would die in childhood.[192]
While at Dedham Newcomen, along with Stephen Marshall, Edmund
Calamy and many other Puritan ministers, enjoyed the protection of
Robert Rich, the second Earl of Warwick and Lord Lieutenant of
Essex.[193] Since four of the Smectymnuans – Stephen Marshall at
Finchingfield, Edmund Calamy at Bury St. Edmunds, Thomas Young
at Stowmarket, and Matthew Newcomen at Colchester, Messing,
Stoke-by-Nayland, or Dedham – were all within about thirty miles of
each other in the late 1620s and 1630s, it is not unlikely that Warwick
enabled them to combine forces to produce the Smectymnuus tracts in
response to Bishop Hall in 1641. The fifth member of the team, William
Spurstowe, was in nearby Buckinghamshire.[194]

Newcomen was invited to preach to the House of Commons on
November 5, 1642, the anniversary of the Gunpowder Plot of 1605. His
sermon was entitled *The Craft and Cruelty of the Churches Adversaries*
and was based on Nehemiah 4:11. Focusing on King Charles, he said:

> As for our Sovereign, Thou O God in whose hands the hearts of Kings are,
> free his heart from the councels and ingagements of mischievous men and
> men of blood. Give him a true understanding of, and a due confidence in
> the loyall affections of his Protestant Subjects. Bring him backe among us,
> rather in the prayers and tears then in the blouds of his people.[195]

That prayer would find answer only in continued warfare. In 1643
Newcomen became a Lecturer at St. Mary Aldermanbury in London
and an assistant there to his brother-in-law, Edmund Calamy.[196] The
financial aspects of this arrangement reveal the kind of secondary and
supportive role that Newcomen was apparently quite willing to play:
Calamy was paid an annual stipend of £160, one of the highest paid to
a London minister, and Newcomen was paid £52 a year, £30 of which
was to be paid him by Calamy.[197]

In the actual work of the Westminster Assembly Newcomen, after
preaching at the opening Fast Day, showed his commitment to Presbyterian distinctives from the beginning.[198] On November 15, 1644 he
was appointed to the committee to consider the 'Reasons' of the
Independents.[199] On April 4, 1645 he made the motion, 'That the
Brethren of this Assembly that had formerly entered their dissent to the
Propositions about Presbyterial Government, shall be a Committee to

bring in the whole Frame of their judgment, concerning Church-Government in a Body, with their Grounds and Reasons.'[200] He also reported on November 27 for the committee preparing an answer to the Dissenting Brethren's *Remonstrance ... Declaring the Grounds and Reasons of their declining to bring in to the Assembly, their Modell of Church-Government*, which was published on November 12.[201]

Newcomen was also very much involved in the committee work dealing with Erastian issues. In August 1645 he was convener of the committee that drew up a petition to Parliament concerning church discipline.[202] On March 20, 1646 Stephen Marshall, Richard Vines, Lazarus Seaman and Newcomen were assigned to prepare the petition to Parliament objecting to the proposed civil commissions to deal with scandalous sins.[203] He also served on the committee to deal with Antinomianism and on the Grand Committee concerned with the treaty obligations to the Scots.[204] Most important of all, on September 4, 1644 he was among those added to the committee to prepare the Confession of Faith, and on July 8, 1645 he was appointed with Edward Reynolds and Charles Herle to reword the draft of the Confession.[205] Jack B. Rogers concludes that Newcomen, along with Anthony Tuckney, Jeremiah Whitaker, and John Arrowsmith, played the largest supporting roles to the seven most responsible for producing the Confession: Reynolds, Cornelius Burgess, Thomas Temple, Herle, Joshua Hoyle, Thomas Gataker, and Robert Harris.[206]

Newcomen continued to exercise his preaching gifts during the Assembly. For a special Fast Day on September 12, 1644, after the defeat of the Parliamentary army of the Earl of Essex in the west, he preached to both Houses of Parliament from Joshua 7:10-11, where the Lord responded to the sin of Achan. William Haller summarizes Newcomen's sermon:

> The answer to the question, what sin, by whom committed, had brought the anger of the Lord upon the parliamentary army in Cornwall, seemed therefore clear. Parliament and assembly had covenanted to extirpate heresy and schism; yet heresy and schism abounded more than ever, and nothing would placate the wrath of the Lord but their immediate suppression and the restoration of order, unity, and discipline in religion with parliament's support.[207]

Newcomen charged that 'the violation of the Covenant of God', just a year after it had been adopted, was a sin so terrible that it might provoke him into 'striking' Parliament.[208] On December 30, 1646 he preached on the regular monthly Fast Day to the House of Commons on Hebrews 4:13, *The All-Seeing Unseen Eye of God*, in which he appealed for the priority of truth and unity over liberty.[209] He dealt with a similar theme when he preached at St. Paul's on Sunday, February 8, 1647 on Philippians 1:27, *The Duty of Such as would Walk worthy of the Gospel, to endeavour Union, not Division, nor Toleration*:

> 'I know ... it hath been said by some, that because a *heart* to *know* and *embrace* the *truth* is the *gift of God*, and the *Magistrate* cannot by *forcible means work* such a heart in man, therefore the Magistrate must use no *compulsion* or *coercion* in matters of Religion. But does this mean that the magistrate may not "*compell* men to *attend* upon those *meanes* where *God* doth *usually give that grace*" or is forbidden to *make Laws* to *restrain* and *punish erreurs and blasphemies* that are against truth?'[210]

Newcomen was part of the Presbyterian 6th Classis in London by virtue of his position at St. Mary Aldermanbury,[211] but by 1648 he was once again active among the ministers of Essex. He and a few others drew up *The Essex Watchman's Watchword* in 1649 protesting against Oliver Cromwell's 'Agreement' because of the proposal of toleration 'which like the fly in the box of ointment may make it abhorrent in the nostrils of every one who is judicious and pious.'[212] Nevertheless, he was appointed an assistant to the commission of 'Triers of Scandalous Ministers' for Essex in 1654, and in 1655 he was Town Lecturer at Ipswich.[213]

In the negotiations toward the restoration of the monarchy in 1660 he was offered a Royal Chaplaincy along with nine or ten other Presbyterians, but he alone declined.[214] When Edmund Calamy was offered the position of Bishop of Lichfield and Coventry, it is reported that he almost accepted, 'but was dissuaded by his wife and Matthew Newcomen, his brother-in-law.'[215] He participated actively in the Savoy Conference to revise the Book of Common Prayer and propose alternate forms for the use of Presbyterians within a comprehensive Church of England, but before May 21, 1661 he left in despair.[216] Unable to conform, he preached two farewell sermons in August of 1662, one on Revelation 3:3 published in the London collection and another on Acts 20:32 entitled *'Ultimum Vale'*; or, *The Last Farewell of a Minister of the Gospel to a beloved people*, which was published in the Country Collection.[217]

In December 1662 he moved with his family to the Netherlands to become Pastor of the English church in Leiden. He had gained the D.D. in October 1661, and his scholarly ministry was well received by faculty members of the University of Leiden.[218] He was among over twenty-five ejected ministers to go to the Netherlands, and his wife was later thanked for her hospitality to preachers who came to Leiden.[219] He was included in a list of fourteen fugitives who were summoned home for trial and punishment in a royal proclamation issued on March 26, 1666, but his name was removed through personal influence. Newcomen prudently took steps to purchase citizenship at Leiden.[220] On March 5, 1667 Sir John Webster wrote to Charles II on his behalf, describing Newcomen as 'a poore preacher at Leyden, that hath a sicke wife and five poore and sicklye children'. These were Stephen, age 21, Hannah, 20, Martha, almost 16, Alice, 14, and Sarah, 11. Webster wrote:

> He came out of England with license, and liveth peaceably, not meddling with anie affaires in England, hath done nothing towards printing or dispersing bookes, and has constantly prayed for the King and Council. He humbly craveth to be exempt from the summons and is ready to purge himself by word or oath before any Commissary yr. Majie. may appoint.[221]

Matthew Newcomen died of the plague, in Leiden, about the first of September, 1669. His funeral sermon was preached by John Fairfax, an ejected minister, at Dedham on September 16, and a large number were present. The sermon was entitled *The Dead Saint yet speaking*. His widow, Hannah, and her children were permitted to return to England in April 1670.[222]

John Ley (February 4, 1583 - May 16, 1662)

On May 1, 1646 John Ley asked permission of the Assembly to be absent for one month 'to visit his people in Cheshire, after four years' absence.'[223] Ley was one of the hardest-working members of the Assembly, chairing the committee for examination of ministers, which S.W. Carruthers claims was, 'next to the production of the great documents, the most important part of the Assembly's work ....'[224] It was not an easy task, yet an urgent one, as the churches needed certified ministers. On September 28, 1643 the Assembly decided that once a name was submitted by the House of Commons' Committee of Plundered Ministers, the next day at 9 a.m. a committee of 'any five of the Assembly, whereof Mr. Ley to be one' was to examine the man;

then they would report to the Assembly before the necessary certificate would be issued for the Parliamentary committee.

> The minutes give reason to suppose that a comparatively few enthusiastic members undertook this extra work, which seems from Lightfoot's journal to have included the hearing of a sermon during the hour before the Assembly sat at ten o'clock.[225]

John Lightfoot was a frequent participant, but the main burden of this examining committee clearly fell on Ley. His well-earned month's leave was granted by the Assembly on May 1, 1646, but this doughty old Puritan was either back in London, or still in London, to preach to the House of Lords on May 12.[226]

John Ley was born on February 4, 1583, in Warwick. On February 12, 1602 he entered Christ Church College, Oxford, where he received the B.A. on October 23, 1605 and the M.A. on May 30, 1608. His earliest publication, showing his Calvinist leanings, was *An Apology in Defence of the Geneva Notes on the Bible*, written about 1612, the year after the publication of the Authorized Version.[227] He became Vicar of Great Budworth, Cheshire in 1616. Sometime later he also became Sub-Dean of Chester and a Friday Lecturer at St. Peter's Church there, and in 1627 he was made a Prebendary of Chester Cathedral.[228] A letter that he wrote to Bishop John Bridgeman in 1635 shows the gradual alienation he was experiencing from Episcopacy and sacramentalism:

> In June of that year he wrote a letter to Bishop Bridgeman, on the subject of an alleged stone altar newly erected in the cathedral .... Ley describes the setting up of an altar as 'schismaticall', and warns that in consequence Puritans 'will be more stiffe in standing out against conformity ... and we that are conformable shall be lesse strong to contest with them.' He goes on to ask 'can there be anything in that heap of stones which may serve to repair the ruines which an altar may make?' Nevertheless the letter is couched in generally respectful terms and Ley quoted the opinion of Aquinas that 'an inferior clerke may sometimes admonish a prelate.' He also refers to the 'great moderation', for which Bridgeman is renowned, and as late as 1641 recalled how they had been preachers together in the Warrington exercise. By this latter date, however, Ley regarded men like his diocesan as exceptions to the general run of bishops, and was himself moving steadily in a presbyterian direction. Two years later he subscribed the Solemn League and Covenant, thus committing himself to the 'extirpation' of episcopacy.[229]

Ley was one of nineteen clergymen who became Lecturers in London as a result of their invitation to the Westminster Assembly.[230] Very soon, however, he made his presence felt. On the Fast Day of April 26, 1643 he preached to the House of Commons a sermon entitled *The Fury of War, and Folly of Sin*, based on Jeremiah 4:21-22.[231] He became Rector of St. Mary at Hill, London in 1643, and in 1644 he was elected President of Sion College,[232] which after October 1643 'seems to have become the centre of Puritan, and later Presbyterian, influence in London.'[233]

Robert Paul comments that in the work of the Assembly itself John Ley 'seems to have carried considerable weight in the First Committee' of the three general working committees into which the entire membership was divided.[234] His Presbyterian inclinations were made evident early in the Assembly, but by November 22, 1643 he, like Herbert Palmer and other conservatives, was still not convinced that the office of ruling elder was mandated by Scripture.[235] When Jeremiah Burroughes argued on January 25, 1644 that the London ministers could not ordain because they did not have the ecclesiastical status, Ley gave the pragmatic answer 'that the ministers of London being set upon this work *is a presbytery.*'[236] On August 9, 1644 he engaged in an exchange with Thomas Goodwin over the definition of 'schisms and sects', Ley offering: 'That that draws Christians from communion with their own pastors' - a definition opposing the concept of the Independents' gathered congregations.[237] On March 18, 1644 Ley took a slap at Congregationalist theologian William Ames for his criticism of ordination without a specific pastoral call, a practice that was commonly accepted in the Church of England.[238]

Ley appears to have been pragmatic about a number of issues. Regarding the requisite education for ministers, he asked whether a man must be able to read his Greek New Testament: Although 'they have forgot their Greek, yet the food of souls is more necessary.'[239] In the discussions about the proper posture for receiving the Lord's Supper, Ley said he 'consented to any posture' though he favored sitting, in imitation of Christ's example, over standing or kneeling; but he commented that different churches follow different practices in this matter. When the committee reported ' – that all the business about coming in companies to the table was left out, and the passage was only this, – "the communicants orderly sitting about the table," &c. and no more mention of any posture ...,' Ley was the only one voting against the recommendation because he felt that it tied communicants 'too strictly to sitting'.[240] In regard to baptism, he and several others were willing to recognize 'dipping' as a legitimate mode in the Directory for Worship, but others including the Scots prevailed because they did not want to encourage doubt about sprinkling.[241]

Ley also served as chairman of the printing committee, which had the difficult and important job of assuring that there was a sufficient supply of accurate Bibles for the populace at a reasonable price.[242] He was appointed on September 4, 1644 to the committee of nineteen men to work with the Scottish commissioners to draw up the Confession of Faith.[243] Ley also preached to Parliament with some frequency, often on the occasions of Thanksgivings for military victories, as to the House of Commons on October 2, 1645, to the House of Lords on February 5, 1646, and again to the Lords on May 12, 1646.[244] He may have preached to the Lords on January 31, 1649 (with Stephen Marshall on the day after the King's execution) and to the Commons on March 13, 1651, but the entries in the Journals of the House of Lords and of the House of Commons are uncertain.[245]

THE WESTMINSTER ANNOTATIONS ON THE BIBLE

A large work entitled *Annotations upon All the Books of the Old and New Testaments*, often referred to as the 'Westminster Annotations' or the 'English Annotations', was published in one folio volume in 1645 with a second edition in two folio volumes in 1651 and a third edition in two folio volumes in 1657. This evidently was not an official work of the Westminster Assembly although it was authorized by Parliament and was produced mostly by members of the Assembly. John Ley did the Pentateuch and the four Gospels, William Gouge did Kings through Esther, Francis Taylor did Proverbs, Edward Reynolds did Ecclesiastes, Thomas Gataker did Isaiah, Jeremiah, and Lamentations, and Daniel Featley did most of the Pauline Epistles. Only the Psalms (Meric Casaubon), Song of Solomon (Mr. Smallwood), Ezekiel, Daniel, and the Minor Prophets (Mr. Pemberton in the 1st edition, John Richardson in the 2nd and 3rd editions), and Acts, the remaining Pauline Epistles, Hebrews, the General Epistles, and Revelation (presumably John Downham and Mr. Reading) were done by others than members of the Assembly, apparently under the supervision of John Downham. The *Annotations*, therefore, can sometimes shed light on how the Westminster divines understood a particular text of Scripture.

One of John Ley's major projects during the Assembly was his part in the production of the English Annotations on the Bible, often referred to as the 'Westminster Annotations' although not an official product of the Assembly.[246] Ley contributed the annotations for the Pentateuch and also for the four Gospels, hence a large proportion of the whole. Other members of the Assembly who contributed were William Gouge (Kings, Chronicles, Ezra, Nehemiah, Esther), Francis Taylor (Proverbs), Edward Reynolds (Ecclesiastes), Thomas Gataker (Isaiah, Jeremiah, Lamentations), and Daniel Featley (the Pauline Epistles, though incomplete). A first edition in one folio volume of 915 pages was issued in 1645, a second edition in two folio volumes in 1651, and a third edition in two folio volumes in 1657. On September 16, 1645 the Assembly's attention was called to 'the Annotations of the Bible' with concern that there were 'Some things in them against the Covenant and the votes of the Assembly.' There was debate about this on the next day, and on the 22nd 'Mr. Palmer made report about the Annotations. The stationers desired that some animadversions may be made suddenly, and they promised to sell no more till tomorrow.' On the 25th 'Mr. Ley gave an account of the antidote prepared against the particulars complained of in the Annotations of the Bible.'[247] Although the Assembly itself was not responsible for the 'English Annotations', there was an awareness of its being produced for a committee of Parliament and of its significance.

In 1646 Ley also published three titles dealing with the views of John Saltmarsh, who had written against the establishment of Presbyterian church government: 1. *Examination of Mr. Saltmarsh's New Query*; 2. *Light for Smoke; or, a clear and distinct Reply to a dark and confused Answer, in a book, made and entitled, 'The Smoke in the Temple' by John Saltmarsh*; and 3. *An After-reckoning with Mr. Saltmarsh*.[248] Also in 1646 Ley was approved to be Rector of Ashfield and of Astbury in Cheshire on September 2, but was not actually placed in the latter until April 22, 1647.[249] Back in Cheshire he produced 'An Attestation to the Testimony of our Reverend Brethren of the Province of London, to the Truth of Jesus Christ and to our Solemn League and Covenant, resolved on by the Ministers of Cheshire at their Meeting, 2nd May, and subscribed at their next Meeting, 6th July, 1648,' which was signed by fifty-nine Presbyterian ministers.[250]

In 1653 Ley contributed his pen to the polemics for tithes against the Fifth Monarchy Men, writing *A Learned Defence for the Legality of*

Tithes and, under the pen-name of 'Theophilus Philadelphus', *Exceptions Many and Just Against two Injurious Petitions Exhibited to the Parliament.* In the latter,

> Ley even opposed the replacement of tithes by a public fund to be managed by commissioners, from which the ministers were to receive yearly stipends. 'It is better to enjoy a revenue of an ancient and well grounded title' he argued, 'then to take a new one of another kind, though of greater valew'; for, Ley warned, 'the inconveniences, and evill consequences of this change, from an Ecclesiasticall to a Politicall Title, are neither few nor small.'[251]

When Edward Hyde (not his kinsman of the same name, the first Earl of Clarendon) was ejected from the valuable rectory of Brightwell, Berkshire, Ley succeeded him there, and this led to a controversy in which he produced three titles: 1. *General Reasons against the Payment of a fifth part to Sequestered Ministers' Wives and Children ... whereto are added special Reasons against the Payment of a fifth part to Dr. E. H. out of the Rectory of Brightwell* (1654); 2. *A Letter to Dr. Edward Hyde, in Answer to one of his, occasioned by the late Insurrection at Salisbury* (1655); and 3. *A Debate concerning the English liturgy, between E. Hyde, D.D., and John Ley* (1656).[252]

Ley later became Rector of Solihull, Warwickshire, where he served for some years before becoming disabled from a ruptured blood-vessel. He then retired to Sutton Coldfield, Warwickshire, where he died on May 16, 1662 at the age of seventy-nine.[253]

George Walker (c.1581-1651)

On May 20, 1641 the case of George Walker came before the Long Parliament. The House of Commons resolved:

> – That his commitment from the Council-table for preaching a sermon, October 14, 1638, and his detainment twelve weeks for the same, is against the law and the liberty of the subject.
> – That the prosecution of the said Walker in the Star chamber, for preaching the said sermon, and his close imprisonment thereupon for ten weeks in the Gatehouse, and the payment of twenty pounds fees, is against law and the liberty of the subject
> – That the five passages marked in the sermon, by Mr. Attorney and Sir John Banks, contain no crime, nor deserve any censure, nor he any punishment for them.

– That the enforcing the said Walker to enter into the bond of one thousand pounds, for confinement in his brother's house at Cheswick, and his imprisonment there, is against law.

– That the sequestration of the parsonage of the said Walker, by Sir John Lamb, was done without any warrant and against the law of the land.

– That Walker ought to be restored to his parsonage, and the whole profits thereof, from the time of the said sequestration, and to have reparation for all such damages as he hath sustained by those several imprisonments, and his case transmitted to the lords.[254]

Thus Walker was freed after two-and-a-half years and restored to his rectory of St. John Evangelist, Watling Street, which he had held since 1614.

Walker had incurred the wrath of Archbishop William Laud when he preached against a book on the Lord's day by Francis White, Bishop of Ely, which reflected the official position of the 'Book of Sports'. In 1635 Laud mentioned in his annual report to Charles I that Walker

had all his time been but a disorderly and peevish man, and now of late hath very frowardly preached against the Lord Bishop of Ely his book concerning the Lord's Day, set out by authority; but upon a canonical admonition given him to desist he hath recollected himself, and I hope will be advised.[255]

In 1638 Walker published in Amsterdam his *Doctrine of the Holy Weekly Sabbath*, a second edition of which would be published in 1641. Larry J. Holley describes this work as 'one of the most extreme statements of Sabbatarian doctrine ever written.'[256] On October 14, 1638 he preached a sermon in his own church in which he taught 'that it is a sin to obey the greatest monarch on earth, in those things which stand opposed to the commands of God.'[257] This teaching was apparently repeated on November 4 at St. Helen Bishopsgate, where he was a Lecturer, for on November 11 he was committed to prison 'for some "things tending to faction and disobedience to authority" found in a sermon delivered by him on the 4th of the same month.' At the trial of Laud in 1643 the imprisonment of Walker was one of the charges against him.[258]

Walker was perhaps the most pugnacious of the Westminster divines, one who apparently was gifted in debate and who could enjoy a good argument. Born about 1581 at Hawkshead in Furness, Lancashire, he attended the Hawkshead Grammar School founded by his kinsman, Archbishop Edwin Sandys. In his youth he was afflicted with small-pox and was expected to die when he suddenly spoke out of a trance, 'Lord, take me not away until I have showed forth thy praise', after which his parents devoted him to the ministry.[259] He went to St. John's College, Cambridge, where he obtained the B.A. in 1609 and the M.A. in 1612.[260] Ordained in 1611, he became Rector of St. John Evangelist, Watling Street, the smallest parish in London, on April 29, 1614. His former tutor, Christopher Foster, had resigned the benefice in his favor. Here he would continue to the end of his life, refusing all higher preferments offered to him.[261]

The year 1614 also marked one of his first controversies, as he accused Anthony Wotton of Socinian heresy and blasphemy. This led to a 'conference before eight learned divines' which ended in the vindication of Wotton.[262] In 1619 Walker received the B.D. and also became chaplain to Nicholas Felton, Bishop of Ely, a position that he would retain until Felton's death in 1626.[263] On May 31, 1623 he had a disputation with a Roman Catholic priest, Sylvester Norris, on the authority of the church. An account of this was published in 1624 under the title *The Summe of a Disputation between Mr. Walker ... and a Popish Priest, calling himselfe Mr. Smith*. Also in 1623 he participated with Daniel Featley in a disputation with the Jesuit Father John Fisher (real name Percy), and afterwards he published *Fisher's Folly Unfolded; or, the Vaunting Jesuites Vanity discovered in a Challenge of his ... undertaken and answered by G.W.*

In the 1630s Walker was one of the few London ministers, along with William Gouge, Cornelius Burgess, Adoniram Byfield, John Downham, Arthur Jackson and some others, who found favor with Puritans.[264] In the first statutory election of Sion College, which would become a center of Presbyterian activity in London, Walker and Burgess were elected Assistants with two others, under the President and two Deans, on May 3, 1631.[265] Walker became a Lecturer at St. Benet Fink and also at St. Helen Bishopsgate, a post he would hold from 1639 to 1647 (except when imprisoned).[266]

In 1638 Walker got into a controversy with John Goodwin, the Vicar of St. Stephen, Coleman Street. Goodwin had Arminian leanings, and the controversy was over the issues of justification and the imputation of Christ's righteousness. According to William Haller,

> The technical point for which Goodwin contended was that the atonement did not impute or transfer to sinners the righteousness of Christ but only the

power to believe that by that righteousness they might be justified and saved if they would. Man was saved by faith, but faith saved him by setting him to the task of seeking truth and obeying it when found.[267]

Walker recognized the affinities of Goodwin's teaching to that of Socinus and of Arminius, met him in public debate, and in 1641 published *A Defence of the True Sense and Meaning of the Words of the Holy Apostle: Rom. 4. ver. 3.5.9*. In this work he alleges that Goodwin is teaching justification by works and that his doctrine is 'more impious than the Pelagian and Popish Heresies concerning justification.'[268] In the process of this controversy Walker brought up again his dispute in 1614 with Anthony Wotton, whose views bore some similarity to Goodwin's. In the earlier controversy Thomas Gataker defended Wotton's opinions, whereas Walker's charges against Wotton were supported by William Gouge, John Downham, and Richard Stock. Now Gataker added a postscript to the defense of Wotton.[269] C. F. Allison in summarizing the discussions of justification and imputation, however, places Walker and Gataker together with John Owen over against the views of Wotton, John Goodwin, and Richard Baxter.[270]

Upon his release from prison in 1641 Walker published half a dozen of his works in the two years before the start of the Westminster Assembly. In the Assembly he played an active role, being seventeenth on the list of most frequent speakers in the debates on church government, after Thomas Temple and ahead of Alexander Henderson.[271] He was one of the leaders in oppositon to the Independents.[272] He gave a strong answer to those who would challenge the ordination that most of the Westminster divines had received from Bishops or who would say that their churches were not true churches.[273] He also served on the committee to consider Antinomianism.[274] When it came to discussion of whom to admit to the Lord's Supper, however, Walker somewhat disgustedly said that 'all our disputation is but a spending of time', for in the last resort each minister must act according to his own conscience.[275]

He did not preach often before Parliament, but on the regular monthly Fast Day of January 29, 1645 he was the first of the preachers to the House of Commons to focus on the subject of heresy and schism.[276] He said that it is no new thing in sacred history for there to be wicked rulers, moved by pernicious counsellors, and with men of violence at their command. But for God to be so merciful 'as to reserve to himselfe a prevayling party, and to put wisdome and courage into the great Counsell of the Kingdome, to resist their violence, to preserve Religion from ruine ...: this,' he said, 'is a mercy proper to the times of the Gospell, and to those Nations and Kingdomes in which Christ ruleth by his holy Spirit, and his church is surely established, by the word of God faithfully preached, & true religion is planted in the hearts of the people.'[277] It is reported that he wrote out all his sermons, but made no use of his notes in the pulpit, although he always had them in his pocket.[278]

In 1645 Walker was elected President of Sion College, having served as Junior Dean in 1643 and Senior Dean in 1644.[279] He also delivered a large gift to the Sion College Library.[280] This is but one example of his generosity in benefactions. On March 11, 1634 he had undertaken to contribute a certain sum annually for five years for repairs at St. Paul's Cathedral.[281] He also engaged in fund-raising for his native Lancashire. He wrote *An Exhortation to Dearely beloved countrimen, all the Natives of the Countie of Lancaster, inhabiting in and about the Citie of London, tending to persuade and stirre them up to a yearely contribution for the erection of Lectures, and maintaining of some Godly and Painfull Preachers in such places of that Country as have most neede.*[282] In that tract he described how the people of Lancashire 'are ready and willing to run many miles to hear sermons when they have them not at home, and lay aside all care of profit, leaving their labour and work on weekdays to frequent public meetings for prophecy and expounding of God's word.'[283] Walker was also aware, on the other hand, of some of the contemporary public opinion about the Assembly; he told of a woman who said of the divines that they 'sit with a price, and are always sitting; but where will they hatch? They will hatch in hell.'[284]

Walker spared neither friend nor foe in his polemical barbs. In 1645 he criticized the Presbyterian Parliamentarian William Prynne in *A Brotherly and Friendly Censure of the Errour of a Dear Friend and Brother in Christian Affection.*[285] On the other hand, he was one of the signers of *A Vindication of the Ministers of the Gospel in, and about London* opposing the actions of the Army leading to the trial and execution of the King in January 1649.[286]

George Walker died in 1651, in his seventieth year, and was buried in St. John Evangelist, Watling Street. Anthony à Wood termed him a 'severe partisan', but Thomas Fuller said he was 'a man of an holy life, humble heart, and bountiful hand.'[287]

Notes

1. [Archibald Alexander], *A History of the Westminster Assembly of Divines* (Philadelphia: Presbyterian Board of Publication, 1841), 222-223.

2. James Reid, *Memoirs of the Westminster Divines*, 2 vols. in 1 (Edinburgh and Carlisle, Pa.: Banner of Truth, 1982 reprint of edition of 1811 and 1815), I, 185.

3. William Haller, *Liberty and Reformation in the Puritan Revolution* (New York and London: Columbia U. Press, 1955), 37.

4. Tai Liu, *Puritan London* (Newark, Del.: U. of Delaware Press, 1966), 74.

5. *Dictionary of National Biography*, eds. Leslie Stephen and Sidney Lee, 22 vols.(London: Oxford U. Press, 1921-22), III, 679. Larry Jackson Holley, 'The Divines of the Westminster Assembly,' (New Haven: Yale U. Ph.D. diss., 1979), 288, says he was born in Wallbrook, Suffolk.

6. Holley, 'Divines', 288; *D.N.B.*, III, 679.

7. Reid, *Memoirs*, I, 166.

8. *Ibid.*, 167.

9. *D.N.B.*, III, 679; Holley, 'Divines', 288; *Calamy Revised*, ed. A.G. Matthews (Oxford: Clarendon Press, 1934), 97; Reid, *Memoirs*, I, 169.

10. Reid, *Memoirs*, I, 171; *D.N.B.*, III, 679.

11. Liu, *Puritan London*, 29, 75-76, 173.

12. *Ibid.*, 151-152.

13. Jacqueline Eales, *Puritans and Roundheads* (Cambridge, New York, etc.: Cambridge U. Press, 1990), 112-113; Paul S. Seaver, *The Puritan Lectureships* (Stanford, Cal.: Stanford U. Press, 1970), 264. Richard L. Greaves, *Saints and Rebels: Seven Nonconformists in Stuart England* (Macon, Ga.: Mercer U. Press, 1985), 15.

14. Reid, *Memoirs*, I, 172. Cf. Haller, *Liberty and Reformation*, 34-35.

15. Tai Liu, *Discord in Zion* (The Hague: Martinus Nijhoff, 1973), 36 n.24.

16. *Ibid.*, 9; George Yule, *Puritans in Politics* (Appleford, Oxfordshire: Sutton Courtenay Press, 1981), 122-123.

17. John F. Wilson, *Pulpit in Parliament* (Princeton, N.J.: Princeton U. Press, 1969), 55-56, Cf. Liu, *Discord in Zion*, 20, 31, 35.

18. Wilson, *Pulpit in Parliament*, 183-184; cf. 63, 158-159. For other references to this sermon, cf. Haller, *Liberty and Reformation,* 68-69; Liu, *Discord in Zion*, 19; H.R. Trevor-Roper, *The Crisis of the Seventeenth Century* (New York and Evanston: Harper & Row, 1968), 306-307.

19. Robert S. Paul, *The Assembly of the Lord* (Edinburgh: T.& T. Clark, 1985), 118-119; *Calamy Revised*, 97. E.H. Pearce, *Sion College and Library* (Cambridge: Cambridge U. Press, 1913), 344, shows the following Assembly members to have been President: John Ley (1644), George Walker (1645), Cornelius Burgess (1647-48), William Gouge (1649) Lazarus Seaman (1651-52), and Edward Reynolds (1659).

20. Wilson, *Pulpit in Parliament*, 70. Cf. Haller, *Liberty and Reformation*, 100-101; Liu, *Discord in Zion*, 23.

21. Wayne R. Spear, 'Covenanted Uniformity in Religion' (Pittsburgh: U. of Pittsburgh Ph.D. diss., 1976), 362.

22. John Richard de Witt, *Jus Divinum* (Kampen: J.H. Kok, 1969), 72, 84.

23. Paul, *Assembly of the Lord*, 243 and n.87.

24. *Ibid.*, 427 and n.190.

25. S.W. Carruthers, *The Everyday Work of the Westminster Assembly* (Philadelphia: The Presbyterian Historical Societies of America and of England, 1943), 62, 64.

26. Cf. Paul, *Assembly of the Lord*, 371, 373-374, 439 n.10, 435 and n.228, 450-451 n.62; Greaves, *Saints and Rebels*, 25-28.

27. Seaver, *Puritan Lectureships*, 273. Newcomen's wife was sister of Calamy's first wife, Mary Snelling, who died between 1638 and '41. They were probably of the same family in Ipswich from which William Ames's mother, Joane Snelling came (*D.N.B.*, III, 681) which was also connected by marriage to the family of John Winthrop (Keith L. Sprunger, *The Learned Doctor William Ames* [Urbana, Chicago, London: U. of Illinois Press, 1972], 3, 9).

28. Yule, *Puritans in Politics*, 139.

29. Wilson, *Pulpit in Parliament*, 177; Liu, *Discord in Zion*, 52. Cf. Yule, *Puritans in Politics*, 142.

30. Reid, *Memoirs*, I, 186-187. Cf. Carruthers, *Everyday Work*, 44.

31. Quoted in C. Gordon Bolam, Jeremy Goring, *et al.*, *The English Presbyterians* (Boston: Beacon Press, 1968), 50.

32. Yule, *Puritans in Politics*, 169.

33. Wilson, *Pulpit in Parliament*, 88-89. In 1641 Calamy had written: 'Blessed be God, we have now our Christian new moons and evangelical feast of trumpets. We have not only our monthly sacrament feast to refresh our souls withal in most of our congregations ... but our monthly fasts in which the word is preached, trading ceaseth, and sacrifices of prayer, praises, and alms are tendered up to God,' thus indicating that the Lord's Supper was observed monthly at that time (Alexander F. Mitchell, *The Westminster Assembly*, 2nd ed. [Philadelphia: Presbyterian Board of Publication, 1897], 243 n.1.

34. *D.N.B.*, III, 680; Haller, *Liberty and Reformation*, 145; Seaver, *Puritan Lectureships*, 281; Geoffrey F. Nuttall, *Visible Saints* (Oxford: Basil Blackwell, 1957), 134; Greaves, *Saints and Rebels*, 23-24.

35. Christopher Hill, *The World Turned Upside Down: Radical Ideas during the English Revolution* (New York: Viking Press, 1972), 85. Cf. also Greaves, *Saints and Rebels*, 29.

36. Liu, *Puritan London*, 74.

37. Paul, *Assembly of the Lord*, 322 n.44.

38. Liu, *Puritan London*, 73.

39. Liu, *Discord in Zion*, 163.

40. Bolam, Goring, *et al.*, *English Presbyterians*, 50, 51, and n.1, 59; A.H. Drysdale, *History of the Presbyterians in England* (London: Publication Committee of the Presbyterian Church of England, 1889), 312 and n.1.

41. Reid, *Memoirs*, I, 175. Both Robert S. Paul, *The Lord Protector* (Grand Rapids, Mich.: Eerdmans, 1964), 264-265 n.4, and Antonia Fraser, *Cromwell, Our Chief of Men* (London: Mandarin, 1993 reprint of 1973 ed.), 416, believe Cromwell's statement to be not so much political cynicism as a sense of providential use of force to support what is right.

42. Cf. Bolam, Goring, *et al.*, *English Presbyterians*, 74-79.

43. George R. Abernathy, Jr. 'The English Presbyterians and the Stuart Restoration, 1648-1663,' *Transactions of the American Philosophical Society*, New Series, 55, Part 2 (1965), 65, 66.

44. Abernathy, 'The English Presbyterians', 68; Drysdale, *History*, 375 and n.1.

45. *Calamy Revised*, 97-98.

46. Abernathy, 'The English Presbyterians', 74-75; Greaves, *Saints and Rebels*, 50-51.

47. Bolam, Goring, *et al., English Presbyterians*, 76; Abernathy, 'The English Presbyterians', 77, says Calamy was dissuaded by his wife and Matthew Newcomen, his brother-in-law.

48. J.I. Packer, *A Quest for Godliness: The Puritan Vision of the Christian Life* (Wheaton, Ill: Crossway Books, 1990), 121.

49. Reid, *Memoirs*, I, 176; Greaves, *Saints and Rebels*, 42-43, n. 49 regards this story as 'probably apocryphal'.

50. Reid, *Memoirs*, I, 177-178.

51. *Calamy Revised*, 16; Seaver, *Puritan Lectureships*, 271-272.

52. *D.N.B.*, III, 681.

53. *Sermons of the Great Ejection*, ed. Iain Murray (London: Banner of Truth, 1962), 34.

54. Reid, *Memoirs*, I, 180-181; *D.N.B.*, III, 681.

55. *D.N.B.*, III, 681; Reid, *Memoirs*, I, 185.

56. *D.N.B.*, III, 678-687.

57. Quoted in Paul, *Assembly of the Lord*, 386.

58. *D.N.B.*, I, 640.

59. Holley, 'Divines', 282; *Calamy Revised*, 16.

60. Reid, *Memoirs*, I, 114-116, 128.

61. J.T. Cliffe, *The Puritan Gentry* (London, Boston, etc. Routledge & Kegan Paul, 1984), 183.

62. *D.N.B.*, I, 640; Reid, *Memoirs*, I, 117.

63. *Calamy Revised*, 16.

64. Holley, 'Divines', 283; Seaver, *Puritan Lectureships,* 271; Liu, *Puritan London*, 131.

65. Seaver, *Puritan Lectureships*, 271; Liu, *Puritan London*, 65, 202.

66. Haller, *Liberty and Reformation*, 30.

67. *Ibid.*, 67.

68. Liu, *Discord in Zion*, 20; Reid, *Memoirs*, I, 118-119, 126-127. Cf. Wilson, *Pulpit in Parliament,* 157.

69. Liu, *Puritan London*, 68; Reid, *Memoirs*, I, 127.

70. Carruthers, *Everyday Work*, 139, 138.

71. Holley, 'Divines', 282.

72. Liu, *Discord in Zion*, 38 n.32.

73. Carruthers, *Everyday Work*, 139.

74. *Ibid.*, 142-143.

75. Liu, *Discord in Zion*, 43.

76. Yule, *Puritans in Politics*, 169. Cf. Liu, *Discord in Zion*, 52, and *Puritan London*, 68.

77. Cf. Robert M. Norris, 'The Preaching of the Assembly,' in *To Glorify and Enjoy God*, eds. John F. Carson and David W. Hall (Edinburgh and Carlisle, Pa.: Banner of Truth, 1994), 75-76.

78. Yule, *Puritans in Politics*, 228.

79. Paul, *Assembly of the Lord*, 505. Cf. Yule, *Puritans in Politics*, 178 and 203 n.196.

80. Seaver, *Puritan Lectureships*, 271; Liu, *Puritan London*,141; Reid, *Memoirs*, I, 118.

81. Seaver, *Puritan Lectureships*, 271.

82. Liu, *Discord in Zion*, 163.

83. Drysdale, *History*, 360.

84. Reid, *Memoirs*, I, 128.

85. *Ibid.*, I, 307.

86. Liu, *Puritan London*, 88-89.

87. *D.N.B.*, I, 641; Reid, *Memoirs*, I, 128.

88. *Calamy Revised*, 16; Seaver, *Puritan Lectureships*, 272.

89. Abernathy, 'The English Presbyterians', 12-13.

90. *Ibid.*, 41; Liu, *Discord in Zion*, 158, 165.

91. Abernathy, 'The English Presbyterians', 45, 48 n.138, 68, 75.

92. Drysdale, *History*, 374.

93. *Calamy Revised*, 16; *D.N.B.*, I, 640.

94. Reid, *Memoirs*, I, 121.

95. *Ibid.*, I, 125-126; Liu, *Puritan London*, 157.

96. Reid, *Memoirs*, I, 126.

97. Leland H. Carlson, 'A History of the Presbyterian Party from Pride's Purge to the Dissolution of the Long Parliament', *Church History,* 11 (1942), 85.

98. Liu, *Discord in Zion*, 14.

99. *D.N.B.*, III, 1174.

100. Reid, *Memoirs*, I, 210.

101. Reid, *Memoirs*, I, 217, says, 'Mr. Case lived the longest of any of those who composed the Assembly of Divines, who continued among the Dissenters.' This allows for John Wallis, who lived until 1703, but who conformed and also was not a voting member of the Assembly. Holley, 'Divines', 291, makes Case second to Robert Crosse, who died in 1683, but Crosse, though a member, seems not to have participated actively in the Assembly (*Minutes*, ed. Mitchell and Struthers, 365-366).

102. Carruthers, *Everyday Work*, 25.

103. Reid, *Memoirs*, I, 211.

104. Quoted in Paul, *Assembly of the Lord*, 91-93. Cf. de Witt, *Jus Divinum*, 57; Liu, *Discord in Zion*, 27. Paul argues that de Witt 'brushes aside' the evidence of Case's openness to some modified form of Episcopacy at this point. Liu, however, makes two points: (1) that Alexander Henderson took no exception to Philip Nye's speech to the House of Commons on the occasion of committing to the Covenant 'in whatever the Word shall discover unto us' and (2) that Nye's and Henderson's speeches were published in Edinburgh (27 and n.105). In other words, Case was saying nothing different from what the Scots would say, and his three sermons were

published with a dedicatory epistle to John Lord Maitland, Henderson, Samuel Rutherford, Robert Baillie, and Gillespie.

105. Reid, *Memoirs*, I, 205.

106. *D.N.B.*, III, 1173.

107. *Calamy Revised*, 104.

108. *D.N.B.*, III, 1173.

109. Liu, *Discord in Zion*, 14-15. Cf. Yule, *Puritans in Politics*, 244; Wilson, *Pulpit in Parliament*, 47-48, and 278-279 where the dating of these two sermons is discussed.

110. Seaver, *Puritan Lectureships*, 279; Liu, *Puritan London*, 139, 78, 141.

111. *Calamy Revised*, 104; Seaver, *Puritan Lectureships*, 371 n.41; Reid, *Memoirs*, I, 208.

112. Holley, 'Divines', 292.

113. Wilson, *Pulpit in Parliament*, 66, 178. Cf. Paul Christianson, *Reformers and Babylon* (Toronto, Buffalo, London: U. of Toronto Press, 1978), 239-241.

114. Wilson, *Pulpit in Parliament*, 77-78.

115. Yule, *Puritans in Politics*, 166.

116. Liu, *Discord in Zion*, 45.

117. Yule, *Puritans in Politics*, 185.

118. James Nichols, ed., *Puritan Sermons, 1659-1689; Being the Morning Exercises at Cripplegate, St. Giles in the Fields, and in Southwark by Seventy-Five Ministers of the Gospel in or Near London*, 6 vols. (Wheaton, Ill.: Richard Owen Roberts, Publishers, 1981 reprint of 1844-45 edition), I, vi.

119. Reid, *Memoirs*, I, 208. Volume V of the modern edition was actually the first one published, in 1660, under the title *The Morning Exercise Methodized*, and is introduced by Thomas Case, who contributed Sermons I and XXVIII.

120. Liu, *Puritan London*, 75.

121. Liu, *Discord in Zion*, 163.

122. Carlson, 'A History of the Presbyterian Party', 87.

123. *D.N.B.*, III, 1174; Reid, *Memoirs*, I, 213.

124. Abernathy, 'The English Presbyterians', 18, regards Coke's sworn statements as 'not too trustworthy.'

125. Carlson, 'A History of the Presbyterian Party', 121.

126. *D.N.B.*, III, 1174; *Calamy Revised*, 104; Carlson, 'A History', 122.

127. Quoted in Leland Ryken, *Worldly Saints: The Puritans As They Really Were* (Grand Rapids, Mich.: Zondervan, 1986), 133. Cf. Reid, *Memoirs*, I, 213. *Correction, Instruction* has been reprinted in 1993 by Soli Deo Gloria of Ligonier, Pa. in *The Select Works of Thomas Case*.

128. Abernathy, 'The English Presbyterians', 16; Liu, *Discord in Zion*, 158, 165.

129. Abernathy, 'The English Presbyterians', 65, 66, 68; Drysdale, *History*, 375 n.1.

130. Quoted in *Calamy Revised*, 104.

131. *The Select Works of Thomas Case*, 2 vols. in 1, II, vii.

132. Bolam, Goring, *et al.*, *English Presbyterians*, 106-107.

133. *D.N.B.*, III, 1175.

134. *Ibid.*

135. Reid, *Memoirs*, II, 137-138. Cf. *D.N.B.*, XVII, 1100.

136. Reid, *Memoirs*, II, 137.

137. Holley, 'Divines', 340, says Seaman 'was second only to Peter Sterry as the youngest nominee to the Assembly of Divines'; however, his own data show Matthew Newcomen, Henry Wilkinson, Jr., Henry Hutton, Francis Cheynell, and Richard Bulkely all to be younger than Seaman. Sterry is the only member of the Assembly younger than the Scottish commissioner George Gillespie.

138. Spear, 'Covenanted Uniformity', 362.

139. *D.N.B.*, XVII, 1100; Holley, 'Divines', 340-341; *Calamy Revised*, 430; Seaver, *Puritan Lectureships*, 254.

140. Holley, 'Divines', 341; Liu, *Puritan London*, 56, 157.

141. Paul, *Assembly of the Lord*, 301.

142. de Witt, *Jus Divinum*, 28, 133; Paul, *Assembly of the Lord*, 119, 137, 144, 146, 150 and n.66, 166 n.132, 282, etc.

143. Paul, *Assembly of the Lord*, 343-345, 164; de Witt, *Jus Divinum*, 79.

144. Paul, *Assembly of the Lord*, 226.

145. de Witt, *Jus Divinum*, 70, 111; Paul, *Assembly of the Lord*, 152-153, 255.

146. Carruthers, *Everyday Work*, 90.

147. Paul, *Assembly of the Lord*, 303, 446 and n.37.

148. *Ibid.*, 420.

149. *Ibid.*, 427-428 n.190.

150. de Witt, *Jus Divinum*, 201-202.

151. Paul, *Assembly of the Lord*, 432.

152. *Ibid.*, 506; Mitchell, *Westminster Assembly*, 313; Carruthers, *Everyday Work*, 11.

153. Paul, *Assembly of the Lord*, 83; Carruthers, *Everyday Work*, 107, 175.

154. Paul, *Assembly of the Lord*, 243 n.87; Carruthers, *Everyday Work*, 157.

155. Paul, *Assembly of the Lord*, 258; cf. 344-348.

156. Paul, *Assembly of the Lord*, 344-348; Carruthers, *Everyday Work*, 75, 76, 77.

157. Quoted in Liu, *Discord in Zion*, 52.

158. Wilson, *Pulpit in Parliament*, 162.

159. Liu, *Discord in Zion*, 46.

160. Quoted in Liu, *Discord in Zion*, 45.

161. Carruthers, *Everyday Work*, 142-143; Paul, *Assembly of the Lord*, 315-316 and n.5; *Calamy Revised*, 430; *D.N.B.*, XVII, 1100-1101.

162. Reid, *Memoirs*, II, 139.

163. *D.N.B.*, XVII, 1101; Reid, *Memoirs*, II, 137.

164. Reid, *Memoirs*, II, 137.

165. *Calamy Revised*, 430.

166. Liu, *Discord in Zion*, 128, 163.

167. Liu, *Puritan London*, 56; *D.N.B.*, XVII, 1100-1101.

168. *Calamy Revised*, 430; Pearce, *Sion College and Library*, 344, 112.

169. Liu, *Discord in Zion*, 126, 128.

170. *Ibid.*, 104, 127-128.

171. *Calamy Revised*, 430; *D.N.B.*, XVII, 1101.

172. Abernathy, 'The English Presbyterians', 15.

173. *Ibid.*, 32-33.

174. *D.N.B.*, XVII, 1101.

175. Reid, *Memoirs*, II, 141.

176. *Ibid.*, II, 139.

177. *Calamy Revised*, 430. Cf. *D.N.B.*, XVII, 1101; Reid, *Memoirs*, II, 140.

178. *Calamy Revised*, 430; *D.N.B.*, XVII, 1101; Reid, *Memoirs*, II, 140.

179. Quoted in Reid, *Memoirs*, II, 140.

180. *D.N.B.*, XVII, 1101.

181. Mitchell, *Westminster Assembly*, 143. Cf. Haller, *Liberty and Reformation*, 103; Wilson, *Pulpit in Parliament*, 71.

182. de Witt, *Jus Divinum*, 30.

183. Quoted in John L. Carson and David W. Hall, eds., *To Glorify and Enjoy God*, 28.

184. Wilson, *Pulpit in Parliament*, 71.

185. Holley, 'Divines', 329; *D.N.B.*, XIV, 324, 325.

186. Seaver, *Puritan Lectureship*, 369-370 n.23; Holley, 'Divines', 329.

187. Reid, *Memoirs*, II, 87.

188. *D.N.B.*, XIV, 324.

189. Holley, 'Divines', 329; Seaver, *Puritan Lectureships*, 273.

190. Mitchell, *Westminster Assembly*, 420, 430-431.

191. William Hunt, *The Puritan Moment: The Coming of a Revolution in an English County* (Cambridge, Mass. and London: Harvard U. Press, 1983), 283.

192. *D.N.B.*, XIV, 325.

193. Haller, *Liberty and Reformation*, 35. On the Earl of Warwick's support of leading Puritans, cf. Hunt, *Puritan Moment*, 163-164, 203.

194. Cf. Haller, *Liberty and Reformation*, 34-35, and Paul, *Assembly of the Lord*, 119 and n.48, on the Smectymnuus tracts.

195. Wilson, *Pulpit in Parliament*, 66-67.

196. Seaver, *Puritan Lectureships*, 273; Liu, *Puritan London*, 73, 137-138.

197. Liu, *Puritan London*, 151-152, 166 n.17.

198. Paul, *Assembly of the Lord*, 119, 164, 166 n.132, 412.

199. *Ibid.*, 427-428 n.190.

200. de Witt, *Jus Divinum*, 150-151; cf. Paul, *Assembly of the Lord*, 473.

201. de Witt, *Jus Divinum*, 156.

202. Mitchell, *Westminster Assembly*, 304.

203. *Ibid.*, 313; Carruthers, *Everyday Work*, 11; Paul, *Assembly of the Lord*, 506.

204. Paul, *Assembly of the Lord*, 180, 244 n.90.

205. *Ibid.*, 399 and n.48; Jack B. Rogers, *Scripture in the Westminster Confession* (Kampen: J.H. Kok, 1966), 174-175.

206. Rogers, *Scripture in the Westminster Confession*, 176.

207. Haller, *Liberty and Reformation*, 131.

208. Wilson, *Pulpit in Parliament*, 185; cf. 79, 205.

209. Haller, *Liberty and Reformation*, 225. Cf. Wilson, *Pulpit in Parliament*, 91.

210. Haller, *Liberty and Reformation*, 225.

211. Liu, *Puritan London*, 73.

212. *D.N.B.*, XIV, 324.

213. *Ibid.*

214. Drysdale, *History*, 375 n.1.

215. Abernathy, 'The English Presbyterians', 77.

216. *Ibid.*, 80.

217. Reid, *Memoirs*, II, 89; cf. *D.N.B.*, XIV, 324-325; *Calamy Revised*, 363.

218. *D.N.B.*, XIV, 324, 325.

219. Keith L. Sprunger, *Dutch Puritanism* (Leiden: E.J. Brill, 1982), 398 and n.9; *D.N.B.*, XIV, 325.

220. *D.N.B.*, XIV, 325; Sprunger, *Dutch Puritanism*, 415.

221. *D.N.B.*, XIV, 325.

222. *Ibid.*

223.Carruthers, *Everyday Work*, 182. The *Minutes*, ed. Mitchell and Struthers, 458-459, show that this was granted.

224. Carruthers, *Everyday Work*, 148. Cf. Paul, *Assembly of the Lord*, 182.

225. Carruthers, *Everyday Work*, 148.

226. Wilson, *Pulpit in Parliament*, 247.

227. *D.N.B.*, XI, 1087; Reid, *Memoirs*, II, 52.

228. *D.N.B.*, XI, 1086; Holley, 'Divines', 332; Reid, *Memoirs*, II, 50.

229. Nicholas Tyacke, *Anti-Calvinists: The Rise of English Arminianism, c. 1590-1640* (Oxford: Clarendon Press, 1987), 223. Ley published his 1635 letter in 1641.

230. Seaver, *Puritan Lectureships*, 272, 369 n.19.

231. Wilson, *Pulpit in Parliament*, 69.

232. Liu, *Puritan London*, 157; Pearce, *Sion College and Library*, 344.

233. Paul, *Assembly of the Lord*, 55 and n.8; cf. 118-119.

234. *Ibid.*, 157.

235. *Ibid.*, 150 n.66, 166 n.132.

236. *Ibid.*, 226. Cf. Carruthers, *Everyday Work*, 122.

237. Carruthers, *Everyday Work*, 77.

238. Paul, *Assembly of the Lord*, 318.

239. Carruthers, *Everyday Work*, 151.

240. Paul, *Assembly of the Lord*, 366 and 373, quoting from Lightfoot's *Journal*.

241. *Ibid.*, 374-375 and n.98.

242. Carruthers, *Everyday Work*, 189-190.

243. Rogers, *Scripture in the Westminster Confession*, 174; Paul, *Assembly of the Lord*, 399 and n.48.

244. Wilson, *Pulpit in Parliament*, 245, 246, 247.

245. *Ibid.*, 251, 253.

246. Cornelius Burgess wrote in the 2nd edition of his *Not sacrilege nor Sin to purchase Bishops' Lands* (1659): 'It is indeed true, that some members of that Assembly, joining with some others, did compile some Annotations upon the Bible, which many take to be the work of the Assembly. But take this for an undoubted truth, those Annotations were never made by the Assembly, nor by any order from it; nor after they were made ever had the approbation of the Assembly; or were so much as offered to the Assembly at all, for that purpose or any other' (quoted in Reid, *Memoirs*, I, 301). Thomas Case, in his 1659 Preface to *The Morning Exercise Methodized*, said that the London ministers 'observed that the larger "English Annotations", in which but some few only of the late "Assembly", together with some others, had a hand, are generally ascribed to the whole

"Assembly", and usually carry the name of "the Assembly's Annotations", as if done by the joint advice of that grave and learned convention' (*Puritan Sermons*, V, 7-8). Burgess and Case may have been inclined to distance the Assembly from the 'Annotations' because it turned out, as acknowledged in the Prefaces to the 2nd and 3rd editions, that the annotator for Ezekiel, Daniel, and the Minor Prophets (one Pemberton) was guilty of plagiarizing from the 'Italian Annotations' of Diodati, and therefore he was replaced by John Richardson, former Bishop of Ardegh.

247. *Minutes of the Westminster Assembly*, ed. Mitchell and Struthers, 132, 133. Carruthers, *Everyday Work*, 192, refers to this work as the *Dutch Annotations* 'ordered and appointed by the Synod of Dort, 1618.' The coincidence of date with the publication of the 1st edition of the 'English Annotations', however, makes it probable that Ley was reporting a correction in the work that he and some other members were producing for a committee of Parliament.

248. Reid, *Memoirs*, II, 53; *D.N.B.*, XI, 1087.

249. Carruthers, *Everyday Work*, 183. Cf. Reid, *Memoirs*, II, 50; *D.N.B.*, XI, 1086.

250. Drysdale, *History*, 332-333 and n.1; *D.N.B.*, XI, 1086.

251. Liu, *Discord in Zion*, 104; *D.N.B.*, XI, 1087.

252. *D.N.B.*, XI, 1087; Reid, *Memoirs*, II, 54.

253. Reid, *Memoirs*, II, 51, 52; *D.N.B.*, XI, 1087.

254. Quoted in Reid, *Memoirs*, II, 202-203.

255. Quoted in *D.N.B.*, XX, 510.

256. Holley, 'Divines', 356; cf. *D.N.B.*, XX, 510.

257. Reid, *Memoirs*, II, 202; Holley, 'Divines', 356.

258. *D.N.B.*, XX, 510; Seaver, *Puritan Lectureships*, 260-261.

259. *Ibid.*; Reid, *Memoirs*, II, 199.

260. Holley, 'Divines', 355. Cf. *D.N.B.*, XX, 510.

261. *D.N.B.*, XX, 510; Reid, *Memoirs*, II, 200.

262. *D.N.B.*, XX, 510.

263. Holley, 'Divines', 355-356.

264. Seaver, *Puritan Lectureships*, 54 and 325-326 n.123.

265. Pearce, *Sion College and Library*, 36-37.

266. Seaver, *Puritan Lectureships*, 236, 260-261; Liu, *Puritan London*, 84.

267. Haller, *The Rise of Puritanism*, 200. Cf. Seaver, *Puritan Lectureships*, 257.

268. C.F. Allison, *The Rise of Moralism* (London: S.P.C.K., 1966), 165-166.

269. Seaver, *Puritan Lectureships*, 236; *D.N.B.* XX, 511.

270. Allison, *The Rise of Moralism*, 176-177, 180, 202.

271. Spear, 'Covenanted Uniformity', 362.

272. Paul, *Assembly of the Lord*, 150 and n.66, 164, 166 n.132.

273. *Ibid.*, 397-398.

274. *Ibid.*, 180, 211.

275. Carruthers, *Everyday Work*, 153.

276. Wilson, *Pulpit in Parliament*, 177-178.

277. Quoted in Wilson, *Pulpit in Parliament*, 203 n.9.

278. Reid, *Memoirs*, II, 204.

279. Pearce, *Sion College and Library*, 344.

280. *Ibid.*, 247.

281. *D.N.B.*, XX, 510.

282. *D.N.B.*, XX, 511.

283. Quoted in Ryken, *Worldly Saints*, 94. Cf. 243 n.27 and Yule, *Puritans in Politics*, 79 and 100 n.53.

284. Carruthers, *Everyday Work*, 75; cf. Paul, *Assembly of the Lord*, 403-404 n.71.

285. *Complete Prose Works of John Milton*, II, ed. Ernest Sirluck (New Haven: Yale U. Press and London: Oxford U. Press, 1959), 123; cf. *D.N.B.*, XX, 511.

286. Liu, *Discord in Zion*, 163.

287. *D.N.B.*, XX, 511. Cf. Reid, *Memoirs*, II, 204.

Chapter 10

The New Englanders

In 1642 a letter signed by five members of the House of Lords and thirty-four members of the House of Commons was sent to New England inviting John Cotton of Boston, Thomas Hooker of Hartford and John Davenport of New Haven to participate in the Westminster Assembly. They had all been significant leaders of the Puritan movement in England before migrating to America. They would not be able to attend, but the theory and practice of their Congregationalism in New England were conveyed by their writings published in London. Two members of the Assembly had spent time in New England. John Phillips of Wrentham, Suffolk, brother-in-law of Dr. William Ames, had been a minister at Dedham, Massachusetts, but seems not to have played a significant part in the Assembly. Sir Henry Vane, Jr., however, played a major role in the Assembly and in Parliament and had previously spent two years in New England, one of them as Governor of the Massachusetts Bay colony. The Puritan movement in America thus had a direct bearing on developments in the Westminster Assembly.

John Cotton (December 4, 1584 - December 23, 1652)

Although some three thousand miles away from London and the Westminster Assembly, ministering in Boston, Massachusetts since 1633, John Cotton exercised an immense influence on the English Puritan movement through his continued writings as well as through his earlier preaching and example. Converted through the preaching of Richard Sibbes, he himself preached the sermon that led to John Preston's conversion. He persuaded John Davenport, Thomas Goodwin and Philip Nye of independency from the ceremonies of the Church of England, and his writings on Congregational polity, although responded to by Presbyterian members of the Assembly, yet still convinced John Owen. Invited to participate in the Assembly in 1642 by five members of the House of Lords and thirty-four members of the House of Commons, Cotton wanted to attend but only if others of those invited from New England would go with him. However, Thomas Hooker was not interested and John Davenport did not have an associate to cover his church and colonial duties.[1]

Cotton was born on December 4, 1584 in Derby, son of Roland Cotton, an attorney who was both godly and wealthy enough to provide John with a good education. He entered Trinity College, Cambridge at about thirteen years of age and obtained the B.A. in 1602 and the M.A. in 1606. From at least 1607 he was Fellow of Emmanuel College, where he became Dean and was an effective tutor and catechist, also preaching occasionally at St. Mary's Church.[2] His conscience had been stirred by the preaching of William Perkins before that Puritan's death in 1602, but not until 1609 was he converted when he heard Richard Sibbes preach on regeneration. The effect of this experience was notable when Cotton's own preaching changed from an elegant, ornamented style, which had gained him attention at his funeral oration for Robert Some, Master of Peterhouse, in February 1609, to a plain, straightforward expository style. This new style was received coldly at a university sermon in 1611, nevertheless John Preston was convicted and forsook medicine for divinity and became a notable Puritan preacher.[3]

Ordained deacon and priest on July 13, 1610 at Lincoln, Cotton was called to be vicar of the large St. Botolph's Church in Boston, Lincolnshire on June 24, 1612, when he was still only twenty-seven years old. Receiving his B.D. in 1613, with further recognition of his scholarship at Cambridge, he began in 1615 to avoid using some of the Anglican ceremonies in St. Botolph's. John Williams, Bishop of Lincoln, who respected Cotton's scholarship, tolerated his practices, and Cotton's ministry became a magnet for those of Puritan inclination. He was able to refute Arminian sentiment within his parish by means of preaching and conference.[4] Scores of people in Boston entered into a covenant with the Lord under Cotton's influence forming, in effect, a congregation within the congregation.[5] His grandson, Cotton Mather, would later report:

> The good *spirit* of God, so plentifully and powerfully accompanied the ministry of this excellant man, that a great *reformation* was thereby wrought in the town of Boston. *Profaneness* was extinguished, *superstition* was abandoned, *religion* was embraced and practised among the *body* of the people; yea, the mayor, with most of the magistrates, were now called Puritans, and the *Satanical party* was become insignificant.[6]

John Preston sent his divinity students to complete their preparation for ministry with Cotton. Among these was Thomas Hill, later a member of the Westminster Assembly.[7] William Ames sent some German students to Cotton from Franeker in the Netherlands.[8] James Ussher consulted with Cotton on theological points related to the doctrine of predestination.[9]

From 1629 he had the assistance of his wife's cousin, Anthony Tuckney, who would eventually succeed him at St. Botolph's and serve as a member of the Westminster Assembly. This was fortunate, for in September 1630 both Cotton and his wife, Elizabeth Horrocks, were afflicted with ague, which disabled him for a year and took her life sometime after October 2, 1630, probably in 1631. Theophilus Clinton, Fourth Earl of Lincoln, was their host while they coped with their fever and chills, and at his manor Cotton became more fully acquainted with the colonization of New England.[10] Already his interest had been manifested in his preaching of the farewell sermon to John Winthrop's company departing from Southampton for New England on the *Arabella* in March of 1630.[11]

After his wife's death Cotton travelled around England while completing his recuperation and came to realize the unusually favorable position he and his church in Boston occupied in the midst of growing ecclesiastical oppression of nonconformity. On April 6, 1632 he married Sarah Hawkridge, widow of William Story.[12] But, soon after his marriage, word came that he was to be summoned before the Court of

High Commission of William Laud. He decided that it was best to go into hiding before deciding on his next step. On his way to London he sought the counsel of the venerable John Dod, who advised flight as a declaration that a sincere profession of faith is preferable to whatever benefits are given up: 'I am old Peter, and therefore must stand still, and bear the brunt; but you, being young Peter, may go whither you will, and ought being persecuted in one city, to flee unto another.'[13] Cotton may have been much younger than Dod, but he was already forty-seven.

By the autumn of 1632 Cotton was safely hidden in London, probably in the home of Henry Whitfield in Ockely, Surrey. To this hiding-place came several Puritans seeking to dissuade him from his nonconformity and his anticipated departure from England. Knowing him to be judicious, they proposed to give him their reasons and to listen to his responses. When he based his arguments for nonconformity to the ceremonies on the Second Commandment, John Davenport, Thomas Goodwin and Philip Nye were persuaded that these were not matters of indifference and thus were united with Cotton in the direction of Independency.[14] All three would serve churches in the Netherlands, Goodwin and Nye eventually returning to England to lead the Independents in the Westminster Assembly and Davenport eventually joining Cotton in America.

After considering for a time whether he should go to Holland, Cotton decided on New England. In a letter of May 7, 1633 he resigned his vicarage of St. Botolph's to Bishop Williams. The date of his resignation entered in the corporation records of Boston is July 8. On July 14 he set sail from Deal in the *Griffin* with his wife, Thomas Hooker, Samuel Stone and a company bound for Massachusetts Bay. Once past the Isle of Wight, Cotton and Hooker, the well-known Puritans, no longer needed to travel incognito, and on the rest of the voyage the three ministers preached to their companions. They arrived at 'Trimountain' (which was renamed Boston in honor of Cotton and his church) on September 4, welcomed by the settlers in the wilderness who said 'that the God of heaven had supplied them with what would in some sort answer their three great necessities; *Cotton* for their *clothing, Hooker* for their *fishing*, and *Stone* for their *building* ....'[15]

On October 10, 1633 Cotton was ordained teacher in the church of Boston, a position he would hold until his death in 1652, almost as long as his twenty-one years as Vicar of St. Botolph's. He immediately became a leading figure in the colony's religious and political life. In 1636 he was appointed to a committee to draft the civil laws for the colony. His *Abstract of the Lawes of New England*, closely derived from the Mosaic code of the Old Testament, was rejected, however, by the General Court in favor of statutes more accommodating to the time. In 1637-1638 he was a key figure in the controversy surrounding Mrs. Anne Hutchinson, a member of his congregation who espoused Antinomian views. Cotton at first defended Mrs. Hutchinson, but eventually he joined with the other ministerial leaders in banishing her from the colony. Cotton also engaged in written controversy with Roger Williams, during the 1640s, over questions of church membership and whether the civil magistrate should have any authority in the religious realm. Cotton argued that it was not necessary to renounce the Church of England to hold church membership in New England and that the authority of the magistrates should extend to the religious realm.[16]

When, in 1642, the invitation came to participate in the Westminster Assembly, to Cotton at Boston, Hooker at Connecticut, and Davenport at New Haven, Cotton was disappointed that his New England colleagues could not, or would not, attend. He decided, however, to influence the Assembly as best he could by writing concerning Congregational polity.[17] In 1644 he published *The Keyes of the Kingdom of Heaven*, a moderate setting forth of the arguments for congregational polity. There was much interest in England in the American experience, for in contrast to the English churches in the Netherlands the churches in Massachusetts Bay and Connecticut were part of the Church of England and yet were Congregational in polity. They purported to be a middle way between Brownism or separatism, 'which reduces the power of the elders by putting church government into the hands of the people', and Presbyterianism, 'which reduces the power of the individual elder in his church by putting church government into the hands of a district presbytery'. According to Everett Emerson:

> For Cotton's English colleagues, the publication of an American work such as *Keyes* had two advantages over the publication of their own efforts, such as *An Apologeticall Narration*. First, it had experience behind it and therefore seemed more authoritative than their own pronouncements. Second, since it was not their own statement that they were issuing, they were less subject to attack for it by the Presbyterians.[18]

The Presbyterians in the Assembly did take note of Cotton's *Keyes of the Kingdom*. Jeremiah Whitaker referred to it, and Samuel Rutherford said, 'When I read through that treatise of the Keys of the Kingdom of Heaven, I thought it an easy labour for an universal pacification, he comes so near to us.'[19]

Cotton's *The Way of the Churches of Christ in New-England* was published in 1645 but actually was written before *The Keyes of the Kingdom* and was circulated for some time in manuscript because of the difficulty in getting works published that favored congregational polity. Twice the length of *The Keyes*, *The Way of the Churches* describes the actual practices of the Congregational churches in New England. After it appeared in England, on April 4, 1645, Cotton regretted its publication because it no longer represented his views on some points. The main difference from *The Keyes* is that it gives less power to the elders and more to the congregations, but Cotton may also have modified his views on the seemingly democratic way of admitting members and on the refusal to receive to the Lord's Supper members of the Church of England who had not joined Congregational churches in New England.[20] In any case, when *The Way of the Churches* appeared in England in 1645, its 'Epistle to the Reader',

THE AMERICAN CONNECTION

The non-separating Puritans who founded Massachusetts Bay Colony, as distinguished from the separatist Pilgrims who founded Plymouth in 1620, viewed their settlement of the 1630s as a 'lighthouse on a hill' to demonstrate to England a reformed church and society. The English Puritans had great interest in America. The American Puritans John Cotton, Thomas Hooker and John Davenport were invited to participate in the Westminster Assembly. John White played a major role in support of the founding of Massachusetts. John Phillips, or Phillip, a member of the Assembly, had served as a pastor in Dedham, Massachusetts between 1636 and 1642. Sir Henry Vane, Jr., a Parliamentary member of the Assembly, had been Governor of the Massachusetts colony for a year, 1636-37. Anthony Tuckney corresponded from Boston, Lincolnshire with his predecessor John Cotton of Boston, Massachusetts concerning the evangelization of the American Indians. Thomas Goodwin almost moved to America and actually had part of his library packed on board the ship in 1647 before he changed his mind. John Lightfoot bequeathed his oriental books to Harvard College in 1675; however, they were destroyed there in a fire in 1769.

signed by N.H. and J.H., evidently English Independents, proved offensive to the Presbyterians in the Westminster Assembly since it seemed to cast aspersions on the Assembly for not considering the 'grounds and reasons' that the dissenting brethren had volunteered to provide. This led to the adoption of Matthew Newcomen's motion for the Independents to present their whole frame of church government with their grounds and reasons, one of the culminating steps to the impasse between the Presbyterians and the Independents in the Assembly.[21]

Thus even from a great distance, John Cotton continued to exert an influence upon England. In 1648 he published *The Way of the Congregational Churches Cleared* in answer to some of his opponents in England, but his remaining influence would be mainly in America. In 1648, with Richard Mather and Ralph Partridge, he was appointed by the Cambridge Synod to draw up a model of church government. The resulting Cambridge Platform agreed with the Westminster Confession in all doctrine except for polity, and although it used Mather's 'platform of church discipline', it reflected the published works of Cotton in large measure.[22]

A man of many parts, Cotton also had a hand in producing the Bay Psalm Book in 1640 and published *Singing of Psalms* in 1647.[23] Postmillennial in his eschatology, as shown in his works on the Book of Revelation,[24] Cotton saw himself and the developments in America as part of God's unfolding plan of redemption. To this cause he gave himself unstintingly. He followed in America the same regimen he had pursued at St. Botolph's: '... besides his ordinary lecture every Thursday, he preached *thrice* more; every week, on the *week-days*; namely, on Wednesdays and Thursdays, early in the morning, and on Saturdays at three in the afternoon.'[25] Like his fellow Independent and correspondent, Oliver Cromwell, he was an activist who believed in waiting on the Lord. On October 2, 1651 Cromwell wrote to Cotton, whom he esteemed:

> Surely, Sir, the Lord is greatly to be feared, as to be praised! We need your prayers in this as much as ever. How shall we behave ourselves after such mercies? What is the Lord a-doing? What prophecies are now fulfilling? Who is a God like ours? To know His will, to do His will, are both of Him.[26]

While preaching to the students at Harvard in the fall of 1652, Cotton caught a heavy cold which developed into respiratory difficulties. He preached in his church for the last time on November 21 and died of asthma and scurvy on December 23. Having no children from his first marriage, Cotton and his second wife, Sarah, had three sons and three daughters. One son, Seaborn, born on their voyage to America, graduated from Harvard in 1651 and was the minister at Hampton, New Hampshire 1660-1686. John Cotton, Jr., born March 13, 1640, was minister at Plymouth, Massachusetts and Charleston, South Carolina, preached to the Indians, and revised the translation of the Bible by John Eliot. One daughter, Mariah, born in 1642, married Increase Mather and was the mother of Cotton Mather. One daughter and one son died in 1649. John Cotton's widow married Richard Mather, whom she also survived.[27]

Thomas Hooker (July 7, 1586 [?] - July 7, 1647)
In the summer of 1642, when Thomas Hooker had been ministering in America for almost nine years,

> There came letters from divers Lords of the upper house and some thirty of the house of commons, and others from the ministers there, who stood for the independency of churches, to Mr. Cotton of Boston, Mr. Hooker of Hartford, and Mr. Davenport of New Haven, to call them, or some of them, if all could not, to England, to assist in the synod there appointed, to consider and advise about the settling of church government.[28]

Hooker immediately informed the messenger who brought the letters of invitation from Boston that he 'liked not the business, nor thought it any sufficient call for them to go 3,000 miles to agree with three men' – by whom he meant fellow Independents such as Thomas Goodwin and Philip Nye who were appointed to the Westminster Assembly. John Cotton and John Davenport were more inclined to go, but the young colony of New Haven could not spare Davenport, and Cotton was eventually persuaded that the relations between Parliament and King were still too volatile and the presence of the Americans might do New England more harm than good.[29] The invitation indicates, however, the continuing reputation of the three American Puritans in England. Hooker, like Cotton, sought to influence the Assembly through his writings, publishing a catechism and two works on the Lord's Prayer in London in 1645 and responding to Samuel Rutherford's *Due Right of Presbyteries* with his *A Survey of the Summe of Church Discipline*, which, however, was published only posthumously in 1648.[30]

Thomas Hooker, who would become known as a powerful preacher, and would also be at the center of controversy, in Essex, in the Netherlands, and then in New England, was born at Markfield (or Mayfield), Leicestershire, probably on July 7, 1586. After attending grammar school at Market Bosworth he entered Queen's College, Cambridge on March 27, 1604 and then moved to Emmanuel College, where he received the B.A. in 1608 and the M.A. in 1611. From 1609 to 1618 he was Dixie Fellow at Emmanuel. It was during his time as Fellow at Emmanuel that Hooker struggled with the question of assurance of his own salvation. This issue was resolved with the help of his younger Sizar, Simeon Ashe (later a member of the Westminster Assembly), and thus he was able to enter a pulpit ministry that would involve the aiding of many others in coming to an assured faith in Christ.[31]

Hooker's first pastoral charge was at St. George's in Esher, Surrey, where he may have come in 1618, but possibly not until 1620. The patron of this small congregation was a Mr. Francis Drake, whose wife, Joan, was struggling with the belief that she had committed the unpardonable sin. The venerable John Dod (1549-1645) had sought to persuade her otherwise, but she had answered with scriptural and theological argumentation and once even hit him with a piece of her bedstead while he was praying for her. Dod recommended to her the young Thomas Hooker, who, 'newly come from the University, had a new answering method'. The income of the parish of Esher being small, Hooker was invited by Mr. Drake to reside in the manor house to be able to counsel more readily with his wife.[32] One result of this arrangement was that Joan Drake became satisfied of her salvation before her death in 1625, and another was that Hooker married, on April 3, 1621, her woman-in-waiting, Susannah Garbrand. Susannah was from Mrs. Drake's hometown of Amersham, and she and Hooker named their first child after her. Francis Drake later left a bequest to be paid to their daughter on her wedding-day; Johanna Hooker would marry the Rev. Thomas Shepard in New England.[33]

Sometime before 1626 Hooker came under the influence of John Rogers, the noted Puritan preacher of Dedham in Essex. Rogers sought to get Hooker a benefice in Colchester, but when that fell through, Hooker accepted a call to St. Mary's in Chelmsford, Essex. Here his career 'was to be brief but spectacular'.[34] He entered into the lectureship at Chelmsford toward the end of 1626, and his family had moved there with the addition of daughters Anne by 1627 and Sarah by 1628.[35]

His fiery preaching attracted people from all over Essex. He also became mentor to a number of younger ministers, including Hugh Peter and also his eventual son-in-law, Thomas Shepard, who became Lecturer in Earls Colne, Essex.[36] The moral tenor of life in Chelmsford was also transformed, particularly in regard to observance of the Sabbath.[37] Cotton Mather describes one of Hooker's sermons at Chelmsford when he, in the presence of the Judges, and before a vast congregation, declared freely the sins of England, and the plagues that would come for such sins; and in his prayer he besought the God of heaven to set on the heart of the King what his own mouth had spoken, in the second chapter of Malachi, and the eleventh and twelfth verses, 'An abomination is committed, Judah hath married the daughter of a strange God, the Lord will cut off the man that doeth this.'[38]

William Hunt comments:

> The audacity is breathtaking. Royal policy might be altered; prelates and councillors could be replaced; but was Charles really supposed to repudiate his wedded queen? No wonder it was said that Hooker, when doing the work of the Lord, would 'put a king in his pocket'.[39]

No wonder also that Hooker should come to the attention of William Laud, then Bishop of London. Two petitions from Essex were addressed to Bishop Laud in November 1629. One, signed by forty-nine clergy (including seven former members of Emmanuel College), described Hooker as 'for doctrine orthodox and life and conversation honest, and his disposition peaceable, in no ways turbulent or factious'. The other, signed by forty-one 'conformable' ministers, complained of widespread 'irregularities' in the diocese of London, 'most men doing what seemeth good in their owne eyes, and fewe regarding the authoritie of the Church or their owne duetie', and it asked Laud 'to enforce those irregulars to conforme'.[40] Already suspended from his lectureship in June, Hooker had retired from Chelmsford to the nearby village of Little Baddow and opened a grammar school, with John Eliot, later the missionary to the Indians in New England, as his assistant.[41]

In July of 1630 Hooker was summoned to appear before Laud's Court of High Commission, and this time his friends, probably including the Earl of Warwick, advised him to go into exile, forfeiting the bond put up for him in the previous year to guarantee his appearance when summoned again. On the eve of his departure alone for the

Netherlands, probably on April 17, 1631, he preached a dramatic fare-well sermon, 'The Danger of Desertion':

> Already the righteous were fleeing the wrath to come. Alluding to the folk who had sailed to New England the preceding year under the leader-ship of John Winthrop, Hooker observed that 'God begins to ship away his Noahs, which prophesied and foretold that destruction was near'.[42]

Hooker had thought that a position awaited him in the English church in Amsterdam pastored by John Paget. It turned out, however, that it was only a segment of the increasingly divided congregation that had extended the invitation and Paget himself, being of Presbyterian senti-ment, was opposed. Although the consistory (elders) of the church issued a call to Hooker on July 2, 1631, and he came and preached to their satisfaction, Paget issued twenty questions for Hooker to answer for the sake of the Dutch Reformed Classis. Some of Hooker's an-swers revealed his developing Congregational polity, with the result that the Amsterdam Classis would not allow him to preach there.[43] Hooker withdrew from this situation and then became the assistant to the Scot John Forbes in the Merchant Adventurers church in Delft, where he served for the better part of two years. He was also associ-ated with Dr. William Ames in Rotterdam.[44]

On the basis of his experience in the Netherlands, Hooker advised his friend John Cotton, now in 1633 being pursued by Laud's agents, not to go to Holland: 'The state of these provinces, to my weak eye, seems wonderfully ticklish and miserable ... the power of godliness, for ought I can see or hear, they know not ....'[45] Instead, the proper destination was America. Already many of Hooker's disciples in Es-sex had migrated to Massachusetts in 1632 and were known as 'Mr. Hooker's company', indicating that his eventual arrival there was ex-pected.[46] But before he could depart for America, he suffered a narrow escape from Laud's agents, as related by Cotton Mather:

> Returning into England in order to a further voyage, he was quickly scented by the pursevants, who at length got so far up with him as to knock at the door of that very chamber where he was now discoursing with Mr. Stone, who was now become his designed companion and assistant for the New English enterprize. Mr. Stone was at that instant smoking of *tobacco*, for which Mr. Hooker had been reproving him, as being then used by few persons of sobriety; being also of a sudden and pleasant wit, he stept unto

the door, with his pipe in his mouth, and such an air of speech and look, as gave him some credit with the officer. The officer demanded, Whether Mr. Hooker were not there? Mr. Stone replied with a braving sort of confidence, 'What Hooker? Do you mean Hooker that lived once at Chelmsford!' The officer answered, 'Yes, he!' Mr. Stone immediately, with a diversion like that which once helped Athanasius, made this true answer, 'If it be he you look for, I saw him about an hour ago, at such an house in the town; you had best hasten thither after him.' The officer took this for a sufficient account, and went his way; but Mr. Hooker, upon this intimation, concealed himself more carefully and securely, till he went on board at the Downs, in the year 1633, the ship which brought him, and Mr. Cotton, and Mr. Stone to New England: where none but Mr. Stone was owned for a preacher, at their first coming aboard; the other two delaying to take their turns in the publick worship of the ship, till they were got so far into the main ocean, that they might with safety discover who they were.[47]

The three ministers were warmly welcomed upon their arrival in Boston on September 4, 1633. John Cotton was ordained teacher in the church there, and Hooker and Samuel Stone were ordained on October 11 to serve the church in Newtown (now Cambridge), Massachusetts, where 'Mr. Hooker's company' had settled. It was not long before Hooker was involved in dealing with a series of controversies, including some surrounding the opinions of Roger Williams, all of which proved distracting to his main purpose of ministering to the souls of those who sought to know the Lord's salvation. Largely for this reason Hooker sought and eventually gained permission to move a hundred miles west to the Connecticut Valley to found what would become Hartford in June of 1636. In August of 1637 he was back in Boston to serve as one of the two moderators of the synod that condemned the Antinomian views of Mrs. Anne Hutchinson, whom John Cotton had at first defended.

Although there was probably some personal rivalry between Hooker and Cotton, as two strong leaders in a context providing limited scope for their leadership,[48] they stood as allies in defence of the evolving Congregational polity. After declining the invitation to attend the Westminster Assembly, they both sought to contribute to it by their writings. Cotton published *The Keyes of the Kingdom of Heaven* in 1644. Hooker was asked by the Cambridge Synod of 1643 to answer Samuel Rutherford's *Peaceable and Temperate Plea for Pauls Presbyterie* (1642), but by the time he could get to the work, Rutherford's *The Due*

Right of Presbyteries (1644) had appeared. Hooker labored to respond to Rutherford's voluminous erudition and had completed his task by late 1645.[49] The manuscript was put on a ship which sailed from New Haven in January 1646, but it was lost at sea. Asked to redo his work, Hooker, in declining health, left unfinished what would be published posthumously in 1648 as *A Survey of the Summe of Church Discipline*, which nevertheless spoke for all of New England in its defence of the autonomy of the local church in matters of discipline, of the 'visible saint' requirement for church membership, and the benefit of synods for advice only.[50]

Sargent Bush argues that three works published by Hooker in 1645 were intended to influence the Westminster Assembly. These were *An Exposition of the Principles of Religion*, which is a catechism, and two works expounding the Lord's Prayer, *A Briefe Exposition of the Lords Prayer* and *Heavens Treasury Opened*, which differ only slightly.[51] He concludes that his catechism may have had some influence on the Assembly's Larger and Shorter Catechisms, but only along with those of several others. The similarities 'undoubtedly depend chiefly on Hooker's being largely in doctrinal agreement with most other Puritan leaders rather than on any thoroughgoing debt of the assembly's catechism committee to Hooker's *Exposition*'.[52]

Favoring the concept of synods or consociations, as well as the power of the civil magistrate to call such bodies, Hooker was unable to attend the Cambridge Synods of September 1646 and June 1647 because of failing health. An epidemic curtailed the latter one, from which Samuel Stone returned to Hartford to find Hooker dying. Almost two weeks after his death on July 7 at sixty-one years of age, Stone wrote to Hooker's son-in-law, Thomas Shepard:

Dearest brother, God brought us safely to Hartford, but when I came hither God presented me a sad spectacle. Mr. Hooker looked like a dying man. God refused to hear our prayers for him, but tooke him from us July 7 a little before sunne-set. Our sunne is set, our light is eclipsed, our joy is darkened, we remember now in the day of our calamitie the pleasant things which we enjoyed in former times. His spirits and head were so oppressed with the disease that he was not able to expresse much to us in his sicknesse, but had exprest to Mr. Goodwin before my returne that his peace was made in heaven and had continued 30 years without alteration, he was above Satan. Marke the upright man for the end of that man is peace! He lived a most blameless life. I thinke his greatest enemies cannot charge

him. He hath done much work for Christ, and now rests from his labours
and his workes follow him, but our losse is great and bitter.

Shortly before his death a comforter said to Hooker, 'Sir, you are
going to receive the reward of all your labors.' But avoiding any Arminianism, Thomas Hooker replied, 'Brother, I am going to receive
mercy!'[53]

John Davenport (April 1597 - March 15, 1670)

In addition to John Cotton and Thomas Hooker, a third New England
Puritan minister to be invited to the Westminster Assembly in 1642
was John Davenport, founder of the colony of New Haven in Connecticut. Like Cotton, Davenport would have liked to attend, but since
he was the only minister of the recently-founded New Haven, he could
not be spared.[54] Unlike Cotton and Hooker, he apparently did not write
any works that would have influenced the Assembly.[55] His invitation
nevertheless indicates recognition of his important contributions to
the Puritan movement in England.

Born at Coventry in Warwickshire, John Davenport was baptized
in the Church of the Holy Trinity there on April 9, 1597. He was the
fifth son of Henry Davenport, who would serve as Mayor of Coventry
in 1613 after having been Chamberlain and Sheriff. He attended the
Free Grammar School of Coventry and then went to Oxford, where he
studied at Merton College, 1613-1615, before transferring to Magdalen
College. He left Oxford without taking a degree because he lacked
sufficient funds to continue. In 1615 he was preaching as a private
chaplain (although only eighteen years old) at Hilton Castle near Durham, and he continued there at least until March of 1616.[56] Late in
1617 we find him preaching in London, where he was cited for lecturing and officiating at St. Mary Aldermanbury without licence. He was
suspended but then restored after humble petition.[57] In 1619 he was
appointed Curate of St. Lawrence Jewry in London, where he became
acquainted with some of the Puritan supporters, including Lady Mary
Vere, whose protege he became.[58]

In 1624 he was elected to be Vicar of St. Stephen's, Coleman Street.
In the controversy over this appointment Davenport wrote to Secretary Edward Conway disavowing any nonconformity: '... if by puri-
tanically affected, be meant one, that secretly encourageth men in opposition to the present government, I profess an hearty detestation of

such hypocrisy.'[59] At this stage his attitude was that it is 'better to unite our forces against those who oppose us in fundamentalls then to be divided amongst our selves about ceremonialls'.[60] His views on even the ceremonial matters would eventually become more firm,[61] but what was definitely non-negotiable for Davenport was the Arminian doctrine which he would see increasing with the elevation of William Laud.[62]

In 1625 he returned briefly to Magdalen College, Oxford to take his B.D.[63] It was also in this year that he gained attention for his faithful and courageous ministry to his parish in London during the great plague. Following the death of the outstanding Puritan preacher John Preston in 1628, Davenport worked with Richard Sibbes in London, and Thomas Goodwin and Thomas Ball in Cambridge, to edit Preston's works for publication.[64] Another Puritan project in which Davenport played an important role was the so-called Feoffees for Impropriations, a committee of four clergymen, four lawyers and four merchants for the buying up of lay endowments in order to support Puritan lectureships in strategic places. The four clergymen included Davenport, William Gouge, Richard Sibbes and Charles Offspring. Laud eventually suppressed this committee as an illegal corporation in 1633.[65]

In 1632 Davenport helped to hide John Cotton in London. It was during this time that the famous conference took place when Davenport, Thomas Goodwin and Philip Nye tried with others to dissuade Cotton from his nonconformity and instead were persuaded by him toward his Congregational principles.[66] When it became clear that Laud would be appointed Archbishop of Canterbury, Davenport decided to leave the country. He resigned his position at St. Stephen's and on August 5, 1633 escaped from London into the country, leaving for the Netherlands three months later. Laud reported to Charles I in 1633 that Davenport, "whom I used with all moderation, and about two years since thought I had settled his judgment, having him then at advantage enough to have put extremity upon him, but forbore it," had declared against conformity and, Laud believed, had left for Amsterdam.[67]

Davenport arrived in the Netherlands by mid-November 1633, bearded and in disguise.[68] Invited to become assistant in John Paget's English church in Amsterdam, he was asked the same Twenty Questions to which Thomas Hooker had been submitted by Paget in 1631.

Roger Williams (c.1604-1683)

Founder of 'Providence Plantation' (later Rhode Island) in 1636 and the first to establish a civil state with liberty of conscience, Roger Williams was an unsettled personality who continually surprised his Puritan colleagues. Educated at Pembroke College, Cambridge and a friend of John Cotton in England, he preceded his friend to Massachusetts, arriving in February 1631. He was invited to be Teacher in the church at Boston, but revealed that he could no longer be associated with the Church of England. His separatist sentiments were less problematic to the church at Salem and then among the Pilgrims at Plymouth. In the autumn of 1633 he served again in Salem, but challenged the lawfulness of the colonists' claim to land belonging to the Indians. His controversial views led eventually to his being expelled from Massachusetts. Fleeing in the winter of 1636, he took refuge with the Indians and founded Providence. In 1638 he became a Baptist, being immersed by Ezekiel Hollyman, whom he in turn immersed. The church he founded was the first Baptist church in America, but within months he renounced his rebaptism as not valid since Hollyman was then unbaptized. Williams became a Seeker, part of the movement that would prove attractive to his friend Sir Henry Vane, Jr. and also to John Milton and Oliver Cromwell.

Williams had an effect on the Westminster Assembly because he was back in England in 1643 to gain the charter for Rhode Island with the help of Vane. In the midst of the Assembly's 'Grand Debate' on church government in 1644 he published his *Bloudy Tenent of Persecution* against the views of John Cotton and the practices of the government of Massachusetts for enforcing religious matters of the First Table of the Law. This was an embarrassment to the Independents in the Assembly, who were themselves seeking an established national church in England which would provide toleration for Congregationalism on the model of Cotton and Massachusetts.

Eventually views like those of Roger Williams on the separation of church and state would come to characterize the United States and much of the Western world.

Davenport proved at first to be acceptable to the Presbyterian-inclined Paget, who said:

> He seemed unto me to accord with us, and to dislike the opinions of *Mr. Hooker* generally. The maine or onely difference which he persisted in for a long time, was about the baptisme of infants, whose parents were no members of the Church, nor would submit unto any private examination by him, further than their publick profession of faith before the whole church.[69]

For some months Davenport served the church as a Lecturer, but differences over the authority of classes and synods, as well as the proper subjects for infant baptism, led to his being excluded from the pulpit. Over one hundred people from the congregation nevertheless attended house meetings under his teaching in the summer and autumn of 1634.[70] When these house meetings were suppressed, he left Amsterdam but stayed in the Netherlands at least until 1636, preaching at The Hague and at Rotterdam. At some unknown date prior to 1619 he had married Elizabeth Wolley, and they had a son, John, who was baptized at The Hague on April 15, 1635.[71] While at Rotterdam, Davenport served in 1635 with Hugh Peter in the Merchant Adventurers Church.[72]

Without prospect of a preaching post consistent with his increasingly Congregational views in either England or the Netherlands, Davenport decided to emigrate to America. John Cotton had written to him about conditions there, and his boyhood friend Theophilus Eaton, now a London merchant, had also been interested in the Massachusetts Bay colony. Having returned to England, probably early in 1637, Davenport sailed with Eaton as joint-leader of an expedition that embarked sometime before May 10 and arrived in Boston on June 26, 1637.[73] Their arrival coincided with the Antinomian controversy, in which Davenport played a part, preaching after the synod in September, 1637 and entering into some of the debates with Mrs. Anne Hutchinson.[74]

In April 1638 his party moved west to Quinnipiac, where they founded the colony of New Haven with Eaton as governor and Davenport as pastor. When a letter came from English ministers asking questions concerning the operation and conduct of the churches in New England, Davenport prepared a full answer which was sent in 1639. This was published in London with the original letter in 1643 by Simeon

Ashe and William Rathband as *A Letter of Many Ministers in Old England*.[75] Unable to accept the invitation to participate in the Westminster Assembly, Davenport devoted his energies to the church and colony of New Haven through the 1640s and '50s.

In the 1660s he took part in two controversies over trends that he felt jeopardized both the church and the colony to which he had devoted so much of his life. He strenuously opposed the 'Half-Way Covenant' which, however, was adopted in 1662, allowing baptism for the children of those who did not live scandalous lives but who had not joined the church. He also sought to avoid the absorption of New Haven by its larger neighbor Connecticut when a new charter was being obtained. When the union was accomplished in 1665, he stated that Christ's interest was 'miserably lost'.[76]

Disappointment over the fate of New Haven may have led to his accepting a call to First Church in Boston in 1667. The New Haven church was not agreed on dismissing him to Boston, and First Church was divided over his appointment because of his opposition to the Half-Way Covenant. He was ordained pastor of First Church on December 9, 1668, but a group withdrew to form Third Church or Old South Church, amidst charges of deception on the part of Davenport. A little over a year later, on March 15, 1670, he died of apoplexy.[77] He was buried in King's Chapel Burying Ground in Boston, sharing a tomb with John Cotton, his companion in so much of this life.[78]

Sir Henry Vane, Junior (May 1613 - June 14, 1662)

In the summer of 1643 the war was not going well for the Parliamentary forces. It was decided to send a delegation to Scotland to achieve an alliance that would bring the Scottish forces into the fray against the King in England. The delegation of four Members of Parliament and two divines included Stephen Marshall and Philip Nye of the Westminster Assembly and was headed by Sir Henry Vane, Jr. The document to seal this alliance became known as the Solemn League and Covenant and was drafted by the Scottish clergyman Alexander Henderson, and the lawyer Archibald Johnston. Several key amendments were offered, however, by Henry Vane. Inserted at a crucial point was the phrase 'according to the Word of God', so that the First Article read:

> That we shall sincerely, really, and constantly, through the Grace of God, endeavour in our severall places and callings, the preservation of the Reformed Religion in the Church of *Scotland*, in Doctrine, Worship, Discipline, & Government, against our common Enemies, the reformation of Religion in the Kingdoms of *England* and *Ireland*, in Doctrine, Worship, Discipline, and Government, according to the Word of God, and the Example of the best Reformed Churches ....

This addition was readily acceptable to the Scots at the time, but later became a basis for Independent argument that Scottish Presbyterianism could yet be improved upon by further light from Scripture. This astute amendment reflected not only the political ingenuity of Henry Vane, but also his Independent inclinations and his sincerely open and tolerant viewpoint.[79] His religious convictions apparently continued to evolve from his privileged childhood through a youthful conversion, two years in New England, membership in the Westminster Assembly, leadership in the House of Commons on several occasions, a checkered relationship with Oliver Cromwell, and finally a courageous testimony on the scaffold before his execution on Tower Hill in 1662 following the Restoration of Charles II.

Henry (or Harry) Vane, Jr. was the eldest son of Sir Henry Vane, Sr. (1589-1655), who became a member of the Privy Council in 1630, was appointed Charles I's Secretary of State on February 3, 1640, and as a member of the Short Parliament served as the King's liaison with that body.[80] Sir Henry Vane, Sr. was also a member of the Long Parliament and of the Westminster Assembly, although not so active in the Assembly as his son. The younger Henry Vane was baptized on May 26, 1613 in the church of Dobden, near Newport, Essex. As a youth he was 'inclined to the vanities of the world' and consorted with those commonly termed 'good fellows' as the appropriate means of becoming a gentleman, but at about age fourteen or fifteen he experienced a conversion, perhaps through the influence of his teacher at Westminster School, Lambert Osbaldeston, a man of Puritan sympathies.[81]

At sixteen he was sent to Magdalen Hall, Oxford, but studied there without becoming a member of the University because he refused to take the oath of allegiance and supremacy. He next spent some time at Geneva or Leyden, and then in 1631 his father sent him to Vienna with the English ambassador. When he returned in February 1632, Sir Tobie Matthew remarked concerning him:

His French is excellently good, his discourse discreet, and his fashion comely and fair; and I dare venture to foretell that he will grow a very fit man for any such honour as his father's merits shall bespeak, or the king's goodness impart to him.[82]

His conscience, however, would not allow him to conform to Anglican ceremonies. In spite of conferences with bishops he abstained from the Lord's Supper for two years because he could get no-one to administer the sacrament to him standing rather than kneeling. In 1635 he resolved to go to New England for the sake of freedom of worship according to his conscience. Although his father was opposed, the King commanded him to allow his son to go, giving royal consent for his spending three years in America.[83]

His aristocratic appearance aroused the suspicions of his fellow-voyagers to America: 'his honourable Birth, long Hair and other Circumstances of his Person rendered his fellow-travellers jealous of him, as a spye to betray their Liberty rather than any way like to advantage their design.'[84] But upon arrival at Boston on October 6, 1635 he was welcomed with open arms. He was admitted to membership in the church at Boston on November 1, and on November 30 an ordinance was passed that any citizens seeking to sue at law should first submit their case to Vane and two elders for arbitration. Vane and the Rev. Hugh Peter, who had also arrived with him on the *Abigail*, also sought, with success, to reconcile the differences between the two former Governors, John Winthrop and Thomas Dudley. On March 3, 1636 he became a freeman of the colony, and on May 25 he was elected Governor of Massachusetts, at the age of twenty-three and after only seven months in the colony.[85]

His term as Governor proved to be both brief and stormy. It started well, as he negotiated an agreement with the sea captains using Boston harbor and, with the help of Roger Williams, achieved a treaty with the Narragansett Indians. Living in the home of John Cotton, Vane as Governor enjoyed regular consultation with the leading minister in a way that seemed appropriate for a theocracy.[86] Just at that time, however, in the autumn of 1636, the controversy over the Antinomian views of Mrs. Anne Hutchinson arose. Most of the clergy opposed her views. Cotton, although first defending her, eventually swung over to the majority. Vane and her brother-in-law, the Rev. John Wheelwright, remained as her main supporters.[87] When letters arrived recalling Vane to England, he sought to resign as Governor, at one point bursting into tears, but was persuaded to remain and fulfil his term. In the elections of the spring of 1637, however, he was defeated by John Winthrop, who succeeded in getting the General Court to pass an act prohibiting any newcomer from staying in the colony more than three weeks without the consent of the magistrates. Favoring civil liberty and religious toleration, Vane wrote against this measure, which was aimed at the supporters of Anne Hutchinson.[88] He sailed for England on August 3, 1637 after less than two years in America.

His somewhat bitter experiences in New England may have confirmed his views on toleration. He believed that his position in favor of toleration was biblically informed.[89] He was known for his 'continual searching' of the Scriptures, and he was capable of citing theologians from Luther, Calvin and Beza to Philip de Mornay and Saravia.[90] His sympathies with Anne Hutchinson and her views, as at least tolerable by the civil magistrate, may account for his not being among the Independent signatories of the invitation in 1642 to John Cotton, Thomas Hooker and John Davenport from Members of Parliament to attend the Westminster Assembly. Even within an established religion he believed there should be toleration of differing opinions.[91]

SIR HENRY VANE, JR.

In January 1639 Vane's father obtained for him the post of Joint-Treasurer of the Navy, a position which increased his wealth and also led to his election to the Short Parliament. On June 23, 1640 he was knighted, and on July 1 he was married at St. Mary's, Lambeth to Frances, daughter of Sir Christopher Wray of Barlings, Lincolnshire. It was when he was searching in his father's papers, with the latter's permission, for a document related to his marriage settlement, that he found some notes from the Council meeting of May 5, 1640 that he allowed John Pym to copy. This evidence was used effectively on April 13, 1641 in the trial of the Earl of Strafford for treason.[92]

Vane, Oliver Cromwell and Oliver St. John drafted the 'Root and Branch' Bill for the total abolition of Episcopacy, which was introduced by Sir Edward Dering on May 27, 1641.[93] In his first printed speech Sir Henry Vane, Jr. argued: 'For the whole Fabrick of this building is so rotten and corrupt, from the very foundation of it to the top, that if we pull it not down now it will fall about the eares of all those that endevour it within a few yeares.'[94] Increasingly Vane became a leader in Parliament, so that after the death of Pym on December 8, 1643 he was the chief political force in the House of Commons.[95] It was in the summer and autumn of 1643 that he played an important role in negotiating and promoting the Solemn League and Covenant. On the scaffold, before his death in 1662, he would still defend it:

> ... the matter thereof and the holy ends contained therein I fully assent unto, and have been as desirous to observe; but the rigid way of prosecuting it, and the oppressing uniformity that hath been endeavoured by it, I never approved.[96]

In the Westminster Assembly Vane served on the Grand Committee for dealing with the treaty obligations to the Scots.[97] He also met informally, along with St. John and Lord Wharton, with Thomas Goodwin, Jeremiah Burroughes, and William Bridge of the Independents in the Assembly, with Stephen Marshall, Richard Vines, and Herbert Palmer of the English Presbyterians, and with the Scottish commissioners in order to build bridges between the developing factions, and perhaps to restrain the Scottish influence.[98] His main concern seems to have been that the power of excommunication did not reside solely in the hands of the clergy.[99] The fear of an enforced uniformity was probably the main reason why the New England experience was not emphasized in the Assembly.[100]

Vane's influence in Parliament rose and fell with the fluctuating fortunes of the Presbyterians and the Army through 1646 and 1647. Striving for a settlement that would preserve a government of King, Commons and Lords, he differed with Cromwell on the King's trial and execution. He absented himself from Parliament after Pride's Purge from December 3, 1648 to February 7, 1649, thus having no part in Charles I's trial and neither approving of, nor consenting to, his execution. He served the Commonwealth energetically, however, handling much of the supply and support of Cromwell's troops in Scotland and then serving as one of eight commissioners to negotiate the union of Scotland and England in 1652 after the conquest. He also served the Commonwealth in other foreign and colonial matters, assisting his old friend Roger Williams in Rhode Island and continuing to manage the Navy.[101]

The dissolution of the Rump Parliament in 1653 produced a lasting breach between Vane and Cromwell. The Army favored the election of an entirely new Parliament, but Vane's proposal was for 400 members representing the different counties, but with the present members of the Long Parliament retaining their seats. In April 1653 Cromwell obtained a promise from Vane and other Parliamentary leaders to suspend passage of the bill in order to discuss a possible compromise, but the House itself insisted on proceeding with the bill. To prevent this, Cromwell dissolved Parliament in a dramatic scene. When he called in his musketeers, Vane cried out, 'This is not honest, yea it is against morality and common honesty.' Cromwell shot back in a loud voice, 'O Sir Henry Vane, Sir Henry Vane, the Lord deliver me from Sir Henry Vane!' As the members were leaving, Cromwell told Vane that he might have prevented this but 'he was a Juggler, and had not so much as common honesty'.[102]

Vane then retired to his estate at Belleau, Lincolnshire, living in seclusion and producing *The Retired Man's Meditations* in 1655. In 1656 he published his *Healing Question Propounded and Resolved*, which argued that the form of government arising out of the Puritan cause was favoring only one particular party, namely the Army. This led to his being summoned before the Council and being imprisoned at Carisbrook Castle on the Isle of Wight from September 4 to December 31, 1656.[103]

After Oliver Cromwell's death in 1658, Vane served in the Parliament of Richard Cromwell and sought to redefine the Protector's role as simply a chief magistrate with no power of veto. He eventually made common cause with the discontented officers of the Army to overthrow the Protectorate and restore the Long Parliament. This, however, led also to the Restoration of the Stuart monarchy, with consequences undesired by Vane. On June 11, 1660 he was excluded from the Act of Indemnity. Imprisoned in the Tower, his property seized, he was at first excepted from capital punishment and transported to the Scilly Isles. The Parliament elected in 1661, however, ruled that he should be proceeded against capitally. He was tried on June 2, 1662 for high treason 'for compassing the death of the King, the subversion of the ancient form of government, and the keeping out of the King from the exercise of his regal power'.[104] Although defending himself skillfully and courageously, he was nevertheless found guilty and sentenced to death.

On the scaffold on Tower Hill on June 14, 1662 he bore himself with dignity and composure, seeking to give the assembled crowd an account of his life in spite of the interruptions of the authorities with trumpets and drums.[105] His written speech and the notebooks of his followers were confiscated, but fortunately he had previously given a copy of his prepared remarks to a friend. Cotton Mather was able to relate the following as his concluding sentiments before the axe fell, ending his life in his fiftieth year:

> As my last words, I leave this with you, that as the present storm we now lye under, and the dark clouds that yet hang over the reformed churches of Christ, (which are coming thicker and thicker for a season) were not unforeseen by me for many years past; (as some writing of mine declare) so the coming of Christ in these clouds, in order to a speedy and sudden revival of his cause, and spreading his kingdom over the face of the whole earth, is most clear to the eye of my faith, even that faith in which I die.[106]

His remains were buried in Shipborne Church, Kent, where his mother, Lady Frances Darcy Vane, was buried after her death on August 3, 1663, and also his wife, Lady Frances Wray Vane, after her death in 1679. They had seven sons and seven daughters.[107]

Notes

1. John Richard de Witt, *Jus Divinum* (Kampen: J. H. Kok, 1969) 22; Robert S. Paul, *The Assembly of the Lord* (Edinburgh: T. & T. Clark, 1985), 125-126 and n.69; Larzer Ziff, *The Career of John Cotton: Puritanism and the American Expe-*

rience (Princeton, N.J.: Princeton U. Press, 1962), 178-179. On Cotton's influence, cf. Geoffrey F. Nuttall, *Visible Saints* (Oxford: Basil Blackwell, 1957), 14-17; Ziff, 197; William Haller, *Liberty and Reformation in the Puritan Revolution* (New York and London: Columbia U. Press, 1955), 151-152; and John F. Wilson, *Pulpit in Parliament* (Princeton, N.J.: Princeton U. Press, 1969), 225-226.

2. *Dictionary of National Biography*, eds. Leslie Stephen and Sidney Lee, 22 vols. (London: Oxford U. Press, 1921-22), XXII, 492-493; *Dictionary of American Biography,* ed. Allen Johnson and Duman Malone, 21 vols. (New York: Charles Scribner's Sons, 1946), IV, 460-461.

3. William Haller, *The Rise of Puritanism* (New York, Evanston, and London: Harper & Row, 1938), 65, 69.

4. Nicholas Tyacke, *Anti-Calvinists: the Rise of English Arminianism, c. 1590-1640* (Oxford: Clarendon Press, 1987), 220.

5. J. T. Cliffe, *The Puritan Gentry* (London, Boston, Melbourne and Henley: Routledge & Kegan Paul, 1984), 94.

6. Cotton Mather, *Magnalia Christi Americana, or the Great Works of Christ in America,* 2 vols. (Edinburgh and Carlisle, Pa.: Banner of Truth, 1979 reprint of 1852 ed.), I, 260.

7. *D.N.B.*, XXII, 493.

8. Keith L. Sprunger, *The Learned Doctor William Ames* (Urbana, Chicago, London: U. of Illinois Press, 1972), 237.

9. *D.N.B.*, XXII, 493.

10. *Ibid.; D.A.B.,* IV, 462; Ziff, *Career of John Cotton*, 64-65. George H. Williams, 'The Life of Thomas Hooker in England and Holland, 1586-1633,' in *Thomas Hooker: Writings in England and Holland, 1626-1633*, Harvard Theological Studies XXVIII (Cambridge: Harvard U. Press, 1975), 17-18, tells of an earlier meeting, on July 25,1629, of Hooker, Roger Williams and Cotton from Boston on the way to the Earl of Lincoln's Sampringham Castle.

11. Ziff, *Career of John Cotton,* 60-62.

12. *Ibid.*, 65; *D.A.B.,* IV, 462 gives the date as April 25.

13. Ziff, *Career of John Cotton*, 67.

14. *Ibid.,* 68; G. H. Williams, 'Life of Thomas Hooker', 30; Cotton Mather, *Magnalia*, I, 256; Robert S. Paul, *An Apologeticall Narration* (Philadelphia, Boston: United Church Press, 1963), 83-85.

15. Mather, *Magnalia,* I, 265.

16. *D.N.B.*, IV, 461-462.

17. Ziff, *Career of John Cotton*, 178-179.

18. Everett Emerson, *John Cotton*, rev. ed. (Boston: Twayne Publishers, 1990), 50.

19. Paul, *Assembly of the Lord*, 435. George Gillespie had earlier cited Cotton's use of Matthew 18 to prove synods in the church (Paul, 420-421).

20. Emerson, *John Cotton,* rev. ed., 45-48.

21. de Witt, *Jus Divinum*, 150-151; cf. Paul, *Assembly of the Lord,* 473.

22. Emerson, *John Cotton*, rev. ed., 57-58.

23. Ziff, *Career of John Cotton,* 162, 248-249; Theodore Dwight Bozeman, *To Live Ancient Lives: The Primitivist Dimension in Puritanism* (Chapel Hill and London: U. of North Carolina Press, 1988), 139, 149.

24. Peter Toon, *Puritans, the Millennium and the Future of Israel* (Cambridge and London: James Clarke & Co., 1970), 34-36.

25. Mather, *Magnalia,* I, 260.

26. Robert S. Paul, *The Lord Protector* (Grand Rapids: Eerdmans, 1955), 251 and n.1.

27. *D.N.B.*, XXII, 494; *D.A.B.*, IV, 462.

28. John H. Ball, III, *Chronicling the Soul's Windings: Thomas Hooker and His Morphology of Conversion* (Lanham, Md., New York, and London: University Press of America, 1992), 67-68, quoting from *John Winthrop's Journal,* ed. J. K. Hosmer (New York: Scribner's, 1908) II, 71.

29. Sargent Bush, Jr. *The Writings of Thomas Hooker: Spiritual Adventure in Two Worlds* (Madison: U. of Wisconsin Press, 1980), 96-97. Cf. Ziff, *Career of John Cotton*, 178-179; Paul, *Assembly of the Lord,* 125-126.

30. Bush, *Writings,* 97-99, 108-109; Frank Shuffelton, *Thomas Hooker, 1586-1647* (Princeton, N.J.: Princeton U. Press, 1977), 272-273, 266-267.

31. Shuffelton, *Thomas Hooker*, 18-25. Ashe entered Emmanuel College in 1613. Shuffelton recounts that 'once when Ashe was to preach to an audience which included Hooker, the older man is said to have encouraged him, "Sim, let itt bee hot".' (25). For biographical data, cf. *D.N.B.*, IX, 1189-1190 and *D.A.B.*, IX, 199-200.

32. G. H. Williams, 'The Life of Thomas Hooker in England and Holland, 1586-1633', 4.

33. Ball, *Chronicling*, 12-13 and n.1; Shuffelton, *Thomas Hooker*, 68-69.

34. William Hunt, *The Puritan Moment: The Coming of Revolution in an English County* (Cambridge, Mass. and London: Harvard U. Press, 1983), 196.

35. Shuffelton, *Thomas Hooker*, 74.

36. Hunt, *The Puritan Moment*, 197.

37. Ball, *Chronicling*, 15.

38. Mather, *Magnalia,* I, 345.

39. Hunt, *The Puritan Moment,* 201.

40. *Ibid.,* 256; Nicholas Tyacke, *Anti-Calvinists: The Rise of English Arminianism, c. 1590-1640* (Oxford: Clarendon Press, 1987), 188-189.

41. Shuffelton, *Thomas Hooker*, 128.

42. Hunt, *The Puritan Moment,* 259-260. For a discussion of this sermon, cf. George H. Williams *et. al., Thomas Hooker: Writings in England and Holland, 1626-1633,* 221, 227.

43. Keith L. Sprunger, *Dutch Puritanism* (Leiden: E. J. Brill, 1982), 102-111.

44. *Ibid.,* 111, 237-238; *D.A.B.*, IX, 199; *D.N.B., IX,* 1189.

45. Ziff, *The Career of John Cotton,* 69; Sprunger, *Dutch Puritanism*, 358.

46. Ball, *Chronicling,* 32-33.

47. Mather, *Magnalia,* I, 340-341.

48. Ball, *Chronicling,* 54.

49. Bush, *The Writings of Thomas Hooker,* 99, 108-109; Shuffelton, *Thomas Hooker*, 266-267; Robert S. Paul, *An Apologeticall Narration* (Philadelphia and Boston: United Church Press, 1963), 48-49.

50. Ball, *Chronicling,* 68-69. Ball summarizes Hooker's congregationalism and

also his 'preparationism', which he finds consistent with Hooker's orthodox Calvinism, on pages 25-28.

51. Bush, *Writings,* 97-99.

52. *Ibid.,* 101.

53. Ball, *Chronicling,* 70-71.

54. Paul, *Assembly of the Lord,* 125-126; Ziff, *Career of John Cotton,* 178-179; Emerson, *John Cotton,* rev. ed., 48; Bush, *Writings of Thomas Hooker,* 73, 96-97.

55. He prepared a response to John Paget's 1641 work *A Defence of Church-government exercised in Presbyteriall, Classicall, and Synodall Assemblies,* but his manuscript was lost at sea with the ship that sailed from New Haven in 1646. His later response, *The Power of Congregational Churches,* was published only posthumously in 1672 (Isabel MacBeath Calder, *Letters of John Davenport, Puritan Divine* [New Haven: Yale U. Press and London: Oxford U. Press, 1937], 9).

56. *D.A.B.,* V, 85; cf. *D.N.B.,* V, 560, and Henry Warner Bowden, ed., *Dictionary of American Religious Biography* (Westport, Conn.: Greenwood Press, 1977), 122.

57. Paul S. Seaver, *The Puritan Lectureships* (Stanford Calif.: Stanford U. Press, 1970), 227.

58. Jacqueline Eales, *Puritans and Roundheads* (Cambridge, New York, Melbourne, etc.: Cambridge U. Press, 1990), 61-62, 65. Cf. J. T. Cliffe, *The Puritan Gentry* (London, Boston, Melbourne, and Henley: Routledge & Kegan Paul, 1984), 163.

59. Seaver, *Puritan Lectureships,* 65.

60. Tyacke, *Anti-Calvinists,* 186-187.

61. Bozeman, *To Live Ancient Lives,* 105.

62. Tyacke, *Anti-Calvinists,* 187.

63. *D.A.B.,* V, 86. *D.N.B.,* V, 560, says that he received both the M.A. and B.D. at this time.

64. Haller, *Rise of Puritanism,* 66, 74, 164.

65. *Ibid.,* 67, 80-81; Seaver, *Puritan Lectureships,* 236-238.

66. G. H. Williams, 'The Life of Thomas Hooker', 30-31; Ziff, *Career of John Cotton,* 68-69; Nuttall, *Visible Saints,* 15; Paul, *Apologeticall Narration,* 84; Seaver, *Puritan Lectureships,* 241.

67. Seaver, *Puritan Lectureships,* 241; *D.A.B.,* V, 86.

68. Sprunger, *Dutch Puritanism,* 112.

69. *Ibid.,* 113.

70. *Ibid.,* 118.

71. *Ibid.,* 119; *D.A.B.,* V, 86; I. M. Calder, *Letters of John Davenport,* 1, which refers to her as Elizabeth Wooley, *D.N.B.,* V, 561 claims that he 'married a daughter of the Rev. Abraham Pierson in 1663 [sic?] and had by her five children'.

72. Sprunger, *Dutch Puritanism,* 167.

73. *D.A.B.,* V, 86; Calder, *Letters,* 5.

74. Shuffelton, *Thomas Hooker,* 251; Ziff, *Career of John Cotton,* 143.

75. Emerson, *John Cotton,* rev. ed., 44; cf. Bush, *Thomas Hooker,* 108, and Shuffelton, *Thomas Hooker,* 264.

76. *D.A.B.,* V, 87; Daniel Reid et al., eds., *Dictionary of Christianity in America* (Downers Grove, Ill.: InterVarsity Press, 1990), 342.

77. *D.A.B.,* V, 87; Bowden, *Dictionary of American Religious Biography,* 122-

123; Calder, *Letters*, 12. *D.N.B.*, V, 561, has March 13 and *Dictionary of Christianity in America*, 342, has March 11 as the date of his death.

78. Mather, *Magnalia*, I, 329.

79. de Witt, *Jus Divinum,* 45-48; Tai Liu, *Discord in Zion* (The Hague: Martinus Nijhoff, 1973), 24-25; Paul, *Apologeticall Narration*, 69-73; Paul, *Assembly of the Lord,* 97-98.

80. *D.N.B.*, XX, 114.

81. Cliffe, *Puritan Gentry*, 16-17; *D.N.B.*, XX, 116.

82. *D.N.B.*, XX, 116.

83. Mather, *Magnalia*, I, 136.

84. Cliffe, *Puritan Gentry*, 202.

85. *D.A.B.*, XIX, 192.

86. Ziff, *Career of John Cotton*, 115.

87. *D.A.B.*, XIX, 192.

88. *Ibid.*

89. Bozeman, *To Live Ancient Lives,* 157-158 and n.11.

90. Cliffe, *Puritan Gentry*, 39; George Yule, *Puritans in Politics* (Appleford, Oxfordshire: Sutton Courtenay Press, 1981), 19.

91. Paul, *Assembly of the Lord,* 125-126 and n.69, 177 and n.13; Yule, *Puritans in Politics*, 209-210.

92. *D.N.B.*, XX, 118.

93. *Ibid.*; Robert S. Paul, *The Lord Protector: Religion and Politics in the Life of Oliver Cromwell* (Grand Rapids, Mich.: Eerdmans, 1955), 51.

94. Cliffe, *Puritan Gentry*, 228-229.

95. *D.N.B.*, XX, 119; Paul, *Assembly of the Lord*, 193.

96. *D.N.B.*, XX, 119.

97. Paul, *Assembly of the Lord*, 243.

98. *Ibid.*, 445, 452; Yule, *Puritans in Politics,* 138-139.

99. Yule, *Puritans in Politics,* 151, 160.

100. Cf. Paul, *Apologeticall Narration*, 110-112.

101. *D.N.B.*, XX, 121-122.

102. *D.N.B.*, XX, 123; Antonia Fraser, *Cromwell, Our Chief of Men* (London, Auckland, Melbourne, Singapore, and Toronto: Mandarin, 1993), 420; Paul, *Lord Protector*, 270.

103. *D.N.B.*, XX, 123-124.

104. *D.N.B.*, XX, 127.

105. Cf. James K. Hosman, *The Life of Young Sir Henry Vane* (Boston and New York: Houghton, Mifflin and Co., 1889), 534-546, for a detailed account.

106. Mather, *Magnalia,* I, 137.

107. *D.N.B.*, XX, 116, 127.

Chapter 11

Other Famous
Contemporary Puritans

For many modern readers the gateway to the world of the English Puritans has been John Bunyan's The Pilgrim's Progress *or John Milton's* Paradise Lost, *or perhaps Richard Baxter's* The Saints' Everlasting Rest *or* The Reformed Pastor. *For the more theologically inclined,it may have been John Owen's* A Discourse on the Holy Spirit *or* An Exposition of the Epistle to the Hebrews. *These writers were all contemporaries of the Westminster divines, generally somewhat younger, and hence productive for the most part in the years following the Westminster Assembly. As part of the Puritan movement, however, they deserve to be included here for the light their lives shed on the spiritual context of the time.*

Richard Baxter (November 12, 1615 - December 8, 1691)

One of the most influential Puritan clergymen of the latter half of the seventeenth century, Richard Baxter commented about the Westminster Assembly:

> The Divines there Congregate were Men of Eminent Learning and Godliness, and Ministerial Abilities and Fidelity: And being not worthy to be one of them my self, I may the more freely speak that Truth which I know even in the Face of Malice and Envy, that, as far as I am able to judge by the Information of all History of that kind, and by any other Evidences left us, the Christian World, since the days of the Apostles, had never a Synod of more Excellent Divines (taking one thing with another) than this Synod and the Synod of *Dort* were.[1]

Whether worthy or not to be a member of the Assembly, Baxter would have been the youngest member since he was but twenty-seven years old when its work began. His respect for the Assembly is significant, however, since he did not fully identify with either the Presbyterians or the Independents, or with the Episcopalians.

Baxter was born at the village of Rowton in Shropshire on November 12, 1615, son of Richard Baxter of Eaton-Constantine, Shropshire and Beatrice Adeney of High Ercall, Shropshire. His father seems to have had a spiritual conversion about the time of young Richard's birth; however, the spiritual state of the local churches in his childhood was deplorable, the clergy being incompetent or immoral. Baxter's education was gained first at the free school of Wroxeter. When ready to go to Oxford, he was instead advised by his teacher to place himself under the tutoring of Richard Wickstead, chaplain at Ludlow. Although largely neglected by the scholar, Baxter made excellent use of the library of Ludlow Castle. He had already been influenced by books, Richard Sibbes's *Bruised Reed* having had a profound effect upon him at about the age of fifteen.[2] Asked later if he were a graduate of Oxford, Baxter responded:

> As to myself, my faults are no disgrace to any university; for I was of none. I have little but what I had out of books, and inconsiderable helps of country tutors. Weakness and pain helped me to study how to die; that set me on studying how to live; and that on studying the doctrine from which I must fetch my motives and comforts.[3]

Though possessing a rigorous intellect, he would not bear the mark of university training, having the drawbacks of those self-taught and the advantages of those who have learned directly from the Lord.

Leaving Ludlow Castle in 1633, he spent a brief time at court in London, but was disgusted with the life of a courtier. His mother's illness caused him to return to Eaton-Constantine, where she died on May 10, 1634. He remained in the vicinity, studying theology, particularly that of the Scholastics, under the guidance of Rev. Francis Garbet, parish clergyman of Wroxeter. In 1638 he became headmaster of a newly established school at Dudley and was ordained by the Bishop of Worcester. Acquaintance with some of the nonconformists in the vicinity of Dudley began to move him from his conformist convictions. While having no problems with kneeling or with liturgy as such, he opposed using the cross in baptism, thought use of the surplice doubtful, and considered his own church's liturgy confused and defective. But what most bothered him was the lack of discipline; drunkards and swearers being admitted to the Lord's Supper. He was also disturbed at the ease of subscription, deciding that he could never again subscribe *ex animo* that there was nothing in the Articles, Homilies, and Liturgy contrary to the Word of God.[4]

With these sorts of conscientious convictions he became assistant minister to Rev. William Medstard at Bridgnorth, Shropshire, 1639-41. Here he was able to preach to a large congregation, but was relieved of all duties he had scruples about or that he thought unlawful. He preached 'as a dying man to dying men', however he found that the people of Bridgnorth

> ... proved a very ignorant, dead-hearted people.... Though I was in the fervor of my affections and never anywhere preached with more vehement desires of men's conversions ... yet with the generality applause of the preacher was the most of the success of the sermon which I could hear of, and their tippling and ill company and dead-heartedness quickly drowned all.[5]

In March 1641 he was invited to become Lecturer of St. Mary's in Kidderminster, Worcestershire, a thriving township of 3,000 people where the Vicar preached only once a quarter. As A. B. Grosart comments:

> The Work done by Richard Baxter in Kidderminster has passed into history. Whereas in the beginning the moral (not to speak of the godly) were

to be counted on the ten fingers, ere very long a passing traveller along the streets at a given hour heard the sounds of praise and prayer in every household.[6]

When the Civil War began in 1642, most of Worcestershire was Royalist. Baxter, though loyal to the monarchy, sided with Parliament. He found it expedient to withdraw from Kidderminster to Gloucester temporarily. Towards the end of 1642 he returned to Kidderminster only to have a country gentleman point him out with the words, 'There goes a traitor.'[7] He then went to Coventry, where he was among some thirty fugitive ministers of the gospel, including later members of the Westminster Assembly Richard Vines and Anthony Burgess. Here he officiated as chaplain to the Parliamentary army garrison, preaching once each Sunday to the soldiers and also once a Sunday to the townspeople and others. He was invited by the officers of Oliver Cromwell's newly raised cavalry troop at Cambridge to be their pastor, as of a gathered church, but he rejected the invitation with a reproof against what he conceived as unlawful.[8]

RICHARD BAXTER

After the Battle of Naseby in June 1645 Baxter visited Cromwell's camp and was appalled at the 'hot-headed sectaries' he found in leading positions in the Army. Cromwell himself received him coolly and confronted him with his refusal to serve his now victorious regiment. As a result he agreed to become a chaplain to Colonel Whalley's regiment and continued with the Army through several siege operations.[9]

His own health collapsed in 1646-1647 with a violent and 'prodigious bleeding at the nose'. Believing that he was near death, he wrote in his retirement the first of his 168 books, *The Saints' Everlasting Rest*, which would be published in 1650. Published before it, in 1649, was his *Aphorisms of Justification* in opposition to the Antinomianism to which he was exposed in the Army. Upon his recovery he returned to Kidderminster, where he provided a model pastorate from 1647 to 1660. In spite of continuing weakness from consumptive tendencies and kidney stones he energetically pursued his labors. He and an assistant catechized 800 families annually by having fourteen or fifteen per week come to his home on Mondays and Tuesdays. On Thursdays he would settle cases of conscience for a group gathering. His preaching drew large crowds and was in demand throughout his ministry, yet he regarded it as the effort of his spare time, every moment being preserved for his writings.

During these crucial years of ministry at Kidderminster, Baxter maintained a very individualistic stance. He opposed the Solemn League and Covenant even though he had rashly signed it at Coventry. Yet he praised the Westminster Confession as 'the most excellent for fulness and exactness he had ever read from any Church', and he took exception only to a few minor points in it.[10] He faulted the Independents for the failure of the Westminster Assembly, naming Philip Nye, Thomas Goodwin, Sidrach Simpson, William Bridge and Jeremiah Burroughes, the last of whom he blamed the least:

> ... Mr. Burroughs being dead, Dr. John Owen arose, not of the same Spirit, to fill up his place; by whom and Mr. Philip Nye's Policie the Flames were encreased, our Wounds Kept open, and carried on all, as if there had been none but they considerable in the World; and having an Army and City Agents sit to second them, effactually hindred all remedy till they had dash'd all into pieces as a broken Glass.[11]

Baxter did contribute to efforts toward greater unity in 1652,[12] and he helped in 1654 to draw up a statement of 'Fundamentals of Reli-

gion'.[13] On the latter occasion in London he met James Ussher, Archbishop of the Anglican Church of Ireland, who urged him to produce a
directory for afflicted consciences, appealing to the unconverted and
to all ranks of professing Christians. (The eventual result of this would
be his *A Christian Directory; or, a Sum of Practical Theology and
Cases of Conscience*, the first edition of which in 1673 had 1,133
folio pages.) He also preached before Oliver Cromwell on 1 Corinthians 1:10 against divisions in the church.[14] Although critical of
Cromwell's policies, he did approve of his system of Triers as generally beneficial for putting good men in as ministers of the churches.[15]
In Kidderminster Baxter had a monthly conference with ministers of
the county, reflected in his 1656 work *Gildas Salvianus: The Reformed
Pastor*: 'If God would but reform the ministry, ... the people would
certainly be reformed.'[16] His Voluntary Association of ministers in
Worcestershire to see to the pastoral care, instruction, and discipline
of the whole county was imitated with similar Voluntary Associations
in a number of other counties in the 1650s.[17]

In 1660 he was summoned to London to aid, as a moderate Puritan,
in the recall of the King. He preached before the House of Commons
at St. Margaret's, Westminster on April 30 and before the Lord Mayor
and Aldermen and all London in St. Paul's on May 10. He was appointed one of ten or twelve Chaplains to Charles II, and he was one of
the four who preached before the King.[18] In the negotiations for a
religious settlement, when a plea was made for the toleration of Independents and Anabaptists, Charles responded by suggesting Roman
Catholics also be included. Before allowing the Bishops to speak first,
Baxter said:

> As we humbly thank your Majesty for your indulgences to ourselves, so
> we distinguish the tolerable Parties from the intolerable: for the former
> we humbly crave greater lenity and favour; but for the latter – such as
> Papists and Socinians – for our parts, we cannot make their Toleration our
> Request.[19]

In 1661 he was among the twelve divines who met with twelve
Bishops to seek compromise on such matters as liturgy, but the Bishops were not accommodating, and there were flaws on the Puritan
side:

> Baxter was far too talkative; he did not concentrate on pressing home a

few demands. And his fellow Puritans, although they reluctantly accepted him as their chief spokesman in the Savoy Conference, were too divided to agree on a single, simple policy which might have been successful.[20]

Having declined the offer of the Bishopric of Hereford, Baxter sought to return to Kidderminster, but was thwarted by his opponents. Shortly before the Act of Uniformity was passed in May 1662 he preached his farewell sermon to the Church of England at the great church of Blackfriars in London. He then retired quietly to Acton in Middlesex, writing many books and preaching when opportunity afforded.[21]

On September 10, 1662 he, at the age of forty-six, married Margaret Charlton, who was twenty years his junior. Theirs was a beautiful relationship for nineteen years, until her death on June 14, 1681. She was a comfort to him during the stress of persecution in the reign of Charles II. He sought to continue preaching, but ran afoul of the Conventicle Act of 1664 and was sentenced to six months in prison in 1669, an imprisonment that was shared by his wife and proved to last only a few weeks.[22] After the King's Indulgence, he gained licence to preach as a Non-Conformist (neither Presbyterian nor Independent) and preached to a lawful public assembly for the first time in ten years on November 19, 1672. Spies and informers hounded him, however, and in 1676 a warrant was issued for his arrest and a guard placed at his chapel door on Sundays. In 1682 his books and property were seized and sold, and he went into hiding in illness. When James II came to the throne in 1685, Baxter was imprisoned and put through a disgraceful trial under 'bloody Jeffreys' in May of that year. 'Richard, I see the rogue in your face,' shouted the Judge. 'I was not aware my face was so true a *mirror*,' shot back Baxter.[23] Although he was spared being whipped through the streets, he was fined and imprisoned for about a year and a half. Released on November 24, 1686, he continued to preach to the end of his life and worked on the completing of his autobiographical *Reliquiae Baxterianae*, much of which had been written in 1664 and which was published posthumously in 1696.[24] When he was dying, a friend comforted him with the reminder of the benefit many had received from his writings. He replied, 'I was but a pen in God's hand, and what praise is due to a pen?'[25] He died on December 8, 1691, having lived into the reign of William and Mary with its new religious toleration.

As J. I. Packer has written, 'Baxter was a big man, big enough to have large faults and make large errors.'[26] In seeking to steer a way between Romanism, Arminianism, and Calvinism he developed a 'Neonomianism' that was criticized by at least sixteen other theologians in his own day and which has not proven satisfactory in our day.[27] As one who admires Baxter greatly, especially as an evangelist, Packer adds:

> Granting that his habit of total and immediate outspokenness ('plain dealing') on all matters of theology and ministry was a compulsion of conscience and not just compensation for an inferiority complex (in fact, it was probably a bit of both), his lifelong inability to see that among equals a triumphalist manner is counter-productive was a strange blind spot.... The plain fact is that Baxter insulted people, treating them as knaves or fools, and that has never been the way to win friends.[28]

On the other hand, Baxter's long acquaintance with death gave him a perspective on what is most important in this life:

> ... when, like Baxter from the time of his majority, one lives with one foot in the grave, it imparts an overwhelming clarity both to one's sense of proportion (what matters, and what does not), and also to one's perception of what is and what is not consistent with what one professes to believe.[29]

Before he died, in the beginning of the reign of William and Mary, Baxter looked back on some of the foolish pride of Puritanism, which God had not allowed to be established. But Richard Baxter could also look forward with a sober hope. He once wrote:

> God will have other generations to succeed us, let us thank him that we have had our time.... The Gospel dieth not when I die: the Church dieth not: the praises of God die not: the world dieth not: and perhaps it shall grow better, and those prayers shall be answered which seemed lost: yea, and it may be that some of the seed that I have sown shall spring up to some benefit of the dark unpeaceable world when I am dead.[30]

John Owen (1616-August 24, 1683)

John Owen was described by a seventeenth-century contemporary as 'the Calvin of England'.[31] Sinclair Ferguson says, 'There is widespread agreement that John Owen was *the* theologian of the Puritan movement.'[32] J. I. Packer comments:

> ... he is by common consent not the most versatile, but the greatest among Puritan theologians. For solidity, profundity, massiveness and majesty in exhibiting from Scripture God's ways with sinful mankind there is no one to touch him. On every topic he handles, apart from the limits he imposes on synods and magistrates, he stands in the centre of the Puritan mainstream, totally in line with the Westminster standards and the developed ideal of godliness.... he was more like John Calvin than was any other of the Puritan leaders.[33]

In another passage Packer adds:

> Owen was a theologian of enormous intellectual energy. His knowledge and memory were vast, and he had an unusual power of organising his material. His thought was not subtle nor complicated, as, for instance, was Baxter's .... Of their content, it is enough to say that for method and substance Owen reminds one frequently of Calvin, frequently too of the *Westminster* and *Savoy Confessions* (the *Savoy* is in fact the *Westminster*, lightly revised, mainly by Owen himself), and time and again of all three together; he is constantly and consciously near the centre of seventeenth-century Reformed thought throughout.[34]

In his *Quest for Godliness*, which collects almost forty years of his writings on the Puritans, from William Perkins to Jonathan Edwards, Packer says, 'The Puritan John Owen, who comes closer than anyone else to being the hero of this book, was one of the greatest of English theologians. In an age of giants, he overtopped them all.'[35]

John Owen was born in 1616, son of the Rev. Henry Owen, of an old Welsh family, the Vicar of Stadham and Chiselhampton, Oxfordshire. Neither the precise date nor the exact place of John Owen's birth is known.[36] After attending a grammar school in Oxford, he matriculated at Queen's College, Oxford on November 4, 1631 and received the B.A. on June 11, 1632 and the M.A. on April 27, 1635. In 1637, already ordained, he became chaplain to Sir Robert Dormer of Ascott, Oxfordshire, leaving the University because he could not submit to Archbishop Laud's statutes. He later served as chaplain to John, Lord

Lovelace at Hurley, Berkshire, but when the Civil War began in 1642, he moved to London.[37]

Having been spiritually depressed for several years, Owen went to St. Mary's Aldermanbury to hear Edmund Calamy preach, but was disappointed when a substitute entered the pulpit. The sermon, from Matthew 8:26, however, brought assurance to Owen of his salvation. Later, despite all his efforts, he was never able to determine the identity of the preacher on that day.[38]

Owen's first publication appeared in March 1642, *A Display of Arminianism*, which Packer calls 'a competent piece of prentice-work, rather of the nature of a research thesis'.[39] Its able defence of Calvinism nevertheless gained him appointment to the sequestered rectory of Fordham in Essex in July 1643. Later that year he married Mary Rooke, daughter of a clothier in nearby Coggeshall. She would bear him eleven children, only one of whom, a daughter, survived into adulthood. A mild Presbyterian in polity at this point, Owen was ejected from the church in Fordham upon the death of the incumbent, and he was recommended in 1646 to the vicarage of St. Peter's Coggeshall. Here he became convinced of Congregational polity, entirely through the study of books rather than through any contacts with Independents. The main book instrumental in his conversion on this point was John Cotton's *The Keyes of the Kingdom of Heaven*.[40]

Some have perceived his transition to Congregationalism in his first sermon preached before Parliament, on April 29, 1646, which was published as *A Vision of Unchangeable Free Mercy ... Whereunto is Annexed a Short Defensative about Church Government*. He was one of the two chosen to preach before the House of Commons on the Fast Day of January 31, 1649, the day following the execution of Charles I.[41] He became thereafter one of the four main preachers to the Rump Parliament, along with Joseph Caryl, John Bond and William Strong, Owen himself preaching on at least eight special occasions from April 1649 to October 1652.[42] At some point he made contact with the remaining 'Dissenting Brethren' of the Westminster Assembly, Philip Nye, Thomas Goodwin, William Bridge and Sidrach Simpson (Jeremiah Burroughes having died in 1646), and eventually became the acknowledged leader of their kind of Congregationalism.[43] Geoffrey Nuttall documents 'the centrality of John Owen' through his network of contacts and comments: 'By his (relative) longevity, as well as by his genuine eminence and his vigour as an apologist, John Owen came

JOHN OWEN

to be accepted as personifying this tradition more notably than any other single man....'[44]

This growing reputation can be accounted for in part by his publication in 1647 of his first masterpiece, *The Death of Death in the Death of Christ*, after more than seven years of hard study. This sets forth the doctrine of 'limited' – that is, definite or particular – atonement and has remained the classic Calvinistic statement of this doctrine.[45] Richard Baxter's *Aphorismes of Justification* of 1649 took issue with Owen's view of atonement, and Owen responded in 1650 with *Of the Death of Christ, The Price He Paid*. Owen's preaching before Parliament on April 19, 1649 attracted the attention of Oliver Cromwell, who invited him to accompany him, as a chaplain, to Ireland. This led to his becoming Cromwell's chief adviser in ecclesiastical matters.[46] On March 8, 1650 he was appointed preacher to the Council of State, and later that year he accompanied Cromwell into Scotland.[47]

In 1651 Owen was appointed Dean of Christ Church, Oxford, and in 1652 he was made Vice-Chancellor of the University. Against his wishes he was made D.D. there in 1653.[48] He also preached regularly, on alternate Sundays with Thomas Goodwin, at St. Mary's in Oxford.[49] He exercised vigorous leadership at Oxford. When a Royalist uprising was rumored in the spring of 1655, he took responsibility for the security of the town and county, riding at the head of a cavalry troop, armed with sword and pistol. Tall and imposing, he dressed more like a layman than a divine. According to Anthony à Wood, at Oxford 'he went cloakless to show off his figure, powdered his hair, and wore large tassels on his bandstrings, pointed ribbons at his knees, Spanish leather boots with large lawn tops, and "his hat mostly cock'd".'[50]

Through the time of the Commonwealth Owen played a prominent part with other Independents in establishing a religious settlement. He was a leader in defining the 'Fundamentals of Religion' in 1654.[51] He was also appointed one of the 'Triers' for approval of candidates for the ministry.[52] In 1657, however, an estrangement occurred between him and Cromwell when he helped draft a petition opposing the offer of the crown to Cromwell. When Cromwell was invested as Lord Protector, Owen was not even an invited guest.[53] Nevertheless, during Cromwell's last days before his death on September 3, 1658, Owen was one of six ministers attending him.[54] In that same month Owen played a key role in producing *The Savoy Declaration* as the official statement of the faith and polity of the Congregational Churches in England.[55] In the collapse of the Protectorate in 1659, Owen took part in the opposition to Richard Cromwell and in support of the English Army in London. He appealed to General Monck on November 19, warning him of the opposite dangers of a Stuart restoration or of Fifth-Monarchy fanaticism. Monck was not swayed from his course, however, and in 1660 the Restoration began.[56]

Ejected from his position as Dean of Christ Church, Oxford on March 13, 1660, Owen moved to his estate at Stadhampton. Although his preaching opportunities were restricted by the Acts of the Clarendon Code, he gained some favor from Lord Clarendon by his writings against Roman Catholicism.[57] He remained true to his Congregational principles, being indicted in Oxford in 1665 for holding religious assemblies in his house. He was able to return to London to preach after the Plague and the Great Fire. In 1667 he wrote on behalf of religious liberty. The Indulgence of 1672 gave him opportunity to see many works to publication, including his commentary on Hebrews, which fills seven of the twenty-four volumes of the modern edition of his works.[58]

In 1673 his congregation in London merged with the church in Leadenhall Street of which Joseph Caryl had been pastor.[59] In 1676 his wife, Mary, died. Over a year later, on June 21, 1677, he married

Michel, widow of Thomas D'Oyley of Chiselhampton near Stadham. With the fortune she brought him, he was able to keep his carriage and villa, first at Kensington and later at Ealing.[60] During his remaining years he continued to write. His great work on the Holy Spirit began to be published in 1674 with remaining parts published posthumously in 1693.[61] Afflicted with both gallstone and asthma, he died on the twenty-first anniversary of the St. Bartholomew's Day Great Ejection, August 24, 1683. He was buried in Bunhill Fields, London, where his tomb's inscription says in part:

> In polemical theology, with more than herculean strength, he strangled three poisonous serpents, the Arminian, the Socinian, and the Roman.
> In practical theology, he laid out before others the whole of the activity of the Holy Spirit, which he had first experienced in his own heart, according to the rule of the Word. And, leaving other things aside, he cultivated, and realised in practice, the blissful communion with God of which he wrote; a traveller on earth who grasped God like one in heaven.
> In casuistry, he was valued as an oracle to be consulted on every complex matter.[62]

Owen and Richard Baxter had differed on many issues, having contrasting conceptions of the church as well as theological differences on the atonement and on justification.[63] Owen's magnanimous spirit is shown, however, in his letter to Baxter when the latter was seeking to promote unity among Nonconformists in 1667:

> Sir, I shall pray that the Lord would guide and prosper you in all studies and endeavors, for the service of Christ in the world, especially in this your desire and study for the introducing of the peace and love promised among them that believe, and do beg your prayers.[64]

Owen was also an admirer and helper of John Bunyan. His connections in high places helped to get Bunyan freed from prison. It was his suggestion that led Bunyan to take his *Pilgrim's Progress* to Owen's publisher, Nathaniel Ponder. When asked by Charles II why he admired the uneducated Bunyan's preaching, Owen said, 'Could I possess the tinker's abilities, please your Majesty, I would gladly relinquish all my learning.'[65]

The main criticism of Owen's writings is of his style. But J. I. Packer suggests as a solution that he be read aloud:

Owen's style is often stigmatised as cumbersome and tortuous. Actually it is a Latinised spoken style, fluent but stately and expansive, in the elaborate Ciceronian manner. When Owen's prose is read aloud, as didactic rhetoric (which is, after all, what it is), the verbal inversions, displacements, archaisms and new coinages that bother modern readers cease to obscure and offend.[66]

Peter Toon, Owen's most recent and thorough biographer, bemoans the fact that none of his diaries was preserved to reveal to us more of the inner man:

So Owen must remain hidden as it were behind a veil. His actions, his concerns and his theology we have gleaned from his letters, his books, and contemporary sources but his secret thoughts remain his own. However, this much can be said: Owen shines through the available information as a truly great man, whose one basic concern in word and deed, book and action, was the proclamation of Jesus Christ and His gospel.[67]

John Milton (December 9, 1608 - November 8, 1674)

Before the Westminster Assembly had concluded its work, the poet John Milton, once a supporter of the 'Smectymnuans' in their opposition to prelacy, had soured on Presbyterianism. He wrote of his former allies:

... you have thrown off your prelate lord
And with stiff vows have renounced his liturgy
To seize the widowed whore plurality
From them whose sin ye invied, not abhorred, ...

But we do hope to find out all your tricks,
Your plots and packing worse than those of Trent,
That so the Parliament
May with their wholesome and preventive shears,
Clip your phylacteries though baulk your ears,
And succour our just fears,
When they shall read this clearly in your charge
New presbyter is but old priest writ large.[68]

Milton had a personal reason to be bitter against the Westminster divines because of their attacks on his books on divorce, but he was also disillusioned that movement for reform of the Church of England was not producing the liberty of which he dreamed.

Milton was born in Bread Street, Cheapside, London on December 9, 1608. His father, also John Milton (1563?-1647), was son of a staunch Roman Catholic and became a Protestant while at Oxford. Disinherited, he went to London to make his fortune as a scrivener. He was successful in this business and also became an accomplished musician, playing the organ and composing.[69] John was the second of three children born to his father and Sarah Jeffrey; his sister Anne marrying Edward Phillips and his younger brother Christopher becoming a judge. John was baptized at All Hallows Church, where the Rector was the Puritan Richard Stock, and he no doubt heard sermons in his youth from nearby Puritan preachers such as William Gouge at St. Anne's, Blackfriars, Richard Sibbes at Gray's Inn, and John Preston at Lincoln's Inn.[70]

Milton's literary gift was evident at an early age, and his father employed as a tutor for him the Scottish clergyman Thomas Young, who was later to be a member of the Westminster Assembly. Young introduced Milton to classical literature and may also have brought him to Christian faith prior to his entrance into St. Paul's School, not later than 1620.[71] He was admitted to Christ's College, Cambridge on February 12, 1625 and received the B.A. on March 26, 1629 and the M.A. on July 3, 1632. As late as July 1628 his plan was to enter the ministry, but he was increasingly alienated by the authoritarian policies instituted by William Laud. Unable in good conscience to take the necessary oaths, he was in this sense 'church-outed by the prelates', as he put it.[72] He decided to serve the cause of truth and reform by using his gift as a writer: 'His experience and the anger and disillusion it brought gave him, he asserted, the right at the appropriate time to speak concerning the church on even terms with any churchman.'[73]

From 1632 to 1638 Milton lived with his father, who had retired to Horton, a village near to Colnbrook, Buckinghamshire, about eighteen miles west of London. His poems *Allegro* and *Penseroso* were probably written in 1632, his *Comus* in 1634, and his *Lycidas* in November 1637. From April 1638 to July 1639 he toured the continent of Europe, visiting Paris, Nice, Genoa, Pisa, Naples, Venice, Verona, Milan and Geneva, with extended stays at Rome and at Florence. He met Hugo Grotius, Galileo, and many leading artists and writers, but it is

JOHN MILTON

reported that he offended the Italians 'by his strict morality and by his outspoken attacks on popery'.[74]

He returned to England in time to join his countrymen in their fight for liberty. Joseph Hall, Bishop of Exeter, published in February 1640 a defence of the *Divine Right of Episcopacy* and followed this in January 1641 with a *Humble Remonstrance* addressed to the Long Parliament. Thomas Young, Milton's former tutor, joined with Stephen Marshall, Edmund Calamy, Matthew Newcomen and William Spurstowe (all soon to become members of the Westminster Assembly) to publish a series of treatises over the name 'Smectymnuus', produced by a combination of their initials.[75] Milton supported this effort by publishing *Of Reformation touching Church Discipline in England* (June 1641), which attacked Episcopacy on historical grounds, *Prelatical Episcopacy* (July 1641), which responded to the arguments of Archbishop James Ussher, and *Animadversions upon the Remonstrance Defence* (July 1641), an attack upon Hall's latest book. While these works were anonymous, though not secret, in February 1642 Milton published under his own name *The Reason of Church-Government urged against Prelacy*, and in April 1642 he published an *Apology*, replying to Hall's latest answer.[76]

At this stage of his development Milton favored Presbyterianism as the best solution to the prelacy of Episcopacy. Everett Emerson sees in his *Of Reformation* a combination of the effective features of earlier Puritan writing: 'Here are the learning of the most learned of them – Cartwright, Travers, and Perkins – and the wit and scorn of Martin Marprelate and John Bastwick.'[77] His arguments are firmly based on the Bible, 'the just and adequate measure of truth, fitted and proportioned to the diligent study, memory, and use of every faithful man'.[78] Although Milton eventually departed from Presbyterianism, he always clung to belief in the full authority of the Bible. It was an authoritative Bible that was, however, subject to interpretation by human reason.[79]

Milton's break from Presbyterianism grew out of the Westminster divines' opposition to his writings on divorce. In May of 1643 he took a trip into the country and returned with a bride, Mary Powell, eldest daughter of a Royalist, Richard Powell of Forest Hill near Shotover, Oxfordshire. At seventeen, Mary was only half Milton's age, and she soon found his home in Aldersgate Street, where he was teaching his two nephews in very spartan and disciplined fashion, a dull place. After just a month she returned to her father's convivial home for a visit which turned out to be of indefinite length. When a messenger from the family 'evilly entreated' Milton, he resolved never to take her back and wrote a book on divorce. His *Doctrine and Discipline of Divorce*, which carries the publication date of August 1, 1643, maintains the thesis that

> indisposition, unfitness, or contrariety of mind arising from a cause in nature unchangeable ... is a greater reason of divorce than natural frigidity, especially if there be no children or that there be mutual consent.[80]

He brought out a second edition, with some additions, on February 2, 1644, and on July 15, 1644 he published another pamphlet, *The Judgment of Martin Bucer on Divorce*, including a translation of the relevant parts of that Reformer's *De regno Christi*, which had been addressed to King Edward VI.

On August 13, 1644 Herbert Palmer, one of the leading figures of the Westminster Assembly, made reference to Milton's book, along with Roger Williams' *Bloudy Tenent* and various others worthy of condemnation, in a sermon before Parliament. Indeed, Milton's former tutor, Thomas Young, may have alluded to it in an earlier sermon be-

fore Parliament, on February 28, 1644.[81] Milton responded to the practice of censorship with his *Areopagitica*, of November 24, 1644 and
offered criticism of Herbert Palmer (and also former Westminster divine Daniel Featley) in his *Tetrachordon* of March 4, 1645, and then in
his *Colasterion* he also castigated Westminster divine Joseph Caryl,
who had licenced and approved of an anonymous answer to Milton.[82]

The Powells, meanwhile, had suffered loss of fortune from the
Royalist reversals, and they sought to restore Mary to the marriage.
She begged his forgiveness on her knees, and he consented to have her
back. They took a larger house in the Barbican, where he was able to
receive more students. It was here that she gave birth to Anne on July
29, 1646, to Mary on October 25, 1648, to John (who died in infancy)
on March 16, 1651, and to Deborah on May 2, 1652, before she died
in 1652, probably from the effects of the final childbirth.[83]

By 1645 Milton had definitely abandoned the Presbyterians, whom
he saw as enforcing their views on the consciences of others as the
Bishops had previously done. The ones in the Assembly with whom
he had the greatest sympathy at this time were the Erastians, such as
Thomas Coleman and John Selden, who represented a Parliamentary
check on Presbyterian discipline.[84] But he eventually favored the Army
over Parliament and championed the cause of Oliver Cromwell. He
defended the execution of Charles I in his *Tenure of Kings and Magistrates* of February 13, 1649. When he was invited to become Latin
Secretary for the newly formed Council of State, he readily agreed
and was sworn in on March 15, 1649. In this capacity he translated the
government's foreign dispatches into dignified Latin, but he also had
to arrange for the publication of replies to various attacks and to prepare some of the replies himself. When Charles II induced Salmasius,
a professor at Leyden, to write the *Defensio Regia pro Carolo I* in
November 1649, the Council had Milton prepare a reply, his *Pro Populo
Anglicano Defensio* of March 1650, over which work he finally lost
his eyesight. His vision had been failing for years, probably from glau-
coma.[85]

Milton continued to serve the Council of State throughout the Protectorate, but his blindness meant that he attended fewer meetings.
Dispatches requiring dignified Latin were nevertheless still brought
to him for translation, the most famous of which were the letters sent
by Cromwell in May 1655 to various governments to protest the persecution of the Waldensians. His loyal commitment to Oliver Cromwell

is shown in his poem *To the Lord Generall Cromwell* of May 1652:

> Cromwell, our cheif of men, who through a cloud
>> Not of Warr onely, but detractons rude,
>> Guided by faith & matchless Fortitude
>> To peace & truth thy glorious way hast plough'd,
>> And on the neck of crowned Fortune proud
>> Hast reard Gods Trophies, & his work pursu'd
>> While Darwen stream with blood of Scotts imbru'd,
>> And Dunbarr feild resounds thy praises loud,
>> And Worsters laureat wreath; yet much remains
>> To conquer still; peace hath her victories
>> No less renowned than warr, new foes aries
> Threatening to bind our soules with secular chaines:
>> Helpe us to save our Conscience from the paw
>> Of hireling wolves whose Gospell is their maw.[86]

Everett Emerson concludes that Milton identified with the variety of Puritanism that Cromwell represented: 'Milton believed that at last the saints were in power, and that Cromwell, a Seeker, was not interested in ruling men's consciences.'[87]

Milton's theology is revealed in his *De Doctrina Christiana*, a work begun no later than 1646 and not completed before 1657 and not published until 1825. As William Haller summarizes it:

> Milton addressed himself to the task of clarifying out of Biblical materials an idea of God, man, and nature, consistent at every point with belief in man's ability to understand himself and his universe sufficiently to permit him to govern himself and determine his own destiny. These convictions Milton felt he must state and prove out of God's Word, namely, that the universe is governed by divine law, that man by his disobedience brought punishment and servitude upon himself under the law, and that Christ set him free again to distinguish true from false, good from evil, and so to obey the law if he would and redeem himself from his subjection to death. Every man had Adam and Christ within him, and every man's fate depended upon the outcome of the struggle of those two with each other and with the evil one.

Thus, Haller concludes, 'Milton could justify his belief that no order of men, no institution or law of state or church, should come between any man and his free obedience to the higher law revealed to him in scripture, in creation, and in his own mind and conscience.'[88] Some have concluded that Milton was Arian in at least parts of his Christology and eventually became Arminian in his soteriology.[89]

In 1658 Milton turned his attention to the composition of his great religious epic, *Paradise Lost*, which he finished in 1663. With the Restoration of the monarchy it had been ordered on June 16, 1660 that Milton's *Defensio* should be burned by the common hangman. He was arrested during the summer, but was eventually released and freed from all legal consequences of his previous actions.[90]

Milton had married a second time, on November 12, 1656, to Catharine Woodcock, who bore him a daughter on October 19, 1657, but both mother and child died in February 1658. He took a third wife on February 24, 1663, Elizabeth Minshull, who was thirty years younger than he.[91] In 1671 his last poems, *Paradise Regained* and *Samson Agonistes* appeared together. By this time his health was declining. He died from the effects of gout on November 8, 1674. Leslie Stephen says of his last years:

> Milton had come to stand apart from all sects, though apparently finding the Quakers most congenial. He never went to any religious services in his later years. When a servant brought back accounts of sermons from nonconformist meetings, Milton became so sarcastic that the man at last gave up his place.[92]

William Haller summarizes: 'In Milton the Puritan revolutionary emerged as the secular humanist concerned less with reforming the church than with liberating men's minds from error and superstition.'[93] He adds:

> Milton had come a long way with the spiritual brotherhood but could not stop at the point where they wished to halt reform. He had been won by the moral idealism of the preachers. With them he exalted preaching, embraced the doctrine of calling and the talent, and eagerly awaited the coming of reform in the church. But he went on from that point to conceive a society ruled by public opinion enlightened not only by preachers but by intellectual and moral leaders of all sorts, lay or cleric, above all by poet-prophets like himself. His Puritanism was a Puritanism transfigured by the idealism which had come to him from the humanist poets and philosophers.[94]

Perhaps a clue to Milton's departure from evangelical orthodoxy is to be found in Haller's account of his youthful poem *On the morning of Christ's Nativity*:

The nativity and the passion have always been associated with the idea of atonement by the son of God for man's sin. But the young Puritan, full of the sense of his own power, felt in reality no need of a redeemer outside his own breast. As his party, when it had the power, permitted little to be made of Christmas or Easter, he would later relegate the Christ child and the crucifixion to a subordinate place in his version of the epic .... For Milton the atonement does not itself directly redeem; it merely starts a truth which redeems as it moves from mind to mind by the aid of prophets and poets.[95]

John Bunyan (November 1628 - August 31, 1688)

When the Westminster Assembly began in 1643, John Bunyan was not yet fifteen years old. As a sixteen-year-old he served in the Parliamentary Army. Although he came to know John Owen, he did not generally travel in the circles of the well-educated Westminster divines. The London Confession of the Calvinistic Baptists, which he may have had a part in producing in 1677, was nevertheless almost identical with the Westminster Confession except with regard to the sacraments and polity. Coming from the lower middle-class, Bunyan reflects the impact of the Puritan movement upon mid-seventeenth-century England, and he in turn has become perhaps the most influential of all English Puritans through his literary works, including his autobiographical *Grace Abounding to the Chief of Sinners* and the allegorical books, *The Pilgrim's Progress* and *The Holy War*.

Bunyan was born in the village of Elstow, Bedfordshire, just south of the town of Bedford, in November of 1628. The ancestors of his father, Thomas Bunyan (1603-1676), had lived in this region since at least the twelfth century. His mother, Margaret Bentley, was also a native of Elstow, born in 1603 of people 'who, though humble in station, were yet decent and worthy in their ways'.[96] His father designated himself in his will a 'brasier', what would later be termed a 'whitesmith, a maker and mender of pots and kettles'. Although John Bunyan would later be styled as 'a tinker and a poor man', he was not a totally itinerant craftsman, but had his forge and workshop by his settled home in Elstow.[97]

Bunyan's mother died in June 1644, and his father remarried within

THE BAPTISTS

Often identified with the Continental Anabaptists, but more closely related to the Puritan movement, the Baptists in England and America were of two types: the General, Free-will, or Arminian Baptists and the Regular, Particular, or Calvinistic Baptists. John Smyth and Thomas Helwys emigrated in 1608 to Holland, where they founded a church based on believer's baptism by immersion and with an Arminian understanding of free will. When Smyth died in 1612, Helwys returned to England to found the first General Baptist church there, at Pinners' Hall, London.

By the 1630s Baptist churches of a more Calvinistic persuasion were emerging from the Puritan movement. In 1633 a group of Calvinistic separatists who had been members of the London church pastored by Henry Jacob adopted believer's baptism. Roger Williams formed a Baptist church in Providence, Rhode Island in 1639.

In 1644 Daniel Featley, Episcopalian member of the Westminster Assembly, held a public disputation with Baptists in London and published his version of it in *The Dippers dipt; or, the Anabaptists Duck'd and Plung'd over Head and Ears at a Disputation in Southwark.*

As a result, a Confession of Faith was produced on behalf of seven London Baptist churches in 1644, with some additions and changes in 1646. Referred to now as 'The First London Confession', it shows the Particular Baptists as in agreement with orthodox Reformed doctrine in all major points except on the sacraments and the church.

'The Second London Confession', first produced in 1677 and reprinted in 1688, was approved by the ministers of over one hundred congregations who met in London in July 1689. Adopted by the Baptist Association in America in Philadelphia in September 1742, it is also referred to as 'The Philadelphia Confession'. It is practically the same as the Westminster Confession, except in the sections on the church and on the sacraments.

In 1693 a Catechism was drafted by William Collins which was based on the Westminster Shorter Catechism. It is sometimes called 'Keach's Catechism' because Benjamin Keach contributed to the work. Among other significant Baptists are Vavasor Powell (died 1670) of Wales, John Bunyan (died 1688),and Hanserd Knollys (died 1690) who preached in Massachusetts from 1638 to 1641 before returning to England.

two months. The arrival of a stepmother may have led to his joining the Army by the time of his reaching the regulation age of sixteen in November 1644. Posted to Newport Pagnell, he seems not to have seen any serious battle action in the Parliamentary Army, although he does refer to a soldier who went to a siege in his place and was shot in the head and killed.[98] Bunyan's regiment was demobilized in July 1647, and he returned to Elstow.

He married a woman whose name is not known, probably in late 1648 or early 1649. She came from a godly home and brought with her two books that were to have a formative influence upon Bunyan's spirituality – Arthur Dent's *The Plain Man's Pathway to Heaven* and Lewis Bayly's *The Practice of Piety*.[99] He gave up his habit of swearing and became regular in his attendance at church. Although he became 'a brisk talker on religion', he realized that he lacked the personal knowledge of God that he sensed in some poor women whose conversation he overheard. His quest for spiritual reality and an assurance of his own salvation led to an agonizing inner conflict for a period of three or four years before he found peace of soul, as described in his *Grace Abounding*.

In 1653 he joined the Nonconformist church to which those poor women belonged. It met for worship in St. John's Church, Bedford, a congregation founded by eleven working-men in 1650 as a result of Oliver Cromwell's policy of toleration for Protestant separatists.[100] The rector was John Gifford, whose ministry before his death in 1655 had a positive influence on Bunyan.[101] It was also in 1655 that he lost his wife, who had borne him four children, Mary (who was blind), John, Thomas and Elizabeth. It was probably in this same year that he moved to Bedford.

In 1655 he was elected one of the deacons and began in private ministry to exercise his gift of exhortation. In 1657 he was formally set apart to the office of preacher, and as he travelled, pursuing his trade as a tinker, he used every opportunity to preach, 'in woods, in barns, on village greens, or in town chapels', and his fame as a preacher spread. In some places the official ministers gave him permission, in other places there was opposition.[102]

Bunyan also began to write. His first published work appeared in 1656, *Some Gospel Truths Opened*, which was an attack upon the mysticism of the Quakers. This was answered by Edward Burrough, and Bunyan responded in 1657 with *A Vindication of Gospel Truths*.

JOHN BUNYAN

These early works show an energetic style, a command of plain English, and a thorough knowledge of the Bible.[103]

With the Restoration in 1660, laws against Nonconformity were
revived, and Bunyan was arrested for preaching without licence on
November 12 at the hamlet of Lower Samsell by Harlington, about
thirteen miles south of Bedford. He was imprisoned in the county jail,
where he would spend most of the next twelve years, although he was
allowed occasional liberty to preach in Bedford and even to visit some
Christians in London.[104]

In 1659 Bunyan had married a second wife, Elizabeth, who cared
for his four motherless children and eventually bore him two more,
Sarah and Joseph.[105] During his lengthy imprisonment she earnestly
and diligently pleaded with the authorities for his release, but to no
avail.[106] To help support his family from prison, he made long tagged
laces, 'many hundred gross of which he sold to the hawkers'.[107] His
imprisonment, however, gave him greater time and incentive to write.
At least eight minor works were published between 1663 and 1665.
Then in 1666 appeared *Grace Abounding to the Chief of Sinners*, Bunyan's spiritual autobiography.

He was released from prison in 1666, but within six weeks he was
arrested again because he would not give up preaching. During the
next six years in jail his writing productivity dropped off, but in 1672

he produced his *Defence of Justification by Faith*, a vehement attack upon a work by Rev. Edward Fowler, Rector of Northill.[108] Also in that year he produced the *Confession of My Faith and Reason of My Practice* as a vindication of his teaching in order to gain his freedom. Thanks to Charles II's covert intention of favoring Roman Catholics in England, Bunyan was among the Nonconformists pardoned in 1672 and finally gained his release after almost twelve years in jail. He was already called to be the Pastor of the Nonconformist church in Bedford, which was no longer able to meet in St. John's Church, but in a barn in the orchard of a member of the congregation.[109]

From his center in Bedford, Bunyan spread his ministry throughout the county and beyond. He applied to the authorities for licenses for preachers and preaching sites in the surrounding country:

> Among these he made stated circuits, being playfully known as 'Bishop Bunyan', his diocese being a large one, and, in spite of strenuous efforts at repression by the ecclesiastical authorities, steadily increasing in magnitude and importance.[110]

He was imprisoned again in 1676, and it was on this occasion that John Owen sought to aid in gaining his release. It was Owen who recommended the manuscript of Bunyan's *The Pilgrim's Progress* to his publisher, Nathaniel Ponder, and who, when asked by Charles II why he listened to an uneducated tinker, said, 'Could I possess the tinker's abilities for preaching, please your Majesty, I would gladly relinquish all my learning.'[111]

The Pilgrim's Progress appeared in 1678, with a second edition in the same year and a third in 1679. According to the author's own claim, it was produced in prison. Edmund Venables, following John Brown's 1885 biography, believes this to be his last, six-months imprisonment, but Christopher Hill argues for its having been written no later than 1672, Bunyan delaying its publication because of concern over the propriety of writing fiction about so serious a subject.[112] He need not have worried. As William Haller points out, Bunyan's 'great allegories were but single items coming from a single practitioner – though a genius – in a vast literature, only a portion of which has been preserved ...,' reflecting the 'similitudes' of many Puritan sermons.[113] J.I. Packer says that 'Bunyan's *Pilgrim's Progress* serves as a kind of gazetteer to the contents of their sermons.'[114] He also says that it reflects the fact that the Puritans were great warriors:

The Puritans fought for truth against error, for personal holiness against temptations to sin, for ordered wisdom against chaotic folly, for church purity and national righteousness against corruption and hostility in both areas. One facet of their greatness was their principled hostility to all evils that stood in the way of godliness and true faith, and their willingness, much as they loved peace, to go out and fight those things, and to keep fighting as long as the evils were there.[115]

Bunyan is usually classified as a Baptist. He himself deplored denominational labels and termed himself 'Congregationall', but this may refer merely to his church's polity. As his 1673 work *Differences in Judgment about Water-Baptism no Bar to Communion* shows, he would not exclude those who differed with regard to the form or subjects of baptism. Calvinistic in his theology, he is to be regarded as a Particular Baptist of an open sort.[116] Alexander F. Mitchell believes that his influence may have softened the 1677 statement, 'a Confession of Faith put forth by the Elders and Brethren of many congregations of Christians baptized upon profession of their faith', which was reprinted in 1688 and approved by over a hundred congregations in London, July 3-11, 1689, commonly known as 'The London Confession of 1688'.[117]

The Pilgrim's Progress was followed in 1680 by *The Life and Death of Mr. Badman* and in 1682 by *The Holy War Made by Shaddai upon Diabolus*. In 1684 there appeared the second part of *Pilgrim's Progress*, in which Chrisitan's wife Christiana makes her pilgrimage to the heavenly city. By this time Bunyan was famous for both his writing and his preaching. His friend Charles Doe reports that when he preached in London,

> if there were but one day's notice given, there would be more people come together to hear him preach than the meeting house would hold. I have seen to hear him preach by my computation about twelve-hundred at a morning lecture by seven o'clock on a working day in the dark winter time.[118]

A contemporary described Bunyan's appearance as follows:

> He was tall of stature, strong-boned though not corpulent, somewhat of a ruddy face with sparkling eyes, wearing his hair on his upper lip after the old British fashion; his hair reddish, but in his latter days had sprinkled with grey; his nose well-set, but not declining or bending, and his mouth

moderately large, his forehead something high, and his habit always plain and modest.

His bearing seems to have been consistent with his message. Another contemporary described him thus:

> He appeared in countenance to be of a stern and rough temper, but in his conversation mild and affable, not given to loquacity or much discourse in company, unless some urgent occasion required it, observing never to boast of himself in his parts, but rather seem low in his own eyes, and submit himself to the judgment of others.

A third contemporary wrote:

> His countenance was grave and sedate, and did so to the life discover the inward frame of his heart, that it was convincing to the beholders, and did strike something of awe in to them that had nothing of the fear of God.[119]

In the spring of 1688 Bunyan had suffered an attack of the 'sweating sickness', from which he was weakened. In August he travelled on horseback first to Reading, where he sought to reconcile a son to his father, and then through forty miles of drenching rain to London. He preached for the last time on August 19, then was seized with a fever and died on the 31st. He was buried in Bunhill Fields, Finsbury, London. During his dying days he continued to share his spiritual wisdom: 'No sin against God can be little, because it is against the great God of heaven and earth; but if the sinner can find out a little God, it may be easy to find out little sins.' At the end it was difficult to say much, and that occasioned this remark: '... when thou prayest, let thy heart be without words than thy words without a heart.'[120]

Notes

1. Robert S. Paul, *Assembly of the Lord* (Edinburgh: T. & T. Clark, 1985), 522 n.1, quoting from Baxter's autobiography, *Reliquiae Baxterianae*, I, i, 73 (#117); cf. Alexander F. Mitchell, *The Westminster Assembly*, 2nd ed. (Philadelphia: Presbyterian Board of Publication, 1897), 122.

2. *Dictionary of National Biography*, eds. Leslie Stephen and Sidney Lee, 22 vols. (London: Oxford U. Press, 1921-22), I, 1349-1350; Marcus L. Loane, *Makers of Puritan History* (Grand Rapids, Mich.: Baker Book House, 1961, 1980), 168-170; William Haller, *Rise of Puritanism* (New York, Evanston, and London: Harper

and Row, 1938, 1957), 66; Geoffrey F. Nuttall, *Richard Baxter* (London: Thomas Nelson and Sons, 1965), 1, 7.

3. *D.N.B.*, I, 1350; Loane, *Makers,* 171.

4. *D.N.B.*, I, 1351-1352.

5. Quoted in Paul S. Seaver, *Puritan Lectureships* (Stanford, Calif.: Stanford U. Press, 1970), 31.

6. *D.N.B.*, I, 1352.

7. *D.N.B.*, I, 1353.

8. William Haller, *Liberty and Reformation in the Puritan Revolution* (New York & London: Columbia U. Press, 1955), 191.

9. *Ibid.*, 194.

10. Mitchell, *Westminster Assembly*, 390; cf. Paul, *Assembly of the Lord*, 542.

11. Quoted in John Richard de Witt, *Jus Divinum: The Westminster Assembly and the Divine Right of Church Government* (Kampen: J.H. Kok, 1969), 164-165 n. 87.

12. Tai Liu, *Discord in Zion* (The Hague: Martinas Nijhoff, 1973), 147.

13. Robert S. Paul, *An Apologeticall Narration* (Philadelphia & Boston: United Church Press, 1963), 94.

14. Loane, *Makers*, 185.

15. Liu, *Discord,* 143 n.91; David L. Edwards, *Christian England*, Vol. II: *From the Reformation to the 18th Century* (Grand Rapids, Mich.: Eerdmans, 1983), 297; George Yule, *Puritans in Politics* (Appleford, Oxfordshire: Sutton Courtenay Press, 1981), 242.

16. Loane, *Makers*, 188.

17. Yule, *Puritans in Politics,* 167-268; Geoffrey F. Nuttall, *Visible Saints* (Oxford: Basil Blackwell, 1957). 122-123.

18. A. H. Drysdale, *History of the Presbyterians in England* (London: Publication Committee of the Presbyterian Church of England, 1889), 375 and n.1.

19. George R. Abernathy, 'The English Presbyterians and the Stuart Restoration, 1648-1663', *Transactions of the American Philosophical Society*, New Series – Vol. 55, Part 2 (May 1965), 75.

20. Edwards, *Christian England*, II, 310-311. Baxter produced his own *Reformed Liturgy* for the Savoy Conference (Edwards, II, 317) which was later much admired by Dr. Samuel Johnson (*D.N.B.*, I, 1354).

21. *D.N.B.*, I, 1355.

22. Loane, *Makers*, 213-214.

23. Drysdale, *History*, 405.

24. Haller, *Liberty and Reformation*, 194; *D.N.B.*, I, 1356.

25. John Charles Ryle, *Bishops and Clergy of Other Days* (London: Charles J. Thynne, 1868), 201.

26. J. I. Packer, *A Quest for Godliness* (Wheaton, Ill.: Crossway Books, 1990), 302.

27. *Ibid.*, 303; C.F. Allison, *The Rise of Moralism* (London: S.P.C.K., 1966), 162-164.

28. Packer, *Quest for Godliness*, 303.

29. *Ibid.*, 306.

30. Quoted in Edwards, *Christian England,* II, 318-319.

31. Cf. Peter Toon, *God's Statesman: The Life and Work of John Owen* (Exeter: Paternoster Press, 1971), 173.

32. Sinclair B. Ferguson, *John Owen on the Christian Life* (Edinburgh and Carlisle, Pa.: Banner of Truth, 1987), 19.

33. J. I. Packer, *A Quest for Godliness: The Puritan Vision of the Christian Life* (Wheaton, Ill.: Crossway Books, 1990), 81.

34. *Ibid.,* 193.

35. *Ibid.,* 191.

36. Peter Toon, ed., *The Correspondence of John Owen (1616-1683), With an Account of His Life and Work* (Cambridge and London: James Clarke & Co., 1970) 3 and n.6.

37. *D.N.B.,* XIV, 1318; Ferguson, *John Owen,* 2.

38. Ferguson, *John Owen,* 2.

39. Packer, *Quest for Godliness,* 145.

40. Ferguson, *John Owen,* 5, 162; Nuttall, *Visible Saints,* 16, 53-54; Paul, *Apologeticall Narration,* 55-56, 84.

41. John F. Wilson, *Pulpit in Parliament* (Princeton, N.J.: Princeton U. Press, 1969), 95, 163; Haller, *Liberty and Reformation,* 339; H.R. Trevor-Roper, *The Crisis of the Seventeenth Century* (New York and Evanston: Harper & Row, 1968), 335, 337.

42. Trevor-Roper, *Crisis,* 329 and n.2; Wilson, *Pulpit in Parliament,* 133; Haller, *Liberty and Reformation,* 337.

43. Nuttall, *Visible Saints,* 16 and n.5; Paul, *Apologeticall Narration,* 108-109.

44. Nuttall, *Visible Saints,* 39, 42.

45. Packer, *Quest for Godliness,* 145; Alan C. Clifford, *Atonement and Justification: English Evangelical Theology 1640-1790, An Evaluation* (Oxford: Clarendon Press, 1990), 5, 9.

46. Robert S. Paul, *The Lord Protector* (Grand Rapids, Mich.: Eerdmans, 1964), 204.

47. *D.N.B.,* XIV, 1318.

48. Clifford, *Atonement,* 5; Ferguson, *John Owen,* 11.

49. Ferguson, *John Owen,* 9.

50. Haller, *Liberty and Reformation,* 337.

51. Paul, *Apologeticall Narration,* 94; Paul, *Lord Protector,* 324. Owen's views on church and state are described in Haller, *Liberty and Reformation,* 339-341, and in Paul, *Lord Protector,* 255-257.

52. Liu, *Discord in Zion,* 143.

53. Ferguson, *John Owen,* 12-13; Paul, *Lord Protector,* 367 and n.4.

54. Paul, *Apologeticall Narration,* 88 and n.29.

55. *Ibid.,* 88; Ferguson, *John Owen,* 13-14.

56. Liu, *Discord in Zion,* 154-156.

57. *D.N.B.,* XIV, 1320.

58. Ferguson, *John Owen,* 16.

59. *Ibid.;* Clifford, Atonement, 7; *D.N.B.,* XIV, 1320.

60. Ferguson, *John Owen,* 17; *D.N.B.,* XIV, 1321, refers to his second wife as Dorothy.

61. Ferguson, *John Owen*, 17.

62. Packer, *Quest for Godliness*, 192.

63. Cf. Allison, *Rise of Moralism*, 174-177, for Owen's position in the discussions of justification.

64. Clifford, *Atonement*, 7.

65. Nuttall, *Visible Saints*, 39; Ferguson, *John Owen,* 16; Toon, *God's Statesman,* 162.

66. Packer, *Quest for Godliness*, 194.

67. Toon, *God's Statesman,* 177-178.

68. Quoted in Everett H. Emerson, *English Puritanism from John Hooper to John Milton* (Durham, N.C.: Duke U. Press, 1968) 285, and in Mitchell, *Westminster Assembly,* 293, n.1, where Mitchell defends the Westminster divines especially against Milton's charge of pluralities.

69. *D.N.B.*, XIII, 470-471.

70. Emerson, *English Puritanism*, 279; Haller, *Rise of Puritanism,* 290-292.

71. Emerson, *English Puritanism*, 279-280; Haller, *Rise of Puritanism*, 293-297.

72. *D.N.B.*, XIII, 472; Emerson, *English Puritanism,* 280.

73. Haller, *Rise of Puritanism*, 295.

74. *D.N.B.,* XIII, 473.

75. Paul, *Assembly of the Lord*, 119, n.48 lists the Smectymnuan titles and exchanges.

76. *D.N.B.,,,* XIII, 475.

77. Emerson, *English Puritanism*, 283.

78. *Ibid.*, 284.

79. Haller, *Rise of Puritanism*, 349; Haller, *Liberty and Reformation,* 44-45.

80. *D.N.B.*, XIII, 476.

81. Haller, *Liberty and Reformation*, 123-128; David Masson, *The Life of John Milton,* new ed. (Gloucester, Mass.: Peter Smith, 1965), III, 262-264, 298.

82. *D.N.B.*, XIII, 476-477; Masson, *Life of Milton,* III, 309-315.

83. *D.N.B.*, XIII, 477.

84. Christopher Hill, *Milton and the English Revolution* (New York: Viking Press, 1977), 151.

85. *D.N.B.*, XIII, 478-479.

86. Quoted in Paul, *The Lord Protector*, 266-267.

87. Emerson, *English Puritanism*, 286.

88. Haller, *Liberty and Reformation*, 239-240.

89. Edwards, *Christian England,* II, 328-329; Mitchell, *Westminster Assembly,* 525-526; *D.N.B.*, XIII, 486-487.

90. *D.N.B.*, XIII, 480-481.

91. *D.N.B.*, XIII, 479, 481.

92. *D.N.B.*, XIII, 483-484.

93. Haller, *Liberty and Reformation*, 239.

94. Haller, *Rise of Puritanism*, 362.

95. *Ibid.*, 312-313.

96. *D.N.B.*, III, 275.

97. *D.N.B.*, III, 275-276.

98. *D.N.B.*, III, 276; Christopher Hill, *A Tinker and a Poor Man: John Bunyan and His Church, 1628-1688* (New York; Alfred A, Knopf, 1989), 45-46.

99. Gordon Wakefield, *Bunyan the Christian* (London: Harper Collins *Religious*, 1992), 13-14.

100. Edwards, *Christian England,* II, 335-336; Wakefield, *Bunyan the Christian*, 66-67.

101. Nuttall, *Visible Saints*, 37.

102. *D.N.B.*, III, 277.

103. *D.N.B.*, III, 277-278. Nuttall, *Visible Saints*, 125, indicates that other 'Congregational men', such as William Bridge, John Owen, and others, participated in the attack upon Quakerism.

104. *D.N.B.,* III, 278-279.

105. *D.N.B.,* III, 282.

106. Hill, *A Tinker and a Poor Man*, 229-230; *D.N.B.*, III, 278-279.

107. *D.N.B.*, III, 279.

108. Allison, *Rise of Moralism*, 145-146, 155, describes this exchange.

109. *D.N.B.*, III, 280.

110. *D.N.B.*, III, 280.

111. Toon, *God's Statesman*, 161-162; Ferguson, *John Owen on the Christian Life*, 16.

112. *D.N.B.*, III, 280; Hill, *A Tinker and a Poor Man,* 197-198.

113. Haller, *Rise of Puritanism*, 150.

114. Packer, *A Quest for Godliness*, 286.

115. *Ibid.*, 335.

116. Wakefield, *Bunyan the Christian*, 70-71; Hill, *A Tinker and a Poor Man,* 292-294.

117. Mitchell, *Westminster Assembly*, 411-412; Philip Schaff, *The Creeds of Christendom*, 6th Ed., 3 vols. (New York and London: Harper & Brothers, 1931), I, 855; A. C. Underwood, *A History of the English Baptists* (London: The Baptist Union Publication Dept., 1947) 103-105.

118. Quoted in Marcus Loane, *Makers of Puritan History* (Grand Rapids, Mich.: Baker Book House, 1980), 161.

119. *D.N.B.*, III, 282.

120. Loane, *Makers of Puritan History,* 161-162; *D.N.B.*, III, 282.

Conclusion

An American Presbyterian friend, when taking the guided tour of Westminster Abbey, asked the tour guide if he could see the Jerusalem Chamber. The guide responded by inquiring why he would want to see the Jerusalem Chamber. When my friend replied, 'Because that is where the Westminster Assembly met,' the guide had to be informed as to what the Westminster Assembly was.

There is a certain irony about the influence of the Westminster Assembly. Half a dozen Scottish delegates come south to London for more than four years to get a group averaging from sixty to eighty Englishmen to produce a Confession of Faith, two catechisms, a Directory for Worship, and a Form of Government which become standards for the Kirk of Scotland, and for Presbyterianism wherever English-speaking Christians take them around the world, but which have only a very momentary influence on England itself. It is perhaps not so unusual that our God would work in such a way 'that no flesh should glory'. Of the fifty-four lives profiled in this book, it is the English Presbyterians described in Chapters 2, 7, 8, and 9 that are probably least well-known and yet did most of the work to produce the Westminster Standards that have had such a profound effect elsewhere.

The lives of the members of the Westminster Assembly help to fill a gap in the story of the English Puritan movement. Because the products of the Assembly were not lastingly adopted in England, they are sometimes overlooked in the study of English Puritanism. Learned articles on English Puritan ethics have been produced, for example, that skip from William Perkins and William Ames to the period of Richard Baxter without commenting on the important statements in the Westminster Larger Catechism on the proper understanding and application of the Ten Commandments. The work of the Westminster Assembly should be seen as reflecting the core of English Puritan theology and spirituality.

For those churches that profess to adhere to the Westminster Standards, the lives of the members of the Assembly shed much light on the foundations of continuing truths. The extended discussions on church government, including such matters as the office and role of the ruling elder, can be studied profitably still today. The same can be said about the Lord's Supper, the reading of Scripture in worship, the conscience, and many other topics. The writings of Joseph Caryl on 'what is good' are still relevant to the study of biblical ethics. The fact that Independents, Erastians, Scots and English Presbyterians - good Puritans all! - did not always agree was a healthy stimulus to study of the Bible in depth and thorough debate as to its meaning and application in the immediate context of the mid-seventeenth century.

The historical context of the Westminster Assembly must not be forgotten. There were differences of theological emphasis and nuance among the members, all of whom were Calvinists. The supralapsarian/infralapsarian issue was not pressed, nor was the matter of the millennium, on which there were differences. It is also interesting to see that there were differences among the members on the specific role of the active obedience of Christ in the justification of the believer.

Most instructive is to realize the strong interest in evangelism and missions on the part of many members of the Assembly. Thomas Hill sought to see missionaries sent not only into the dark corners of the realm, but also abroad. John White, Anthony Tuckney, William Gouge, Edmund Calamy and others maintained an active interest in the American missions to the Indians. Herbert Palmer's dying prayers were for the spread of the gospel around the world.

It was a rare collection of God's servants with a rich variety of gifts that gathered in the Westminster Assembly to produce the documents that continue to bear fruit in the understanding and living out of God's Word. As the Apostle Paul wrote in Ephesians 4:7, 11-16:

> ... to each one of us grace has been given as Christ apportioned it .... It was he who gave some to be apostles, some to be prophets, some to be evangelists, and some to be pastors and teachers, to prepare God's people for works of service, so that the body of Christ may be built up until we all reach unity in the faith and in the knowledge of the Son of God and become mature, attaining to the whole measure of the fullness of Christ.
>
> Then we will no longer be infants, tossed back and forth by the waves, and blown here and there by every wind of teaching and by the cunning and craftiness of men in their deceitful scheming. Instead, speaking the truth in love, we will in all things grow up into him who is the Head, that is, Christ. From him the whole body, joined and held together by every supporting ligament, grows and builds itself up in love, as each part does its work.

The members of the Westminster Assembly, imperfect as they were, were nevertheless gifts to the church from the ascended Christ, to whom be thanks and all glory given.

INDEX

Abbot, George, Archbishop of
Canterbury: 48, 173.

Aberdeen: 102, 103.

Abernathy, George: 184.

active obedience of Christ: see
obedience of Christ.

Act of Uniformity of 1662: 64, 128,
189, 192, 203n.170, 216, 233,
293; nonconformists
disobeyed, 217.

Act Rescissory of 1661: 104, 109.

Acton, Middlesex: 49, 79.

Acts of the Clarendon Code: 298.

Adderlay, Humphrey and daughter
Katherine: 136.

Adenay, Beatrice: 288.

adoption, doctrine of: 165.

Aeschylus: 156.

Aldersgate Street, London: 303.

Alexander, Archibald: 15, 64, 101,
129, 147, 208.

All Saints Church, Oxford: 46.

All Hallows, London: 211.

All Hallows, Bread Street: 49, 154,
230, 232, 233, 301.

All Hallows, Lombard Street,
London: 73.

All Hallows, Staining: 78.

allegorical interpretation: see
Scripture.

Alleine, Joseph: 188.

Allison, C. F.: 247.

Amanuensis (assistant to scribes):
17, 43, 192, 194.

America: 23; adoption of Westminster Standards, 11; see
descriptive insert on 264.

Amersham: 267.

Ames, William: 20, 86, 92n.35, 121,
250n.27, 259, 261, 269, 318;
chastised, in absentia,
over definition of pastoral
call, 241.

Anabaptists: 161, 191, 222, 292.

analogy of faith: see Scripture.

Anglicanism: 10, 44, 183, 184, 196, 260.

*Annotations upon all the books of
the Old and New Testament*:
50, 185, 256n.246; Assembly
members who contributed to,
199n.31; Parliament orders
preparation of, 37, 159; quote
from Burgess concerning,
256n.246; see descriptive
insert on 242.

anointing with oil: 72.

antinomianism: 103, 159, 160, 198n.25,
210, 222, 230, 263, 270, 275,
278, 291.

apocrypha: 61.

Apologetical Narration: 29, 73, 79, 125.

apologist: 296.

Aquinas, Thomas: 209, 240.

Arabella (ship): 23, 261.

Archbishop of Canterbury: 10, 48, 64,
120, 162, 187, 273.

Archer, John: 72, 78, 86.

Arian theology: 306.

Arminianism: 10, 18, 19, 20, 26, 158,
161, 180, 208, 210, 222, 261,
272, 294, 296, 299; Baptists,
308; Laud's theology, 46, 102,
273; many following it ejected
from Cambridge, 221; Milton
and, 306; quote concerning,
144; Socinus and, 247.

Arnold, John, and his widow
Margaret: 86.

Arrowsmith, John: **144-148**, 14, 153,
175, 177, 180, 190, 194, 207,
221, 232; similarity of birth to
Lightfoot's, 145; glass eye, 146.

Arundal, Lieutenant: 31.

Ascott, Oxfordshire: 295.

Ashe, Simeon: **218-224**, 109, 140, 192,
267; died, 216, 276; he gave

Christian Focus titles by
Donald Macleod
Principal of the Free Church College, Edinburgh

A Faith to Live By
In this book the author examines the doctrines detailed in the Westminster Confession of Faith and applies them to the contemporary situation facing the church.

ISBN 1 85792 428 2   *Hardback*   *320 pages*

Behold Your God
A major work on the doctrine of God, covering his power, anger, righteousness, name and being. This book will educate and stimulate deeper thinking and worship.

ISBN 1 876 676 509   *paperback*   256 pages

Rome and Canterbury
This book assesses the attempts for unity between the Anglican and Roman Catholic churches, examining the argument of history, the place of Scripture, and the obstacle of the ordination of women.

ISBN 0 906 731 887   *paperback*   *64 pages*

The Spirit of Promise
This book gives advice on discovering our spiritual role in the local church, the Spirit's work in guidance, and discusses various interpretations of the baptism of the Spirit.

ISBN 0 906 731 448   *paperback*   *112 pages*

Shared Life
The author examines what the Bible teaches concerning the Trinity, then explores various historical and theological interpretations regarding the Trinity, before indicating where some of the modern cults err in their views of the Trinity.

ISBN 1-85792-128-3   *paperback*   *128 pages*

Reformed Theological Writings
R. A. Finlayson

This volume contains a selection of doctrinal studies, divided into three sections:

General theology
The God of Israel; God In Three Persons; God the Father; The Person of Christ; The Love of the Spirit in Man's Redemption; The Holy Spirit in the Life of Christ; The Messianic Psalms; The Terminology of the Atonement; The Ascension; The Holy Spirit in the Life of the Christian; The Assurance of Faith; The Holy Spirit in the Life of the Church; The Church – The Body of Christ; The Authority of the Church; The Church in Augustine; Disruption Principles; The Reformed Doctrine of the Sacraments; The Theology of the Lord's Day, The Christian Sabbath; The Last Things.

Issues Facing Evangelicals
Christianity and Humanism; How Liberal Theology Infected Scotland; Neo-Orthodoxy; Neo-Liberalism and Neo-Fundamentalism; The Ecumenical Movement; Modern Theology and the Christian Message.

The Westminster Confession of Faith
The Significance of the Westminster Confession; The Doctrine of Scripture in the Westminster Confession of Faith; The Doctrine of God in the Westminster Confession of Faith; Particular Redemption in the Westminster Confession of Faith; Efficacious Grace in the Westminster Confession of Faith; Predestination in the Westminster Confession of Faith; The Doctrine of Man in the Westminster Confession of Faith.

R. A. Finlayson was for many years the leading theologian of the Free Church of Scotland and one of the most effective preachers and speakers of his time; those who were students in the 1950s deeply appreciated his visits to Christian Unions and IVF conferences. This volume contains posthumously edited theological lectures which illustrate his brilliant gift for simple, logical and yet warm-hearted presentation of Christian doctrine (I Howard Marshall).

272 pages   ISBN 1 85792 259 X   large format

MENTOR TITLES

Creation and Change – Douglas Kelly

A scholarly defence of the literal seven-day account of the creation of all things as detailed in Genesis 1. The author is Professor of Systematic Theology in Reformed Theological Seminary in Charlotte, North Carolina, USA.

large format   ISBN 1 857 92283 2   *272 pages*

The Healing Promise – Richard Mayhue

A clear biblical examination of the claims of Health and Wealth preachers. The author is Dean of The Master's Seminary, Los Angeles, California.

large format   ISBN 1 857 923 002   *288 pages*

Creeds, Councils and Christ – Gerald Bray

The author, who teaches at Samford University, Birmingham, Alabama, explains the historical circumstances and doctrinal differences that caused the early church to frame its creeds. He argues that a proper appreciation of the creeds will help the confused church of today.

large format   ISBN 1 857 92 280 8   *224 pages*

Calvin and the Atonement – Robert Peterson

In this revised and enlarged edition of his book, Robert Peterson examines several aspects of Calvin's thought on the atonement of Christ seen through the images of Christ as Prophet, Priest, King, Second Adam, Victor, Legal Substitute, Sacrifice Merit, and Example. The author is on the faculty of Covenant Seminary in St. Louis.

large format   ISBN 1 857 923 77 4   *176 pages*

Calvin and the Sabbath – Richard Gaffin

Richard Gaffin of Westminster Theological Seminary in Philadelphia first explores Calvin's comments on the Sabbath in his commentaries and other writings. He then considers whether or not Calvin's viewpoints are consistent with what the biblical writers teach about the Sabbath.

large format   ISBN 1 857 923 76 6   *176 pages*

MENTOR COMMENTARIES

1 and 2 Chronicles
Richard Pratt

The author is professor of Old Testament at Reformed Theological Seminary, Orlando, USA. In this commentary he gives attention to the structure of Chronicles as well as the Chronicler's reasons for his different emphases from that of 1 and 2 Kings.
hardback, 512 pages   ISBN 185792 1518

Psalms
Alan Harman

The author, now retired from his position as a professor of Old Testament, lives in Australia. His commentary includes a comprehensive introduction to the psalms as well as a commentary on each psalm.
hardback, 456 pages   ISBN 185792 1917

Amos
Gary Smith

Gary Smith, a professor of Old Testament in Baptist Seminary, Kansas City, USA, exegetes the text of Amos by considering issues of textual criticism, structure, historical and literary background, and the theological significance of the book.
hardback, 400 pages   ISBN 185792 2530

Territorial Spirits and World Evangelization
Chuck Lowe

ISBN 1 85792 399 5   *192 pages*   *large format*

Over the last decade, a new theory of spiritual warfare, associated primarily with the teaching of Peter Wagner, has become popular around the world. This teaching concerns the role of 'territorial spirits', who are said to rule over specific geographical areas. Along with this theory has come a new practice of spiritual warfare: ruling spirits are named, their territories identified, and they are then bound or cursed. evangelism and mission are then said to proceed rapidly with dramatic results. Chuck Lowe, who teaches at Singapore Bible College, examines the full range of biblical, intertestamental and historical evidence cited in support of this new teaching. He affirms the need to be involved in spiritual warfare, but proposes a more biblical model.

'This is a methodologically-clear, admirably lucid, and mission-hearted challenge; a challenge not merely to our theories about Strategic-Level Spiritual Warfare, but to our evangelical technocratic quest for successful 'method'. Lowe argues that the floodtide of confidence in this 'method' has swept away exegetical, historical and empirical caution, and that it has unwittingly produced a synthesis uncomfortably closer to *The Testament of Solomon* and to animism than to any *biblical* understanding of demonology and spiritual warfare. In place of this questionable construction, with its quick-and-easy answers, Lowe points to the grittier, more robust example provided by James O Fraser, a CIM missionary to the Lisu in China. A great read!'

Max Turner
Vice Principal and Senior Lecturer in New Testament,
London Bible College

'So easily do many accept the new and the novel! To all who care deeply about world mission, Chuck Lowe's evaluation of strategic-level spiritual warfare is a needed clarion call; a call to reject what is built on a foundation of anecdote, speculation and animism, and to walk in the established paths of biblical truth and practice.

'Lowe has set himself up as a target for those who follow the SLSW theology. It will be interesting to see how they respond to this book.'

George Martin
Southern Baptist Theological Seminary
Louisville, Kentucky

'I am pleased to commend this careful examination of a controversial subject. The new interest in demons and the demonic, lately fanned by Peretti's novels, obliges Christians to reflect carefully on the biblical basis of all contemporary thought and practice. Not every reader will agree with the conclusions, which are sharply critical of Peter Wagner and others. But you do not have to go along with their theology to take seriously the devil and his minions.'

Nigel M. de S. Cameron
Distinguished Professor of Theology and Culture,
Trinity Evangelical Divinity School, Deerfield, Illinois

'The evangelical community at large owes Chuck Lowe a huge debt of gratitude. With his incisive, biblical analysis of strategic-level spiritual warfare, he shows clarity and sanity. He thoughtfully analyses the biblical, historical and theological tenets of our times with regard to spiritual warfare, showing them to be the re-emergence of the inter-testamental period and the medieval age. He makes a complex subject readable and concise, while remaining charitably irenic toward other Christians with whom he takes issue.

'The greatest strength of this book is the author's dogged insistence that, whatever one's approach to SLSW, one must not build doctrine on vague texts, assumptions, analogies or inferences, but on clear, solid, biblical evidence alone. I fully endorse the contents of this exceptional work.'

Richard Mayhue
Senior Vice President and Dean,
The Master's Seminary, Sun Valley, California

'The Bible makes it very clear that the forces of evil are strong, and that the followers of Jesus are engaged in an unrelenting battle against them. But little attention is given to this struggle in a good deal of modern writing, so Dr. Lowe's study of spiritual warfare is important. He is concerned with modern approaches that do not do justice to what the Bible teaches about the forces of evil. Specifically he deals with those who advocate strategic-level spiritual warfare. His book clarifies many issues, and encourages readers in their task of opposing evil.'

Leon Morris
Ridley College,
Australia

Christian Focus Publications publishes biblically-accurate books for adults and children. The books in the adult range are published in three imprints.

Christian Heritage contains classic writings from the past.

Christian Focus contains popular works including biographies, commentaries, doctrine, and Christian living.

Mentor focuses on books written at a level suitable for Bible College and seminary students, pastors, and others; the imprint includes commentaries, doctrinal studies, examination of current issues, and church history.

For a free catalogue of all our titles, please write to
Christian Focus Publications,
Geanies House, Fearn,
Ross-shire, IV20 1TW, Great Britain

For details of our titles visit us on our web site
http://www.christianfocus.com